THE
AMERICAN SECRETARIES OF STATE
AND THEIR DIPLOMACY

VOLUME VII
VOLUME VIII

THE AMERICAN SECRETARIES OF STATE AND THEIR DIPLOMACY

SAMUEL FLAGG BEMIS

EDITOR

J. FRANKLIN JAMESON

H. BARRETT LEARNED

JAMES BROWN SCOTT

ADVISORY BOARD

NEW YORK

COOPER SQUARE PUBLISHERS, INC.

1963

MANUFACTURED IN THE UNITED STATES OF AMERICA
NOBLE OFFSET PRINTERS, INC., 400 LAFAYETTE ST., NEW YORK, N. Y.

VOLUME VII

TABLE OF CONTENTS

EDITOR'S PREFACE

TO VOLUME VII

THE incoming of the Lincoln Administration in March 1861 and the precipitation of the Civil War in April marked an entirely new chapter in American foreign relations. With the secession of the Southern states the influence of slavery on our diplomacy with Great Britain, Spain, and Mexico—such a constant orienting factor in the diplomatic history of the United States recounted in the two preceding volumes of this series—ceases once and for all, and the United States with Secretaries Seward and Fish appears at last as the ardent champion of abolition. The primary task of the new Administration was that of putting down the rebellion and of preventing foreign intermeddling in it. The important role which William H. Seward played in the directing councils of the Republican party and the part which foreign relations bore to his plans of healing the domestic break, or at least of saving the secession of the border states—plans which seem so fantastic to us today—have justified Dr. Temple in devoting considerable space and emphasis to Seward's activity in the weeks preceding the inauguration and to that involved series of quasi-relations with the Confederate commissioners prior to the fall of Sumter.

Seward's great problem of preventing foreign recognition of the Confederacy—a problem solved for him, really, by the success of the Union army at Antietam—

his astute handling of the violations of the Monroe Doctrine while the United States had its hands tied at home, his expansionist ambitions in the Carribbean and the Pacific—not to mention the purchase of Alaska— make his eight years in the Department of State one of the three most important periods of American diplomatic history, and raise him to a high rank among the men who have held the office of Secretary of State. Despite the wealth of material that has been printed about Seward, it is here submitted that Dr. Temple has given a fresh treatment of his diplomacy and has contributed several new interpretations.

After the few days of Elihu B. Washburne's tenure of office as Secretary, in 1869, Hamilton Fish, fellow New Yorker to Seward, became Secretary of State for eight years more. Curiously enough, Dr. Fuller's sketch of Fish is the first serious study of this able and interesting man's diplomacy. It was the somewhat prosaic task of Secretary Fish to wind up the issues left over from the Civil War—the *Alabama* arbitration question, for example—and to lend a sedative influence to the frequent disturbances in our relations with Spain over the subject of Cuba. He also had to be a shock-absorber between the Senate and President Grant's Carribbean expansion policy. Dr. Fuller shows us that though Secretary Fish's service presents a record less spectacular than that of Seward, he also stands well up in the long list of Secretaries of State. It was a period of transition from war-time hysteria to the normal processes of peaceful development, the prelude to that quiet time of diplomatic doldrums between 1877 and the Spanish-American war.

William Maxwell Evarts has long needed a biographer. The authors of the sketch presented in this volume, Mr. Bowers and Miss Reid, do not attempt the whole of this ambitious duty, but they have ransacked the official papers of the Department of State so as to present, within the space allowed, a reasonably definitive account of this aspect of that witty statesman's career—four years in the Department of State under President Hayes, those four years of quiet and routine work, the most colourful phase of which perhaps was that of the Chinese exclusion question.

The Republican regime was still continuing unbroken when James G. Blaine accepted the office of Secretary of State for President Garfield and served over for a few weeks under Acting-President Arthur. Blaine's dynamic personality and quick and comprehensive intellect would have lent animation and verve to any office, but his first administration of the Department was largely a series of disappointments, the most notable of which was the failure of his attempt at mediation in the War of the Pacific, and with it of his Pan-American project. Nor was his exchange of arguments with Lord Granville over the Clayton-Bulwer Treaty any more successful; other turns in the wheel of world policy were necessary before England could be brought to see the American point of view in regard to the future control of the Panama Canal. Professor Lockey will resume his study of Blaine, in his second administration of the Department, in the next volume.

S. F. B.

WILLIAM H. SEWARD

SECRETARY OF STATE

MARCH 5, 1861, TO MARCH 4, 1869

BY

HENRY W. TEMPLE, D.D., LL.D.

MEMBER OF THE HOUSE OF REPRESENTATIVES

WILLIAM H. SEWARD

William H Seward

WILLIAM H. SEWARD

CHAPTER I

LINCOLN SELECTS SEWARD FOR SECRETARY OF STATE

WHEN Lincoln asked Seward to become his Secretary of State, it had not yet become apparent to either of them, or to other political leaders, that the conduct of our foreign affairs during the new Administration would present problems so perplexing and dangerous as those which actually developed a few months later. The obvious crisis was domestic.

Turmoil had increased since the election, barely a month past, and it was certain that the session of Congress just beginning would be full of dangers. The inauguration of the President-elect was three months in the future; action might be taken in the mean time that would preserve the federal Government; or the advocates of disunion might shatter it beyond repair. The interval until the fourth of March must be bridged or by March there might be no government to administer. Policies must be fitted to actual conditions, and there must be an understanding between the President-elect and the men who were to support him after he took his seat. It was imperative that Lincoln have a trustworthy source of information concerning influences at work in Washington and also a recognized and influential spokesman there. Seward's long experience in public life and acquaintance with public men, his influence in the Senate and the country, and his reputation for political sagacity seemed to fit him for the needs of the time.

Seward was born in Orange County, New York, in 1801. His father, of Welsh descent, occupied himself at the same time as a physician, a magistrate, and a country merchant. His mother was of Irish ancestry. In 1816 he entered Union College, Schenectady, but broke his college course in 1819 to teach for six months in an academy in Georgia, after which he returned and was graduated Bachelor of Arts in 1820. He read law in New York City and began the practice of his profession in Auburn in 1823. He was active at once in the tangled politics of New York, and his own abilities and the political management of his friend Thurlow Weed made him state senator, governor, and United States senator, and fell short of nominating him for the presidency only because his anti-slavery views were supposed to be too radical for the doubtful states.

Seward had now been twelve years in the United States Senate, where, until the formation of the Republican party, he had been the recognized leader of the anti-slavery Whigs. The spirit of his speeches could sometimes be condensed into an aphorism, and his assertion that "there is a higher law than the Constitution," and that there is "an irrepressible conflict" between slavery and freedom, had shaped the convictions of many people. His long public career was not solely the result of his oratory. He had been trained from his youth in the art of politics, at a time when one political party after another was organized and after a time dissolved to be merged into another by the various elements in New York which were opposed to the powerful "Albany Regency." Active in the National Republican party which supported Adams in 1824, elected to the state senate by the Antimason party in 1830, and chosen governor of New York for two terms by the Whig party, he had constantly increased in popularity and power. Each of these parties in turn had furnished a large part of the material out of which he, with Thurlow Weed and other leaders, had built successive larger parties, the last of them the Republican. Of this one also he was a leader, and more influential in it at that time than Lincoln.

A keen and not too friendly political observer who knew Seward well in those days, wrote of him: "He made upon me as well as upon many others, the impression of a man who controlled hidden, occult powers which he could bring into play if he would. Indeed I heard him spoken of as a sort of political wizard who knew all secrets and who commanded political forces unknown to all the world except himself and his bosom friend, Thurlow Weed, the most astute, skilful and indefatigable political manager ever known." [1] The new Administration must assume responsibility before it had power, and all the resources both of statesmanship and of political strategy might be required to make Lincoln's inauguration possible. Seward and Seward's political manager would be of great value to Lincoln's Administration.

Threats of disunion had not been lacking in former controversies over slavery, but they had been quieted by conciliatory measures. Now, however, a new political party had arisen on the ruins of the Whig party, wrecked by the compromise of 1850, and the South did not expect further yielding. Even before the election Governor Gist of South Carolina had announced that if a majority of Lincoln electors should be chosen, South Carolina would withdraw from the Union, provided there should be a good prospect of like action by other states. As soon as the result was known, the legislature called a convention to determine what action the state should take. Nor was disunion sentiment confined to the South, or to the supporters of slavery. Some of the anti-slavery leaders, wearied by the long controversy, found relief in the prospect of a separation of the cotton states from those of the North. Even Horace Greeley wrote: "We must ever resist the right of any state to remain in the Union and nullify or defy the laws thereof; to withdraw from the Union is quite another matter. And whenever a considerable section of our union shall deliberately resolve to go out, we shall resist all coercive measures designed to keep it in. We hope never to live in a republic whereof one section is pinned to the residue by bayonets." [2]

When Congress met, on December 3, no state had yet actually withdrawn, but the expected action of South Carolina and other states could not be ignored. President Buchanan discussed it in his annual message. After arguing at length that a state had no right to secede he affirmed that nevertheless neither Congress nor any other department of the federal Government had the power by force of arms to compel a state to remain in the Union. The message provoked violent discussion throughout the country, and the danger increased that not only South Carolina, but also several other states would withdraw at once.

Prior to the meeting of Congress, but after the publication of the Greeley editorials, Thurlow Weed began a series of articles in his newspaper, the Albany *Evening Journal*, at that time "probably the most powerful organ of public opinion outside of New York City," in which he recognized the earnestness and seriousness of the secession movement and urged upon the victorious Republican party the necessity of moderation and concession. He was willing to restore the Missouri Compromise line and extend it to the Pacific, and to require counties in which fugitive slaves were rescued to compensate the owners. He suggested a constitutional convention to provide a permanent basis for agreement between the two sections. These proposals, he said, were intended to draw out, strengthen, and unite the Union sentiment, north and south, and to allay the suspicion that the new Administration would enforce radical anti-slavery policies. He hoped at least to hold the border states in the Union and to prevent a disastrous division of the Northern people, who, he believed, could be united against disunion even though they were not agreed as to anti-slavery measures. There was a general belief, based on the known political partnership of Seward and Weed and supported by an assertion made at the office of the New York *Tribune*, that the articles were Seward's, and on the first day of the session of Congress the Republican senators held a caucus for the purpose of finding out whether Seward agreed with Weed's proposals.[3] Seward gave them no satisfaction, but wrote to his wife: "Mr. Weed's articles have brought perplexities about me which he, with all his astuteness, did not foresee."

Such was the situation when, five days after the opening of the session of Congress, Lincoln wrote to Seward asking him to become Secretary of State in the new Cabinet, and about the same time sent Weed an invitation to come to Springfield to discuss policies and appointments. To Seward, in addition to the brief official note, there was a private and confidential letter in which Lincoln said it had been his purpose from the date of his nomination at Chicago to assign Seward, if he was willing, to the Department of State. He added cordially: "I now offer you the place in the hope that you will accept it, and with the belief that your position in the public eye, your integrity, ability, learning and great experience, all combine to render it an appointment pre-eminently fit to be made."[4] The offer found Seward not wholly unprepared. He shared the general expectation that he would be offered a seat in Lincoln's Cabinet. In fact, he had discussed the probability of it with Weed, to whom he wrote immediately: "I have now the occasion for consulting you that you expected. I shall be in New York Friday evening. Not finding you there, I shall look for you at Albany Saturday."[5]

At the interview thus arranged Seward learned of Weed's invitation to go to Springfield. It had come through Leonard Swett, one of Lincoln's most intimate friends, who wrote: "Mr. Lincoln would be very glad to see you. He asks me to tell you so. . . . I do not think it at all necessary for you to come, so far as recognition of Mr. Seward's friends by him may be affected by that interview. This I mention as it may be inconvenient for you to make the journey. Still, it was Mr. Lincoln's wish that you should come, and it strikes me that it would be much better. . . . Besides Mr. Lincoln wants your advice about the Cabinet, and the general policy of his administration."[6] This invitation was reinforced by a letter from Judge David Davis, afterward by Lincoln's appointment a justice of the Supreme Court of the United States, in which he said: "I would advise you, inasmuch as Mr. Lincoln requests it, to go to Springfield at once."[7]

The prospective Secretary of State and his political manager had ample opportunity to consult and did consult as to the significance of this request. It had come almost simultaneously with the invitation to Seward to become Secretary of State, and both had followed within a few days the publication of Weed's articles concerning compromise, of which rumour said Seward was either the author or the inspirer. Before the Republican convention had met in May, it had been confidently expected that Seward would be its nominee. Lincoln had been chosen instead largely because the leaders of the doubtful states declared Seward's record, and especially his "irrepressible conflict" and "higher law" speeches proved him too radical and uncompromising. It was therefore somewhat surprising when Weed— it was supposed, with Seward's consent—had proposed conciliation and compromise. If Seward was to be the senior member of Lincoln's Cabinet and his spokesman during the intervening session of Congress, it was necessary that there should be as soon as possible an understanding as to the policies of the new Administration. Seward and Weed conferred together for two days, December 15 and 16. Weed's newspaper, the Albany *Evening Journal*, had an editorial, on December 17, which summed up and elaborated Weed's earlier proposals for compromise. That evening Weed started west, and he and the editorial, he tells us, reached Springfield about the same time. Meanwhile Seward postponed his final reply to Lincoln's offer of the State Department. He proceeded to his home in Auburn and wrote to Lincoln, saying that Weed would go to Springfield, adding: "I have had some conversation with him concerning the condition of public affairs, and he will be able to inform you of my present unsettled view of the subject on which you so kindly wrote me a few days ago. I shall remain at home until his return, and shall then in further conference with him have the advantage of a knowledge of the effect of public events certain to occur this week." [8]

The principal public event referred to was doubtless the South Carolina convention, which met that week and on December 20, the first day of the conference between Lincoln and Weed, issued its ordinance of secession. In spite of the progress of events and of what he called "much muttering in the cotton states," Lincoln expressed the hope that "by wisdom and forbearance the danger of serious trouble might be averted, as such danger had been in former times." [9] Weed suggested that one of the measures which might tend to avert it would be to select at least two members of the Cabinet from slave-holding states. Lincoln asked if there were any such men who could be trusted if their states should secede, and when Weed answered that there were men who could be relied on in any circumstances, Lincoln said: "Well, let us have the names of your white crows." Weed mentioned, among others, John A. Gilmer of North Carolina, whom Lincoln afterward tried to secure for the Cabinet, but he, like most Southern men, "went with his state" when North Carolina seceded.

For five days Seward had been in Auburn, where he waited anxiously for Weed's return. Business was coming up in the Senate on Monday for which he could not ask postponement, and on Saturday he started for Washington. He met Weed at Syracuse returning from the west, and they travelled together for several hours. Of the conversation between them in these circumstances Seward wrote to Lincoln a few days later: "I had only the opportunity for conferring with Mr. Weed which was afforded by our journeying together on the railroad from Syracuse to Albany. He gave me verbally the substance of the suggestion you prepared for the consideration of the Republican members, but not the written proposition. This morning I received the latter[10] from him, and also information for the first time of your expectation that I would write to you concerning the temper of the parties and the public here."[11]

CHAPTER II

O N December 18, 1860, while Seward was at Auburn
and Weed was on his way to Springfield to discuss policies and Cabinet appointments with Lincoln,
Senator Crittenden of Kentucky introduced a plan of
compromise. His first article, which dealt with slavery
in the territories, did not differ in substance from the
plan suggested by Weed in the Albany *Evening Journal,*
except that it proposed to do by constitutional amendment, which by special provision should be irrevocable
by any future amendment, what Weed had thought
might be accomplished by legislative enactment. Crittenden's proposed amendment would restore the Missouri Compromise line, extend it to the Pacific, and
provide that during the continuance of territorial
government slavery should be prohibited north of the
line and recognized and protected south of it. States
organized either north or south of the line should be
admitted with or without slavery as their constitutions
might provide. The plan included other constitutional
amendments, which provided that Congress should
have no power to abolish slavery in the District of
Columbia without compensating the owners or without
the consent of the adjoining states of Virginia and Maryland; that it should have no power to prohibit or hinder
the transportation of slaves from one state to another

or to or from the territories; that no future amendment
should affect any of these provisions, nor should any
future amendment give Congress power to abolish or
interfere with slavery in any state.

This plan, with other proposals, was referred to a
committee of thirteen senators, of whom five were
Republicans, three Northern Democrats, three from
the border slave-states, and two, Jefferson Davis and
Robert Toombs, from cotton states. On motion of Davis
it was agreed that no report should be adopted unless
it had the assent of a majority of the Republican members and also of a majority of the other eight. Seward,
absent from the first two meetings of the committee,
came back to Washington bringing the suggestions
which Lincoln had made for the consideration of the
Republican members.

Reporting on these suggestions, he wrote to Lincoln:
"I met on Monday my Republican associates on the
committee of Thirteen, and afterwards the whole committee. With the unanimous consent of our section I
offered three propositions which seemed to me to cover
the ground of the suggestion made by you through Mr.
Weed as I understood it. First: That the Constitution
should never be altered so as to authorize Congress to
abolish or interfere with slavery in the states. This was
accepted. Second: That the fugitive slave law should
be amended by granting a jury trial to the fugitive.
This, in opposition to our votes, was amended so as to
give the jury in the state from which the fugitive fled,
and so amended was voted down by our own votes.
Our Third resolution was that Congress recommend
to all the states to revise their legislation concerning

persons recently resident in other states, and to repeal all such laws which contravene the Constitution of the United States or any laws passed in pursuance thereof. This was rejected by the pro-slavery vote of the committee." [12]

Prior to his appointment as a member of the committee of thirteen, in spite of many attempts to lead him to a declaration of his views with regard to the proposals for compromise, Seward had maintained a cautious silence. Though never an abolitionist, he had long been considered a radical anti-slavery man and had sometimes used the language of the agitator; but he had always had sufficient political flexibility to accommodate himself to actual conditions. Now that his own party was coming into power, and therefore had become responsible, he ceased to be an agitator. He realized the serious purpose of the extreme secessionists and thought it wise to refrain, and to persuade other Republicans, from saying too much, especially at a time, as he said, "when concession, or solicitation, or solicitude would encourage, and demonstrations of firmness of purpose would exasperate." He knew that public opinion in the North was divided; he overestimated the strength of union sentiment in the South, which he hoped would rise, if not alarmed by radical utterances, to energetic opposition to the secession movement; but his strongest hope was that at least the border slave-states might be saved for the Union. To accomplish all this he believed that compromise, or at least negotiation about compromise, was necessary, and he was willing to compromise. The only question was how far it would be necessary to go.

It seems safe to say that he was willing to go the full length of Weed's proposals. It was immediately after long conferences between Seward and Weed that the two most important articles in the *Evening Journal* had been published. Weed assumed full responsibility for them, but it is exceedingly probable, in view of all the circumstances, that Seward concurred in the design of publishing them—for a purpose. They would test public sentiment, and Seward need not express approval of them unless the responses proved sufficiently favourable. The circumstances under which the article of December 17 was prepared indicate that it was intended to serve as a text for Weed's conference with Lincoln and to draw out the opinions of the President-elect. Weed's account of the conference shows something of Lincoln's reaction to this editorial, but does not give as full a report as could be desired of their discussion of its proposals. Lincoln's letters, however, written within a few days before and after the meeting with Weed, show that even at that time he was not unyielding except on the question of the admission of slavery into the territories.

One of these letters had been written to Weed, but not received by him before their conference. Weed had asked for an expression of Lincoln's views that might be presented to the convocation of governors. In spite of numerous requests for a public declaration of policies, Lincoln, like Seward, had been silent since the election. Maintaining still the same course as to a public announcement, he furnished no statement to be delivered to the governors, but merely authorized Weed to tell them "that you judge from my speeches that I will be inflexible on the territorial question; that I probably think either the Missouri line extended, or Douglass's and Eli Thayer's popular sovereignty would lose us everything we gain by the election; that filibustering for all south of us and making slave states of it would follow, in spite of us, in either case. Also that I probably think all opposition, real and apparent, to the fugitive slave clause of the Constitution ought to be withdrawn. I believe you can pretend to find but little, if anything, in my speeches about secession. But my opinion is that no state can in any way lawfully get out of the Union without the consent of the others; and that it is the duty of the President and other functionaries of the government to run the machine as it is."[13] To John A. Gilmer of North Carolina he had written, on December 15: "I have no thought of recommending the abolition of slavery in the District of Columbia, nor the slave trade among the States. . . . On the territorial question I am inflexible. As to State laws . . . if any of them are in conflict with the fugitive slave clause, or any other part of the Constitution, I shall certainly be glad of their repeal. . . . "[14]

Weed came back from Springfield having full knowledge of Lincoln's attitude toward proposals for conciliation. Lincoln still "hoped to avert serious trouble by wisdom and forbearance," but there were definite limits beyond which he would not consider compromise. He would not accept Greeley's proposal to consent to secession; he intended to "run the machine as it is"; he was "inflexible on the territorial question"; slavery must not be extended. He was willing at the proper time to give assurances to the South on every other aspect of the questions at issue. Weed gave to Seward Lincoln's views as he had expressed them fully and freely and delivered the message Lincoln had sent for the consideration of the Republican members of the committee of thirteen.

As a member of the committee Seward must now speak out. From his own point of view also there was no further necessity for silence. He had received the expected offer of the chief place in the Cabinet; he knew the views of the President-elect and was the agent through whom these views were communicated confidentially to other Republican senators; and Lincoln's request that he keep him informed about the temper of parties and the public gave opportunity for a correspondence which would make their relations even more intimate and confidential. With sublime confidence in his own powers Seward cheerfully accepted responsibility. His activity became incessant. In the committee of thirteen he offered compromise resolutions based on Lincoln's proposals; in the Senate in his speech of January 12 he urged the same proposals, suggested a constitutional convention "when the eccentric movements of secession shall have ended—then and not till then—one, two, three years hence." He even offered, if Kansas were admitted as a free state, to consolidate all the other territories into two states and admit them without restriction as to slavery. In addition to these public activities he renewed his intimate social intercourse with old friends among the Southern Whigs, cultivated other union men of the South, and, without actually committing himself, talked about a "truce with slavery"[15] to such an extent that it was generally believed that Seward would go much further than any compromise he had yet offered, and might ultimately accept the Crittenden proposals.

Southern men opposed to secession now brought him valuable information about the disunion movement in their states, hoping to convince him even more fully of the necessity of compromise. He established confidential relations with Secretary Jeremiah S. Black, then recently transferred to the State Department, and with Edwin M. Stanton, who had succeeded Black as Attorney-General, from whom he learned daily what was going on in the Cabinet. He reported to Lincoln: "At length I have gotten a position in which I can see what is going on in the councils of the President. It pains me to learn that things there are even worse than is understood. . . . A plot is forming to seize the capital on or before the 4th of March, and this, too, has its accomplices in the public councils. . . . You must not imagine that I am giving you suspicions and rumours. Believe me, I know what I write. In point of fact the responsibilities of your Administration must begin before the time arrives."[16]

Of Seward's speech of January 12, 1861 Sumner, Chase, and other Republican senators expressed disapproval; even his wife reproached him for his concessions; but Lincoln wrote: "Your recent speech is well received, and, I think, is doing good all over the country."[17] To his wife Seward insisted that he was not "making any compromise whatever," and with perhaps some impatience wrote: "Once for all, I must gain time for the new Administration to organize and for the frenzy of passion to subside."[18] It was to the same sympathetic correspondent that he wrote: "The revolution grows apace. It has its abettors in the White House, the Treasury, the Interior. . . . I have assumed a sort of dictatorship for defense";[19] and later: "I am trying to get home, but as yet see no chance. It seems to me that if I am absent but three days, this Administration, the Congress and the District fall into consternation and despair. I am the only hopeful, calm, conciliatory person here";[20] and a few days later: "Mad men North and mad men South are working together to produce a dissolution of the Union. The present Administration and the incoming one unite in devolving upon me the responsibility of averting these disasters." His egotism was like that of William Pitt, the elder, who, when he took over the leadership of the Ministry and the House of Commons in 1756, said to the Duke of Devonshire: "I know that I can save this nation, and that nobody else can." It must be admitted that in both cases, Seward's no less than Pitt's, there was some ground to excuse, if not to justify, such astounding self-confidence.

As he had explained "once for all," Seward was playing for time. Until the new Administration should be organized, the border states must be held in the Union and there must be no actual conflict with the states which had already seceded. Compromise was perhaps even then impossible on any terms short of complete surrender, but it was Seward more than any other man who kept alive the hope of compromise in the breasts of Union men in the border states. There were many such men in North Carolina, Tennessee, and Virginia, and it was to them that Virginia appealed with the call for a convention to meet on February 4 to adjust the differences between the sections. There was no better prospect for agreement in the convention than in the Senate, but the bare fact that such a convention was in progress worked advantage to Seward's purpose of gaining time. Neither Virginia, North Carolina, Tennessee, nor any other state represented at the convention would secede while its sessions continued. So long as both Maryland and Virginia remained in the Union, there would be no attempt by conspirators to seize the capital.

That there was such a conspiracy, to prevent the formal counting of the electoral votes and the inauguration of the President-elect, was believed by General Scott and many others in responsible positions. The House committee which investigated the subject reported that if such a plot existed, it had been rendered contingent on the secession of Maryland or Virginia, or both, and on the sanction of one of those states. In Lincoln's opinion the critical time would not be the fourth of March, but the day fixed for the formal counting of the electoral votes. He wrote to Seward: "It seems to me the inauguration is not the most dangerous point for us. Our adversaries have us now clearly at disadvantage. On the second Wednesday of February, when the votes should be officially counted, if the two Houses refuse to meet at all, or meet without a quorum of each, where shall we be? I do not think that this counting is constitutionally essential to the election; but how are we to proceed in the absence of it?"[21] The convention was still in session when the danger point was reached and passed. The electoral votes were counted and Lincoln's election was officially announced.

Seward congratulated himself that his play for time had thus far been successful. He joyfully wrote to his wife: "We have passed the 13th safely. I am at last out of direct responsibility. I have brought the ship off the sands and am ready to resign the helm into the hands of the captain the people have chosen." [22]

CHAPTER III

SEWARD AS "PRIME MINISTER"

SEWARD'S readiness to resign the helm was only momentary. It was publicly known that he was to be Secretary of State, and it was generally believed, north and south, that this meant that Seward was to be the real head of the Administration. Lincoln was still an unknown quantity, and outside of his own state there were few who had regarded his nomination over Seward as other than "the sacrifice of commanding ability in favor of respectable mediocrity."[23] Seward himself shared in the belief that Lincoln would be guided by his advice. He told Preston King, his New York colleague in the Senate, that Lincoln wanted him for his "Prime Minister."[24] He elaborated the idea when he said to Rudolph Schleiden, minister from the Republic of Bremen, that "there is no great difference between an elected president of the United States and an hereditary monarch. The latter is called to the throne through the accident of birth, the former through the chances which make his election possible. The actual direction of public affairs belongs to the leader of the ruling party, here as well as in any hereditary principality."[25] Throughout the winter of '60 and '61 there had been nothing to indicate to Seward that his estimate of the situation was erroneous. Intimate relations had been established with Lincoln, and frequent interchange of letters had brought out no great differences of policy. Lincoln submitted his inaugural address to Seward and modified it in accordance with some of Seward's suggestions. A few days before the inauguration, however, there was a flare-up that threatened trouble. It became known that Lincoln intended to name both Seward and Chase for Cabinet positions, and factional hostilities threatened to disrupt the Administration before it could be organized. Greeley and some other Chase men attempted to prevent Seward's appointment. The suggestion was made that Seward might be sent as minister to England. On the other hand, some of Seward's friends told Lincoln that Seward would not serve in the Cabinet with Chase. On March 2 Seward withdrew his acceptance of the secretaryship. Lincoln wrote to Seward saying that this was "the subject of the most painful solicitude with me; and I feel constrained to beg that you will countermand the withdrawal. The public interest, I think, demands that you should; and my personal feelings are deeply enlisted in the same direction." Following the inauguration there was a long conference between Seward and the President. Lincoln prevailed. Both Chase and Seward were given the places in the Cabinet for which Lincoln had tentatively chosen them on the night of his election. On March 8 Seward wrote to his wife: "The President is determined that he will have a compound Cabinet. . . . I was at one time on the point of refusing—nay, I did refuse, to hazard myself in the experiment. But a distracted country appeared before me and I withdrew from the position. I believe I can endure as much as anyone; and maybe I can endure enough to make the experiment successful. At all events I did not dare to go home, or to England, and leave the country to chance."

When Lincoln was inaugurated, only seven of the fifteen slave states had seceded—South Carolina in December; Mississippi, Alabama, Florida, Georgia, and Louisiana in January; and Texas on the first of February. In Virginia, North Carolina, and Tennessee the union men had thus far been strong enough to defeat the strenuous efforts of the secessionists. When the final test came, it proved concerning most of these union men that their fealty to the federal Government was secondary to their devotion to their states; yet that fealty was honest, and so long as there was a prospect of compromise, they continued to hope that they would not be forced to choose between their two allegiances. Many of them believed, with Gilmer of North Carolina, that if a collision could be avoided, the border states would stay in the Union and the seceding states, if "let go out into the cold for a while," would come back. He believed this would happen in less than two years.[26] The letter to Seward in which Gilmer expresses this opinion sounds like an echo of Seward's own policy and especially of his speech of January 12, in which he proposed a convention to be held "one, two, three years hence . . . when the eccentric movements of secession and disunion shall have ended . . . and the angry excitement of the hour shall have subsided."

If the Confederacy had taken possession of Fort Sumter at Charleston and Fort Pickens at Pensacola without a struggle and before the inauguration of Lincoln, as it took thirty other fortifications, together with the custom-houses within its borders, it is probable that Lincoln would have made no attempt to retake them. In his inaugural address he had said there would be no

"invasion" beyond what would be necessary to "hold,
occupy and possess the property and places belonging
to the Government," and he explained afterward to a
committee from the Virginia convention that by "property and places belonging to the Government" he meant
chiefly "the military posts and property which were in
the possession of the Government when it came into
my hands."[27] If there had been no "invasion," Virginia
and the border states would not have had this incentive
to secede. But Sumter and Pickens remained in the
possession of the federal forces and thus gave the seceded
states an opportunity to force the issue.

The Confederate Congress, soon after it convened,
expressed the opinion that immediate steps should be
taken to obtain possession of these forts either by negotiation or by force. On February 27 Davis appointed
a commission, headed by Martin J. Crawford of Georgia,
to open negotiations on the subject, and after Lincoln's
inauguration they sought in many ways to secure an
interview with Seward. He avoided meeting them even
informally, but on March 13 the commissioners sought
to force a decision by presenting a written request that
the Secretary of State receive them officially as delegates
from an independent nation. This formal demand was
embarrassing, for Seward had learned that if these men
should go back without acknowledgment as commissioners, Davis would not be able to prevent his people
from attacking the forts.[28] There could of course be no
recognition of the Confederacy as an independent nation, but an answer to the commissioners refusing their
request would precipitate a conflict and thus destroy
the basis of all Seward's hopes. He delayed his reply,

and twice the secretary of the commissioners called for it at the State Department only to be told that it was still in preparation. Such was the status of this affair on March 15, when the situation with regard to Fort Sumter had reached a stage which would allay the impatience of the commissioners if it could be revealed to them.

Lincoln was seriously considering the surrender of Fort Sumter without resistance. The day after his inauguration, Judge Holt, still Secretary of War, transmitted a report from Major Anderson, commanding at Fort Sumter, informing the President that the food-supply there would last only a few weeks, and if the place were to be held, it would require reinforcements of twenty thousand men. Attention to the clamour of office-seekers was permitted to consume the time that should have been given to more serious matters, and the first Cabinet meeting was not held until four days had gone by. The situation was then brought to the attention of the President's advisers, and naval and military officers were consulted. General Scott advised that Fort Sumter be evacuated. Captain Gustavus Fox, afterward the very able Assistant Secretary of the Navy, advised that supplies could be delivered to the fort. On March 15 Lincoln asked each member of the Cabinet to prepare a written opinion in answer to the question: "Assuming it to be possible now to provision Fort Sumter, under all the circumstances, is it wise to attempt it?" Postmaster-General Blair emphatically favoured the attempt. Chase's reply was conditionally affirmative. Seward, Cameron, Welles, Smith, and Bates advised against the attempt.

Lincoln received the written opinions, but announced no decision. Seward, however, finding his views supported by the judgment of the commanding general of the army and by the opinion of the Attorney-General and the heads of the War and Navy Departments, was convinced that his policy would prevail and that Fort Sumter would be evacuated within a few days. Nevertheless, Seward's anxiety was not much relieved; the Southern commissioners were pressing for an answer to their demand for a formal interview. They had been sent to negotiate for the possession of the two forts. Seward was willing to abandon Fort Sumter to them, but not to negotiate with them about it and thus recognize their claim to be representatives of an independent nation. He addressed no reply to the commissioners, but filed in the State Department a memorandum of his reasons for not receiving them, with instruction that a copy should be delivered to them at their request.

This memorandum was filed on March 15, the same day on which the President received the opinions of the members of the Cabinet on the provisioning of Fort Sumter. Later, but still on the same day, two justices of the Supreme Court, Nelson of New York and Campbell of Alabama, called on Seward and urged him to receive the Southern commissioners and assure them that the Government was for peace. Seward expressed regret that he was unable to do this and said there was not a member of the Cabinet who would consent to it. In his perturbation he added: "If Jefferson Davis had known the state of things here, he would not have sent those commissioners; the evacuation of Sumter is as much as the administration can bear." Campbell

afterward went over to the Confederacy, but at the time
of this interview he was still a justice of the Supreme
Court and was one of the Southern union men of the
type depended on by Seward to bring the seceding
states back into the Union. His attention was attracted
by the apparently inadvertent revelation that Sumter
was to be evacuated. He said he would see the commissioners and urge them not to press their demand for an
interview. He offered to write to Davis and asked what
he might say. Seward replied: "You may say to him
that before that letter reaches him the telegraph will
have informed him that Sumter will have been evacuated." Seward also assured him that no action was
contemplated as to the forts on the Gulf of Mexico.
Campbell saw the commissioners, told them that he
was confident Fort Sumter would be evacuated within
five days, and persuaded them not to send their secretary for Seward's reply to their letter.[29]

Lincoln in the mean time sent Captain Fox to Fort
Sumter to confer with Major Anderson and to investigate the feasibility of the plan Fox had proposed for
provisioning the fort. Captain Fox came back fully convinced that his plan was sound. On the other hand
General Scott about this time recommended the abandonment of both Fort Sumter and Fort Pickens, though
on March 12 he had ordered the landing of troops to
reinforce the latter. On March 28 Lincoln told the
members of the Cabinet of Scott's recommendation and
the next day again asked for opinions about provisioning Fort Sumter. By that time the protests of members
of the Senate, the expressions of public sentiment, and
the report of Captain Fox were having an effect. Of all

the members of the Cabinet only Seward and Smith were in favour of withdrawing the garrison. Lincoln was still undecided, but went so far as to order the fitting-out of an expedition which, if required, should be ready to sail by April 6. He permitted Seward to say to Judge Campbell that Sumter would not be supplied without notice previously given, but Seward realized that this would not save his credit with the Southern men on whom his fading hope of conciliation depended.

Seward was in desperate alarm. He was still of the opinion that his was the only policy and he the only man by whom the country could be saved, as he had been when he withdrew his refusal to hazard himself in the experiment of a "compound Cabinet" because he "did not dare to go home or to England and leave the country to chance."[30] Chagrin at the defeat of his personal plans was not the chief cause of his disturbance. He saw the end of the policy that had arrested dismemberment after seven states had seceded and that while Virginia, North Carolina, Tennessee, and the border states remained in the Union, gave hope to him, if to none of his associates, that the others might yet be brought back through their good offices. He was sure that the attempt to provision Fort Sumter, whether successful or not, would bring on immediate hostilities, drive the remaining slave states into the Confederacy, and so strengthen it that reunion would be hopeless.[31] With characteristic persistence he still cast about for anything that might yet be done to save the situation.

The time-worn expedient of rousing national sentiment by means of foreign war had more than once occurred to Seward during the winter. One day he said to

Schleiden, minister from Bremen, that if the Lord would only give the United States an excuse for such a war, that would be the best means of uniting the country; but Schleiden was not much concerned, for he thought the plan too intricate to be dangerous.[32] Lord Lyons, minister from Great Britain, reported to his Government a similar remark on another occasion.[33] Seward's floating dream became a definite purpose when he found what he thought an opportunity for foreign war at a moment when nothing short of desperate measures could save the policy that was his only hope. It was Friday, March 29, when the Cabinet members reversed their advice about Fort Sumter. On Saturday Campbell reminded Seward of his unfulfilled assurance based on the former advice. On Sunday morning Seward received from C. J. Helms, consul-general at Havana, a dispatch saying: "The Spanish Government despatched a vessel of war from this port, two days since, with several companies of artillery for the island of Santo Domingo, with the view of taking possession of that island," adding that other troops would soon be sent from Spain or from Cuba with the same object.[34] Seward at once interpreted this military action of Spain in the light of several dispatches received during the previous Administration by Cass, Secretary of State, from McLane, the American minister to Mexico. McLane had expressed the confident opinion that Spain, aided by France and Great Britain, would intervene in Mexico and that "the project will be converted into a scheme for acquisition." Cass had assured McLane that these powers had disavowed such a design, but added: "If attempted, it will be met by the armed action of the

United States."[35] Seward considered the Santo Domingo expedition as evidence of a scheme for acquisition. Here was a chance for a war which, remembering the Ostend Manifesto and the persistent Southern desire for American expansion southward, he believed the cotton states might support. Foreign war in a cause of such vital importance to the South might yet bring the seceding states back into the Union. He wrote to Tassara, the Spanish minister at Washington, saying that this expedition "cannot fail to be taken as a first step in a policy of armed intervention by the Spanish Government in the American countries which once constituted Spanish America," and added that the President would be obliged "to meet the further prosecution of enterprises of that kind, in regard to either the Dominican Republic or any part of the American continent or islands, with a prompt, persistent, and, if possible, effective resistance."[36]

If there was to be war with Spain, it was not Sumter, but the Gulf forts that must be strengthened—Pickens at Pensacola, and especially Taylor at Key West and Jefferson in the Dry Tortugas, both of which were nearer the coast of Cuba than to our own mainland. And there was no time to lose. It was Sunday morning. Captain Meigs, an engineer officer whom Seward had already recommended for the command of these three forts, was about to start for church when Colonel Keyes, General Scott's military secretary, called and took him to Seward. He told them to consult General Scott and prepare plans and carry them to the President before four o'clock that afternoon. The time was short, and they submitted their plan to Lincoln without seeing

Scott. Lincoln heard the plan and directed them to take it to the General. "Tell him," said Lincoln, "that I wish this thing done, and not to let it fail unless he can show that I refused him something that he asked for as necessary."[37] The plans were perfected and the required orders were drawn up by Colonel Keyes, Captain Meigs, and Lieutenant David D. Porter of the Navy, in consultation with Seward and General Scott, and were signed by Lincoln on April 1. It was part of the plan that no one but the officers named, not even the secretaries of War or Navy, should have knowledge of them.[38] The order to the commandant of the navy yard at New York directed him to fit out the *Powhatan* for Lieutenant Porter, who was to relieve Captain Mercer in command of her, and continued: "She is bound on secret service, and you will under no circumstances communicate to the Navy Department that she is fitting out."[39] Porter was ordered to proceed to Pensacola harbour and at any cost prevent any expedition from the mainland reaching Fort Pickens, but General Scott's order to Captain Harvey Brown of the Army, signed by Scott on April 1 and approved by Lincoln on April 2, directed Brown to take command of the expedition and to secure Fort Pickens "against all attacks foreign and domestic." He was further directed to make Fort Jefferson in the Dry Tortugas (more than four hundred miles' sail from Fort Pickens and about a hundred from Havana) his main depot and base of operations, and to be "careful not to reduce too much the means of the fortresses in the Florida Reef, as they are deemed of even greater importance than Fort Pickens."[40] On the same date an order from Lincoln directed Seward to furnish Captain Meigs ten thousand dollars from the secret-service fund of the State Department.[41]

There was one order about which the Secretary of the Navy must know; it was addressed to him. It bore Lincoln's signature, though Secretary Welles says the body of the order was in the handwriting of Captain Meigs of the Army. It directed him to issue instructions to Captain Pendergrast of the Navy, commanding the home squadron, to go to Vera Cruz—"important complications in our foreign relations rendering the presence of an officer of rank there of great importance." Until recently there had been two Governments in Mexico, Juárez's, with a capital at Vera Cruz, and Miramón's, with his capital at Mexico City. Juárez had driven out his antagonist and taken possession of the ancient capital, but this had made no change in the essential situation. It was against Juárez that McLane had expected Spain to begin military operations and there were already rumours of the purpose of France to put a European prince upon a Mexican throne.[42] Welles did not know at that time of the other orders interfering with the Navy, but against this one he protested, saying that he knew of no foreign complications and Pendergrast could not be spared from his present duty. Welles records that Lincoln "seemed disinclined to disclose or dwell on the project," but authorized him to treat the order as if it had never been written.[43] A few days later, when Secretary Welles wanted the *Powhatan* for the Sumter expedition, he found that her commander, Captain Mercer, had been displaced and the ship had been given to Lieutenant Porter for a purpose of which Welles was to know nothing. He went to Seward, and together they went to Lincoln. Over Seward's protest Lincoln said that Welles must have the ship. Seward telegraphed to Porter on April 6: "Give the *Powhatan* up to Captain Mercer.—Seward"; but Porter replied: "I received my orders from the President and shall proceed and execute them." He proceeded, and could not again be overtaken by orders. Lincoln's messenger informed the Governor of South Carolina, April 8, that an attempt would be made to supply Fort Sumter with provisions. The expedition, delayed by the confusion about the *Powhatan*, reached a point near the mouth of the harbour in time to hear the guns of the bombardment. After a gallant defence the fort was surrendered, April 13, to the Confederate forces. The Civil War was on.

Seward did not follow up his threatening correspondence with Tassara and nothing more was heard of war with Spain. But surely these astonishing orders of April 1 throw light on the more astounding "Thoughts for the President's Consideration" which Seward placed in the President's hands on the same day. The opening sentences of this paper speak of the delay in deciding on policies: the closing propositions offer a remedy. Between these two portions of the paper Seward outlines his policies, domestic and foreign. The home policy is that which Seward had pursued ever since the consultation of Weed and Lincoln in the preceding December and which Lincoln had followed since his inauguration— namely, to "change the question from one upon slavery or about slavery to one upon union or disunion." The evacuation of Sumter, Seward said, though not in fact a slavery or party question, was so regarded. He would therefore evacuate the fort as a safe means of changing the issue; but he would reinforce all the Gulf forts, recall the navy from foreign stations, and put the island of Key West under martial law. Lincoln replied that this was the exact domestic policy he had been following, except for Fort Sumter, and he did not perceive how that was a slavery or party issue, while the reinforcement of Fort Pickens would be a more national and patriotic one.

The foreign policy suggested by Seward is this: "I would demand explanations from Spain and France, categorically at once. I would seek explanations from Great Britain and Russia, and send agents into Canada, Mexico, and Central America to rouse a vigorous spirit of independence on this continent against European intervention. And if satisfactory explanations are not received from Spain and France, would convene Congress and declare war against them." To this proposal Lincoln replied in one sentence: "The news received yesterday in regard to St. Domingo certainly brings a new item within the range of our foreign policy; but up to that time we have been preparing circulars and instructions to ministers and the like, all in perfect harmony, without even a suggestion that we had no foreign policy."

Seward's criticism of the President's delay was severe. He had said: "We are at the end of a month's administration and yet without a policy, domestic or foreign"; further delay would "bring scandal on the administration and danger upon the country." But it was his final proposal that was most astounding. He said: "Whatever policy we adopt, there must be energetic prosecution of it . . . it must be somebody's business to pursue it and direct it incessantly. Either the President must do it, and be all the while active in it, or devolve it on some member of his Cabinet. Once adopted, debates on it must end, and all agree and abide. It is not in my special province: but I neither seek to evade nor to assume responsibility."

Seward's offer to assume control was not limited to the foreign policy, but applied, as he said, to matters not in his special province. His demand that debates must end when a policy was once decided upon was a reference to Lincoln's second request for opinions on Fort Sumter after five out of seven members of the Cabinet had once given their judgment that the fort should be evacuated. The proposal was a very blunt expression of Seward's belief, which, it must be admitted, was that of many public men of the day, that he and not Lincoln was to be the real head of the Administration. Lincoln's reply was in few words of unmistakable meaning: "Upon your closing proposition . . . I remark that if this must be done, I must do it. When a general line of policy is adopted I apprehend there is no danger of its being changed without good reason, or continuing to be a subject of unnecessary debate; still, upon points arising in its progress I wish, and I suppose I am entitled to have, the advice of all the Cabinet."

In a few days, as we know, the decision was made. The delayed expedition arrived too late to aid in resisting the attack. Fort Sumter was surrendered, and, whatever may have been true before, there was no longer any possibility of avoiding civil war. It had begun with an attack on the flag, and the North was for a time almost as thoroughly united as the South.

CHAPTER IV

PRIVATEERS AND THE DECLARATION
OF PARIS

AFTER the fall of Fort Sumter the situation developed rapidly and in a manner which at once made possible serious difficulties between the United States and the maritime powers of Europe. The fort was surrendered on Saturday. On Monday Lincoln called seventy-five thousand men to the colours to put down the insurrection. Two answers to this action came from the South on Wednesday, when Virginia passed an ordinance of secession and Jefferson Davis issued a proclamation announcing that the Confederacy, which had no navy, would commission private ships to prey on Northern commerce. In prompt rejoinder Lincoln on Friday declared that the United States would treat the privateers as pirates, and proclaimed a blockade of Southern ports. Thus, within one week the situation had developed beyond the control of any power in America and demanded consideration by foreign governments.

A privateer's commission might authorize the ship holding it to capture not only merchant ships of American ownership, but also goods owned by an American though carried in foreign merchant ships. Consideration was at once given on both sides of the Atlantic to means by which sea-borne commerce might be delivered from this form of warfare. The first article of the Declaration of Paris, signed in 1856 in connexion with the treaty which ended the Crimean War, had abolished privateering, but the declaration was binding only on those powers that had signed it or formally acceded to it, and the United States was not one of them.

Both to Russell, the British Minister of Foreign Affairs, and to Seward, neither knowing what was in the mind of the other, it occurred that we might even yet adopt it, and Russell thought of proposing such accession to both American belligerents.[44] Seward acted promptly. Seven days after the proclamation of the Confederacy was issued, Seward instructed the American diplomatic representatives to all the maritime powers of Europe, including Adams in London and Dayton in Paris, to enter into an agreement, each with the government to which he was accredited, for the United States to accede to the "Declaration of the Paris Congress, with the conditions annexed by that body to the same."

The Declaration consisted of four articles. The first abolished privateering; the second and third declared that, with the exception of contraband of war, enemy goods on neutral ships and neutral goods on enemy ships should not be subject to capture; the fourth recognized the principle that blockades to be binding must be effective. When the seven powers which signed the declaration submitted it to the United States in 1856, President Pierce expressed the willingness of this Government to accede to it on condition that the first article be amended. The surrender of the right to use privateers was of little consequence to a strong naval power, he said, so long as it could use its public armed cruisers against the property of private citizens of an enemy country; but the United States maintained no great navy and was unwilling to give up an effective weapon so long as crippling an enemy's commerce remained a legitimate means of making war. President Pierce therefore proposed to add to the first article, which abolished privateering, an amendment suggested by Marcy, Secretary of State, providing that the private property of subjects and citizens of a belligerent on the high seas should be exempt from capture by the public armed vessels of the other belligerent. The proposal was favourably considered by France, Prussia, Austria, Russia, and other powers, but was not acceptable to England. Negotiations were still in progress when Buchanan became President, but were "suspended" by his direction in 1857. Seward now instructed the American diplomatic representatives abroad to renew the negotiations and accept the four articles without modification.

He explained that President Lincoln believed the Marcy amendment still desirable, but would not urge it because time and circumstances were not propitious; a portion of the American people had raised the standard of insurrection and had "taken the bad resolution to invite privateers to prey on the peaceful commerce of the United States," and he thought it wise in the circumstances to "secure the lesser good offered by the Paris Congress without waiting indefinitely to obtain the greater one offered" in the proposed amendment.[45] Seward thus made it known from the beginning that his purpose in offering to accept the Declaration of Paris was to render the use of privateers by the Confederacy unlawful by treaty obligation, as it was already piracy by the law of the land if Lincoln's proclamation was to have the force of law.

The instructions were sent April 24. At that time no foreign government had issued a proclamation of neutrality or in any other way taken official cognizance of the existence of the Confederacy. The situation had changed before the proposal could be made to either Great Britain or France. Charles Francis Adams did not arrive in London until May 13, and his first interview with Russell was five days later. England's proclamation of neutrality had already been issued, recognizing the existence of a war, with, of course, two contending parties, each of which might exercise the rights of a belligerent in dealing with British ships. Russell was concerned, however, at the prospect of privateering and had already been trying to devise ways to prevent it. He had proposed, through Lord Cowley, British ambassador at Paris, that England and France unite in asking from both American belligerents an agreement to observe the Declaration of Paris. Thouvenel, the French Minister of Foreign Affairs, thought it unwise to include the article on privateering, on the ground that France and England would get into difficulties if the North should agree and the South should refuse, but he was willing to make the attempt so far as the other articles were concerned and suggested that the Confederacy might be approached through the British and French consuls at Charleston or New Orleans. In spite of this objection, a private letter from Russell accompanied the instructions sent to Lyons on May 18 and authorized him to encourage any disposition which the United States might have to recognize the declaration with regard to privateering. Russell added: "You will clearly understand that Her Majesty's Government cannot accept the renunciation on the part of the Government of the United States if coupled with the condition that they should enforce its renunciation on the Confederate States." [46]

From the outset the negotiations were doomed to failure. Seward's letter of April 24 had made it plain that it was the Confederate resolution to use privateers that made him willing to accede to the Declaration of Paris and thereby "secure the lesser good"—namely, the outlawing of this mode of warfare. On the other hand, Russell was careful to say to Lyons that England would not consider the Southern privateers outlawed even if the United States should accede to all the articles of the Declaration. Yet in spite of the definiteness of the instructions on both sides, misunderstandings arose, and when the negotiations had failed, Russell said of Seward, in a note to the Prime Minister, Lord Palmerston: "It all looks as if a trap had been prepared"; [47] and as for Adams, "his faith in the straightforwardness of any portion of the Palmerston-Russell Ministry was gone." [48] The suspicions and distrust thus aroused on both sides made negotiations on any question more difficult for many months to come. How did the misunderstandings arise?

The first meeting between the new American minister and Russell took place May 18. Towards the close of the interview Adams told Russell, not that he was instructed to accept the Declaration of Paris, but that he was "authorized to negotiate in regard to the rights of neutrals in time of war," and had been given a form of a convention which he would submit if there was any disposition to pursue the matter further. Russell "expressed the willingness of Great Britain to negotiate. But he seemed to desire to leave the subject in the hands of Lord Lyons, to whom he intimated that he had already transmitted authority to assent to any modification of the only point in issue which the Government of the United States might prefer." [49] If Adams had explained at this point that the United States did not ask any modification at all and that the form of convention which he was directed to submit was in the exact words of the Declaration of Paris, later misunderstandings might have been avoided. Adams did not do this. There was some difference afterwards between his recollection and that of Russell concerning the conversation, but on this point they agreed, as is shown by Adams's account of his later interview of July 18. Adams reported that after comparing their respective recollections of the facts in dispute he handed to Russell the draft of the convention he was authorized to sign. Russell examined it. "The first remark he made was that it was essentially the Declaration of Paris. He had never known until now that the United States were disposed to accede to it. He was sure I had never mentioned it. To this I assented but observed that the reason why I had not done so was that my Government had directed me to make a preliminary inquiry, and that was whether Her Majesty's ministers were disposed to enter into any negotiations at all." [50]

As Russell had not learned the situation from Adams, neither had he heard of it from Paris, though he had been in constant communication with France about the policy the two countries were to pursue in common. Dayton, the American minister in Paris, had disregarded his instructions. On May 22 he acknowledged the receipt of Seward's circular of April 24, together with a form for a treaty identical with that sent to Adams, but he protested against the course he had been instructed to pursue, saying that he felt he ought to attempt once more to secure the Marcy amendment. On May 30 he reported that he had actually followed this course. He had told Thouvenel that he was authorized to accept the Declaration of Paris, "but with the desire expressed by the President that the provisions should be added exempting private property afloat, except contraband, from seizure and confiscation. I did not say, nor did he ask, whether the four propositions would be accepted without change." [51]

To this communication Seward replied, saying: "The instructions contained in my despatch No. 4, dated 24th of April, required you to tender to the French Government without delay our adhesion to the Declaration of Paris Congress, pure and simple," and directed him to carry out that instruction without further loss of time. Dayton still demurred and said that since he had heard that Adams had referred the question back to Washington, it would be "more convenient in every respect that you should take charge of the whole question." Seward still insisted, and at last Adams in London and Dayton in Paris were ready for the signing of the treaty. Both France and England proposed to accompany the signature with a statement in writing to the effect that they were undertaking no "engagement that would have any bearing, direct or indirect, on the

internal differences now prevailing in the United States."
Russell explained that Great Britain had declared her
neutrality, thereby recognizing the belligerent rights of
the South; but that the North, refusing to recognize the
status of belligerency, might expect Great Britain to
treat the privateers of the Confederacy as pirates. Both
Adams and Dayton refused to sign, and Seward approved their action. The negotiation thus closed was not
again renewed.

When Seward proposed accession to the declaration,
no government had proclaimed its neutrality or recognized the neutral rights of the Confederacy. The chief
object of his diplomacy for the first few months of his
administration was to prevent recognition; and that
was his original purpose in this negotiation. Seward, like
many others of his time and later, did not at first distinguish clearly between mere recognition of belligerency
and recognition of full sovereign powers. Indeed, he
sometimes wrote as if either form of recognition were
hardly to be distinguished from actual intervention. He
maintained that there was in this country, as there
always had been, one and only one political power
competent to make war—namely, the United States of
America—and that its treaty accepting the Declaration
of Paris would be "obligatory equally upon disloyal as
upon loyal subjects." He had offered an assurance that
we ourselves would not make use of privateers, and
that we would punish as piracy such "depredations by
the insurgents." He felt that any foreign power which
should deny our full sovereignty over the South, and
our right to make a treaty which would be legally binding on our "insurgent" citizens, would by that denial

interfere in our domestic quarrel. He had hoped that by offering this treaty at the very moment we were presenting our protest against the recognition of the Confederacy, such recognition might be prevented.[52] Such was Seward's own explanation of the motives which led him, on April 24, to send the original instructions to the American representatives to European powers. But there was delay in presenting the offer, in both London and Paris, and Seward's persistence in the negotiations after the belligerent rights of the Confederacy had been recognized led to the belief that another purpose had developed afterward and accounts for Russell's feeling that a trap had been laid.

Before dismissing the subject it may be well to add that the whole question of privateering soon lost its importance. Great Britain, whose example was followed by other powers, issued an order, June 1, 1861, which prevented privateers or other armed ships of either belligerent from taking prizes captured by them into the ports of the British Islands or of any of the British colonies or possessions. This order worked to the disadvantage of the Confederacy. The ports of the North were always available to United States ships of war and prizes captured by them, while the Southern ports were closed by the blockade, and Confederate privateers and cruisers could find no place to which to take their prizes. The *Alabama* and other vessels of the Confederate Navy, when the navy had been created, did much damage as commerce-destroyers; but privateers, which are not maintained by appropriations, but are entirely dependent on the sale of prizes, soon ceased to be profitable to the owners and were no longer used.

The ever-recurring question of recognition came up with the negotiation about the Declaration of Paris. The British consul at Charleston was Robert Bunch. In accordance with Russell's instructions Lyons authorized him to get the Confederacy to accept the two articles which deal with neutral commerce. Lyons warned him to avoid anything like recognition; he was not to go to Richmond nor to deal with the central authorities, but was to make the proposal to Governor Pickens and ask him to get action by President Davis. Mercier, the French minister at Washington, directed the consul of his Government at Charleston to co-operate with Bunch. The two consuls engaged William H. Trescot, who had been in the American diplomatic service, to broach the subject to Davis. Trescot was successful and the Confederate Congress soon accepted all the articles of the declaration except the one on privateering. Bunch was elated, talked of the "negotiations," and said that this was the first step towards recognition.

A few days later one Robert Mure was arrested in New York with a sealed bag from the Charleston consulate for the Foreign Office in London, and a large number of private letters and papers. The consular bag was sent to Adams unopened to be delivered to Russell. Among the other papers was one which described Bunch's recent activities. All consuls in Southern cities were doing business under exequaturs granted by the Washington Government, for no foreign power had recognized the Confederacy. Seward asked Great Britain to remove Bunch from office, but Russell declined, avowing the Government's responsibility for his action on the declaration, but denying responsibility for any assertion that this action was a step towards recognition. Russell wrote: "Her Majesty's Government have already recognized the belligerent character of the Southern States, and they will continue to recognize them as belligerents. But Her Majesty's Government have not recognized and are not prepared to recognize the so-called Confederate States as a separate and independent nation." The right to communicate with the South in case of necessity was asserted, but the practice seems to have been discontinued because of the American protest. Seward cancelled Bunch's exequatur on the ground that his utterances showed partisanship for the South, and Bunch disappears from the public records.

LINCOLN'S proclamation of a blockade gave more concern to the maritime powers than the anticipated dangers from Southern privateers. The cotton supply of the world was furnished largely by the plantations of the seceding states, and the textile industries of England and France would be seriously affected if their supply of raw material should be interrupted. An effective blockade meant, of course, that any ship, foreign or American, would be captured if after due warning it should attempt to enter or leave a blockaded port. Before the question was decided, there had been some discussion in the Cabinet about the relative advantages of two proposed methods of cutting off the trade of the Southern seaports. Secretary Welles and some others advised that the Government close them by statute or by a mere proclamation that they were no longer ports of entry, so that ships attempting to deliver goods in any of them might be seized as smugglers; but Seward advised a formal blockade as less likely to bring complications with foreign governments because the right of blockade was well established and recognized by all nations. In spite of this, Seward evidently did not realize that by proclaiming a blockade the United States

Government had declared itself a belligerent and was claiming rights over foreign vessels that are admitted only in time of war, and that the relations of other powers to the United States would thereafter be governed, not by the law of peace, but by the law of neutrality. He insisted that they recognize our blockade and permit us to exercise war rights in dealing with their merchant ships, but he protested when foreign nations recognized the situation by proclaiming their neutrality.

If Seward would not admit or hoped by diplomacy to avoid the normal implications of this step, he nevertheless had good reasons for preferring blockade to an attempt to close the ports by municipal law. Nearly a month earlier he had said to Lord Lyons, the British minister in Washington, that the ports might be closed and vessels attempting to enter might be seized on a charge of violating the revenue laws. Lyons replied that this would "amount to a paper blockade, and would place the foreign powers in the dilemma of recognizing the Confederacy or submitting to the interruption of their commerce." Even a formal blockade, though recognized as lawful in time of war, might not avoid trouble with England, Seward feared, for Lyons had told him that if the United States determined to stop by force so important a commerce as that of Great Britain with the cotton states, Lyons "could not answer for what might happen." [53] In this remark, which was half a threat, Lyons evidently said more than he meant, for when he reported to Russell two months later that Lincoln had proclaimed a formal blockade, he said: "If it be carried on with reasonable consideration for foreign flags, and in strict conformity with the Law of Nations,

I suppose it must be recognized."[54] The fear of serious trouble with England as a result of the blockade had, however, been planted in Seward's mind, and doubtless had an influence on the instructions he gave later to Adams.

Recognition by the European powers had, of course, been hoped for from the beginning by the seceding states. It was four months since South Carolina, as she declared, had "resumed her separate and equal place among the nations," and it was more than a month since Jefferson Davis had appointed special commissioners and sent them to Europe to secure recognition of the independence of the Confederacy. These commissioners, Yancy and Rost, arrived in London on April 29, almost simultaneously with the news of the outbreak of hostilities at Fort Sumter. At the same time Russell heard of the design of the Confederacy to commission privateers and of Lincoln's proclamation of blockade. He sent for Dallas, still the American minister, but awaiting the arrival of Adams as his successor, and told him that he had not yet seen the commissioners from the Confederacy, but was "not unwilling to do so unofficially," and that there existed between Great Britain and France an understanding which would lead both to take the same course as to recognition, whatever that course might be. At the same time Russell mentioned the rumour of a meditated blockade of Southern ports and their discontinuance as ports of entry. Dallas replied that he had heard nothing from his Government of these matters. He informed Russell that Mr. Adams would probably arrive in less than two weeks, whereupon, Dallas reported, "his lordship acquiesced in the expedi-

ency of disregarding mere rumor and waiting the full
knowledge to be brought by my successor," and added
that the motion of Mr. Gregory might be further postponed at his lordship's suggestion.[55]

Seward's attention was again turned by this communication to the danger that recognition might follow
the enforcement of a blockade. The motion which Mr.
Gregory had offered in the House of Commons was only
to be postponed, and it was a motion to recognize the
Confederacy not merely as a belligerent, but as a fully
sovereign, independent nation. Seward knew that England's greatest industry was absolutely dependent on
the cotton of the Southern states, and if the attempt to
isolate the South should be at all successful, English
manufacturers would bring enormous pressure upon
their Government to break the blockade and secure a
supply of their essential raw material. Russell was even
now willing to meet the Confederate commissioners,
though as yet unofficially, and recognition might follow
very soon. The situation was made worse by the understanding between England and France, announced to
Dallas by Russell, that these two powers would take
the same course with regard to recognition. It was by
no means certain, Seward thought, that recognition
would be the limit of their action. It might be only the
first step towards an actual alliance with the Confederacy. Had not Lord Lyons told him that if an attempt
were made to stop by force the commerce of Great
Britain with the cotton states, he "could not answer for
what might happen"?

There was much in the situation to cause anxiety.
Seward expressed his fears in a letter to his wife, dated

May 17, in which he said: "They have misunderstood things fearfully in Europe. Great Britain is in grave danger of sympathizing so much with the South, for the sake of peace and cotton, as to drive us to make war against her as the ally of the traitor. . . . My last despatches from Great Britain and France have shown that they were almost ready, on some pretext, to try and save cotton at the expense of the Union. I am trying to get a bold remonstrance through the Cabinet before it is too late."[56]

The bold remonstrance referred to was the dispatch to Adams, dated May 21. Adams had landed at Liverpool on May 13 and had proceeded at once to London, where he immediately assumed the duties of his office. This dispatch as at first prepared by Seward contained several sharp expressions and vigorous instructions, some of which were omitted when the original draft was revised by Lincoln, but even in the amended form, which was approved by the President, it placed heavy responsibilities on Adams, and its harsh tone caused him much uneasiness. After reciting the chief items of information communicated by Dallas under date of May 2, the dispatch gave Adams instructions as to his attitude with regard to each of them. Concerning the Confederate commissioners, Seward said that intercourse of any kind with them was likely to be construed as a recognition of the authority that appointed them, and it would be none the less hurtful to the United States for being called unofficial. "More, unofficial intercourse is useless and meaningless if it is not expected to ripen into official intercourse and direct recognition. . . . You will, in any event, desist from all intercourse, unofficial as well as official, with the British Government so long as it shall continue intercourse of either kind with the domestic enemies of this country."

When Adams received and read this dispatch, he wrote in his diary: "The Government seems almost ready to declare war with all the Powers of Europe, and almost instructs me to withdraw from communication with the ministers here in a certain contingency." That was very true. The situation would be serious if that contingency should arise; but the instructions just received did not require him to go much further than he had already told Russell he might have to go, when on his arrival he learned that England had recognized the belligerency of the Confederate states. It was May 18, at his first official interview with Lord John Russell, some days before the disturbing dispatch of May 21 was written and nearly a month before it came into his hands. Adams had then said to Russell that if there was on the part of Great Britain an intention to extend the struggle by giving encouragement in any form to the Confederacy, "I was bound to acknowledge that in that contingency I had nothing further to do in Great Britain."[57] This language, if well considered, indicated a purpose to withdraw from communication with the Ministers, and even to withdraw from the country, in a certain contingency, which was practically the same as that now feared by Seward.

As to the blockade, Seward's dispatch insisted that this was a proper means of suppressing insurrection when national ports had been seized by the insurgents; and he added: "You will not insist that our blockade is to be respected if it be not maintained by a competent force; but passing by that question as not now a practical, or, at least an urgent one, you will add that the blockade is now, and it will continue to be so maintained, and therefore we expect it to be respected by Great Britain." Returning to the question of recognition, the dispatch continued: "It is, of course, direct recognition to publish an acknowledgment of the sovereignty and independence of a new power. It is direct recognition to receive its ambassadors, ministers, agents, or commissioners officially. A concession of belligerent rights is liable to be construed as a recognition of them. No one of these proceedings will pass unquestioned by the United States in this case."

The privateers, about which instructions had been sent a month before, presented still another problem. If Great Britain would not accept his proposal that we accede to the Declaration of Paris, Seward saw the possibility that British subjects might accept commissions or serve on board such ships, and groundlessly feared that foreign ports might be open to them. He said: "As to the treatment of privateers in the insurgent service, you will say that this is a question exclusively our own. We treat them as pirates. They are our own citizens, or persons employed by our citizens, preying on the commerce of our country. If Great Britain shall choose to recognize them as lawful belligerents, and give them shelter from our pursuit and punishment, the laws of nations afford an adequate and proper remedy."

Then came the paragraph which, with the instructions to discontinue intercourse with the British Government in a certain contingency, made Adams wonder at the warlike tone of the dispatch. Only a sentence or two need be quoted: "We are not insensible of the grave importance of this occasion. We see how, as the result of the debate in which we are engaged, a war may ensue between the United States and one, two or even more European nations. War in any case is exceptional from the habits, as it is revolting from the sentiments of the American people. But if it come it will be fully seen that it results from the action of Great Britain, not our own; that Great Britain will have decided to fraternize with our domestic enemy either without waiting to hear from you our remonstrances and our warnings, or after having heard them. War in defense of national life is not immoral, and war in defense of independence is an inevitable part of the discipline of nations."

Many judicious writers, careful in forming opinions on historical matters, have expressed the belief that this dispatch is evidence that Seward had not abandoned or was now returning to the policy of foreign war as a means of reuniting the hostile sections at home. It is with some diffidence that the suggestion is here made that another understanding of the instructions to Adams is at least possible, which does not do so much violence to Seward's sanity or to the keen shrewdness which all students of the man and his achievements recognize. The dispatch does speak very plainly of the possibility of war with "one, two or even more European nations," but this language was approved by Lincoln as well as by Seward. If it had been a revival of Seward's foreign-war proposal of April 1, it seems improbable that Lincoln would have failed to recognize it or would have approved in May what he had rejected in April.

In his "Thoughts for the President," Seward had spoken of war against nations about to intervene in Latin America—an intervention to which the South was even more antagonistic than the North. Both Lincoln and Seward were anxious now because of the possible necessity of war with England or any European nation that should become what Seward had called "an ally of the traitor," or, as this dispatch expressed it, should have "decided to fraternize with our domestic enemies." It was one thing, before any fighting had occurred, for Seward to hope, however mistakenly, that if sufficient attention was called to the ambitions of France and Spain with regard to Latin America, the South might be convinced of the necessity of returning to the Union in order that the united force of the nation might be ready to oppose the threatened intervention; it would have been quite another thing if he had expected the South, after hostilities had actually broken out and after three more states had gone over to the Confederacy,[58] to join the North in fighting one or more European nations whose only offence would have been that they had become allies of the South in our domestic strife.

The alarm which Adams expressed on receiving the dispatch was caused chiefly by the paragraph which instructed him to withdraw from all intercourse with the British Government so long as it continued official or unofficial intercourse with the Southern envoys. In the original draft, as written by Seward, there was an additional instruction. When Adams withdrew, he was to emphasize the breach by delivering to Russell a copy of the dispatch. Lincoln struck out that portion of the sentence, but the order to discontinue his functions if the Southerners were permitted any kind of intercourse with the British Government was permitted to stand. This was not new to Adams. Seward had written him, April 10, before Fort Sumter had been fired on: "If, as the President does not at all apprehend, you shall find Her Majesty's Government tolerating the application of the seceding states, or wavering about it, you will not leave them to suppose for a moment that they can grant that application and remain the friends of the United States. You may even assure them promptly in that case that if they determine to recognize, they may at the same time prepare to enter into an alliance with the enemies of this republic. You alone will represent your country at London, and you will represent the whole of it."[59]

Adams approached the subject with directness, saying to Russell that the continued stay of the Southern envoys in London, and still more the knowledge that they had been admitted to interviews with the Foreign Minister, was calculated to excite uneasiness. Indeed, it had already given great dissatisfaction to the American Government. "I added as moderately as I could," reported Adams, "that in all frankness any further protraction of this relation could scarcely fail to be viewed by us as hostile in spirit, and to require some corresponding action accordingly." Russell replied that it had long been the custom to receive such persons unofficially, but that this did not imply recognition. He added that he had seen the gentlemen on two occasions, and that he "had no expectation of seeing them again."[60]

It is interesting to observe in this connexion that

when news of the Confederate victory at Bull Run reached London, the commissioners again asked Russell for an informal interview. He asked them to put their communication in writing. About that time they reported that they had "not received the least notice or attention, official or social, from any member of the Government."[61] Russell would in all probability have taken this course without urging, but Seward's protest as presented by Adams brought to his attention the strong feeling of the United States on any matter implying or approaching the recognition of the Confederacy.

It was not only from Adams that Russell knew of this feeling. Lyons had reported the rumours that were floating in Washington about the warlike note that had been discussed in the Cabinet, but Lyons was uncertain how the situation should be understood. On May 21, in a private letter to Russell, he interpreted Seward's threats as mere bluster, but the next day he wrote to Sir Edmund Head, Governor of Canada, urging him to prepare for defence against attack by the United States.[62] There was already uneasiness in Canada as to Seward's intentions, though the Duke of Newcastle, then Colonial Secretary in Palmerston's Cabinet, doubted whether there was much ground for it. In order to quiet Sir Edmund Head's apprehensions Newcastle related the incident that later, in England, at the height of resentment over the *Trent* affair, was used to stir up suspicion against Seward. Newcastle wrote: "I entirely agree with you in what you say in your letter of 18th of May about Mr. Seward's speculations and unfriendly views toward Canada, but I think you hardly make sufficient allowance for his hyper-American use of the policy of bully and bluster. When I saw him at Albany last October he fairly told me he should make use of insults to England to secure his own position in the States, and that I must not suppose he meant war. On the contrary he did not wish war with England, and he was confident we should never go to war with the States—we dared not and could not afford it."[63] It has been assumed sometimes that Newcastle misunderstood what Thurlow Weed called Seward's *badinage* and took it seriously. It is evident from this letter that he did not mistake Seward's meaning, but his displeasure at the remark is readily understood.

The uncertainty as to Seward's intentions continued through several months to influence the attitude of the British Government towards the United States. Bluster might be met with arrogance; and some of Russell's replies to American claims seem to have been written in that spirit; yet Seward might really mean war, and Russell was careful not to give unnecessary provocation. The attitude of Great Britain in several matters about which Seward had been anxious was more favourable than he had expected. There was no recognition of the Confederacy as an independent nation; the Minister of Foreign Affairs had no expectation of seeing the Southern commissioners again; and our blockade was to be respected. As to the fear that Southern privateers would find shelter in British ports, Lyons assured Seward that no such shelter would be given. The Queen's proclamation of neutrality, which roused much resentment in the North at the time, covered most of these points. It warned British subjects that they were forbidden to enter the military service of either of the contending parties, or to fit out or equip any ship to be employed as a ship of war or privateer, or to break or endeavour to break any blockade lawfully established. All persons subject to British jurisdiction were warned that if they committed any of these acts, they would not only be subject to the penalties imposed by British law, but would not obtain any protection from Great Britain against any liability or penal consequences imposed by the offended belligerent.

Nevertheless, the proclamation of neutrality did of necessity recognize that there were two belligerents and that the Confederacy was one of them. It was this "granting belligerent rights" to the South that grieved Seward. When France also had proclaimed her neutrality, Seward wrote to Dayton: "This Government insists that the United States are one whole undivided nation, especially so far as foreign nations are concerned, and that France is, by the law of nations and by treaties, not a neutral between two imaginary parties here, but a friend of the United States." Many American writers of those days and for a generation afterwards accepted Seward's position, not recognizing that it was necessary, especially for Great Britain, with her great shipping interests, to determine whether our blockade should be recognized, and if it were, then to notify her shipowners that they could not expect British protection if they should attempt to enter or leave a blockaded port. It is difficult to find any just ground even for the belief that the Queen's proclamation was issued with unfriendly haste.

CHAPTER VI

THE *TRENT* AFFAIR

THE Trent affair, which in point of time closely followed the Bunch incident, roused to a point of dangerous resentment the distrust of Seward already prevalent in England, and for a time seemed to confirm the suspicion that it was the deliberate intention of the American Government to provoke Great Britain to war. Captain Charles Wilkes, commanding the United States warship *San Jacinto,* had overhauled the *Trent,* a British mail-steamer, on the high seas, bound from Havana to St. Thomas in the Danish West Indies, and compelled her to bring to, which she did only after he had fired the second shot across her bow. He compelled her to surrender the Confederate envoys, James M. Mason of Virginia and John Slidell of Louisiana, and their secretaries, George Eustice and James MacFarland, all of whom were on their way to England. These men refused to leave the British vessel, claiming the protection of the neutral flag, and Captain Moir of the *Trent* protested vehemently against their seizure. Lieutenant Fairfax, executive officer of the *San Jacinto,* had boarded the *Trent* alone, but found it necessary not only to bring up the guard of marines whom he had left in his small boat, but also to call on the *San Jacinto* for additional men. There was no actual physical resistance, but even after the arrival of the larger guard Mason and Slidell refused to go until hands were laid on their shoulders, and thus they were taken, without violence, but technically by force, to the *San Jacinto*. The wife, son, and three daughters of Slidell, and the wife of Eustice, were on the steamer. Lieutenant Fairfax offered them the use of the cabin of the *San Jacinto*, but they preferred to proceed on the *Trent* to St. Thomas, whence they sailed by another vessel to England.

Captain Wilkes had acted without instructions and without the knowledge of his Government. For many months he had been cruising off the coast of Africa with the *San Jacinto*, a part of the squadron for the suppression of the African slave trade. Returning, he touched at St. Thomas and there heard that Mason and Slidell had slipped out of Charleston on the blockade-runner *Theodora* and made their way safely to Havana. Proceeding to that port, he learned of their intention to sail on the *Trent* and determined to seize them, though his executive officer, Lieutenant Fairfax, protested, fearing the unlawful act would cause trouble or even war with Great Britain. Mason and Slidell seemed to Wilkes to be very important men and he thought their seizure worth the risk. Mason, before he was expelled from the United States Senate for participation in secession, had been for ten years chairman of the Committee on Foreign Relations; and Slidell, formerly a senator from Louisiana, was considered a master in political strategy. Their appointment to replace the earlier envoys, who had made little progress towards securing European recognition of the Confederacy, had raised high hopes throughout the South and apprehensions in the Northern states.

The seizure took place on November 8, 1861, but noth-

ing was known of it in America until the *San Jacinto*
arrived at Fortress Monroe, November 15. It is difficult
now to understand the wave of triumphant rejoicing
that swept the country. Seward made no statement,
Postmaster-General Montgomery Blair thought the seizure unlawful, and Sumner, chairman of the Foreign
Relations Committee, would have ordered Wilkes to
make amends by taking the captured envoys to England
on the *San Jacinto*. These adverse opinions were not expressed publicly and the whole country went wild with
exultation. The military successes of the South had
caused much depression, England was believed to be in
full sympathy with the Confederacy, there had been unreasonable fears for the results that might be expected
from the mission of Mason and Slidell, and this spectacular incident appealed to the imagination of the multitude.
It was not the unthinking alone who were carried away:
the Secretary of the Navy congratulated Wilkes and assured him that his act had "the emphatic approval" of
the Navy Department; Edward Everett, who had been
Secretary of State and ambassador to Great Britain, said
there was "not the slightest ground for any apprehension
that there is any illegality" in the act, and Caleb Cushing, Attorney-General in Pierce's Cabinet, ponderously
affirmed that Wilkes was "amply justified by the principles and doctrines of international jurisprudence." In an
ecstasy of delight the New York *Times* said in an editorial article: "As for Commodore Wilkes and his command, let the handsome thing be done. Consecrate
another Fourth of July to him."

Far different was the sentiment in England. The
possibility of the seizure of the envoys had been

foreseen there, but not the circumstances which actually occurred.

The *James Adger*, a fast United States cruiser, was at Southampton and seemed to be waiting for something. Lord Palmerston suspected that it might be her purpose to intercept the British mail-steamer from the West Indies on which Mason and Slidell were expected, and the Government asked the Advocate-General what might be done in such a case. The preliminary opinion of the law-officers, as Palmerston understood it,[64] put little limit on the belligerent right of visit and search. Palmerston wrote to Delane, editor of *The Times*, for his private information, that "this American cruiser might, by our own principles of International Law, stop the West India packet, search her, and if the Southern men and their despatches and credentials were found on board, either take them out, or seize the packet and carry her back to New York for trial." This was by no means the opinion acted upon by the British Government when the facts about the stopping of the *Trent* became known. With this opinion in mind Palmerston sought an interview with Adams and urged the unwisdom of stopping a foreign vessel for such a purpose as was indicated. The presence of one or two more Southern men, he said, would scarcely make a difference in the action of the Government after once having made up its mind. Adams assured him that the *James Adger* had been sent to intercept the *Nashville*, a Confederate cruiser, but "had no instruction" to interfere with the British packet. Palmerston seems to have understood Adams to say that the *James Adger* had positive instructions not to interfere with any foreign vessel, and this

mistaken impression, by allaying Palmerston's apprehensions, may have prepared the way for a reaction to
more intense feelings when he learned, twelve days later,
that the *San Jacinto* had actually done off the coast of
Cuba what he had at first feared might be done by the
James Adger in nearer waters.

Information of the seizure of the envoys reached
England on November 27, when the mail-steamer from
the West Indies arrived at Southampton bringing
Slidell's family and certain officers of the *Trent*. The
London *Times* of the 28th published it, together with a
leading article that was evidently written under the
influence of the opinion communicated to Delane by
Palmerston seventeen days earlier. This article[65] said:
"The intention of the Federal Government evidently
was to act on their strict right, and to do so in as little
ceremonious manner as might be. . . . Unwelcome as
the truth may be, it is nevertheless a truth, that we
have ourselves established a system of International
Law which now tells against us." The same article
added, however: "It is and always has been vain to
appeal to old folios and bygone authorities in justification of acts which every Englishman and every Frenchman cannot but feel to be injurious and insulting." Two
days later *The Times* said editorially: "We hear that
there is a possibility that the seizure was the act of the
American commander, and was not expressly directed
by his Government. Lieutenant Fairfax said, we are
informed, on board the *Trent*, that his commanding
officer acted on his own responsibility."[66]

The first draft of the instructions to Lyons was modified and softened in accordance with a paragraph

written by the Prince Consort at the request of the Queen. The dispatch, dated November 30, was supplemented by another of the same date and by a private letter of the day following, December 1, the day on which the Queen's messenger sailed to bear them to Washington. The supplementary instructions were important, but the date of sailing evidently gave no time for rewriting the original. The first dispatch demanded the release of the prisoners, with an apology; the second authorized a delay of seven days rather than insistence upon an immediate answer from Seward; the private letter instructed Lyons to abstain from anything like menace. There was a strong desire to avoid war, but such expectation of it that orders were issued to hold the fleet in readiness, several thousand troops were sent to Canada, and war-supplies for America were cut off by a proclamation that prohibited further export of arms and ammunition. The exultation in America over the seizure of the envoys was not known in England until three days after the Queen's messenger had sailed with the demand for their release, but it brought on increased anger and resentment, which continued with little abatement until the American reply was received.

The danger was well known to Seward. Anxious warnings had come to him from Adams as to British sentiment and from Dayton in Paris as well as from Weed, who was in London as an unofficial but authorized agent of President Lincoln. Weed had written: "It is again said that you want to provoke a war with England for the purpose of getting Canada," people are "fortified with evidences of your hostility to England. . . . Everything here is on a war footing. Such prompt and gigantic preparations were never known. . . . I was told yesterday repeatedly that I ought to write the President demanding your dismissal."[67] Seward had given no hint to Adams or Weed of what the policy of the Government would be, but was waiting to learn what the British Government might have to say. Lyons "unofficially" communicated his instructions on December 19. Two days later he called to deliver them formally, but at Seward's request there was a further postponement until December 23. The seven days for consideration would have expired December 30. There was a consultation with the President, at which Lincoln said: "Governor Seward, you will go on, of course, preparing your answer, which, as I understand it, will state the reasons why they ought to be given up. Now, I have a mind to try my hand at stating the reasons why they ought not to be given up. We will compare the points on each side."[68] Seward's draft was presented to the Cabinet on December 25 and earnestly discussed with much difference of opinion. Sumner was present and urgently supported Seward, reading private letters from Bright, Cobden, and others of his English correspondents who earnestly wished for an amicable settlement, but had no hope of it except by the surrender of the envoys. The Cabinet adjourned without agreement, but the next day, after further discussion, came to the unanimous opinion that the prisoners must be given up.

Seward's position was difficult. As a statesman he saw that he must yield to England's demand, or America must fight an unjust war, and even a righteous war with Great Britain at that time would have made the restoration of the Union very doubtful. As a politician he must gain support for a statesmanlike decision, which even the American correspondent of the London *Times* thought he dare not make in the face of popular sentiment so violent that "such a concession, even in this extremity, would prove fatal to its authors and destroy their Government."[69] Seward's reply was of course addressed to Lord Lyons, but it was almost immediately given to the newspapers because the greater part of it was intended not for the British Government, but for the American public. The letter was adroit rather than sound. Some of its arguments will not bear analysis, and some of the positions taken with regard to international law would not be defended by a scientific student of that subject. Seward maintained that persons as well as goods might be contraband, and that even neutral destination does not change their contraband character nor modify the right to capture them. He affirmed without qualification that a neutral vessel carrying contraband is itself subject to capture and confiscation, and applied that principle to the *Trent*, whose only "contraband" was the persons of Mason and Slidell. Wilkes's sole error, as Seward saw it, was that "after capturing the contraband persons and making prize of the *Trent* in what seems to be a perfectly lawful manner," he released her instead of sending her into port, where an American prize court would have passed upon the case. Seward affirmed that England was at last adopting American principles and asking us to do what she had refused to do for us in former times. He expressed his satisfaction that "a question is finally and rightly settled . . . which heretofore, exhausting not only all forms of peaceful discussion but also the arbitrament of war itself, for more than half a century alienated the two countries from each other, and perplexed with fears and apprehensions all other nations." The multitude that had been jubilant over the seizure of Mason and Slidell rejoiced again over the manner of their release. In giving up the case Seward had apparently committed England to the abandonment of her own precedents and the acceptance of a cherished American policy. It is true that Russell later made reply to Seward's argument, but for the moment Great Britain was interested only in that part of the dispatch which read: "The four persons in question are now held in military custody at Fort Warren, in the State of Massachusetts. They will be cheerfully liberated. Your lordship will please indicate a time and place for receiving them." The reply was that it gave "Her Majesty's Government great satisfaction to be able to arrive at a conclusion favourable to the maintenance of the most friendly relations between the two nations."

Seward knew why he had answered as he did. To Weed he wrote: "I am under the necessity of consulting the temper of parties and people on this side of the water quite as much as the temper of parties and people in England. If I had been as tame as you think would have been wise in my treatment of affairs in that country, I should have had no standing in my own." [70]

There was much in the dispatch which made the judicious grieve. Hamilton Fish, some years later Secretary of State, said its style was verbose and egotistical and its argument flimsy; but the change in public sentiment is better represented by R. H. Dana's attitude. In November he had written to Adams: "Wilkes has done a noble thing and done it well." Of this dispatch he wrote: "Seward is not only right but sublime."[71] The Secretary of State had accomplished what seemed impossible. He had secured enthusiastic popular support for an act which without his pen would have roused a storm of disapproval.

In England the decision brought relief. The difficulties of overseas war, the openness of Canada to attack, the prospect of further injury to commerce and industry, already crippled by the blockade, and, above all, the reluctance to make war against a kindred people had all been brought home when the rush of immediate preparation began. The reaction brought something like resentment towards Mason and Slidell, who had been the occasion of the alarm. The London *Times* recounted their earlier careers, saying that they more than any other men were responsible for the traditional American "insane prejudice against England," and expressing the hope that the English people would "not give these fellows anything like an ovation." The incident also cleared away, at least temporarily, the suspicion that Seward sought an excuse for war with England, and it strengthened the British policy of strict neutrality. The act of Wilkes, which had threatened disaster, had actually made for progress towards better understanding. To Seward belongs the credit for the unpopular but just and wise decision. The adroit appeal of the politician by which he won support for it cannot rob the statesman of his laurels.

IN his "Thoughts for the President's Consideration," Seward had suggested work which he thought must be done by the President or devolved upon some member of the Cabinet, and had offered to assume responsibility for the energetic prosecution of it, though it was not within his special province. The President rejected the offer, saying: "If this must be done, I must do it." Yet the relations between the two men remained cordial. More than that, a mutual respect and confidence grew up which endured through many troubles to the end. Lincoln never ceased to depend on Seward for miscellaneous work, and Seward never avoided it, even though by its nature it belonged to other departments than that presided over by the Secretary of State.

To meet the emergency of the time, Lincoln by proclamation suspended the privilege of the writ of habeas corpus. It was Seward—not the Attorney-General or the Secretary of War—who developed the system under which hundreds of men were arrested and without trial or hearing confined in forts or military prisons. The commanding officer of Fort McHenry refused to obey a writ issued in the case of John Merryman by the Chief Justice of the Supreme Court of the United States, who thereupon delivered an opinion declaring that Congress alone, and not the President, had authority to suspend the privilege of the writ. Lincoln defended his action as in complete harmony with the Constitution, but added that even if it were unconstitutional, the question to be decided was: "Are all the laws but one to go unexecuted and the government itself to go to pieces lest that one be violated?"

Seward's activity in ordering arrests was such that the brunt of all criticism fell on him. In putting the system into effect he appointed special agents and stationed them at various ports of entry to examine the passports required of persons entering or leaving the country. These agents were given authority to intercept and arrest suspicious persons. Elsewhere, within limits which were widely extended by successive proclamations, a telegram signed by Seward and sent to a United States marshal, or to a military officer, or even to a local chief of police, ordering that a man named in the message be arrested and sent for imprisonment to a military post, was obeyed without question. Hundreds were imprisoned on such orders. Some arrests were made also by order of the Secretary of War or by some military commander, but even in such cases the prisoners came generally under the control of the Secretary of State. Arrests were made on suspicion of having given or even intending to give substantial aid to the enemy by supplying arms or ammunition, or for selling bonds of the Southern states, or for expressing sympathy for the Confederacy, or for other reasons, such as belonging to a disloyal organization. Alien residents were arrested on suspicion as well as our own citizens, and of course they appealed to their diplomatic representatives in Washington, some of whom undertook to discuss with Seward the constitutionality of the President's action. He firmly declined to permit any foreign power to interpret for us our own fundamental law, and the attempt was not renewed.

It was inevitable that mistakes should be made. Conditions required prompt action, and innocent men were sometimes caught up in the machinery when rumour and plausible suspicion pointed to them. Provisions for reviewing the evidence were so inadequate that errors were not promptly corrected, and it was Seward who was the target for criticism, deserved and undeserved, so long as he controlled the system. It was all turned over to Stanton, February 14, 1862, less than a month after he succeeded Cameron as Secretary of War, and Seward was pleased to be relieved of an unpleasant task. Seward had already released many whom he thought improperly held, but Secretary Stanton appointed commissioners to examine the remaining cases, and within two months nearly a hundred were discharged on the report of the commissioners that they had been "long in prison and are detained without just cause."

It was while he had charge of these arrests that Seward sent a circular letter of instructions to the marshals and district attorneys of the federal courts which brought a protest from Attorney-General Bates. He wrote Seward a formal note saying that the officers of the courts might be "embarrassed by discrepant instructions from different sources," and reminding him that it was the Attorney-General who was charged by the act of Congress with the superintendence of attorneys and marshals of all the districts of the United States.

In the affair of the *Powhatan* and the expedition to the Gulf forts Seward had procured the issuing of naval and military orders without the knowledge of the Secretaries of War and Navy, and the heads of these departments on other occasions had his help, sometimes with and sometimes without their consent. Seward described his own occupation in the spring of 1862 when he wrote: "I dare not, because I cannot safely, leave this post from which all supplies, all directions, all inquiries must radiate to armies and navies at home and legations abroad."[72] The astonishing element in the situation is that so much of this activity was so long accepted as a matter of course. It was still generally supposed that Seward was the guiding spirit of the Administration. Seward himself had learned that this was true only within a limited sense, had adjusted himself to the situation, and was supporting Lincoln loyally; but he did not underestimate his own value. He wrote to his wife, June 5, 1861: "You have no idea how incessant my labors are to keep the conduct of it [the war] up to the line of necessity and public expectation. Executive skill and vigor are rare qualities. The President is the best of us, but he needs constant and assiduous cooperation."[73] Lincoln was in complete control as the final arbiter of policies, but he trusted Seward, and, finding him resourceful, energetic, and willing, he depended on him much more than on some other members of the Cabinet for details of management and administration for which he felt his own more limited experience had not prepared him.

Even Stanton gave his complete approval to a plan devised by Seward for securing additional recruits under the peculiar difficulties presented by the military situation in June and July 1862. McClellan's advance on

Richmond had failed because, as he affirmed, he had not been given the additional forces he had demanded. After the disastrous Seven Days' Battles the sorely disappointed and angry General had reported to the Secretary of War: "I have not a man in reserve, and I shall be glad to cover my retreat. . . . If I save this army now, I tell you plainly that I owe no thanks to you or to anyone in Washington. You have done your best to sacrifice this army."

McClellan's losses had been heavy and troops must be had. The censorship of the press and of the telegraph had been so strict that the people did not yet know what had been happening. Lincoln decided that he must have at least one hundred and fifty thousand men for three years' service, but to call for them by proclamation at the moment the people were learning that the beaten army was in retreat would cause, he feared, "a general panic and stampede." It was arranged that Lincoln should address a letter to Seward setting forth the need for additional troops and that Seward should get it before the governors of the states without attracting too much public notice. Telegraphing to Governor Morgan of New York and Thurlow Weed to meet him, Seward hurried to New York by special train. Governor Curtin of Pennsylvania joined them. There the plan was modified, Lincoln's consent being obtained by telegraph, so that the increase of military forces might seem to be made at the suggestion of the governors and on their initiative rather than in response to a cry for help. A joint letter was prepared, and signed by most of the governors of the loyal states, expressing their earnest desire that the "recent successes" of the federal army might be followed up by measures which must insure the speedy restoration of the Union, and requesting the President to call for as many men as might be "necessary to garrison and hold all of the numerous cities and military positions that have been captured by our armies, and to speedily crush the rebellion." Lincoln immediately replied, and the correspondence, apparently showing a spontaneous offer of troops and a grateful acceptance, was published widely before reports from the army made the actual results of McClellan's battles known. Three hundred thousand men were called.

Recruiting was slow, and in a few weeks Stanton announced a draft of three hundred thousand of the militia, but only enough would be conscripted to make up in each state its quota of the original call for volunteers under the offer of the governors. July and August of 1862 were gloomy months for the North. The Army of the Potomac had been withdrawn from the Peninsula, with McClellan still calling for reinforcements. General Pope had been brought from the West and placed in command of the forces about Washington and severely beaten at the second battle of Bull Run. Lee was preparing an invasion of the North. Early in September McClellan was again given command of all the forces in the East, and, following Lee, defeated him at Antietam. This victory, though incomplete, gave Lincoln an opportunity to issue his preliminary proclamation of emancipation, which had long been prepared, but was withheld on the advice of Seward until it could be "borne on the bayonets of an advancing army, not dragged in the dust behind a retreating one." Even then the proclamation did not have immediately the effect which Lincoln had anticipated. It failed to satisfy the abolitionists and the radical Republicans, for it proposed to free no slaves except in the states which were in arms against the Union, and in those states Lincoln had no control; yet it displeased the border states—the slave states which had not seceded—because they saw in it the ultimate extinction of slavery.

Elation over the victory at Antietam, which stopped the invasion, was soon followed by disappointment when Lee's army was permitted to recross the Potomac and get away without further loss. The general lack of success in the field, and to some extent the emancipation policy, led to dissatisfaction, which was reflected in the November elections. Several states which had cast their electoral vote for Lincoln two years before, now showed a reaction, and the Republican majority in the House of Representatives was much diminished.

Deep feeling must find an expression and must have an object—a hero for every victory and a scapegoat for every defeat. The most active and conspicuous member of the Cabinet was held responsible for the failures of the year, and the same political elements which had tried in vain to prevent his appointment to the Cabinet combined, both before and after the election, to compel his removal or resignation. Joseph Medill of the Chicago *Tribune* wrote to Schuyler Colfax: "McClellan in the field and Seward in the Cabinet have been the evil spirits which have brought our grand cause to the very brink of death. Seward must be got out of the Cabinet. He is Lincoln's evil genius." A committee from New York came to Lincoln with a similar message, but Lincoln said: "There is not one of you who would not see the country ruined if you could turn out Seward."

The most strenuous effort came a few weeks later, after General Burnside's disastrous defeat at Fredericksburg. The country was grieved at the useless slaughter and angry at the mismanagement of military affairs. Roused by the public indignation, a caucus of Republican senators, having failed to agree on a resolution asking that Seward be dismissed, adopted one that, without mentioning any names, requested the President to make such changes in the Cabinet as would secure better results in the prosecution of the war. Seward heard of the action and at once sent his resignation to the President.

The committee sent to the White House by the caucus spoke very plainly. They were all of the radical wing of the party and opposed to Seward. Wade of Ohio said that the President had placed the conduct of military affairs in the hands of bitter and malignant Democrats, and this was the cause of the Republican defeats in the recent elections. Fessenden of Maine said that the Senate had entire confidence in the patriotism and integrity of the President, but believed that Seward exerted an injurious influence on the conduct of the war. Sumner, Grimes, and other senators expressed their lack of confidence in Seward. Lincoln called a meeting of the Cabinet the next day and reported what had happened. He told them that the complaint of the senators was against Seward; they charged him "with indifference, with want of earnestness in the war, with lack of sympathy with the country, and especially with too great ascendancy over the President and meas-

ures of administration."[74] Lincoln asked the members of
the Cabinet to meet the senatorial committee face to
face at another conference in the evening. At the appointed hour, with the secretaries and the senators
present (except Seward, who had not attended since his
resignation), Lincoln defended the Administration and
the members of the Cabinet. "Secretary Chase endorsed
the President's statement fully and entirely,"[75] to the
surprise of those senators who were opposed to Seward.
They had looked on Chase as their leader and had been
influenced by his criticism of the President and the
Secretary of State.

The next morning the President sent for Chase and
said to him: "This matter is giving me much trouble."
Chase replied that he, too, was "painfully affected by
the meeting last evening" and had prepared his resignation. "Let me have it," said the President, reaching his
long arm and fingers toward Chase, who held on, seemingly reluctant to part with the letter. The President
took and hastily opened the letter. "This," said he, "cuts
the Gordian knot. . . . I can see my way clear." Then
Stanton, who was in the office at the time, offered his
resignation. "You may go to your Department," Lincoln
replied, "I don't want yours. This," holding out Chase's
letter, "is all I want; this relieves me; my way is clear;
the trouble is ended."[76]

The attack on Seward, made by the radicals of whom
Chase was the leader, had threatened to divide not only
the Cabinet, but also the country. Lincoln needed the
support of every political group that could be united in
his one chief purpose—the maintenance of the Union.
The new turn which the situation had taken gave him

an opportunity to retain the services of both Chase and Seward, and the support of their followers, without appearing to value one above the other. He refused to accept either resignation and almost ordered both men back to their duties.

Among those who watched the crisis with interest was Lord Lyons, and in view of his earlier suspicions of Seward his comment upon it has a peculiar value. He wrote to Russell: "I shall be sorry if it ends in the removal of Mr. Seward. We are much more likely to have a man less disposed to keep the peace than a man more disposed to do so. I should hardly have said so two years ago"; and Russell replied: "I see Seward stays in. I am glad of it."[77]

CHAPTER VIII

DANGER OF FOREIGN WAR; RECOG-
NITION, THE *ALABAMA*, AND THE
"LAIRD RAMS"

THE blockade proclaimed April 19 and actually begun in May was not at first very effectively maintained. Delay was inevitable, for until merchant ships were purchased and hastily converted into cruisers, the whole force of the United States Navy had been forty-two vessels in commission, tenders and store-ships included. There were four at Pensacola and six in Northern ports; the rest were scattered over the seven seas. Besides, there were twenty-seven frigates, sloops, brigs, and schooners that were not in commission, and twenty-one that were pronounced unfit for duty.[78] The day the blockade was proclaimed, orders were issued to purchase and arm twenty steamers. More were bought later and the blockade was rapidly extended. From the beginning it interfered to a considerable extent with the commerce of the South because shipowners, uncertain of the termination of their voyages, avoided Southern ports.

The effect of the blockade on the textile mills of England was not felt as early as the South had expected, and the hoped-for protests against it by Great Britain were not made. In fact, the British Government recognized the blockade as legitimate, and could do so with little complaint from her manufacturers because at first no shortage of cotton was felt. The fear of war had led to an early moving of the crop of 1860, which had been unusually large, and the Liverpool importers of raw cotton were unable to sell it to the mills in great quantities because of the over-production and accumulation of manufactured cotton goods in the preceding two years. It was not until the autumn of 1861 that the cotton-manufacturing districts of Lancashire and adjoining counties felt seriously the burden of unemployment, and it came even then more from the glut in the market for the finished product than from a shortage of raw material. Later, in the summer of 1862, when the accumulated surplus had been sold and the more effective blockade had almost completely cut off the supply of raw cotton, the continued and increasing distress in the Lancashire district gave the British Government good reason for its earnest wish to end the war. But Seward had from the beginning left no room for doubt that intervention would only mean a greater war and that offers of mediation would be rejected. Lyons had made the situation plain to Russell, and the British Government proceeded cautiously.

It was France that showed the first inclination to break the blockade. The proposal came to the British Government from the Emperor, Louis Napoleon, in October 1861, at the time when Thouvenel, Minister of Foreign Affairs, was protesting to Seward against the disturbance to the commerce of France. It was not favourably considered by Russell, who wrote to Palmerston: "If we do anything it must be on a large scale. It will not do for England and France to break a blockade for the sake of cotton."[79] Palmerston agreed with him, and replied: "Our best and true policy seems to be to go on as we have been doing and keep quite clear of the conflict between the North and the South. It is true, as you say, that there have been cases in Europe in which the allied powers have said to the fighting parties, like the man in the Critic, 'In the Queen's name, I bid you drop your sword,' but those cases have been rare and peculiar. . . . I quite agree with you that the want of cotton would not justify such a proceeding unless, indeed, the distress created by the want was far more serious than it is likely to be."[80]

At first the vessels used in running the blockade were Southern coasting steamers, whose regular business was gone, or small craft not suitable for such an enterprise; but when many of these were captured and the sea-borne trade of the South became more difficult to maintain, the opportunity for large profits attracted adventurous men to the business of systematic blockade-running. Vessels cleared from British ports for Havana, Nassau, or other ports in the West Indies, and delivered cargoes of arms, ammunition, blankets, and other supplies, which were afterward carried to the Southern states by small, swift ships, many of which were built for that business in the ship-yards on the Clyde. There were numerous inlets along the coast which these vessels of light draft could use, but which had no harbours equipped for heavy traffic; the principal ports also were frequently entered, however, by the faster blockade-runners, which, painted a dull grey colour, were almost invisible even by day and had a fair chance at night of slipping through the blockading squadron and making port safely. They could bring in arms and ammunition, but cotton, value for value, is a bulkier cargo, and no great quantity of it was moved. It required larger vessels or more of the small ones than were safely running the blockade. At the end of November 1861 Lyons reported to Russell that he was puzzled as to how he ought to answer the question whether he considered the blockade effective. He said: "I suppose the ships which run it successfully are more numerous than those which are intercepted. On the other hand it is very far from being a mere paper blockade. A great many vessels are captured; it is a most serious interruption to trade."[81]

So many small inlets gave access to the Southern ports that Welles decided to make the blockade more effective by blocking some of the harbour entrances. Old whaling ships were bought, loaded with stone, chained together bow and stern, and sunk in channels of Charleston harbour and the entrances to Pimlico Sound. Much indignation was expressed in England and Russell instructed Lyons to protest, saying that he had it on apparently good authority that the purpose was to destroy the harbour for ever, that it showed the North had despaired of restoring the Union, and that such revengeful and irremediable injury of an enemy was unjustifiable. Seward replied that the main channels were not closed, that the measures were only temporary, and that the obstructions would be removed by the federal Government on the restoration of the Union. As evidence that the entrance to Charleston harbour had not been destroyed he added that a British steamer laden with contraband had just succeeded in getting in.

In the spring and summer of 1862 vigorous efforts were made by the Confederates and by their friends to bring French pressure to bear on the British Government for joint action to break the blockade. W. S. Lindsay, one of the principal shipowners of England and the Member of Parliament for Glasgow, went to Paris and obtained an interview with the Emperor. Lindsay told Lord Cowley, British ambassador to France, that the Emperor was ready to recognize the South and had expressed a desire that Lindsay should lay his views before Palmerston and Russell, as such matters were better arranged by private than by official hands. Cowley was not favourably impressed, either with the proposal or with Lindsay himself, and warned Russell of Lindsay's probable attempt to make capital with the opposition, who might be heard from in Parliament. Lindsay also told Slidell of his interview with the Emperor, and Slidell on April 14 wrote to Benjamin, the Secretary of State of the Confederacy, giving information which, if known to Cowley, would have confirmed his suspicions. The Emperor, Slidell said, had asked Lindsay to see not only Palmerston and Russell, but also Derby and Disraeli, leaders of the opposition, and inform them of his views. Slidell believed that even if the British Government should fail to co-operate with him, the Emperor might act separately in recognition of the South.[82] Before Benjamin could have received this dispatch, he had sent instructions to Slidell to attempt the negotiation of a treaty with France permitting free access of French goods to the Confederacy for a limited period and also offering the Emperor one hundred thousand bales of cotton of five hundred

pounds each, which would furnish funds to maintain a
fleet, Benjamin thought, for a time sufficient to open
the Atlantic and Gulf ports to French commerce.[83]

The military successes of the South in the summer of
1862—the defeat of McClellan and later of Pope at the
second battle of Bull Run—had been enough to give
Seward warning even if positive information about the
activity of the diplomatic agents of the Confederacy
had been lacking. He wrote to Dayton, July 10, saying:
"If intervention in any form shall come, it will find us in
the right and in the strong attitude of self defense. . . .
European statesmen, I am sure, before waging war
against us, will consider their rights, interests and resources as well as ours."[84] To Adams he wrote that the
United States continued to rely upon the practice of
justice and the respect of our sovereignty by foreign
nations, but added: "It is not necessary for me to say
that if this reliance fails, this civil war will, without our
fault, become a war of continents—a war of the world."[85]
A few days later he gave Adams specific instructions:
"If the British Government shall in any way approach
you, directly or indirectly, with propositions which assume, or contemplate an appeal to the President on the
subject of our internal affairs, whether it seem to imply
a purpose to dictate, or to mediate, or to advise, or even
to solicit or persuade, you will answer that you are forbidden to debate, hear or in any way receive, entertain
or transmit any communication of the kind. . . . If,
contrary to our expectation, the British Government,
either alone or in combination with any other government, should acknowledge the insurgents, while you
are without further instruction from this department,

you will immediately suspend the exercise of your functions, and give notice of that suspension to Earl Russell and to this department. . . . I have now in behalf of the United States and by the authority of their chief executive magistrate performed an important duty. Its consequences have been weighed, and its solemnity is therefore felt and freely acknowledged. This duty has brought us to confront the danger of a war with Great Britain and with other states allied with the insurgents who are in arms for the overthrow of the American republic. You will see that we have approached the contemplation of that crisis with the caution which great reluctance has inspired, but I trust you have also seen that the crisis has not appalled us."[86]

The policy expressed in this dispatch is that which Lincoln and Seward had adhered to without wavering from the beginning of the war, and before it. On April 10, 1861, Seward had instructed Adams to say that if the British Ministers determined to recognize the Southern states they might at the same time prepare to enter into an alliance with them; the much discussed instruction of May 21, 1861 was not a temporary brain-storm, as it has been called, but a vigorous and definite expression of a fixed policy, which brought forth renewed instructions of the same nature every time the prospect reappeared that the Confederacy might be recognized. Repeatedly, to Adams, to Dayton, and in his intimate correspondence with Thurlow Weed, Seward expressed the purpose to resent with war any recognition of the independence of the Confederacy. In the autumn of 1862 the danger was real.

Palmerston and Russell agreed that the time had

come to propose an arrangement in America "on the basis of a separation,"[87] and Russell believed that "in case of failure, we ought ourselves to recognize the Southern states as an independent State,"[88] but a few days later, when Palmerston had learned of Lee's attempt to invade the North, but before the result at Antietam was known to him, he wrote again to Russell saying: "It is evident that a great conflict is taking place northwest of Washington, and its issue must have a great effect on the state of affairs. If the Federals sustain a great defeat, they may be at once ready for mediation, and the iron should be struck while it is hot. If, on the other hand, they should have the best of it, we may wait a while and see what may follow."[89] The plan was still only tentative, but it was so far advanced that Palmerston wrote to Gladstone that he and Russell were in agreement that mediation should be offered, though no actual step would be taken without the sanction of the Cabinet. Gladstone's Newcastle speech of October 7, in which he said that Jefferson Davis had made an army, and was making a navy, and had created something greater still—a nation—was taken as an indication of early recognition of the new nation by the Cabinet of which he was a member.

Adams had not communicated his instructions to Russell, but on October 12, a few days after Gladstone's speech was delivered, he gave the substance of them, in confidence, to William E. Forster, a Member of Parliament and a staunch friend of the North, who thought they should be made known to the Government before they committed themselves. Adams replied that "he had been thinking of it but waited to see how far Mr. Gladstone should appear to be sustained." It is not unlikely that Forster found a way to communicate the purpose of these instructions to the Cabinet, and that this knowledge, together with the failure of Lee at Antietam and some other considerations not so influential, led the British Ministers to drop the project of mediation at that time. Russell told Adams, October 23, that Great Britain intended no change of policy. The Emperor Louis Napoleon persisted in the project and it was again discussed in the British Cabinet on November 11 and 12, but it was then definitely abandoned. The following February the French minister in Washington made an offer of mediation, but without the support of any other power, and when Seward politely but firmly declined it, the matter was not pressed. In June 1863, Roebuck's motion, which was to request the Queen to negotiate with other powers for the recognition of the Confederacy, had no support from the Government or from the leaders of the opposition, and was withdrawn because it was certain to be overwhelmingly defeated if brought to a vote. The definite plan of Russell and Palmerston in October 1862 was the last serious purpose of interference by any foreign power.

Another danger was already manifest, however, which proved even more threatening. The lawfulness of our blockade was never brought in question, though its injurious effects on French and British industry and commerce made the two Governments anxious to bring it to an end if that could be done without provoking more serious consequences; but our own shipping trade was suffering because of what was considered in America the failure of Great Britain to fulfil the obligations of a neutral.

The Confederate Government recognized the value of commerce-destroyers, and, since few could be bought in Southern ports and there were no facilities there for building them, they determined to buy them or build them abroad. This business was committed to Captain James D. Bulloch, formerly of the United States Navy. He went to England in June 1861, and soon began to send large shipments of arms and ammunition. His more important mission was to make contracts for the Confederate Government with private ship-builders in England for warships, which were to be regularly commissioned and operated as cruisers of the newly-created navy of the South.

The Queen's proclamation of neutrality forbade "fitting out, arming, or equipping any ship or vessel to be employed as a ship of war" by either of the contending parties, but when the sympathy of the builders, the community, and the port officials was with the South, it was difficult to get legal evidence of the contract, even though the facts were common knowledge. The first ship contracted for by Bulloch was called the *Oreto* while she was building, and it was given out that she was for the Italian Government. Adams was convinced that she was intended for the Confederacy and asked that she be detained, but was unable to secure such proof of ownership as was required by the authorities. She cleared for Palermo, but proceeded to Nassau in the Bahamas, where she awaited her arms and equipment, which came from England in another vessel. After some delay and further interesting adventures she received a new name, the *Florida*, and began energetically and successfully the work for which she was intended.

A second and more powerful warship, afterward known as the *Alabama*, was launched May 15, 1862, and on June 23 Adams presented evidence which justified him in asking that she be detained.   The papers were referred to the proper department and, following the usual routine, were sent to the surveyor of the port with a request for an investigation and a statement of the facts.   On the basis of his report, which took no notice of what was common knowledge, but accepted the face of the records, the legal authorities decided that there was no ground for detaining the ship.   With the efficient aid of Dudley, the American consul at Liverpool, Adams secured additional evidence.   Still insufficient, said the authorities.   Adams retained Sir Robert Collier, an eminent Queen's Counsel, and submitted to him the affidavits and other papers in the case.   In his written opinion he said: "It appears difficult to make out a stronger case of infringement of the Foreign Enlistment Act, which, if not enforced on this occasion, is little better than a dead letter." The port authorities at Liverpool still refused to act.   Adams had sent duplicates of all the papers, including Collier's opinion, to Russell, who referred them to the law-officers of the Crown.   They lay five days at the home of the Queen's advocate, who had been suddenly stricken with an illness from which he never recovered.   Other advisers were called in, and on July 31 orders were telegraphed to Liverpool to hold the vessel.   It was too late.   The order had been anticipated and careful plans had been laid to evade it.   With a party of guests on board to cover her real purpose, and under pretence of making a trial trip, the *Alabama* steamed down the

Mersey and stood out to sea. The guests were sent back on a tug, but the *Alabama* did not return. Two years later, in June 1864, she was destroyed by the United States steamer *Kearsarge*, but in the mean time she had sunk, burned, or captured and released under bond more than sixty American merchant ships, making a record that so far surpassed that of the *Florida* and the other cruisers bought or built in England that even their names are half forgotten. "The *Alabama* claims" was the phrase commonly used to include the damage done by all of them when indemnity was demanded of Great Britain.

Success in building commerce-destroyers in British ship-yards encouraged the Confederacy to attempt the construction by the same method of a fighting navy which would be able to dispose of the wooden warships with which the blockade was maintained. Even before the escape of the *Alabama* work had already been begun by the Laird brothers at Birkenhead on two formidable armoured steamers, each to carry four nine-inch rifled guns and to be provided with a sharp projection at the prow for piercing the hull of an enemy. From this method of attack and from the name of the builders the ironclads were spoken of as "the Laird rams." They were to be ready for delivery in the summer of 1863. Neither the ordinary warships nor the monitors of the United States Navy of that period were able to cope with such vessels, and our naval authorities were seriously alarmed. Captain Fox, Assistant Secretary of the Navy, wrote from Washington that the departure of these warships must be prevented at all hazards, "as we have no defense against them . . . as to guns, we have

not one in the whole country fit to fire at an ironclad. . . .
It is a question of life and death."[90]

As the serious depredations of the *Alabama* became
known, Seward instructed Adams to lay the facts before the British Government. It was not the intention
of the United States, he said, to harass Great Britain
with impatient demands for immediate reparation, but
to prevent similar injuries hereafter. With rare discretion Adams carried on the difficult work in complete
harmony with the spirit of his instructions. The burning of American ships and cargoes was persistently
brought to the attention of the Foreign Office, redress
was asked for the national and private losses caused
by the *Alabama* and her sister ships, and Adams urgently insisted on the necessity for more effective precau-
tions against further violations of the British neutrality
laws. Russell officially disclaimed for the British Government any responsibility for the damage, but he wrote
to Lyons: "I must feel that her roaming the ocean with
English guns and English sailors to burn, sink and destroy the ships of a friendly nation is a scandal and a
reproach."[91]

Several influences had combined to convince Russell
that energetic measures must be taken to prevent the
departure of Confederate warships from British ship-
yards. It was now obvious, whatever doubts may have
existed formerly, that the *Florida* and the *Alabama* had
been built and delivered to the Confederacy in defiance
or in evasion of the law of England, or that the law
was not sufficient to enable the Government to maintain its neutral obligations. By this time, too, another
influence was affecting British public opinion, and the

opinion of Russell along with others. The emancipation proclamation of January 1863 had followed the preliminary proclamation of September 1862 and its meaning was better understood. In consequence the sympathies of anti-slavery England were turning again to the North.

Besides all this, there was a new turn in American policy which was giving much concern both to Russell and to Lyons. In July 1862, about the time the *Alabama* evaded Russell's order and escaped from Liverpool, a bill had been introduced in Congress which would give President Lincoln authority to issue letters of marque. Little attention was paid to it then, but in January 1863 it was revived and urged as an Administration measure. Senator Grimes, its sponsor, said the Administration wanted the bill to pass because the Confederates were building a fleet in England to break the blockade, and the privateers were needed to maintain it. The bill passed the Senate February 17. It immediately attracted the attention of Lyons, who told Seward that it would probably have a bad effect in Europe, to which Seward replied that some remedy must be found for the fact that the law did not appear to enable the British Government to prevent the issue of Confederate privateers.[92] Again on March 9, after the bill had become a law, Lyons protested against the commissioning of privateers and expressed the fear that war might result. "Mr. Seward said," Lyons reported, "that he was well aware of the inconvenience, not to say the dangers of issuing letters of marque; that he should be glad to delay doing so, or to escape the necessity altogether; but that really unless some intelligence came from England to allay the public exasperation, the measure would be unavoidable."[93] Adams also was alarmed when he received his instructions from Seward, and expressed to Forster his apprehension that there would be a clash "unless the ministry here could be persuaded to act with more energy in restraining the outfits from this kingdom." He feared there "would be a demand in America for the issue of letters of marque which the Government would find it hard to resist. But if the President should yield, the chances of a collision on the ocean would be much increased. . . . I urged him therefore," wrote Adams, "to do something to make the ministry alive to the nature of the difficulty."[94] Russell had received Lyons's reports and was already aware of the danger.

Privateers were not public armed vessels, maintained by appropriations from the national treasury, but were privately owned and operated for the profit of the owner. Their operating expenses and their profits came from the sale of captured merchant ships and their cargoes. It was obvious that there were no Confederate merchant ships to be captured. What commerce was to be their prey? When such questions as this were asked of Adams or of Seward, the reply was that they would pursue vessels like the *Alabama*. Russell instructed Lyons to inquire further about them and "find out whether in any case they will be authorized to interfere with neutral commerce, and if in any case in what case and to what extent."[95] There was reason for this anxious inquiry. Privateers might be authorized to visit and search neutral merchant ships anywhere on the open ocean and to capture any vessel and bring her in for adjudication by a prize court, provided her clearance papers or other satisfactory evidence should indicate that she was bound for a port at which an effective blockade was then actually in existence; for as international law was interpreted at that time, both in British and American courts, it was not necessary that a vessel be intercepted while actually attempting to enter a blockaded port; she became liable to capture the moment she left neutral waters for the forbidden destination.[96] Also any merchant ship, including neutrals, might be seized and brought before a prize court if bound for any port in the Confederacy, whether blockaded or not, provided her cargo was contraband.

Neither Seward nor anyone else in authority ever committed the Government definitely to any statement as to the use that might be made of privateers, but Seward made it plain that the building of Confederate warships in England had a very close relation to the new privateering policy, whatever that policy might be. Doubtless other considerations such as have already been mentioned had their weight with Russell, but concern as to the use intended for the proposed privateers was influential in persuading him to adopt more energetic measures to prevent further violations of neutrality by British ship-builders.

The enforcement of the Foreign Enlistment Act was discussed in the House of Commons March 27, when the Government was severely criticized by John Bright, Forster, and other friends of the North. Anticipating the debate, Russell had said to Palmerston that since the escape of the *Alabama* was clearly an evasion of the law, the Prime Minister could have no difficulty in declaring that the Government disapproved all such attempts to elude the law with a view to assist one of the belligerents. The attack on the Government was so sharp, however, that Palmerston found it necessary to defend its course. He reminded the House that seizure by the Government would have to be followed by condemnation proceedings in the courts, and said: "You cannot seize a vessel under the Foreign Enlistment Act unless you have evidence on oath confirming a just suspicion.... When a vessel is seized unjustly, and without good grounds, there is a process of law to come afterwards, and the Government may be condemned in heavy costs and damages." He assured the House that the Government had "no indisposition to enforce the provisions of the Foreign Enlistment Act."

Adams and the friends of the North in Parliament were discouraged by the debate, but unnecessarily so, for if the Government showed an unwillingness to be driven to a declaration of new policy, there was nevertheless a willingness to act, as was shown within a very few days. On March 30 Adams placed in Russell's hands evidence tending to prove that the *Alexandra*, then almost ready to sail, was intended for the Confederate Navy. The prompt action in this case showed a remarkable contrast with the delays concerning the *Alabama* the preceding summer. In six days all the preliminary proceedings had been completed and the *Alexandra* seized. This action was gratifying to Seward, but it was by no means the end of the case. It was tried in the Court of Exchequer, which decided there was no sufficient ground for holding the ship. The Government appealed the case and, though after long delays the law proved inadequate, found means to prolong the proceedings so that the *Alexandra* was never delivered to the Confederacy. Lyons was able also to inform Seward of new orders of a general nature that indicated an attitude more favourable to the North in future cases. Russell had written him: "The orders given to watch, and stop when evidence can be procured, vessels apparently intended for the Confederate service will, it is hoped, allay the strong feelings which have been raised in Northern America by the escape from justice of the *Oreto* and the *Alabama*."[97]

This information somewhat relieved Seward's anxiety, but work was still in progress on the Birkenhead rams and there had been no assurance that these vessels would be seized. The success of Northern arms at Gettysburg and Vicksburg encouraged Seward to speak in a still higher tone of the possibility of conflict with Great Britain. He wrote to Adams that the United States must protect itself and its commerce against armed cruisers proceeding from British ports as against the naval force of a public enemy. To this end the Government was preparing a naval force with the utmost vigour, and if it should not be sufficient for the emergency, then must the United States use such private armed ships as the merchant marine might afford. British ports were now open, under certain restrictions, to the visits of piratical vessels. Could it be a matter of surprise, or a subject of complaint, if this state of things continued, that the Navy of the United States "receive instructions to pursue these enemies into the ports which thus, in violation of the law of nations and the obligations of neutrality, become harbors for the pirates"?[98] Adams, exercising the discretion already given him, did not communicate this threat to Russell, and it is probable that Seward did not intend that it should be communicated to him directly. Adams did find an opportunity, however, after receiving this and other instructions of a like nature, to say to the Duke of Argyle, who was a member of the Cabinet, that the situation was "grave and critical," and that his instructions were far more stringent than he had yet been disposed to execute; and Adams suspected that Argyle at once communicated this to Russell.[99]

In the mean time Russell had done much more than Adams knew. He had collected evidence relating to the Birkenhead rams in addition to that submitted to him by Adams, and had twice referred to the law-officers of the Crown what he believed sufficient evidence to justify the seizure of the vessels, but received opinions that there was no evidence capable of being presented to a court of justice. On September 1 he wrote Adams that the Government was advised that they could not in any way interfere with these vessels, but that they would nevertheless be watched carefully. On receipt of this note Adams was much perturbed, and it was then, September 5, that he wrote to Russell the long communication containing the much quoted sentence: "It would be superfluous in me to point out to your lordship that this is war." The threat, fully revealed, though draped with ingenious ambiguity, was not needed. On September 3, two days before the date of Adams's letter, Russell had written to Palmerston: "The conduct of the gentlemen who have contracted for the two ironclads at Birkenhead is so very suspicious that I have thought it necessary to direct that they be detained. The Solicitor-General has been consulted, and concurs in the measure, as one of policy, though not of strict law. We shall thus test the law, and if we have to pay damages, we have satisfied the opinion which prevails here as well as in America, that that kind of neutral hostility should not be allowed to go on without some attempt to stop it. If you do not approve, pray appoint a Cabinet for Tuesday or Wednesday next."[100] Palmerston did not object, and two days later Russell confirmed the preliminary order and specifically required that the vessels be prevented from leaving Liverpool on a trial trip or any other pretext "until satisfactory evidence can be given as to their destination." This order was merely for detention of the vessels, but in October they were formally seized by the Government and to prevent escape were anchored under the guns of a British warship. The courts never passed on the question of their condemnation. The two ironclads were purchased by the Government in May 1864 and commissioned as ships of the British Navy.

The efforts to build ships for the Confederate Navy had not been limited to British ship-yards. Two rams and four vessels of the *Alabama* type were under contract in France with the knowledge and consent of the Emperor Louis Napoleon, but in September 1863, about the time the Confederate ship-building came to an end in England, full evidence of ownership came into the hands of John Bigelow, then United States consul at Paris, and Mason, Slidell, and Bulloch decided to get rid of the vessels. One of the rams was sold to Denmark. The other and two cruisers were bought by Prussia, and two building at Nantes were bought by Peru.[101] The policy of England was now set toward a more complete observance of the obligations of neutrality, though handicapped by an inadequate statute, and Napoleon, influenced by that policy, was not willing openly to countenance such a violation of his obligations as would have amounted to an overt act of war. The leading men of the Confederacy perceived that it was England's policy that controlled, and Davis in his message to Congress in December expressed his dissatisfaction with the British Government. Several months earlier Benjamin, Secretary of State in the Confederacy, made a similar complaint and paid a grudging compliment to Seward's diplomacy when he wrote: "It is impossible not to admire the sagacity with which Mr. Seward penetrated into the secret feelings of the British Cabinet, and the success of his policy of intimidation which the world at large supposed would be met with prompt resentment, but which he with deeper insight into the real policy of that Cabinet foresaw would be followed by submissive acquiescence in his demands."[102]

CHAPTER IX

THE END OF THE WAR. FRENCH INTER-VENTION IN MEXICO. TERRITORIAL EXPANSION. REST

RUSSELL'S order to seize warships when they were "evidently intended" for the Confederacy, together with the Government's purchase of the rams in May 1864, when the evidence was insufficient to make sure their condemnation in the courts, relieved Seward of the fear of foreign war. The privateering bill disappears from diplomatic correspondence. Lyons, however, was not completely reassured, for he continued throughout the spring and summer to call Russell's attention to the formidable development of the military and naval power of the North. The war was prosecuted with increased vigour, but the end was not yet. Lee's strong resistance and Grant's heavy losses at the battles of the Wilderness and Cold Harbor in May and June threw the North into despondency and encouraged the Confederate Government and its friends in Europe to make one more attempt to secure recognition. They found that the French Emperor would not act alone and every effort to change the policy of Great Britain was without result.

There was nevertheless much discouragement throughout the North, and Lincoln expected his Administration to be repudiated at the November election, 1864.

The tide turned in time. Farragut's hard-earned victory at Mobile in August, followed a few weeks later by Sherman's capture of Atlanta and Sheridan's successful operations in the Shenandoah Valley, renewed the hopes and energies of despondent men of the Union party and brought back the wavering so that Lincoln was reelected by a large majority both of the popular vote and in the electoral college. The congressional election gave Lincoln's supporters more than two-thirds of the House of Representatives. There could no longer be any doubt, at home or in Europe, that the Lincoln policies would be supported and the Union restored.

Operations in December 1864 brought the end of the war very near. Sherman's destructive march through Georgia cut off a great part of the food-supply of Lee's army, and Thomas's victory at Nashville crushed and disintegrated the Confederate forces under Hood. The South was sorely discouraged and nearly exhausted. Francis P. Blair, father of the Postmaster-General, conceived a fantastic scheme which he wished to present to the Confederate Government with a view to ending the war. Lincoln refused to discuss or even to hear the plan, but gave Blair a pass to go through the lines. He went to Richmond and explained his scheme to Davis. He would have an armistice in order that Davis might take a combined force of Union and Confederate soldiers to Mexico, form an alliance with Juárez, and "expel the Bonaparte-Hapsburg dynasty from our southern flank." Davis might mould the Mexican states so that they could be received into the Union.[103] Davis did not commit himself to the plan, but expressed a willingness to enter into a conference with a view to peace. Lincoln was also willing and the conference at Hampton Roads was arranged. Lincoln and Seward met the commissioners appointed by Davis. The Mexican scheme was not seriously considered. Lincoln insisted on the restoration of the national authority, no receding on the slavery question, and no cessation of hostilities short of an end of the war. The Hampton Roads conference ended without result.

There remained only Sherman's difficult march northward from Savannah and Grant's persistent hammering at Petersburg and Richmond to bring the four years' tragedy to an end. Lee at last decided to abandon the hopeless defence of Richmond and to form a junction with the forces under Joseph E. Johnston, who after giving much annoyance to Sherman was being forced steadily northward towards the Virginia boundary. Pressed by Grant and Sheridan, Lee made the attempt, but Grant overtook him and he surrendered his exhausted army at Appomatox. Johnston's surrender to Sherman followed inevitably, and the war was over.

On April 5, 1865, two days after the federal army entered Richmond, Seward was thrown from his carriage and seriously injured. His right shoulder was dislocated and his jaw broken on both sides, so that it could be held in place only by an iron frame. There were serious doubts as to his recovery. On April 14, the night of Lincoln's murder, one of the assassins forced his way into Seward's house, fought his way to the bed of the helpless man, and slashed furiously at his throat. Seward was severely cut about the head and neck, and his life was probably saved by the iron brace about his jaw. Four unarmed men, including Seward's two sons, the nurse, and a messenger from the State Department, were wounded, Frederick W. Seward almost fatally, while attempting to restrain or capture the assassin. He escaped, but was taken and hanged later for his part in the conspiracy.

Andrew Johnson's accession to the presidency made no immediate change in the Cabinet. Seward recovered slowly from his injuries, but he had no desire to turn over to a successor certain unfinished foreign problems about which he had definite policies. One of these, and probably the most important, was the presence of a French army in Mexico to establish an Austrian prince as emperor of that country.

Mexico had been free from Spanish rule for forty years and in that period had suffered thirty-six changes of government and seventy-three presidents. Outrages on foreigners had become insufferable, and by 1861 intervention had been contemplated in both Europe and America. Benito Juárez, an honest and able man of unmixed Indian blood, was the constitutional ruler. He overthrew a rival claimant in January 1861 and began to restore order, but in July the Congress, lacking funds, passed an act suspending for two years all payments on the foreign debt. This brought matters to a crisis and gave France and Spain a long-sought opportunity for intervention with the help of England, the anticipation of which in the preceding April had turned Seward's thoughts towards foreign war.

England would intervene only to secure redress for actual injuries. Spain would have been willing to regain some part of her former possessions, but it was only a few weeks since she had been notified by Seward

that the Santo Domingo intervention "must be regarded as threatening Hayti, Mexico," and other former Spanish colonies, and such attempts would be held
to manifest "an unfriendly spirit toward the United
States."[104] To secure joint action the French Emperor
concealed his purpose, and the three powers signed a
convention agreeing that they would not exercise any
influence in the internal affairs of Mexico of a nature to
interfere with the "right of the Mexican nation to choose
and constitute freely the form of its government." It
was not long before the English and Spanish leaders
became convinced that the real purpose of France was
not set forth in the convention. They reached an agreement with Mexico with regard to the claims and withdrew, leaving France to do what she would. Sharp
fighting with Juárez, large reinforcements from France,
and the capture of the Mexican capital led to the organization of a provisional Government under French
influence. The provisional authorities voted to establish
an empire, and Maximilian, brother of Francis Joseph
of Austria, accepted the crown.

The situation required careful handling on the part
of the United States. If Seward should protest too
strongly, Napoleon might offer the Confederacy an
alliance; if he should say nothing, he would give up a
permanent American principle. It was necessary to
avoid both extremes. He instructed Dayton to intimate
to Thouvenel that disquieting rumours had reached the
President's ears and had awakened some anxiety. Dayton was to say that he was not authorized to ask for
explanations, but was sure that any which could relieve
that anxiety would be welcome. He might account for

his suggestion by calling attention to statements made to the three powers when joint action was undertaken that the United States could not look with indifference upon any armed European intervention for political ends in a country so near as Mexico. Thurlow Weed saw the instructions and wrote from Paris: "Your despatch on Mexican matters breaks no eggs. It makes a record, and there, I hope you are at rest." Weed and Seward were in constant communication, always understood each other, and seldom differed seriously in judgment. So long as the war lasted, Seward said no more than was necessary to make the record. When Bigelow urged him, in the spring of 1864, to be more outspoken, he replied: "With our land and naval forces in Louisiana retreating before the rebels instead of marching toward Mexico, this is not the most suitable time for offering idle menaces to the Emperor of France. We have compromised nothing, surrendered nothing and I do not propose to surrender anything. But why should we gasconade about Mexico when we are in a struggle for our own life?"[105]

Many were displeased with Seward's attitude, and the demand for vigorous measures was growing. The House of Representatives passed resolutions against the erection of a monarchy by any European power on the ruins of an American republic. After Lee's surrender there was a growing sentiment in favour of sending an army into Mexico. General Grant told President Johnson that the attempt to establish a monarchy on this continent by means of foreign bayonets was "an act of hostility against the United States." Grant initiated measures not wholly unlike Blair's fantastic proposals prior to the Hampton Roads conference. He gave General Schofield twelve months' leave of absence with permission to go beyond the limits of the United States with the understanding, says Schofield, that he was to "organize on Mexican territory an army corps under commissions from the Government of Mexico, the officers and soldiers to be taken from the Union and Confederate forces, who were reported to be eager to enlist in such an enterprise."[106]

General Sheridan, who had been sent to Texas with fifty-two thousand men, was to furnish arms and equipment for men who might be mustered out for the purpose of volunteering in Schofield's force.[107] Seward was alarmed at the prospect. His heart was set on getting the French out of Mexico without war. Reports from Bigelow, who after Dayton's death had been appointed minister to France, indicated that opposition to Napoleon's Mexican venture was increasing in the French parliament. This opposition might vanish and all France might rally to his support if humiliating conditions were demanded or if French troops were attacked in Mexico by American soldiers. Seward upset Grant's plans by persuading Schofield that he could do more in Paris than in Mexico. The essence of a long interview between Seward and Schofield may be summed up in Seward's words, as reported by Schofield: "I want you to get your legs under Napoleon's mahogany and tell him he must get out of Mexico."[108] Seward had instructed Bigelow to assure Drouyn de Lhuys, the new Minister of Foreign Affairs, that the death of Lincoln and the accession of Johnson had made no change in the American policy with regard to France and Mexico, but he had also kept Bigelow informed of the increasing disposition of the people, of Congress, and especially of the Army, to demand "initiatory action toward France in regard to Mexico," and had asked Bigelow not to withhold the information from Drouyn de Lhuys. Perhaps such information as Schofield could give, if he could "get his legs under Napoleon's mahogany," would make Bigelow's communications more effective. At any rate no harm would come of his visit to Paris and much mischief would have followed if he had gone to Mexico.

Carefully watching the effect of his preparatory moves, in successive instructions to Bigelow Seward spoke with increasing plainness. On September 5 he wrote that the time had come when both nations might well consider whether the permanent interests of international peace and friendship did not require thoughtful intervention. Two months later he said that the maintenance of an authority in Mexico resting on force and maintained by a French navy was "a cause of serious concern to the United States." In December he wrote that the President desired that France should be respectfully informed upon two points: first, that the United States earnestly desired to continue to cultivate sincere friendship with France; second, "that this policy would be brought into imminent jeopardy unless France could deem it consistent with her interest and honor to desist from the prosecution of armed intervention in Mexico."

About two weeks after this message had been communicated to Drouyn de Lhuys, the Emperor wrote to Bazaine, commander of the French forces with Maximilian, that his difficulties compelled him to fix a time for withdrawal from Mexico. The troops were with-drawn—not at once, but all too soon for Maximilian. Napoleon urged him, and Bazaine entreated him, to abdicate and return to safety in Europe, but he refused. His forces were overwhelmed by Juárez, he was tried by court martial, and shot, June 19, 1867. Seward en-deavoured to save his life, but Juárez thought to make him a terrifying example against future attempts on the integrity of the Mexican republic.[109]

Seward never ceased to urge upon Great Britain the settlement of the *Alabama* claims. Adams supported him ably, but it was not until there had been a change of ministry in England that Seward obtained any recogni-tion of them. The first treaty, signed by Lord Stanley and Reverdy Johnson, Adams's successor, was entirely unsatisfactory to Seward; but another, signed by John-son and Lord Clarendon, under the close supervision of Seward, who cabled minute detailed instructions to Johnson, while it did not expressly mention the *Alabama* claims, provided for the settlement of all claims arising since July 26, 1853. President Johnson's Administration was in great disfavour by that time, and the Johnson-Clarendon convention had only one vote in the Senate. Sumner spoke against it, though he wrote John Bright afterward that if it had been submitted a year earlier, it would have been ratified without dissent.[110]

The unseemly quarrels between the President and Congress grew partly out of Johnson's personal qualities and partly out of radical differences on the question of reconstruction, which had begun to give trouble even in Lincoln's lifetime. Johnson's reconstruction policy substantially followed Lincoln's, which was based on the abiding conviction, expressed by Lincoln before his first inauguration, that "no state can in any way lawfully get out of the Union without the consent of the others," and that the Southern states had been resisting the lawful authority of the national Government. This had been the controlling principle of Seward's diplomacy, constantly set forth in his correspondence with foreign powers, to whom he as constantly asserted the purpose of the United States to resent by force of arms any foreign recognition of the Southern states as an independent power. Seward, of course, supported the reconstruction policy founded on that doctrine, and as he also opposed the impeachment of the President, he too was exposed to bitter censure. Seward's support of Johnson's policies lacked the lively interest and the energy that was always shown in his co-operation with Lincoln. There was little in either Johnson or Seward that could appeal to the social instincts of the other. Johnson was pugnacious and intolerant of opposition, while Seward could enjoy the friendly fellowship of his most active opponents. Seward was a master of compromise, but no compromise was possible in the quarrel between Johnson and his enemies in Congress. Therefore Seward gave his attention almost exclusively to territorial expansion and other external policies. It was fortunate for his Alaskan treaty that it was submitted to the Senate and ratified before the disposition shown in the vote on the Johnson-Clarendon convention became manifest.

During Seward's eight years in the State Department the Far East was the theatre of important international developments, which, in spite of the burdens of the

Civil War, demanded and received his attention. In 1860 the close of China's war with England and France made many changes in the condition of foreigners throughout the Orient, and Seward was willing to enter heartily into agreements with other treaty powers for co-operation in a common policy. He approved an understanding by which the powers would protect the treaty ports, give China moral support, but no military aid, against the Tai-Ping rebels, and man with foreigners the war steamers recently purchased to put down piracy along the Chinese coasts. He proposed a joint naval expedition against Japan, subject to the sanction of hostilities by Congress, to enforce the treaties of 1858, and he approached France on the subject of a punitive expedition to Korea to collect indemnities for the murder of French missionaries and the killing of the crew and the burning of the American steamer *Sherman*. Equal opportunities, the preservation of the territorial integrity of China, and co-operation in protecting foreigners, were the elements of his policy. It is not difficult to agree with the careful student of the Far East who says that, in 1899, "when Hay turned to this difficult problem he must have been made aware that all its paths had been traversed in the sixties, either by Seward or by his able representative at Pekin, Anson Burlingame. . . . Absolutely no new principles have been added to American Far Eastern policy since 1869."[111]

The purchase of Alaska had been discussed with the Russian minister in 1859 by the Assistant Secretary of State and Senator Gwin of California, whose constituents were attracted by the fisheries of the northern Pacific and the possibilities of the fur trade in Russian

America,[112] but it was probably the destruction of whaling vessels in Bering and Okhotsk seas in 1865 by the Confederate cruiser *Shenandoah* which opened Seward's ears to a revival of the California request in 1866. Frederick W. Seward says that his father, during the Civil War, "had found the Government laboring under great disadvantages from the lack of advanced naval outposts in the West Indies and the North Pacific; so at the close of hostilities he commenced his endeavors to obtain such a foothold in each quarter."[113] Negotiations were completed between Seward and Stoeckl, but the approval of the Czar was necessary. One evening in March 1867 the Russian minister called at Seward's house and informed him that the Czar had consented and that the treaty might be prepared the next day. Seward pushed away the table at which he was playing whist and said: "Why wait till tomorrow, Mr. Stoeckl. Let us make the treaty tonight." Sumner, chairman of the Senate Committee on Foreign Relations, was sent for; the necessary clerks were summoned. The treaty was signed at four o'clock the next morning and sent by the President to the Senate the same day. There was a great deal of opposition at first, but in the end it was ratified with only two dissenting votes.[114]

Seward's other attempts to add to the national domain were not successful, but in two cases the islands he wished to acquire are now United States territory. When the reciprocity treaty with Hawaii was under consideration in 1867, Seward expressed a strong preference for annexation, but he realized that his wish could not then be gratified. In 1869, while one of the frequent civil wars of Santo Domingo was in progress, the

Government of that republic asked that it be taken under our protection. At Seward's request a joint resolution providing for the annexation of Santo Domingo "on the application of the people and government of that republic" was introduced in the House and favourably reported by the Committee on Foreign Affairs, but failed to pass. In pursuance of his policy of acquiring a naval outpost in the West Indies, and after long-continued efforts, Seward succeeded in negotiating a treaty for the transfer of the Danish West Indies to the United States. It was ratified by the Danish Rigsdag and signed by the King, but the Senate was reluctant even to consider it. After long delay the Committee on Foreign Relations reported unanimously against ratification, but this was not until 1870, when Seward was no longer Secretary of State.

At the end of President Johnson's Administration Seward was free for the first time in many years from the burdens of high position. He had rejoiced in responsibility when he was in health and associated in difficult labours with Lincoln and other men for whom he had profound respect. It was conviction and not personal advantage that led him to support Johnson's reconstruction policy and oppose his impeachment, but Johnson's mode of conducting controversy made it impossible, after the first few months, for Seward to give him more than perfunctory support. Sumner with his strong sympathies, and Thaddeus Stevens with his bitter hatreds, did not understand a man who would go to neither one extreme nor the other, and because Seward's abiding principles were moderate, they thought him indifferent and without conviction. It was a time of intense hatreds and Seward, because of his moderation, was very unpopular.

For more than two years he travelled. He saw Alaska, which he had made American territory. He was for many weeks the guest of the Mexican republic, which he had freed from foreign rule. In Japan and China he was received with unusual honours. In Turkey he was treated as the guest of the Empire. He was cordially received in France and England by the statesmen who had known him as an opponent in diplomacy. After returning to his own city he explained his travels by saying that at his age and in his condition of health rest would be rust, and he must keep in motion. He had "selected the way that would do the least harm, give the least offense, enable me to acquire the most knowledge, and increase the power, if any remained, to do good."[115] Seward's health was failing rapidly. He spent the last months of his life working on his unfinished autobiography and writing an account of his recent travels. Unconscious of the approaching end, he was at his literary work on the morning of October 10, 1872; in the afternoon he was at rest, indifferent for ever to the blame or praise of men.

ELIHU BENJAMIN WASHBURNE

SECRETARY OF STATE

MARCH 5, 1869, TO MARCH 10, 1869

BY

JOSEPH V. FULLER, Ph.D.

DIVISION OF PUBLICATIONS, DEPARTMENT OF STATE

ELIHU B. WASHBURNE

FROM AN ENGRAVING BY G. E. PERINE

ELIHU B. WASHBURNE

MONG President Grant's original appointments of Cabinet officials, one of those subjected to severe criticism was that of Elihu
Benjamin Washburne as Secretary of State;
nevertheless, the appointment was confirmed by the Senate and his commission was issued
on March 5, 1869. While his ability and integrity as a
public servant, demonstrated by fifteen years' service in
Congress, were recognized, his character, education, and
experience were not considered such as to fit him for
the office conferred upon him.

Born in Livermore, Maine, September 23, 1816, one
of seven brothers, four of whom were to enter Congress
from different states, Washburne's early life had been
rather migratory and his education fragmentary. After
leaving the primary school and working for a time on
his father's farm, he spent two years in newspaper work
and one in teaching school before he took up the study
of law. A year in Kent's Hill seminary, two in a law-
office, and one in the Harvard Law School prepared
him for admission to the bar in 1840, when he set up
practice in Galena, Illinois. He was elected to Congress
in 1853, where he was retained continuously by his district until his resignation to enter Grant's Cabinet.
This long period of service gained for him the title
"Father of the House," while his persistent scrutiny of
appropriation bills and opposition to extravagance made
him known in his day as the "Watch-dog of the

Treasury." As chairman of the Committee on Commerce since 1855, he had displayed his interest and competence in economic matters, and he had served on other important bodies, such as the sub-committee for investigation of the Frémont frauds in Missouri and the joint committee on reconstruction. It was his belligerent and headstrong advocacy of President Johnson's impeachment, during which he acted as chairman of the committee of the whole, that principally raised doubts as to his temperamental fitness to conduct the country's foreign relations. His title to recognition by the new Administration rested chiefly upon the zeal he had displayed throughout the war in fostering the military career of his distinguished fellow-townsman U. S. Grant, defending his conduct in Congress and taking the initiative towards his successive promotions up to the highest rank.

The Cabinet post for which Washburne's qualifications made him most eligible was probably that of Secretary of the Treasury, but Grant had set his heart on placing in that department the successful New York merchant A. T. Stewart. The attempt of the President and his supporters to push through an exemption in Stewart's favour from the Act of September 2, 1789 excluding business men from the office met with a formidable opposition, led by Charles Sumner. This clash marked the beginning of a conflict between the President and the redoubtable Senator from Massachusetts which was profoundly to influence the foreign policy of the United States. It also let loose a flood of criticism, which brought about a reconstruction of the Cabinet. Washburne's appointment, the President soon let it be known, was only temporary, intended as a compliment to him personally and as giving him prestige for a diplomatic post. James F. Wilson of Iowa agreed to accept the succession, provided Washburne confined himself to a nominal incumbency and made no decisions or appointments; but, alleging that this condition had been violated, Wilson suddenly left Washington and declined to return. Whatever hopes Washburne may have had of retaining his office after this development were shattered by Grant's defeat over Stewart's appointment. He accepted the post of minister to France and quietly withdrew when his successor, Hamilton Fish, arrived to assume his functions, on March 16, leaving no impression on the foreign policy of the United States.

Washburne fulfilled his ministerial duties with a dignity and tact which indicated that the strictures on his original appointment were perhaps unwarranted. The most important period of his mission was that of the Franco-Prussian War, some of the problems connected with which are touched upon in chapter iii of the following sketch of Fish's administration. With equal restrained firmness Washburne confronted the French authorities, in protecting the interests of North German subjects, and Bismarck, in contending for the freedom of diplomatic intercourse with his own Government through the German lines round Paris. During the ensuing civil disturbances he unofficially interceded, alike in vain, with the Commune for the liberation of the Archbishop of Paris and with the Versailles Government for the release of Blanqui by way of exchange. So thoroughly did he win the esteem of the statesmen with whom he came into contact during his mission that upon his retirement, in 1877, he was presented with portraits of Emperor William I, Bismarck, Thiers, and Gambetta. His last years, spent in private life in Chicago, where he died in 1884, were partly devoted to the writing of his diplomatic reminiscences, published under the title *Recollections of a Minister to France.*

HAMILTON FISH

SECRETARY OF STATE

MARCH 11, 1869, TO MARCH 11, 1877

BY

JOSEPH V. FULLER, Ph.D.

DIVISION OF PUBLICATIONS, DEPARTMENT OF STATE

HAMILTON FISH

HAMILTON FISH

CHAPTER I

THE NEW SECRETARY—THE GENERAL SITUATION

THE selection of Hamilton Fish, who was commissioned as Secretary of State on March 11, 1869, came as a general surprise to political observers. Prior to his appointment he had had no experience in diplomatic affairs, and he had held no public office for twelve years.

Born in New York City, August 3, 1808, son of Colonel Nicholas Fish, a Revolutionary officer, and Elizabeth Stuyvesant Fish, descendant of the last Dutch governor and heiress of a large part of his estate, Hamilton Fish enjoyed all the advantages in life that family and wealth can bestow. His early education under a French schoolmaster gave him a somewhat unusual qualification for the office which came to him in his last years—a command of the French language. Following his graduation from Columbia University, in 1827, he took up the study of law, and in the course of his later practice he formed a partnership with W. B. Lawrence, formerly secretary of legation at London and editor of Wheaton's *International Law*. After the death of his father, in 1833, however, much of his attention was occupied by the management of the family property. At about the same time he entered actively into politics, identifying himself with the newly-organized Whig party and becoming a candidate for the state assembly in its unsuccessful campaign of 1833. In 1836 he married Julia Kean, of a prominent New Jersey family, a woman of intelligence and social charm.

Although Fish maintained a keen interest in the affairs of his political party, he did not again run for office until 1842, when he was elected to Congress, where he served out his term, but he failed of re-election. In 1846 he was defeated as candidate for lieutenant-governor, mainly because of his opposition to the agitation against feudal land-tenures, but in the following year he was successful in a special election for the same office, which had been vacated. In 1848 he was elected governor, owing to a split in the Democratic party. He served a single uneventful term, not being nominated at the next election. His most notable statements on public questions during this time were those in his two annual messages against the introduction of slavery into the newly-acquired territories of California and New Mexico. When, in 1851, he was sent to the Senate by an election carried through during the absence of two of his opponents in an equally divided upper house, he maintained his opposition to the extension of slavery, though he deplored making a political issue of its existence. But the forces of his times were too strong to be denied, and Fish's own party went to pieces beneath his feet. Only after a careful weighing of the policies of both principal parties left in the field did he cast in his lot with the Republicans; and it is significant that in

HAMILTON FISH 127

his private letters debating the choice he laid great stress upon the issue of foreign policy, characterizing that of the Democratic party, symbolized by the Ostend Manifesto, as "unsafe and belligerent," a policy "of the pirate and the bandit." Although he co-operated loyally enough with his chosen organization, he harboured reservations on many of its doctrines and did not become its candidate for re-election upon the expiration of his term in 1857.

After his retirement from office Fish went abroad with his family and spent two years in Europe, giving much of his time to the study of political questions, particularly foreign affairs. He returned to take an active share in the election of President Lincoln and he played a certain unofficial part in the councils of the changing Administration, being concerned in the outfitting of the *Star of the West* for the relief of Fort Sumter. After the outbreak of the Civil War he became an organizer, and later chairman, of the Union Defence Committee of the state of New York, one of the private organizations which rendered indispensable help to the Government in mobilizing the public sentiment and material resources of the North in the chaotic conditions of the early months of the struggle. In 1862 he was appointed member of a commission to look after the welfare of Federal prisoners, which eventually arranged an agreement for the exchange of prisoners.

Although Fish supported the election of General Grant as President and entertained him in New York during the campaign, he was not regarded as in line for an administrative office. In the perplexity which followed Wilson's withdrawal of his acceptance of the office of Secretary of State, Grant unexpectedly turned to his urbane and cultivated recent host. Fish promptly declined the proffered honour, but when the President, nevertheless, sent his name to the Senate, and the appointment was confirmed, he yielded in order to avoid adding to the already considerable difficulties that had appeared in constructing the new Cabinet. He came to Washington, as he wrote to his friend Senator Sumner, "with a heavy heart and with unnumbered misgivings." He hoped to retire as soon as he could do so without embarrassing the Administration, but, though his resignation was offered several times, he remained in office throughout both of Grant's terms.

When Secretary Fish took charge of the foreign relations of the United States, he found himself called upon to deal with a situation in which the country faced the choice between a course of peaceable development and one of adventurous imperialism. A complicated set of questions beckoned it along the latter road.

The most serious of these questions affected our relations with Great Britain. The outstanding issue between the two countries was that of the claims for damages arising out of the depredations of the *Alabama* and other Confederate cruisers which had sailed from British ports during the Civil War, but the specific claims merely symbolized a mass of grievances founded on the conviction that Great Britain's conduct, beginning with her recognition of Confederate belligerency, had been unfriendly and largely responsible for the prolongation of hostilities. The recently signed Johnson-Clarendon convention for a settlement of these claims was generally regarded as inadequate to appease this

resentment, and its rejection by the Senate was a fore-
gone conclusion. Beneath this widespread sense of injury ran a strong current of feeling that the only proper
reparation should include the withdrawal of Great Britain from Canada, opening the way to its annexation by
the United States. This feeling was only strengthened
by the existence of boundary disputes with Canada
and the embarrassing activities of the Fenians. In view
of the generally prevailing impression as to the indifference of Gladstone's Government towards the Empire,
it is comprehensible that those who cherished such
sweeping imperialistic aspirations could have hoped to
realize them by a peaceable arrangement; but there
were not wanting those who did not shrink from war as
a means of attaining the desired solution. In any case,
a policy of holding the entire question open, subject to
such a condition of settlement, was fraught with grave
danger.

Opportunity for movements of expansion in another
quarter was afforded by the problems of the Caribbean
area. The insurrection raging in Cuba since 1868, with
consequent injuries to American interests, invited intervention; and a strong pressure exercised by Cuban
sympathizers for recognition of the rebels as belligerents
greatly embarrassed the Government in its attitude
with respect to the British recognition of Confederate
belligerency. The internal troubles of the Dominican
Republic had brought precariously into power the
Government of President Baez, which was frankly prepared to turn over the country to the United States
rather than succumb to its rivals. The "forward policy"
in the Caribbean region which these conditions invited

presented special possibilities of serious complications if carried on under the circumstances of strained relations with Great Britain.

The situation within the country, particularly in the North, favoured the development of an enterprising foreign policy, to which a strong impetus had already been given by Seward. The restless aftermath of a victorious war was succeeding to the first relaxation of peace with its problems of reconstruction and its restriction of spectacular economic opportunities. A soldier President had entered the White House with a suite of adventurers civil and military, the latter chafing in the dull inactivity of arrested careers. Projects of expansion beyond the frontiers, with opportunities for action, glory, profit, escape from the humdrum problems of peace, found plenty of advocates in Congress and in the Cabinet, not to mention the miscellaneous swarm of hangers-on about the President. And all these advocates found the President accessible to their persuasions.

Among this raffish company Hamilton Fish moved, a dignified but uncertain figure. Unfamiliar with the work he had undertaken and undecided as to the courses he should pursue, he leaned heavily upon others more experienced than himself for advice and even for the formulation of his policies and the drafting of instructions—especially upon his friend Charles Sumner, chairman of the Senate Committee on Foreign Relations, and Caleb Cushing, stormy petrel of American diplomacy, at this time agent of the United States in the Puget Sound Agricultural Company case with Great Britain. His Assistant Secretary, J. C. Bancroft Davis, brought to bear upon his duties an experience of three years' service, in the fifties, as secretary of the legation in London. Bound to President Grant by a strong sense of personal and party loyalty, Fish made himself the instrument of presidential policies without consulting his own convictions and continued in office despite his distaste for the tasks he had to perform. But beneath his deference to the judgments of others his policy was largely moulded in the long run by his inherent qualities of caution and patience—the caution and patience bred of a lifetime spent in the management of a secure estate, in association with conservative business men, and of a personal disinterestedness in his tenure of office. His caution led him to distrust all adventurous undertakings, even while lending himself to their pursuit; his patience enabled him to await the proper moment for discomfiting projects with which he did not sympathize, but which he did not feel able to defeat by open opposition at the outset. The interplay of conflicting policies, interests, and personalities in the stormy political drama in which he moved ultimately made it possible for him to steer the Government into a safe and peaceful course of foreign policy, which, if not regarded as one of lost opportunities for achieving "manifest destinies," must be called successful and salutary.

CHAPTER II

THE *ALABAMA* CLAIMS AND SUMNER'S
POLICY—THE CUBAN QUESTION—GRANT'S
DOMINICAN POLICY—THE DEFEAT OF
RECOGNITION OF CUBAN BELLIGERENCY

I

THE question of the *Alabama* claims came to a crisis on April 13, 1869, when the Senate practically unanimously rejected the Johnson-Clarendon convention. Not only was the negotiation of a settlement rendered more difficult by the agitation of public opinion on both sides in connexion with the failure of this attempt, but the difficulty was greatly increased by the speeches delivered against the convention. Although its defeat was sufficiently certain, Senator Sumner seized the occasion to take a comprehensive review of the American case against Great Britain. Reviving all the contentions of Seward and Adams in regard to British conduct during the Civil War, he held the country liable for the direct damage inflicted by cruisers sailing from its ports and for the general damage suffered by American trade through the hazards created by their operations, and also for half the cost of the war itself, on the ground that its duration had been doubled by the moral and material support given by Great Britain to the South. The estimated total of these claims was well over two billion dollars. Sumner made no attempt to indicate the manner in which this enormous account might be cleared, but the kind of settlement he desired was well enough known and was clearly indicated by other speakers. As he outlined it in a letter to Francis Lieber somewhat later, he mentioned among the factors of reparation a payment of money, an apology, the acceptance of a definition of international law under which the British practices would stand condemned, and "territorial compensation." There can be little doubt that the underlying purpose of Sumner's presentation of the case in its most extreme form was to commit the Government to a set of demands which could be satisfied only by a general settlement including Great Britain's renunciation of Canada, rather than by any recognition and satisfaction of specific claims.[1]

As such a policy found much support in the country, in governmental circles, and with the President, Fish felt obliged to adopt it, though he did so with serious misgivings as to the difficulties and dangers involved in carrying it through. When it became necessary to draw up instructions for John Lothrop Motley, who was to succeed Reverdy Johnson, negotiator of the rejected convention, as minister to Great Britain, Fish was able to agree to a statement of the American case acceptable to Sumner in all respects save its treatment of the British Government's recognition of Confederate belligerency. Sumner adhered unreservedly to the contention that this act, from which flowed all the others prejudicial to the Northern cause, had been unjustifiable from every point of view. He believed that any restrictions upon the condemnation of it would impair the success of the policy of settlement he had in mind. Fish, on the other hand, besides being by no means enthusiastic about pressing the case against Great Britain to the extent Sumner favoured, was embarrassed by his reluctance to make any general statements which would hamper the Government's freedom of action in recognizing the belligerency of the Cuban insurgents if it should decide upon such a step. He himself did not believe the step was warranted by existing conditions, but he knew Grant to be inclining towards it and felt that a free hand must be kept for the future.

A lively controversy arose over the language of the instructions on this point, which, thanks to Cushing's good offices, finally resulted in a compromise statement, admitting "the right of every power, when a civil conflict has arisen within another state, and has attained a sufficient complexity, magnitude, and completeness, to define its own relations and those of its citizens and subjects toward the parties to the conflict, so far as their rights and interests are necessarily affected by the conflict." This left an opening for action in Cuba; but, in order to maintain the case against Great Britain, the assertion was added: "The necessity and the propriety of the original concession of belligerency by Great Britain at the time it was made have been contested and are not admitted." In language still condemnatory, Fish managed, however, to restrict the role of that question in the debate by stating that it formed "a part of the case only so far as it shows the beginning and the animus of that course of conduct which resulted so disastrously to the United States." Emphasis was laid repeatedly upon "acts causing direct damage" as the real subject of the settlement, in a manner which indicated Fish's disposition to narrow the issues so broadly stated by Sumner. The desire for a definition of neutral rights and duties as a feature of the eventual settlement was also stated. The advisability of a temporary suspension of negotiations was pointed out.[2]

When the British minister, Sir Edward Thornton, attempted, on June 11, 1869, to obtain a definite statement of the bases upon which the American Government was prepared to resume efforts towards a settlement, the exchange of views took a form which was to remain virtually unchanged for months. "Fish said to him that our claims were too large to be settled pecuniarily, and sounded him about Canada, to which he replied that England did not wish to keep Canada, but could not part with it without the consent of the population."[3] Sumner's policy was thus laid before the British Government and met with a demurrer which was to be maintained throughout.

Although the Secretary of State was thus expounding Sumner's views, it was something of a shock to himself and the President to find that the new minister in London was doing the same to an extent far exceeding his instructions. The report of his first interview with Lord Clarendon, on June 10, showed that he had spoken far more strongly than he had been authorized to do, particularly in defining more stiffly the right of a government to "issue proclamations of neutrality between an insurgent portion of a nation and the lawful government." So angered was Grant, who was at that very time canvassing opinion on the question of recognizing Cuban belligerency, at this mangling of the carefully drafted formula of Motley's instructions that he

urged the minister's immediate recall. But Fish contented himself for the time with a mild rebuke and a
notification that any further negotiations were to be
conducted in Washington, rather than through the
legation in London.[4]

The official expression by the Secretary of State of a
policy in accordance with Sumner's desires was accompanied by unofficial intimations that he did not intend
these expressions as the final word in regard to his willingness to arrive at an agreement. The most important
of these intimations was conveyed in a conversation on
July 8 with John Rose, a Canadian politician of Scottish
birth, then serving as commissioner in the arbitration
between the Hudson's Bay and the Puget Sound companies, who offered through Caleb Cushing his private
good offices for arriving at a settlement of the larger
question at issue. He discussed with Fish the advisability
of the British Government's sending a special envoy of
high rank to express regret for its actions of the past,
and Fish accepted the idea without attaching any drastic conditions.[5] Somewhat later, in a letter to a friend,
Fish described the essential basis of a settlement as
Great Britain's acknowledgment of her errors "by a
definition of what *shall* be Maritime International Law
in the future and a few kind words."[6]

Senator Sumner was not minded to let the negotiation
take such an easy course. He advised Fish that it was
time to lay before the British Government a fresh statement of the case, and upon his declining to draft one,
the task was entrusted to Cushing, who produced the
instruction to Motley of September 25, 1869, to which
Sumner pointed the moral by a speech of the 22nd

voicing his expectation of a union with Canada. The instruction followed closely the lines of Sumner's speech, laying stress upon the necessity of reparation for the "*national* injuries" inflicted by Great Britain's conduct as well as of "indemnities . . . to individual citizens."[7] The burden of the references to relations with Great Britain in President Grant's first annual message to Congress was much the same. The hope of a settlement was reiterated, but definition of its bases was confined to such references as that to "what is due to the rights, dignity, and honor of both nations." In his further conversations with Sir Edward Thornton, in the latter months of 1869, Fish continued to evade specific discussion by referring to the necessity of consulting with the chairman of the Senate Committee on Foreign Relations and his colleagues. When he mentioned the question of Canada again, the minister replied in his former vein: "The Canadians find fault with me for saying so openly as I do that we are ready to let them go whenever they shall wish; but they do not desire it."[8] In spite of a conciliatory correspondence carried on between Fish and Rose since their conversation, a settlement seemed as remote as ever.

II

The difference of opinion between Sumner and Fish over the question of denying Great Britain's right to recognize Confederate belligerency, in the circumstances of May 1861, was intimately connected with the development of American policy regarding the situation in Cuba. The two men were agreed in feeling that the extension of a belligerent status to the unorganized insurgent movement there was unwise; but, while Sumner was quite prepared to see all possibility of such action precluded by a sweeping doctrinal pronouncement on the general subject, Fish believed that he must hold the way open by reserving the question of right and making judgment turn upon questions of fact. He realized that recognition of a state of war in Cuba would subject American commerce to greater interference by the Spaniards than if the situation were regarded as one of mere internal disorder, and that such interference was practically certain to lead to war with Spain. It would be the first step in a course of intervention such as he had termed piratical in 1856. But it was a step advocated by many from idealistic as well as interested motives and urged upon Grant by intimate advisers, chief among whom was General Rawlins, Secretary of War. Unable to make his own cautious views prevail, Fish felt obliged to follow in dealing with Spain a policy holding in view the possibility of recognition of the rebels and assistance in the liberation of Cuba, just as he followed in dealing with Great Britain a policy looking towards her elimination from Canada.

As early as April 1869, in his correspondence with the Spanish minister, largely made up of protests against measures of the local authorities in Cuba regarded as inhumane and injurious to American rights and interests, the Secretary of State alluded to the insurgents as "enemies of Spain" and frankly admitted that "there pervades the whole American people a special desire to see the right of self-government established in every region of the American hemisphere, so that the political destiny of America shall be independent of transatlantic control." [9]

The necessity of taking an immediate decision was averted by Grant's acceptance of the scheme of a private citizen personally acquainted with General Prim, the Spanish Regent, for a mediation between the Government and the rebels. In his instruction of June 29, 1869, to the minister in Spain, General Sickles, Fish proposed the use of the American Government's good offices in the negotiation of an arrangement based upon Cuban independence and the abolition of slavery. He referred advisedly to the conflict as a "civil war" and authorized Sickles to give the Spanish Government to understand that, if the struggle was not ended one way or another, "an early recognition of belligerent rights is the logical deduction from the present proposals." The Spanish Government met these overtures, in August, with a program of its own, imposing the conditions that the insurgents should lay down their arms as the preliminary to any arrangement and that the possible grant of independence should be subject to a popular referendum.[10] Fish argued strongly the impracticability of these conditions, which revealed a wide divergence between the views of the American and Spanish Governments, but he applied himself to a sustained effort to devise concessions and compromises which would bring the two together. The exchange of views thus opened with the Spanish Government proceeded haltingly to the accompaniment of a continued series of protests against the measures of the authorities in Cuba. A number of gunboats built for use in Cuban waters were detained by the American Government, on representations from the Peruvian minister that their release would free other Spanish vessels for use in the war then in progress between Spain and Peru, in violation of American neutrality.

While the negotiations with the Spanish Government were hanging on its counter-proposals, Fish's policy was nearly upset by the President's intervention. On the night of August 19, while travelling north in a Fall River boat for his vacation, Grant succumbed to the persuasions of the partisans of recognition of Cuban belligerency and signed a proclamation effecting it. When this document reached Fish, he countersigned it, but withheld its promulgation, an action to which Grant later referred as one of the occasions on which "your steadiness and wisdom have kept me from mistakes into which I should have fallen." [11] In his message of December 6 the President included a passage deprecating intervention in the troubles between European states and their possessions in the New World, despite the natural sympathy with their efforts for independence, and stating that, while the Government maintained it should "be its own judge when to accord the rights of belligerency" to the Cuban insurgents, it did not believe they had yet developed "a *de facto* political organization . . . sufficient to justify a recognition of belligerency." Its hands were thus left free with respect to the Cuban situation, while maintaining the case against Great Britain's action set forth in Fish's instructions to Motley.

The attempt at a pacification in Cuba through American good offices had meanwhile been brought to nothing through difficulties raised by the Spanish Gov-

ernment and the Cortes. The dispatch of reinforcements
to the island was, at the same time, pushed energetically, and profuse assurances were given of benevolent intentions to execute reforms, with which Fish
expressed satisfaction. Awaiting the outcome of these
efforts and promises, Fish informed Sickles, on January
26, 1870, that the Government reserved its freedom of
action for the future, insisting upon the abolition of
slavery as a "*sine qua non* of any Cuban settlement." [12]

III

Although the question of annexation of the Dominican Republic was of smaller scope than those of the
Alabama claims and the recognition of Cuban belligerency, it was for a time to obscure these others in political
significance and to afford Fish, through the practice of
his methods of compromise, opportunity to make his
moderate policies prevail in other fields—and, in the
long run, in this one as well. The question had arisen
under the preceding Administration and was pressed
from the beginning of Grant's term by agents of President Baez, who freely offered to deliver his country for
annexation as the price of aid against his rival, Cabral.
Complicated with the question of annexation was that of
the acquisition of a naval base at Samaná Bay, offers of
which had repeatedly been made by past governments
anxious for American support. The Navy Department had a special interest in this latter question, and
advocates of annexation on one ground or another were
numerous. These soon won Grant entirely to their side
through mixed motives, one of which was a conviction

that bringing this black republic under the American flag would contribute to a solution of the Negro problem by affording a field of emigration from the mainland. The President's views were bitterly contested by Senator Sumner, who could see only injury to the Negro cause in the extinction of this outpost of political independence.

Secretary Fish, with his accustomed loyalty tempered by distrust of adventurous undertakings, accepted the President's direction of policy in this matter, only endeavouring to restrain him from undue haste. When the Secretary of the Navy ordered a warship to proceed on an investigation of the feasibility of a coaling station at Samaná Bay, he agreed to a broadening of the mission to include a general survey of conditions in the country, with particular attention to popular feeling "in regard to annexation to the United States, or the sale or lease of the Bay of Samaná."[13] When the ship's mission was prevented by an accident, it was decided to dispatch a special agent instructed to make similar but more thorough inquiries, and the choice finally fell upon General Orville E. Babcock, one of Grant's military aides. In addition to the formal instructions for his inquiry given him by Fish, Grant told Babcock personally that the execution of his mission should be made contingent upon his obtaining from President Baez personal assurances favourable to annexation of the country.[14] Babcock also carried a letter from the Secretary of the Navy to the commanding officer of a cruiser then in Dominican waters instructing him to stand by during the General's visit and "give him the moral support of your guns."[15]

Babcock returned in due course, bringing with him, in addition to a set of financial statements and glowing reports furnished by the Baez Government, an extraordinary document, signed by himself and the Dominican secretary in charge of foreign relations, which he defined as a memorandum embodying their common understanding of the terms of an ultimate agreement, but which both Fish and Grant commonly alluded to as a "treaty." It might be termed an "option" agreement. It provided two alternative choices for the American Government: annexation upon assumption of the public debt of $1,500,000, or purchase of Samaná Bay for $2,000,000. The Baez Government undertook to deliver the "national consent" to annexation within four months, while Babcock pledged President Grant "privately to use all his influence" for the acceptance of annexation by Congress. As consideration for the "option," Babcock undertook to agree that "his Excellency President Grant assumes the obligation to remit forthwith" $100,000 in cash and $50,000 worth of arms, to be credited against the ultimate payment on either alternative. It was further provided: "In either case the United States will guarantee the safety of the country and of the government against every foreign aggression or machination [the Cabral movement being regarded as supported by Haiti], in order that the present cabinet may carry into effect the obligation it contracts, to obtain from the people the expression of the national consent."[16]

Fish was greatly disturbed by Babcock's usurpation of diplomatic authority in signing this document, with its commitments of the executive power to political, financial, and military action without congressional authorization. He was in favour of ignoring it as a factor in whatever transactions might be undertaken with regard to the Dominican question. But Grant, now won completely to the cause of annexation, stubbornly insisted on considering himself bound by the agreement and directed that it be converted into regular diplomatic form. After a brief discussion of the matter with the Cabinet, in which he found no one to support his views, the President simply carried on the policy single-handed, making it an issue of party harmony. The Cabinet members were thus enabled to stand aside in attitudes, of more or less benevolent neutrality, with the exception of the Secretary of State, who was obliged to direct the necessary diplomatic procedure. While Fish had concurred in a mission clearly enough designed to pave the way towards annexation, he had been so unprepared for its far-reaching results that he had actually assured opponents of the measure that no definite steps were being taken. Regard for his personal sincerity, as well as for the slighted prerogatives of his office, impelled him to offer his resignation rather than carry out the President's instructions. Grant was able, however, to dissuade him from a course which so threatened to discredit the Administration and disrupt the party. Reluctantly the Secretary assumed such shade of responsibility for the President's policy as devolved upon his department.[17] In recognition of his support in this matter Grant deferred to his views on the Cuban question, dropping the idea of recognizing the rebels' belligerency and agreeing to the inclusion in his message to Congress of the passage referred to above.

The upshot of Fish's understanding with Grant was that Babcock was sent back to Santo Domingo carrying instructions for the negotiation of a treaty of annexation and an alternative convention for a lease (rather than purchase) of Samaná Bay, together with full powers for their signature by the American Government's representative in the Republic. He also brought with him a cargo of arms and a draft for $100,000, and an authorization to instruct the commander of a naval force dispatched for the purpose to take whatever action he judged proper for protecting the existing Government and assuming possession of either the entire country or the coaling station as might ultimately turn out to be the case. The documents were duly signed on November 29, 1869, and the station was at once set up at Samaná Bay under the American flag, while Baez's forces, re-equipped with American arms and supported in their operations by American warships, proceeded to pacify the country and to supervise the voting in a popular referendum which, by February 1870, was rolling up a safe majority for annexation.[18]

In Washington, however, matters went less smoothly. When the agreements negotiated by Babcock arrived, President Grant took the extraordinary step of calling personally on Senator Sumner to solicit his support for their approval. All he obtained was Sumner's assurance as "an Administration man" that he would give the measures "the most careful and candid consideration."[19] Grant interpreted these remarks as an assurance of support; and Sumner's failure to make his attitude clearer, after the documents were shown to him by Babcock next day, made possible the development of a misunderstanding which was to have the most painful results. The treaty and convention were transmitted to the Senate without comment on January 10, 1870; on March 14 the President sent in a brief reminder that the time for ratification would expire within another fortnight and expressing "the sincere hope that your action may be favorable." Next day the Committee on Foreign Relations rendered an adverse report, in which four of his six colleagues concurred with Sumner, who made a four-hour speech condemning annexation.

Grant, whose pugnacity was roused by what he regarded as Sumner's breach of faith, exerted himself to undo its effects, even to the extent of using the President's room at the Capitol for conferences with senators. Failing to obtain the Senate's consent to ratification within the stipulated time, he procured an extension of the annexation treaty until the end of June. In communicating this additional article, on May 31, he accompanied it with a lengthy message dilating upon the advantages of the acquisition. He announced privately that all members of the party would be held to support of his policy; and Attorney-General E. Rockwood Hoar, whose neutrality was held not sufficiently benevolent, was informed, in the middle of June, that his resignation was requested.[20] Fish remained loyal in his support of the President, even calling on Sumner and pleading with him to forgo his opposition in the interest of party harmony, but with no result.[21] The entire imbroglio was so painful to the Secretary that he again expressed his desire to resign, but once more was dissuaded.[22]

All Grant's efforts proved unavailing. When the treaty of annexation came to a vote, it failed to receive the two-thirds majority necessary for ratification and expired. Grant did not yet acknowledge himself beaten, but turned to devising other means for attaining his end. As for Fish, the material results of this phase of the affair had been that, without seeing an actual victory for the doubtful project he had reluctantly supported, he had been able to take advantage of it to make his Cuban policy prevail, and that he could feel sure of the President's support in putting through a settlement with Great Britain over any difficulties that Sumner might raise—for the mere reason that it was he who raised them.

IV

The most immediate incidental effect of the Dominican controversy was on the development of the Cuban question. Fish's initial suport of the President's annexation policy for the Dominican Republic had been rewarded, we have said, by the concession to his views against recognition of Cuban belligerency in the message of December 6, 1869. A fresh campaign by the Cuban sympathizers in the ensuing year corresponded most fortunately for Fish with the final crisis over the Dominican treaty, in which the President felt anew his need of the fidelity of his Secretary of State.

In spite of all Fish's efforts to dissuade them from their purpose, the advocates of according belligerent rights to the Cuban rebels had rallied their forces and presented a joint resolution in Congress calling upon the President to take the action they desired. On the advice of their opponents, Fish prepared a counter-attack in the form of a special presidential message; but he found Grant again disposed to recur to his stand of the previous August. Fish was supported by the rest of the Cabinet in his argument that if the injuries inflicted by the Spanish authorities upon Americans merited retaliation, it should be by direct action rather than by proceeding towards war through a recognition of belligerency unjustified on the very grounds that were being alleged against Great Britain's act of 1861. After three days of debate Grant yielded and signed the message of June 13, 1870.[23]

Referring to the statements in his message of December 6, the President affirmed that there had been no change of conditions since that date such as would warrant recognition of the rebels as belligerents. While deploring the barbarities of the conflict and the injuries sustained by Americans, he also deprecated the efforts of the rebels and their partisans to involve the United States in hostilities with Spain, which he indicated in plain terms would be the probable result of the interference with American commerce made possible under the Spanish treaty of 1795 in the event of recognition of belligerency. The matter of principle was discussed from the point of view of the facts, leaving untouched the question of the right of recognition, in such fashion as to prejudice future action neither in this case nor in the controversy with Great Britain over her actions in the past. "The question of belligerency," it was stated, "is one of fact, not to be decided by sympathies for or prejudices against either party. The relations between the parent state and the insurgents must amount in fact to war in the sense of international law. Fighting, though fierce and protracted, does not alone constitute war. There must be military forces acting in accordance with the rules and customs of war, flags of truce, cartels, exchange of prisoners, etc.; and to justify a recognition of belligerency there must be, above all, a *de facto* political organization of the insurgents sufficient in character and resources to constitute it, if left to itself, a state among nations capable of discharging the duties of a state. . . . It is a well-established principle of public law that a recognition by a foreign state of belligerent rights to insurgents under circumstances such as now exist in Cuba, if not justified by necessity, is a gratuitous demonstration of moral support to the rebellion."

Despite this pronouncement the House Committee on Foreign Affairs reported the resolution next day, with a lengthy argument in its favour signed by the majority. An acrimonious debate ensued which was finally brought to a close by invoking the machinery of party discipline recently strengthened for use in the Dominican question. It worked better at this time in the House than later in the Senate on the question for which it was specially furbished up, and on June 16 the resolution passed, but with amendments which reduced it to a mere authorization to protest against the barbarous conduct of hostilities.[24] The pressure for recognition of belligerency was thus definitely relieved, leaving the way open for Fish's conciliatory policy.

The continued acceptance of this policy depended, however, upon its success in obtaining from the Spanish Government concessions calculated to pacify Cuba and redress for the injuries sustained by American persons and property in the island. Fish's insistence upon the

abolition of slavery was met, in June 1870, by a law
providing for emancipation, though on such a limited
and gradual scale that Fish instructed Sickles to inform
the Spanish Government that "this Government is disappointed in this project . . . that in the opinion of the
President . . . it will fail to satisfy or to pacify Cuba,"
although it would be regarded as an "entering wedge"
for more serious reform.[25] His gloomy predictions were
fulfilled the more surely because of the obstructions
placed in the way of even this limited measure. The
revolt continued, to the accompaniment of outrages
upon American citizens and their property.

With a view to neutralizing the effects of these, Fish
addressed to General Sickles, on June 24, an instruction
to demand immediate satisfaction on all outstanding
cases and the restoration of an interrupted arrangement
under which the Spanish minister in Washington was
empowered to pass on all such cases and give direct
orders to the authorities in Cuba. When Sickles took
it upon himself to proceed to a negotiation for the
establishment of an arbitral board, Fish approved his
action, upholding likewise his refusal of the Spanish
proposal that claimants be required first to establish
their American citizenship in the Spanish courts. After
much discussion an agreement was finally reached,
through an exchange of notes, on February 11, 1871, for
the establishment at Washington of a board, consisting
of two commissioners representing the respective Governments and an umpire selected by them, empowered to
pass on both the citizenship of claimants and their right
to indemnity.[26] This agreement, replacing a policy of
intervention, formed a fitting prelude to the treaty

concluded with Great Britain in the same year for arbitration of the claims against its Government. The commission functioned throughout the rest of the period of rebellion, reducing greatly the causes of international friction, although it was unable to overcome the dilatoriness and ineffectiveness of the Spanish Government in carrying out its obligations.

CHAPTER III

THE FRANCO-PRUSSIAN WAR—THE UNITED FRONT IN THE FAR EAST

I

WHILE the Dominican controversy, which had opened the way for the success of Fish's Cuban policy, was also creating a situation in Washington favourable to a moderate settlement with Great Britain, the British were being brought to a more conciliatory attitude by the Franco-Prussian War. That conflict, bringing serious preoccupations to the British Government and anxieties concerning the observance of neutrality by the United States if England should be involved, imposed also certain problems and responsibilities upon the American Government.

As sea-power played little part in the course actually taken by the war, no serious questions affecting neutral duties or the rights of neutral trade arose. After the investment of Paris a question of the right of legation was raised by the attempt of the German authorities to require that correspondence with the American minister, who remained in the city, should pass the lines only if unsealed and subject to scrutiny. Fish's insistence that the right of a neutral government to correspond with its agents was subject to "no exception or reservation looking to the possibility of blockade of a capital by a hostile force" brought about an arrangement for the passage of dispatch bags, which Bismarck, after first treating it as a "privilege," finally referred to in a note to Washburne as a "right." [27]

Washburne was authorized at the beginning of the war to assume the protection of North German and Saxon subjects in France and to act in conjunction with the Swiss and Russian representatives, who were acting for other German Governments, in moderating the harsh measures of the French authorities for deporting enemy nationals. When, however, the new French Government of September 4, which had been promptly recognized, requested the United States to "join the other powers in intervention for peace," Fish replied: "It is not the policy or interest of the United States to act jointly with European powers in European questions." [28] Nevertheless, he asked Bancroft, the minister in Berlin, to ascertain if America's good offices for peace would be welcome there, and upon receiving an unfavourable reply, instructed the minister to lose no opportunity of bringing to the North German Government's attention his own Government's desire to see an early and moderate peace, and "to contribute what you may to the presentation of such terms of peace as befit the greatness and the power which North Germany has manifested, and as shall not be humiliating or derogatory to the pride of the great people who were our earliest and fast ally." [29] Had the counsel been heeded, occasion might never have arisen for the more fateful correspondence engaged upon with the German Government forty-five years later.

II

The war in Europe was partly responsible for the necessity which devolved upon Secretary Fish of redefining American policy with respect to China. His first pronouncements on that subject had been in accord with the new spirit of consideration expressed in the Burlingame treaty concluded shortly before his entrance into office. In instructing the American minister in Berlin, on August 31, 1869, to render what assistance he could to the efforts of the Burlingame mission there, he admitted that the treaty involved a departure from the previous policy of maintaining a united front with the European powers "in so far as that policy was aggressive and attempted to force upon China measures which could not be forced upon a European or American state." Nevertheless, he supported certain British demands for an extension of trade facilities in the interior, and in transmitting a copy of the instruction to the minister in China, on December 3, Fish told him to "be unyielding in demanding the extreme protection to American citizens, commerce, and property which is conceded by the [earlier] treaties."[30] The hand of Caleb Cushing, negotiator of the Chinese treaty of 1844, is here clearly enough evident. In the spring of 1870 the United States entered into an arrangement with Great Britain, Germany, and other powers for co-operation with their naval forces against pirates in Chinese waters.

The Tientsin riot of June 21, 1870, in which a score of foreigners, mainly French, lost their lives, and for which France was powerless to enforce redress, owing to her preoccupations at home, caused much alarm concerning the stability of the position of all foreigners in China. On November 1 Fish telegraphed to Berlin instructing Bancroft to endeavour to secure a suspension of hostilities between Germany and France in the Far East and co-operation of their naval forces there for the protection of foreigners, on the ground that "hostilities between France and Germany . . . will operate on the minds of the Chinese to put in peril the lives of Europeans and Americans in that empire." The advice was followed and the united front of the Western powers in China was maintained until forty years later, when Germany's proposals of 1914 for neutralizing the Far East were rejected by the Allies, with incalculable results. The place of the United States in the closed rank was reaffirmed by Fish on November 29, when he informed the minister in China that his language in protesting against the threats to American missionaries that forced them to leave Tsungchow had been too moderate; in place of warning the Chinese Government only that a flagrant violation of the rights of American citizens might move his Government from its traditional policy, he was instructed to state that "any violation of the rights of our citizens and any flagrant violation of treaty stipulations of other powers may cause a change." [31]

In 1871 an attempt was made to secure from the Korean Government, through a mission backed by naval forces, a convention for the humane treatment of shipwrecked sailors, which resulted only in an armed clash and a punitive expedition in which five forts were destroyed and some two hundred and fifty Koreans and three Americans were killed.

CHAPTER IV

THE ABANDONMENT OF SUMNER'S POL-
ICY REGARDING THE *ALABAMA*
CLAIMS—THE DEFEAT OF
GRANT'S DOMINICAN
POLICY

I

THE influence of the Franco-Prussian War upon the progress towards a settlement of the *Alabama* claims was greater in anticipation of the event than in its actual occurrence. This influence was indicated by Sir Edward Thornton's response, in March 1870, to Fish's reiteration of the suggestion that a grant of independence to Canada would open the way to a solution. The minister stated anew that his Government could not take the intiative in such a separation, but he added: "They are willing, and even desirous, to have one. Europe may at any moment be convulsed; and if England became involved, it would be impossible to prevent retaliation, and the ocean would swarm with *Alabamas*. England would then be compelled to declare war." The Secretary agreed that, in the event foreseen, commerce destroyers would be fitted out in American ports by England's enemies, in spite of all the Government's efforts to prevent them.[32]

Notwithstanding these gloomy forebodings, the British Government showed no signs of receding from its position with respect to Canada. No steps were ever taken actually to ascertain the will of the Canadians in the matter, while the actions of the governmental authorities were such as to influence public opinion against the United States. Among the reasons for the new Canadian fishing-regulations and the revival of the claim to exclusive rights in navigation of the Saint Lawrence River, which, in the spring of 1870, exacerbated relations with the Dominion, the Consul-General in Montreal perceived an intention "to create a Canadian sentiment in antagonism to the ... spread of American sentiment here looking to ultimate annexation." [33] The raising of these issues, moreover, created a new, indirect approach to the question of the *Alabama* claims, by introducing additional subjects of negotiation between the two Governments, and tying the settlement up with the Canadian question in such a way as actually to turn the tables on the annexationists and obtain a fresh recognition of the Imperial connexion.

While the British Government was thus strengthening its resistance against the proposal of giving up Canada, the insistence of the United States upon the point as a condition of reconciliation was being weakened by the decline in influence of the principal champion of such a policy. Senator Sumner's very efforts to conserve the national expansionist energies for his favourite project by blocking all others were defeating themselves by discrediting him with the Administration. When, in June 1870, his opposition to the President's Dominican policy showed itself inflexible, Grant's vindictive desire to strike at his power took the form of a renewed demand for the recall of Sumner's protégé in

London, Motley. Fish opposed the action, preferring to let the unsatisfactory situation presented by Motley's position clear itself up through less drastic means, but Grant was determined upon showing that he would not "allow Sumner to ride over" him. Fish's attempt to patch up the matter by persuading Sumner to abandon his opposition to the treaty of annexation failed, as did likewise his suggestion that Sumner himself should take the London post. On July 1, immediately following the rejection of the Dominican treaty, Fish addressed a letter to Motley regretfully requesting his resignation. When the minister indignantly refused to give it, Fish put off recalling him in the hope of escaping the painful step by his own retirement from office.[34]

The proposal to send Sumner to London and the idea of resignation at this time indicate how little prospect Fish perceived of reopening negotiations with Great Britain upon more promising lines than those followed during the past year. The President, despite his hostility to Sumner, still clung to the idea championed by the Senator of exacting Great Britain's renunciation of Canada as a condition. He discussed with Fish the possibility of resuming conversations at London, through Motley's successor, on bases including a Canadian referendum on independence. When Fish broached this idea to the British minister in September, Thornton replied: "It is impossible to connect the question of Canadian independence with the *Alabama* claims; not even to the extent of providing for the reference of the question to a popular vote of the people of the Dominion."[35] This firm language could leave no doubt in Fish's mind that there was little hope of ever securing a settlement to which such a condition was attached. This fact was the more evident now that the war in Europe had passed the stage where Great Britain might fear being drawn into it through an invasion of Belgium or damage to her commerce.

The situation was given a new turn at the end of October, by Russia's taking advantage of the general disturbance to denounce the provisions of the treaty of 1856 excluding warships from the Black Sea. Great Britain's denial of her right to take such action single-handed brought on a new menace of war, which was cleared away, after a month of suspense, only by Bismarck's proposal of an international conference. While the tension was at its greatest, the Russian minister suggested to Fish that the opportunity was favourable for pressing Great Britain to settle the *Alabama* claims.[36]

Fish by this time was prepared to take the suggested course, but he had decided to drop from the negotiation all mention of Canadian independence, the obstacle which had held it up so long. A negotiation on any other basis was certain to encounter objections from Senator Sumner, but Fish was now prepared to discount these objections and to rely upon the President's animosity towards Sumner to assure his support of the resulting agreement against any opposition the Senator might offer. That animosity had increased rather than diminished since the defeat of Grant's Dominican policy in the summer, and its further growth was assured by the new schemes being hatched for reviving the policy in the next session of Congress. Fish's decision to risk a breach with Sumner was marked by his notification to Motley of his recall, on November 10, 1870. The step

was to be attended by even more unfortunate consequences than had been anticipated. When Motley
undertook to defend himself and Sumner, Fish was
prompted by his irritation and his desire to cover up the
President's responsibility and motives in the case to
sign, on December 30, a lengthy polemical dispatch
which, after repudiating any connexion with the Dominican controversy by alleging reasons for the recall,
valid enough, but inadequate by themselves, went on
to make a thinly veiled accusation against Sumner of
dishonesty towards the President in connexion with
that controversy.[37] When these statements came to the
Senator's knowledge, as they did early in the following
year, a difference in political views was converted into a
rupture of personal friendship.

The abandonment of Sumner's policy with respect to
the *Alabama* claims took definite shape ten days after
the notice of Motley's recall, when, in a conversation
with Sir Edward Thornton, Fish alluded to the Russian
minister's suggestion and, for the first time, met the
familiar request for a statement of America's terms of
settlement without any reference to Canada. He spoke
only of an expression of regret, a redefinition of the
principles of international law involved, and financial
reparation.[38] This intimation of the American Government's new stand was followed up by the inclusion of a
paragraph in the President's message of December 5
alluding to the claims without reference to other questions and expressing "an earnest desire for a conclusion
consistent with the honour and dignity of both nations."
The recommendation that the Government itself should
assume the claims by settling with the individual claim-

ants gave notice to Great Britain that the matter might take more serious form if not settled speedily.

The gesture proved unnecessary, for, four days later, Fish reported to the Cabinet the receipt of a letter from Sir John Rose intimating that the British Government was disposed to enter upon negotiations. Its willingness had been inspired by Fish's statement to Thornton, which, omitting mention of Canada, had coincided with his statements to Rose of over a year before. In another month Rose himself was back in Washington, still in an unofficial capacity, but fully primed to prepare the way for official negotiations. As the weakening of Sumner's influence, due to his quarrel with Grant over Santo Domingo, had made possible this new turn in the controversy with Great Britain, so that further development of that quarrel was to affect the progress of the negotiations thus initiated.

II

In the final act of the fateful drama of the President's Dominican policy, Fish played no direct role, since it never reached the point of diplomatic action. In the same message of December 5, 1870 that contained the invitation to Great Britain for renewal of negotiations on the *Alabama* claims, Grant had recurred to his thwarted project for annexation of the black republic. He presented extravagant estimates of the value of the acquisition from the commercial and strategic points of view as well as from that of its effect upon the Negro problem, and he predicted that the "folly of our rejecting so great a prize" would result in a European establishment at Samaná Bay. He suggested a joint resolution for the appointment of a commission to negotiate a new treaty and annexation by joint resolution, as had been done in the case of Texas.

This device for evading the requirement of a two-thirds majority, which a treaty would require, proved too much for even the President's supporters to sponsor. They temporized by introducing a resolution for a commission of investigation. Sumner opposed even this, flaying the President's policy in his speech of December 21, 1870 in a fashion which embittered their quarrel still further. Despite his opposition the resolution passed, and in January 1871 the commission was appointed and departed on its tour, which lasted until the end of February.

Before its report could be presented, measures were taken to diminish the effectiveness of Sumner's opposition to the President's designs. On March 4 the Forty-second Congress entered upon its existence and, in the organization of its committees, an action against Sumner was carried out that had been projected three months earlier. On March 9 the Republican caucus voted to exclude him from the Committee on Foreign Relations. Although the step had an important bearing on the progress of the Anglo-American agreement, then in process of conclusion on bases not fully approved by Sumner, the impelling force behind the caucus's action was the President's solicitude for his Dominican policy and his desire to break the power of its principal opponent.

Sumner's loss of the position which gave him such great control over the destinies of diplomatic agreements did not affect his influence over policies which had not yet reached that stage, and he opened fire again on the new Dominican project before the commission's report was submitted. On March 27, submitting resolutions against the misuse by the executive of the military power, he denounced the employment of naval forces to coerce the Dominican people and to bully the neighbouring republic of Haiti. His resolutions were tabled, but the exposition which accompanied them had discredited the whole policy of annexation. When Grant transmitted, on April 5, 1871, the highly favourable report of the commission of investigation, he recommended only its publication with a view to informing the people as to the merits of the case. With a couple of speeches on the subject, it was laid to rest and not heard of again until in his last annual message Grant expressed his regret that the opportunity for annexation had been neglected.

CHAPTER V

THE TREATY OF WASHINGTON—
THE GENEVA ARBITRATION

I

AFTER the arrival of Sir John Rose in Washington, on January 9, 1871, negotiations for an agreement with Great Britain moved forward rapidly. They began with an unofficial understanding as to the formal procedure. The British Government, to spare itself an open capitulation, should approach the matter indirectly by proposing the appointment of a joint commission to settle the questions in dispute affecting Canada, whereupon the American Government should propose the inclusion of the *Alabama* claims. No understanding was arrived at in respect of Fish's desire to obtain a preliminary expression of regret and admission of liability; and the confidential memorandum embodying the plan, which Rose transmitted on the 11th, provided only that the agreement to be reached should determine the methods by which the various disputes and claims were to be settled, including the question of liability.[39]

As the propositions laid down in this memorandum contained no mention of a British withdrawal from Canada, the issue with Sumner was now fairly drawn. The Senator's influence was at this time rapidly declining, owing to his opposition to the President's new Dominican projects and the already developing plans for ousting him from his committee; nevertheless, after conferring with the newly-appointed minister to Great Britain, General Schenck, and with Sumner's rivals in the Senate, Fish decided to lay the memorandum squarely before him and obtain either an approval of the new basis of negotiations or an outright statement of his objections. As friendly relations with the Senator had now been broken, owing to his having learned of the Motley dispatch of December 30, 1870, the interview of January 15 had to be arranged through another member of his committee. It resulted in a note from Sumner, written two days later, which committed him more deeply against the project than could have been anticipated. After approving of Rose's suggestions as a "starting point" for a full settlement of differences, he referred to the Fenian menace to Canada as a cause of friction not touched upon and concluded: "Therefore the withdrawal of the British flag cannot be abandoned as a condition or preliminary of such a settlement as is now proposed. To make the settlement complete, the withdrawal should be from this hemisphere, including provinces and islands." [40]

This startling document merely served to strengthen Fish's position. Shown to Grant, it was enough to turn him against the idea Sumner stood for and to transform his doubtful approval of Fish's new course into active co-operation. He authorized the Secretary to inform Rose at once that the Administration was prepared to adopt his suggestions without qualification. [41] The Senate leaders whom Fish consulted were of the same opinion. Accordingly, on January 24, 1871, Fish met Rose again and, after reading him a statement reiterating the American Government's desire for an expression of regret and an admission of Great Britain's liability, added that it would not stand out against deferring all the questions covered by the latter point for ultimate decision by the arbitral process to be agreed upon, providing it were confidentially understood that the American claims should be liberally interpreted to include the cost of capturing the Confederate raiders. He showed Sumner's note to Rose, but assured him that the Administration would make every effort to reach a settlement on the agreed basis, "even if it involved a conflict with the Chairman of the Committee on Foreign Relations in the Senate." Lord Granville, consulted by cable, agreed only to the conditions of an expression of regret and a restatement of the rules of international law; but, rather than hamper the progress of negotiations by insisting on an admission of liability and a definition of the extent of the claims, Fish took the statement as satisfactory and proceeded to open the formal diplomatic exchanges in accordance with the scheme outlined by Rose.[42]

The agreed procedure of proposals and counter-proposals was carried out in two exchanges of notes between the British minister and the Secretary of State, beginning January 26, 1871. With Fish's final note of February 3 the warrant was complete for the appointment of a joint high commission, consisting of five representatives of each Government, to agree upon means for settling all outstanding questions. The only ones to occasion serious difficulties, in fact, were those connected with the *Alabama* claims.

Some advance towards a meeting of minds on this crucial issue had been made, in that the American

Government had renounced the design of exploiting it to obtain Canada and in that the British Government had conceded an expression of regret for the occurrences giving rise to the claims. But on two fundamental questions those Governments still took conflicting views. These were: (1) Had the British Government failed to observe its obligations under international law? (2) Was the American Government entitled to claim compensation for anything more than the damage directly inflicted by the *Alabama* and other cruisers of similar antecedents? On both points the American position had consistently been that expressed by Senator Sumner nearly two years before, in his speech against a convention which had departed from it, although all reasonable basis for hope of satisfaction of the claims he then outlined disappeared with the abandonment of his dream of territorial compensation. The billion-dollar indemnity demanded of France by Germany at this time staggered the world; a conservative estimate of the claims stated by Sumner would amount to more than twice as much. Yet the American Government could not simply abandon them. Fish afterwards wrote to General Schenck that the American commissioners "would at any time willingly have waived the indirect claims for any equivalent." The British knew well enough what equivalent was desired, although it was no longer openly spoken of. Since they made no move towards offering it and even refused to make any admission of liability in advance, the Americans felt obliged to maintain their position and to refuse to admit any preliminary limitation of the claims presented. Fish told his colleagues privately that "he supposed it was pretty well agreed that there were some claims which would not be allowed by the arbitrators, but he thought it best to have them passed upon."[43]

On the two points indicated, most of the discussions turned, and upon each they threatened at one time and another to be broken off. Both were raised by Fish in the first business session of March 8. An agreement on the first was reached on April 6, when the British commissioners produced a draft of definitions of the duties of a neutral government with respect to the fitting out of belligerent ships in its ports, which was acceptable to both sides, and declared that their Government, while not admitting that these represented the generally accepted state of international law of ten years before, was willing to have them applied to the cases under consideration. On the second point no real understanding was reached at all. The British commissioners succeeded in keeping out of the treaty any provision for payment of expenses involved in capturing cruisers whose escape should be ruled illegal or for the submission of any other "national claims"; but the vague reference to "differences" between the two Governments in the formula of agreement to accept arbitration opened a wide loop-hole; while, in a special protocol, the American commissioners recorded their contention that the general language of the agreement allowed the submission of claims such as those for the expense of pursuit of the cruisers.[44]

The Treaty of Washington, which stands as the greatest monument of Fish's career as Secretary of State, was signed on May 8, 1871. It provided for the reference of what were "generically known as the '*Alabama*

claims'" to five arbitrators named by the heads of the
American, British, Italian, Swiss, and Brazilian states.
It registered "the regret felt by Her Majesty's Government for the escape, under whatever circumstances,
of the *Alabama* and other vessels from British ports,
and for the depredations committed by those vessels."
The principles by which the arbitrators were to be guided
in determining the British Government's responsibility
for the escape of these ships were laid down in the
famous "three rules" of Article VI:

"A neutral Government is bound—

"First, to use due diligence to prevent the fitting
out, arming, or equipping, within its jurisdiction, of
any vessel which it has reasonable ground to believe
is intended to cruise or to carry on war against a
Power with which it is at peace; and also to use like
diligence to prevent the departure from its jurisdiction
of any vessel intended to cruise or carry on war as
above, such vessel having been specially adapted, in
whole or in part, within such jurisdiction to warlike use.

"Secondly, not to permit or suffer either belligerent
to make use of its ports or waters as the base of naval
operations against the other, or for the purpose of the
renewal or augmentation of military supplies or arms,
or the recruitment of men.

"Thirdly, to exercise due diligence in its own ports
and waters, and as to all persons within its jurisdiction, to prevent any violation of the foregoing obligations and duties."

In cases in which it should be found that the British
Government had failed to fulfil the duties thus defined,

the arbitrators were empowered to award a gross sum
for the resulting damages or to refer the separate claims
to a board of assessors. The character of the claims to
be considered was not defined in any precise manner,
thus leaving each side free to maintain its own stand-
point with regard to the various classes of "indirect
claims." The issue on this point was left to be fought
out before the arbitrators at Geneva.

The other questions with which the treaty dealt—
claims against both Governments not connected with
operations of the Confederate cruisers, boundaries, fishing-rights, navigation of lakes and rivers, the coasting
trade, transit of goods in bond—were either settled outright or referred to commissioners or arbitrators. The
most serious difficulty encountered in drafting these
articles concerned the use by citizens of the United
States of the inshore fisheries. The British commissioners had insisted on a restoration of the reciprocity
treaty of 1854, terminated by the United States in 1866,
which the Americans pronounced themselves unable to
accord. Various American proposals for the purchase of
these rights by a lump sum or by the admission free of
duty of certain Canadian products were rejected as
inadequate. Agreement was at last reached on the
eventual reference to a special commission of the question as to what sum the United States should pay in
consideration of the greater value of the inshore fishing-
rights, for a period of ten years, over the rights granted
in other articles to British citizens.[45] The settlement
of all these questions in a treaty concluded by representatives of the British Government constituted a
new recognition of the relations between that Govern-

ment and the Dominion of Canada and the colony of Newfoundland.

When the treaty was referred to the Senate, Sumner, the champion of a policy of holding out for the British Government's renunciation of all connexion with those territories, was no longer chairman of the Committee on Foreign Relations. The Administration's anxiety as to his reception of the agreement had been partly responsible for his removal. Nevertheless, his influence, which had still availed to defeat the latest Dominican project, continued to be important, and he was, throughout the negotiations, the recipient of many private attentions from both the American and the British commissioners. He proved a good loser. The great hope which underlay his attack on the Johnson-Clarendon convention had been frustrated, but all his specific criticisms of that agreement were met by the new treaty. He did propose some amendments broadening the pronouncements on international law, but refrained from pressing them in order not to imperil the whole result, which he characterized as promising. The treaty was approved without change on May 24 and ratified on June 17, 1871.

II

The "cases" of the contending Governments in regard to the *Alabama* claims were presented at Geneva, on December 15, 1871, to the board of distinguished arbitrators chosen as provided in the Treaty of London. The American case, drawn up by Assistant Secretary J. C. Bancroft Davis, followed the lines taken from the beginning. Proceeding from a condemnation of the British recognition of Confederate belligerency, as an act unjustified by the existing situation and prompted by "a conscious unfriendly purpose toward the United States," it passed to a review of the conduct of the British authorities, with particular reference to the fitting out of the *Alabama* and other cruisers, "wherein Great Britain failed to perform its duties as a neutral." In conclusion it stated claims to reparation, not only for the damage actually done by the cruisers, but also for the expenses of their pursuit, for the reduction of the American merchant marine by transfers to foreign flags to escape capture, for the enhanced premiums on marine insurance, and for the cost of "the prolongation of the war."

The British Government, which in its case had contested its liability even for the direct damage done by the raiders, was taken aback by the sweeping character of the American claims. Public opinion was roused by their staggering scope and indignant at the reference to a "conscious unfriendly purpose." The Government made known its belief that consideration of the indirect claims was not within the province of the tribunal of arbitration created by the treaty and intimated the possibility of asking for withdrawal of the American case. Fish insisted on having the whole matter "judicially decided and . . . forever removed from the possibility of disturbing the perfect harmony of relations between the two countries." The American Government could recede from its position out of court only in consequence of some sort of transaction. The equivalent of the "indirect claims" intended by Sumner was now out of the question, but Fish suggested something very much less considerable—a withdrawal of the British contentions regarding the disputed water boundary in the Strait of San Juan de Fuca.[46] When this concession was refused, he fell back upon a still more reduced bargain. In instructions of April 23 and 27, 1872, he asserted that the American Government itself desired assurance against ever being held liable for similar claims, and he stated that no damages would be asked under them if the British Government would engage never to present any such claims in the future. After lengthy correspondence an understanding on these lines was actually formulated in the shape of an additional article to the Treaty of Washington and communicated to the Senate, on May 13, with the request for "an expression . . . of their disposition in regard to advising and consenting to the formal adoption" of such an article. In the debate Sumner, who realized the untenability of the "indirect claims" as such, characterized the American conduct of the case as unskilful, disingenuous, and tactless, but was for leaving the Administration to find its own way out. By resolution the Senate approved the article, but with amendments which the British Government declined to accept.

The deadlock remained unbroken on June 15, the date set for submission of arguments to the tribunal. The American counsel presented theirs, but the British argument was delayed with the intention of asking an adjournment of some months in order to negotiate further. Fish, who was interested only in having the question of the indirect claims passed upon by the tribunal, believed that longer wrangling might imperil the entire settlement. He had no expectation of an actual award under them, and no desire to press for one; but he felt that a decision of the arbitrators ruling them out would conserve the consistency of the American Government's position, besides giving assurance against future claims of the kind against it, better than any bargain that could now be patched up with the British Government out of court for their withdrawal. He had informed the American arbitrator, Charles Francis Adams, of these views before his departure for Geneva and asked him to make, on his way through London, a final effort to convince the British Government of the wisdom of allowing the matter to take such a course. Adams found the British statesmen as timorous and as obstinate on the point as ever, but he continued his efforts upon reaching Geneva. After three anxious days of consultation among the arbitrators and counsel, an agreement was reached on a form of declaration acceptable to both sides, and, on June 19, the tribunal assembled to pass on the question of the indirect claims. It rendered the opinion that "these claims do not constitute, upon the principles of international law applicable to such cases, good foundation for an award of compensation or computation of damages between nations." Fish at once instructed the American counsel to make it known that their Government accepted this judgment and considered the indirect claims adjudicated and disposed of. The British counsel were thereupon instructed to withdraw their motion for adjournment and present their argument, which they did on the 27th.

With these simple gestures was swept away the whole mass of ill-defined grievances which had stood between the two countries for so many years and prevented their coming to grips with the concrete problem of direct damage resulting from the British Government's failure to fulfil its duties as a neutral. This problem was itself by no means easy of solution. It remained to be established that the "due diligence" had not been employed in the observance of neutrality as related to the acts of various Confederate cruisers and to determine the amount of damage done by them which could be traced to the negligence of British authorities. Moreover, the costs of pursuit of such cruisers had not been included in the indirect claims ruled out by the decision of June 19. But these matters had now passed out of the field of diplomatic consideration into that of arbitral procedure.

They were actually dealt with in the course of about six weeks of intensive work after the tribunal took up definite consideration of them on July 15. In the "decision and award" formally rendered on September 14, 1872, it was found that "Great Britain has . . . failed, by omission, to fulfill the duties prescribed in . . . the rules established by the VIth article of the Treaty of Washington" in the cases of the *Alabama* and two other cruisers. The costs of pursuit of these were left out of consideration as indistinguishable from the general cost of carrying on the war. As the result of a calculation based upon various items and tempered by mutual concessions, an award was made to the United States of $15,500,000 in gold. The British arbitrator, Sir Alexander Cockburn, refused to sign the award and submitted a dissenting opinion, but his Government made no attempt to contest it. The payment was made a year later in United States bonds purchased by bankers under contract with the British Government.

The important controversy which had disturbed relations with Great Britain for a decade was thus brought to an end. Settlement of the other questions dealt with in the Treaty of Washington had either been completed by the close of the year or appeared well on the way to being so. Outstanding among these was the dispute over the San Juan Strait boundary, decided in favour of the United States by the German Emperor on October 21. In his annual message of December 2, 1872 the President declared that the disappearance of these issues "leaves these two Governments without a shadow on the friendly relations which it is my sincere hope may forever remain equally unclouded."

CHAPTER VI

FURTHER CONTROVERSIES WITH
SPAIN CONCERNING CUBA—THE
VIRGINIUS AFFAIR

I

THE international settlements of 1872, which made
Hamilton Fish a notable figure in the public eye,
reflected credit on the Administration in general and
contributed to Grant's success in the bitter electoral
campaign of that year. Without great difficulty the
President prevailed upon Fish to retain his office for
the second term. The Secretary of State had become
one of the strongest pillars of the Administration, inspiring, as did few of his colleagues, public confidence
in his ability, integrity, and stability. His influence in
the direction of caution and conservatism extended beyond the limits of his own department. In 1874 he was
largely instrumental in inducing the President to veto
the so-called "inflation bill" inspired by the recent
financial panic, and in the following year helped restrain him from further military intervention in the
reconstruction troubles of Louisiana.

Fish himself was finding his duties less onerous than
in the earlier years. From experience and success he
gained self-confidence and facility in diplomatic affairs.
The President had come to trust his judgment. The two
questions of the *Alabama* claims and the Dominican

annexation, which had presented the most serious difficulties and entailed the most embarrassing and painful
political and personal complications, were out of the
way. But one problem of major importance continued
to trouble our foreign relations—that presented by the
Cuban insurrection, which blazed as stubbornly as ever
in spite of the augmented efforts put forth by the
Spaniards towards the close of the year 1869 to quench
it by military force and to deprive it of fuel by reforms.
American interests and lives continued to be menaced
by the prevailing disorder and the arbitrary acts of
the Spanish authorities, while American sympathies on
interested and humanitarian grounds remained engaged
on the side of the rebels.

So exasperating was the situation that Fish had felt
constrained to address, on October 29, 1872, to General
Sickles, our minister at Madrid, a lengthy instruction
directing him to call the Spanish Government's attention to various unsatisfactory aspects of its conduct:
its failure to execute laws for the emancipation of slaves
and for the liberalization of colonial government, the
brutal and extortionate proceedings of local authorities,
affecting in many cases American citizens, the intolerable delays in affording redress for such wrongs. He was
further to give the Government to understand that, if
such delays continued, "Spain must not be surprised to
find . . . a marked change in the feeling and in the temper of the people and of the Government of the United
States." [47] Satisfaction was promised on all points, and
the Spanish Government, early in 1873, even asked
American approval of a new plan of pacification in
Cuba, which Fish expressed, with some reservations. [48]

But all developments were interrupted, in February 1873, by the abdication of King Amadeo and the formation of a republican Government. Fish promptly recognized the republic and awaited the definition of its colonial policies before pressing further the complaints he had put forward.

Fair promises were made, but, as usual, their fulfilment proved halting, and before long Fish was renewing his representations with mounting impatience. On March 21 he instructed Sickles to present a long memorandum from American shipowners against the system of customs fines imposed in Cuba and to endeavour to secure common action with the British and other European ministers in this connexion.[49] The desired co-operation did not take effect until October, owing to the fact that the other governments had not recognized the Republic, and the American requests were rebuffed. Some advance in colonial reform was made with the abolition of slavery in Porto Rico and the emancipation of some ten thousand Cuban slaves.

Though these acts received due acknowledgment, Fish's tone continued to rise in the instructions he dispatched to be read to the Spanish Minister of Foreign Affairs. On April 23 he wrote of the forbearance of the United States under the persistent delays in affording redress of grievances and "in the face of events . . . which might possibly have presented justification for something more than remonstrance." He pointed out that the repeated failures in execution of the Spanish Government's promises indicated that it did not really control the Cuban Administration. He put the question: "If the authorities in Cuba do not recognize the

authority of Spain over the Island . . . who else should?"
He called attention, on June 27, to the Government's
failure to rebuke those authorities, who continued to
thwart its assurances even while they were being given.
On August 27 he attributed the unsatisfactory situation to the Captain-General's power of suspending the
measures of the home Government and directed Sickles
to present "the inconvenience, perhaps I might say
the danger, which lies in this extraordinary power
vested in the Captain General by the Decree of 1825,
and urge its repeal." With reference to a ministerial
declaration that reforms in Cuba would be deferred,
Sickles was to "urge . . . the disavowal or abandonment
of a policy so inconsistent with the possibility of a
restoration of peace," which must compel other powers
"to consider its bearing and its effects with reference to
their own interests and duties." He concluded by saying
that "the President hopes that the United States may
not be the first of the nations which may be forced" to
take notice of the hopelessness of a situation in which
this country was most closely concerned.[50]

Lavish promises of amendment of the conditions complained of were once more made, with particular reference to the release of embargoed American property,
but the performance continued to lag. When, on October 11, Sickles telegraphed that as a proof of friendship
the Spanish Government proposed to raise its legation
in Washington to the rank of embassy, Fish tartly replied by cable: "It would be additional evidence of
friendship if the promises mentioned . . . were fulfilled."
In a dispatch of the 15th he elaborated on the theme of
broken promises at some length, remarking: "I must

frankly say that the present state of things cannot last. Our patience and endurance are sorely tried." Referring anew to the inability of the Government to control the authorities in Cuba, he intimated that the President might be forced into "recognizing the right of anti-slavery Republicans to carry on war for the dominion of a territory which in that event would have been practically abandoned by the Power hitherto recognized as its sovereign." Sickles was left to use his own discretion in impressing these views upon the ministers. One of Fish's suggestions was met, on the very day this dispatch was written, by the repeal of the decree of 1825. Nevertheless, he continued his pressure, stating, on the 25th, that if satisfaction on the point of the embargoed estates was not speedily forthcoming, "this Government may be forced to act in its own defense. Its probable action is the subject of consideration." [51]

Thus relations with Spain appeared to be approaching a crisis in the latter days of October 1873. The partisans of intervention in Cuba, whose pressure upon the Administration is indicated by these vigorous efforts to obtain redress of grievances, were also acting in other ways to promote their cause. From the beginning the Government had been embarrassed by the filibustering operations of a Cuban revolutionary committee in New York, financed from American sources. One of the most spectacular of the committee's ventures was the acquisition of the steamer *Virginius*, which, under American registry and with a mainly American crew, had, in 1871, both taken part in a Venezuelan revolution and landed an expedition in Cuba. The vessel had since been dodging about from one Caribbean port to another, obtaining the escort of American warships when too closely pressed by Spanish pursuers. On October 31, 1873 she was captured by a Spanish cruiser on the high seas between Jamaica and Cuba with a large party of revolutionists and a cargo of arms on board. Orders sent by the Spanish Government, upon representations from the American minister, to impose no death sentences without authorization, were delayed in transmission, and the authorities in Cuba, on the 7th and 8th of November, summarily executed fifty-three of the persons taken aboard, including the captain and thirty-six of the crew. A crisis seemed to have been brought about that must surely result in the most serious consequences.

II

When Secretary Fish learned of the seizure of the *Virginius*, he at first regarded the incident as merely another troublesome item in the long account with Spain. On November 7 he telegraphed Sickles that the case required investigation, that any hasty executions "will attract attention as inhuman," and that the wrongful execution of any American citizens "will require most ample reparation."[52] So little did he realize the development of any extraordinary situation that in another telegram of the same date he recurred to the subject of his previous correspondence as still the most pressing issue to be settled before the opening of Congress, saying: "Important that the official notice of release of embargoed estates be received here by 27th of this month."[53] When news of the executions arrived,

Fish denounced them, in a telegram of the 12th, as "butchery and murder," instructing Sickles to protest and to declare that "this Government will demand the most ample reparation of any wrong which may have been committed upon any of its citizens or upon its flag." But he added that there were grave doubts as to the right of the *Virginius* to fly the American flag, which required investigation.

This relatively calm attitude could not be maintained in the face of the rising popular excitement which seized upon the Government and led to the decision to present an ultimatum and to put the navy on a war footing. On the 14th, Fish telegraphed Sickles to demand the release of the ship and of the surviving persons taken aboard, a salute to the American flag, and the signal punishment of officials concerned in the capture and executions. If these demands were not granted within twelve days, he was to close the legation and leave Madrid. In a telegram of the following day Fish stated: "If Spain cannot redress the outrages perpetrated in her name in Cuba, the United States will." In adding that Sickles should use his instructions discreetly, "avoiding unnecessarily exciting any proper sensibilities and avoiding all appearance of menace," it must be admitted that he was imposing a caution practically impossible without contradicting their spirit. It is not surprising, therefore, that by rendering his instructions too literally in his notes to the Spanish Minister of Foreign Affairs, Sickles did give considerable offence and became involved in a dangerously acrimonious discussion that disturbed his own judgment.

The Spanish Government answered Fish's demands,

November 18, 1873, by stating that it could not meet those based upon the allegation of insult to the American flag until the right of the *Virginius* to fly that flag had been established. Although the period of grace allotted by Fish had still a week to run, Sickles proposed to regard this answer as a definite refusal and to close his legation forthwith. Popular feeling was rising high in both countries. A mass meeting held in New York on the 17th endorsed speeches demanding energetic action, and a crowd demonstrated on the next night before the American legation in Madrid. As Fish perceived how rapidly and rashly the Governments threatened to be carried along, his caution reasserted itself. He was assisted in stemming the tide by a communication received through the Spanish legation on November 18, differing notably from the *staccato* telegrams coming in from Sickles, in which the Spanish Government earnestly affirmed its intention to abide by the principles of international law and to make full reparation for any infractions as soon as the facts concerning them were established. On the 19th and 20th, Fish telegraphed to Sickles that the expectation of more time for ascertaining the facts was judged reasonable and that he should defer his departure, the Spanish minister having been informed that a satisfactory settlement was expected by the 26th.

When Sickles protested against any wavering and urged the efficacy of his departure as a means of bringing Spain to terms, Fish, after consulting the President, ordered him again to remain and informed him that the negotiation would thenceforth be pursued primarily through the Spanish legation in Washington, whence

the most promising assurances had come. The next communication from the minister, Admiral Polo de Bernabé,
however, proved to be a proposal for arbitration, which
was rejected as inapplicable to a question of "national
honor." When two days more had passed without further developments, Fish fell in with the suggestions
urged by Sickles to the extent of asking the Italian
Government to authorize its minister to take over the
custody of the legation in Madrid. Admiral Polo's
attempt, on the 24th, to obtain still more time was rebuffed on the ground that, according to past experience,
allowing the Spanish Government to take its own time
"amounts to an indefinite postponement." In a conversation on the following day, Fish stated flatly that
reparation for the indignity to the American flag must
precede the inquiry into the vessel's right to fly it and
that justice to Spain would afterwards be done according to the results of the investigation. In the evening he
instructed Sickles by cable to ask for his passports if no
accommodation had been reached by the close of the
next day, but to defer this action if he received any
further proposal, until it could be referred to Washington for reply.

Before Fish's telegram reached Madrid, on November 26, 1873, Sickles had already asked for his passports
and agreed to a postponement of their delivery until he
could obtain an answer to a new note which had crossed
his request. In this note the Spanish Government agreed
to deliver the vessel and crew and render the demanded
salute if by the 25th of December the illegality of the
registry of the *Virginius* had not been proved, and to
punish all officials concerned in the affair if convicted

of violation of laws or treaties. Understanding from the telegrams relating these developments, partially garbled in transmission, that Sickles had actually left Madrid, Fish conveyed to him no reply beyond transmitting at noon on the 27th, "for information of whom it may concern," the text of a Senate resolution of June 16, 1858, asserting that any interference with a vessel flying the American flag "is in derogation of the sovereignty of the United States."

No further communications had been received from Madrid when, in the afternoon of the 27th, the Spanish minister called to discuss the new proposals. Fish showed him the telegram from Sickles and told him that the Government could not consent to Spain's detention of the *Virginius* while the investigation was being carried on. When Admiral Polo answered that he was empowered to offer immediate surrender of the ship and men, Fish hurried to the White House to consult the President. Still believing that Sickles had left Madrid, and thinking that this concession was the most that had been effected by the step, he advised that the Spanish offer as thus amended should be accepted. Grant agreed, and he returned to assure the minister that a settlement proposed with the new condition would be agreed to and that if the illegality of the ship's registry was proved by December 25, the salute demanded would be dispensed with and all concerned in the violation of American laws would be prosecuted. On the whole, in view of the more than dubious status of the *Virginius*, this settlement appears fortunate; yet it may be doubted if the negotiations would have reached such an outcome but for Fish's defective communications with Madrid.

In fact, General Sickles had inferred from the laconic message of the 27th that Fish had found the new proposal inadmissible and intended that he should recur to the project of departure. Accordingly he intimated to the Spanish Minister early in the morning of the 28th that he would renew his request for passports in the afternoon unless the original demands had been accepted in full by that time. He was convinced, from the information which came to him, that the Spanish Government was prepared to yield and that an inflexible course would lead to an unconditional acceptance of the demands. Instead, he received a communication informing him of the new arrangement arrived at in Washington, which was confirmed by a telegram from Fish instructing him further that "the supposed negotiations must therefore drop at Madrid and be conducted hereafter here." His suggestion that an unconditional acceptance might yet be obtained was met by a simple order to remain at his post and await instructions.

The final agreement, on the lines laid down in their conversation of the 27th, was reached between Secretary Fish and Admiral Polo on November 29. The protocol of this agreement was transmitted to Congress with the President's annual message of December 1, together with a statement that the principle laid down in the Senate resolution of 1858 had been successfully maintained. Arrangements for the surrender of the ship and men were not finally completed until December 8. She was delivered to American authorities a week later and wrecked on her voyage to New York. On December 22 Fish informed the Spanish minister that the Government was convinced by the proofs transmitted of the fraudulent nature of the registry of the *Virginius*, actually under the ownership and control of Cuban insurgents throughout her career, and that the salute to the flag was "spontaneously dispensed with." The most serious diplomatic features of the incident were thus disposed of, although the questions of indemnity for the executions and of the punishment of the responsible officials remained open.

CHAPTER VII

CUSHING'S MISSION TO SPAIN—FISH'S
INSTRUCTION OF NOVEMBER 5, 1875
AND PLAN FOR COMMON ACTION WITH
THE EUROPEAN POWERS—A PARTIAL
SETTLEMENT WITH SPAIN

I

BESIDES the unsettled issues left over from the *Virginius* controversy, there were enough questions concerning Cuba still outstanding at the close of the year 1873 to render relations difficult between the United States and Spain. In his message of December 1 the President had referred with satisfaction to the liberation of some thousands of slaves, the repeal of the decree of 1825, and the steps taken to release embargoed estates, in regard to which fresh assurances had been received in November. But he indicated the persisting institution of slavery as the greatest obstacle to peace and the execution of other reforms. In fact, it soon became apparent that the passing of the crisis of November simply left matters in the state indicated by Fish's impatient instructions of the preceding month. The chance of improvement, moreover, was impaired by the serious disorders which developed in Spain in 1874.

Early in that year a new minister was sent to Madrid.

Feeling that Fish had concluded the *Virginius* settlement over his head, on less advantageous conditions than he could have obtained, and that he no longer possessed his Government's confidence, General Sickles had insisted upon tendering his resignation, which was accepted on December 20. As his successor, in what had become the most critical post of the service, was chosen Caleb Cushing, a diplomatist of proved ability, who was one of Fish's most trusted counsellors, and who was known to be *persona grata* with the Spanish Government because of his antipathy to filibustering. That this appointment was intended to inaugurate a policy of bringing about a drastic solution of the Cuban problem is indicated clearly enough by the general instructions on the subject furnished to the new minister on February 6, 1874, the date of his formal appointment.

In this document Fish reviewed the course of developments in Cuba, pointing out the intimate interest of the United States, the sympathy of the American people and Government with the causes of independence and emancipation, and the difficulty of preventing violations of the neutrality laws. He stated that, while the United States would prefer the complete independence of Cuba as a solution of the problem, "we might well accept" self-government under Spain accompanied by the abolition of slavery. "But," he added, "the President sees little cause to believe that Spain will consent to cease to exploit Cuba for the benefit of herself or of peninsular Spaniards, or that the Cubans will be content to ... accept anything less than absolute independence of Spain." He concluded, therefore, that "the President cannot but regard *independence,* and emancipation, of course, as the only certain, and even the necessary, solution of the question of Cuba." He repudiated any designs of the United States on the island in connexion with these views. As for the Government's immediate policy, he defined it as "one of expectancy," and notified Cushing that specific instructions would be given "when the time or emergency of action shall arrive."[54]

While awaiting its arrival Fish followed up this general exposition with instructions concerning questions still at issue under the existing situation. On the same date he directed Cushing to press for the promised release of embargoed estates, which was still obstructed. On February 10 he transmitted to him the documents on the basis of which he was to demand reparation for the deaths and mistreatment of American citizens in the case of the *Virginius*. These and similar matters occupied all the attention Cushing could claim from the harassed Spanish Government for months following his arrival at his post, late in May. The question of indemnities was complicated by a partial arrangement effected with Great Britain in regard to the British subjects on the *Virginius*, and no settlement had yet been reached when Alfonso XII was installed as King early in 1875. Fish then instructed Cushing to defer presenting his credentials to the new Government until an agreement on satisfactory terms had been concluded.[55] It was finally signed on March 9, and Cushing's credentials were presented on the following day. The agreed sum of $80,000 was paid in full by May 5. All accompanying efforts to bring about the punishment of responsible officials met the usual fate of such attempts. In regard to the recognition of Alfonso's Government,

Fish, on April 12, answered Cushing's discussion of the subject by saying: "The practice of the United States in recognizing that government of a people which is the *de facto* one, is founded upon the only true and wise principle and policy."[56]

The prompt payment of the *Virginius* indemnity was acknowledged as a demonstration of friendliness, but did not long suffice to improve the tone of relations between the two countries. In addition to repeated futile representations regarding the punishment of responsible officials, the question of embargoed estates and that of trials of American citizens by court martial, when the existence of a state of war was not recognized, continued to occasion voluminous correspondence. Fish concluded a long instruction of May 21, 1875, on the subject of embargoes, with a statement that, if not soon satisfactorily disposed of, it "cannot fail to be a seriously threatening question to the relations which the President desires to have surely established between the two Governments." Cushing undertook negotiations for a general settlement of the cases involved, and had high hopes of success when the Ministry with which he was dealing fell from power in September. Fish replied on October 1, 1875 to his dispatch reporting the change of ministers, with a despairing commentary on the difficulty of dealing with so unstable a government and notified him that a general reconsideration of relations was under way. On the 6th he wrote: "They are delaying the settlement beyond the possible endurance or patience of either the government or people of the United States." And, with particular reference to the question of trials by court martial, he ominously observed that the conduct and language of the Spanish authorities had impressed upon the struggle "all the characteristics of a state of legal war."[57]

II

The further presentation of the American Government's views on the Cuban situation, promised on October 1, 1875, was forwarded to Cushing on November 5 in the comprehensive instruction which became generally known as "No. 266." In it the preceding developments were reviewed at even greater length than in Cushing's original instructions, and with special attention to the questions most recently under discussion: embargoed estates, trials by court martial, and the prosecution of General Burriel, the officer held responsible for the *Virginius* executions, concerning which another long instruction was sent on the same date. The rejection of American good offices and the refusal of all measures of reconciliation on terms acceptable to the insurgents, he said, made a pacification hopeless. The failure to redress wrongs to American citizens, he continued, had gone on until it must be asked whether "longer endurance ceases to be possible." He again referred to the contradiction between the Spanish Government's denial of a state of war and its exercise of the rights and privileges of belligerency. He announced that "such a state of things cannot continue," and that, while still awaiting spontaneous measures for its termination, "the maintenance of our relations with Spain, even on their present footing," demanded a speedy end. These relations, he resumed after some discussion, "are in that critical position that [even a minor incident] . . . may suddenly produce a feeling and excitement which might force events which this government anxiously desires to avoid." Failing an immediate settlement, he concluded, the President "feels that the time is at hand when it may be the duty of other governments to intervene. . . . He will, therefore, feel it his duty to submit the subject in this light . . . for the consideration of Congress."[58]

The instruction itself authorized Cushing to read it to the Minister of State, but another instruction accompanying it directed him to defer this action if co-operation with Great Britain could be secured. To this end, as Cushing was informed, a copy of No. 266 was sent to General Schenck, at London, to be read to Lord Derby, with the suggestion that "the expression by Great Britain to Spain of its approval of the view of this Government, and its influence to induce a settlement, will tend to a more speedy adjustment." Communication of the instructions to the other principal European governments was to follow.

The warning given to Spain of proposals to be laid before Congress was accompanied by naval preparations of pronounced significance. Winter quarters for the fleet were established at Port Royal, South Carolina. Orders were sent, on November 13, 1875, to the commanding officer in European waters to send two of his ships there and to take two others to Lisbon for further orders "as if on your own authority and without attracting attention if possible." Two ships in the South Atlantic were ordered to Key West "for fleet exercises."[59]

The Government had been impelled to take these

steps by pressure from various interested and sympathetic quarters in favour of intervention on behalf of the Cuban insurgents. This pressure had been successfully counteracted in 1870, but had gradually reasserted itself until it reached a climax in the *Virginius* crisis. Although frustrated at that time, it had not ceased, but had translated itself into the series of impatient instructions which now culminated in Fish's No. 266. The Administration was anxious to show, by the time Congress reassembled, either some more substantial results of its policy of forbearance than promises and isolated cases of redress, or else a definite plan for obtaining them which would keep the initiative in its hands. Fish, with the support of most of his colleagues in the Cabinet, had consistently maintained that any action taken should be direct, rather than in the underhanded form of a dubious recognition of belligerency. He realized, however, that the European governments could not disinterest themselves in any intervention by force in the colonial affairs of Spain. By informing them in advance and presenting the American side of the case first, he thought to forestall the Spanish Government, to gain their sympathy, and perhaps to enlist their aid in obtaining satisfaction peaceably.

The decision to invite particularly the co-operation of Great Britain was by no means without precedent, as there had been a constant tendency towards common action in affairs regarding Cuba. Fish had instructed Sickles early in 1870 to make representations against slavery in conjunction with the British minister. The two Governments had arranged for simultaneous protests against excessive customs fines in Cuba. The British

Government had supported the American demands in the *Virginius* case by refusing Spain's request for good offices unless they were complied with. Its separate settlement of claims had hampered rather than helped Fish's negotiations on that score, but it had seconded his efforts to secure the punishment of General Burriel. Moreover, the co-operation with European states, which was refused in regard to European affairs, had been admitted by Fish, particularly as concerned Great Britain, in the affairs of the Far East. He had, in the first year of his secretaryship, supported the British demands for trading privileges in the interior of China. His affirmation, in 1870, of adherence to the principle of the "united front" was reinforced in his instructions of December 21, 1872 to the minister in China to act in concert with the representatives of other powers in demanding an audience with the new Emperor under threat of suspending intercourse, and the principle was again reaffirmed in instructions to the minister in Japan on April 20, 1874. The tendency may be observed towards a tacit understanding for co-operation with Great Britain in the Far East, accompanied by British support of American policy in the Caribbean.[60]

The expectation of results in this case from such a system of co-operation was frustrated, in part by a counter-move of the Spanish Government which disconcerted Fish's diplomatic campaign. Whether forewarned of the dispatch of his No. 266, which had not yet reached Madrid, or merely desirous of giving matters a more friendly turn, as it had repeatedly sought to do, before the assembling of Congress, it conveyed to Cushing, under date of November 15, 1875, a conciliatory note meeting all the points he had raised in recent correspondence and containing specific undertakings of redress and reform. Rather upset by this sudden withdrawal from the positions against which he had disposed his attack, news of which was telegraphed in summary on the 16th, Fish finally instructed General Schenck to delay communication of No. 266 to the British Government until he could readjust himself to the new state of affairs. He also added a postscript of the same nature to the instructions to ministers in other countries, already prepared on the 15th, directing them to communicate the document and invite the governments to join in conveying the "friendly expression of such views to Spain."

After some ten days of perplexed deliberation in Washington it was decided that Fish's elaborate plan should nevertheless be pursued, in the hope of obtaining more complete concessions to the American demands than were contained in the Spanish note, and that the President's message to Congress, while it could not announce a complete victory or present definite recommendations for action, should yet be strong and suggest the possibility of intervention. In the interest of obtaining quicker results it was also decided that the communication of No. 266 to the Spanish Government should not be deferred until the chances of British cooperation had been ascertained. On November 27 both Cushing and Schenck were directed by telegraph to carry out their original instructions. But Cushing was now authorized to accompany his presentation of No. 266 by a declaration that it "is not intended as minatory in any sense but in the spirit of friendship," and to convey an intimation of the nature of the forthcoming presidential message, as Schenck was likewise to do.

The Spanish Minister, Calderón, received Cushing's communication of No. 266, on November 30, quite calmly, expressed his accord with the observations it contained, and promised a detailed reply after it had been studied. Lord Derby, the British Foreign Secretary, who had naturally been informed of the Spanish note of the 15th, told Schenck, on December 2, that he would defer discussion of Fish's document until the President had time to consider that note, which he thought might modify the pending message. He added that his Government was "willing ... to co-operate in any way that promises to bring about a settlement of troubles in Cuba, but is not prepared to put any pressure on the Spanish Government or to put forward proposals which he has reason to think it would not be inclined to accede to." Declining to admit the failure of his expectations which this statement clearly implied, Fish returned to the charge in a telegram of the 6th, asserting that, while the Spanish note offered hope of "adjustment of our particular grievances," it did not affect the President's intended statements "upon general questions of the condition of Cuba and continuance of struggle." At the same time he instructed the American ministers to communicate No. 266 to the principal European governments.

The President's message was transmitted to Congress December 7, 1875. It referred anew to the unsettled American grievances and the hopelessness of an end to the strife in Cuba. It discussed frankly the possibilities of recognition of independence or of belligerency, rejecting both on the grounds alleged six years before. Then it raised the question: "What course shall be adopted should the conflict not soon be brought to an end by the parties themselves?" The answer given was that "other nations will be compelled . . . to seriously consider the only remaining measures possible, mediation and intervention." The President announced that his good offices were always available and concluded by saying, with reference to the recent Spanish proposals, that if American complaints were not soon remedied and the hopes of "restoration of peace" by promised reforms fulfilled, he would have a further communication to make "at some period not far remote" as to "what may then seem to me to be necessary."

These statements and Fish's telegram to Schenck made the objects of his No. 266 clearer than its language had done. What the American Government desired was not assurances of respect for its citizens' rights by the authorities combating the insurrection in Cuba, which indeed were held impossible of fulfilment, but the ending of hostilities on the bases outlined in Fish's original instructions to Cushing: independence (or possibly self-government under Spain) and emancipation. The Spanish Government must consider whether it would grant these; the other governments, whether they would help to obtain such a settlement. That Spain would freely grant what he sought, Fish himself had earlier declared was not to be expected; and Cushing had telegraphed his frank opinion that, if Fish's appeal to the other powers failed to align them with the United States, Spain would fight rather than yield much more than was promised in the note of November 15. As for the other powers, preoccupied just then with the troubles in Herzegovina which threatened a revival of the Eastern question, those whose action counted for most Great Britain and France, had interests of their own in the Caribbean which would not be furthered by such a program. Vaguely favourable responses from Russia, Italy, and Germany did not greatly advance Fish's case. The French Minister of Foreign Affairs declared that the Spanish Government could not yield without playing into the hands of the Carlist opposition, which still held the field against it. All Fish's further appeals to the British Government brought only a repetition, on January 25, 1876, of Lord Derby's refusal to support any proposals which Spain was unwilling to accept.

It was by this time clear enough that Fish's great diplomatic plan had broken down and that recommendations to Congress for intervention in Cuba, hinted at in the President's message, could not be made without danger of provoking a war in which the sympathies of the European governments would be with Spain. Moreover, Fish's diplomacy was discredited at home by the revelation in the press of his approaches to those governments, which were widely censured as a departure from the Monroe Doctrine. His only retort was to attribute the authorship of that doctrine to Canning.[61] The Democratic House of Representatives called for communication of the correspondence in two resolutions of January 21 and 23, 1876. In answer to the first, Fish transmitted his No. 266 and the instructions to Schenck and Washburne, with a note stating that the latter had also gone to the ministers in certain named countries, and an abbreviated selection of other papers. In answer to the second, he stated that, while the ministers had been instructed to communicate No. 266 orally to the governments to which they were accredited, "no correspondence has, however, taken place upon the subject with these Governments."[62] The approximately complete collection of documents was not published until twenty years later, upon the demand of another Congress.

No debate took place upon the subject of these resolutions, probably for the reason that Congress speedily became too engrossed in the spicier business of unearthing various noisome scandals in the field of internal administration. Fish was content to let the matter rest. Had the Administration sought to divert attention from its shortcomings by embarking the country upon a foreign war, it would doubtless not have been blocked in its course by Congress; but it found itself disarmed by the conciliatory attitude taken by the Spanish Government. When that Government undertook, with Cushing's eager connivance, to treat Fish's formidable instruction as an object of friendly negotiations rather than as a peremptory summons, there was no seemly choice but to meet its advances and seek to obtain the most satisfactory outcome possible.

Cushing reported, on January 16, 1876, that Calderón had asked of Fish point-blank: "What is the precise thing he would wish Spain to do under the circumstances?" And on February 3 the Spanish Government addressed to the United States and the principal European countries a memorandum in answer to Fish's No. 266. It contested in dignified terms many of his charges against the Government and its officials in Cuba. It asserted that the insurrection had lost its Cuban

character and degenerated into indiscriminate brigand-
age under nondescript foreign chieftains, which would
soon be suppressed by the adequate forces now available.
It declared that material evidences of the institution of
reforms had already been given, and that economic
recovery was actually under way, as revealed by increasing production and trade. With Fish's reply to Calderón's inquiry the negotiations entered upon a new
stage.

III

In an instruction of March 1, 1876, Fish undertook
to reduce the vague and sweeping demands of No. 266
to concrete proposals of a diplomatic character. They
came down to four points: (1) a satisfactory understanding as to rights of persons and property under existing
treaties; (2) administrative reform in Cuba, in the
direction of self-government and accompanied by a
general amnesty; (3) effective emancipation; (4) improvement of commercial facilities. Nearly complete
agreement on all these points was expressed by the
Spanish Government in a note of April 16, 1876. Meanwhile, alongside the negotiations arising out of Fish's
instructions of November 5, 1875, another set had been
proceeding in desultory fashion on the basis of the
Spanish note of November 15, which had dealt with
specific grievances, such as embargoed estates and trials
by court martial. On the former issue substantial satisfaction was given by awards in favour of practically all
claimants. The latter question was not settled until
February 4, 1877, when a protocol, signed by Calderón

and Cushing, provided that American citizens should be tried only before civilian tribunals unless taken with arms in hand, and even then should enjoy such rights as acquaintance with the accusation, employment of counsel, and appeal.[63]

The principal complaints as to injuries suffered by American citizens in consequence of the disturbances in Cuba were thus eliminated, but on the score of measures to conciliate the insurgents the Spanish Government continued to elude all attempts to pin it down to immediate performance of its pledges. Instead, as it had done towards the close of 1869, it put forth new efforts for suppression of the rebellion by force. A special loan was raised for the purpose, and the dispatch was begun of reinforcements destined to reach the number of forty thousand men. By the time Fish gave up his office the Cuban problem itself was well on the way to a temporary solution as a result of these efforts, and its complications affecting American interests had been fairly well disposed of. One of his last official acts was his approval of an arrangement reached by Cushing for payment of the awards made by the claims commission of 1871.

CHAPTER VIII

UNFULFILLED CLAUSES OF THE TREATY OF WASHINGTON—INTEROCEANIC CANAL PROJECTS—RELATIONS WITH MEXICO—FISH'S RETIREMENT

I

ALTHOUGH matters connected with the rebellion in Cuba presented the most serious diplomatic problems of Grant's second Administration, certain of the other subjects that engaged Fish's attention deserve notice.

Two clauses of the Treaty of Washington still remained unexecuted. One of these was the agreement of the United States and Great Britain, not only to observe the "three rules" of Article VI as between themselves in the future, but "to bring them to the knowledge of other maritime Powers, and to invite them to accede to them." A long discussion had taken place regarding interpretations to be advanced in the note of presentation. No mutually satisfactory conclusion was ever reached, and the only outcome was an exchange of notes between Sir Edward Thornton and Fish, in 1876, in which each Government charged the other with responsibility for the delays and failure to reach agreement. In Fish's note of September 18 he even stated that his Government held the obligation to communicate the rules indivisible from that to observe them, "so that a failure to comply with one part thereof may, and probably will, be held to carry with it the avoidance and nullity of the other."[64]

The execution of Article XXIII, calling for the appointment of a commission to fix the amount of compensation payable by the United States for the greater value of the concessions made in its favour in the fisheries compromise, had been delayed by various factors. One of these was an attempt made in 1874 to supersede the article by a new reciprocity treaty similar in terms to that of 1854, which the American commissioners had refused, in 1871, to restore. This project was submitted to the Senate in draft form, practically as presented by the British negotiators, on June 18, to "determine . . . whether it will give its constitutional concurrence" to such an agreement in the form proposed or in any other found more acceptable. Not until after the Senate, on February 3, 1875, resolved that "it was not deemed expedient to recommend the negotiation of the treaty" were efforts made to complete preparations for putting Article XXIII into effect by the appointment of commissioners. Discussions regarding the impartial third member, which had been begun and interrupted, were resumed, but were not concluded until a few days before Fish left office, when he accepted the Belgian minister at Washington, to whom he had previously objected on the ground of "the political relations between his government and that of Great Britain."[65]

II

The subject of a Central American canal connecting the two oceans came under especially active consideration during Grant's presidency, owing to the interest aroused by the completion, in 1869, of the Suez Canal. In that year an advisory board of experts was appointed which carried on its studies of the various possibilities until 1876, when it reached a conclusion in favour of the Nicaraguan route. Meanwhile Fish had taken over the dreary attempt to come to an agreement with Colombia for use of the Panama route, to take the place of the treaty of January 14, 1869, which had been rejected by the Colombian Senate.[66] Owing to the length of time required for communications, a practically free hand was left to the minister at Bogotá, Mr. S. A. Hurlbut, who assumed the initiative in the affair. A new treaty was signed by him, on January 26, 1870, under which the United States was to "construct or cause to be constructed said projected canal" and to guarantee it against attacks, but other powers were to be invited to participate in this guaranty. This agreement was at once subjected to criticism on various grounds by the Colombian Senate. The article of guaranty, which constituted the United States an "ally" of Colombia for the purpose and provided that the canal should be closed to the flags of nations at war with either contracting party, gave rise to apprehensions that it might involve Colombia in hostilities against enemies of the United States. The American negotiator agreed that it was fair and "in accordance with the principles of the Clayton-Bulwer treaty" to confine this exclusion to warships and to provide that merchant ships of other guarantor powers should be allowed passage free from the exercise of belligerent rights against them even when at war with one of the contracting parties; but the Colombians insisted that, in addition, other powers should be allowed to participate in the guaranty on such terms that, in case of war with one of the contracting parties, the canal should be closed to the warships of *both* belligerents. With the naval importance of the project thus practically annulled, the treaty became unacceptable to the United States and was not ratified.

The break-down of this project, attributed in part by Hurlbut to British influence behind the Colombian opposition to the original treaty, averted a possible controversy over it with Great Britain at a time when relations were still strained. It constituted a rather bold initiative on the part of the United States and, while reconcilable with the limitations imposed by the Clayton-Bulwer Treaty, was open to conflicting interpretations on several points. The difficulty of making the canal of any military advantage was implicit in that treaty. Had the United States and Great Britain not become reconciled in 1871, Fish might have been led into even wider departures from their agreement of 1850, but as matters turned out, he displayed no further tendencies in that direction. He himself invoked its limitations against Great Britain. In calling the British Government's attention, in 1873, to reported trespasses from British Honduras into Guatemalan territory, he stated that these, if verified, would be considered "an infringement of the Clayton-Bulwer treaty, which will be very unacceptable in this country."[67]

After the canal board's report in favour of the route through Nicaragua, Fish turned, late in the year 1876, to the task of reaching an agreement with that country which should replace the inadequate clauses of the treaty of 1867. This negotiation was carried on in Washington with an envoy, Dr. Adan Cárdenas, accredited by Nicaragua for this purpose. The draft convention submitted to him provided no special position for the United States such as was aimed at in the earlier negotiations with Colombia. It was simply designed, as Fish described it in a note of February 16, 1877, to secure "a guarantee of the neutrality of the work by the chief maritime powers and by grants from Nicaragua such as would be sufficient to tempt the cupidity and inspire the confidence of capital." The guaranty was to be obtained from the "principal maritime powers" in common, and the canal was to be open to ships of all nations and classes at all times, without qualification. The neutrality of the canal was to extend to the waters within a radius of a hundred and fifty marine miles from each entrance and to an inland zone ten marine miles wide along its course, within which Nicaragua should retain sovereignty and jurisdiction, but permit an armed police maintained by the company. A board of control appointed by the guarantor governments should have authority over all regulations "affecting the general enjoyment and use of the canal."

The objections offered by Dr. Cárdenas to these impairments of Nicaraguan sovereignty and the counter-proposals he put forward to safe-guard it were such that Fish decided it would be impossible to reach an agreement attaining the objects he had in view. The negotiations were broken off, and, on February 28, 1877, Fish sent out a circular to the American ministers in all capitals informing them of his reasons for action and enclosing copies of his correspondence with Cárdenas to be shown to the authorities of the governments to which they were accredited in case the subject was discussed with them. In his remarks on an article of the Nicaraguan counter-draft making specific reference to the Anglo-American treaty of 1850, Fish declared this mention to be "unnecessary, because the obligations of the Clayton-Bulwer treaty . . . are still subsisting."

III

Relations with Mexico had been especially troubled by outrages upon American citizens on both sides of the border ever since the renewal of revolutionary disturbances attending the re-election of President Juárez in October 1871. Fish's action in regard to these had been confined to forwarding the correspondence concerning particular cases to the legation in Mexico for presentation to the Government with demands for redress and requests that measures be taken to prevent further occurrences of the sort. On January 16, 1873, he wrote that, if Indian raids across the border were not stopped, the marauders would be pursued on Mexican soil, but he directed that no official representations be made to this effect. In May an incursion of American troops took place, giving rise to a protest from the Mexican Government, which was rendered early in the following year. Counter-complaints, moreover, began coming in of raids into Mexico by Apaches living on the northern side of the border. Arrangements were made, in January 1875, for co-operation of the military forces of both countries in fighting hostile Indians. Charges and counter-charges concerning lawless acts and violations of territory were not diminished by this limited arrangement. In a note of March 18, 1875, to the Mexican minister, dealing with certain reported murders of Mexicans in Texas, Fish was obliged to invoke the very excuses so frequently alleged by the Mexican Government: the difficulty of policing vast, sparsely populated regions and of keeping in order "a border population . . . comprising but too often lawless persons of the nationalities of each of the coterminous states, and refugees from the laws of all nationalities, who alternately assume the character of citizens of either of the bordering states." He added that people taking residence in such regions "must be presumed to be aware of the risks thus incurred." Yet, after admitting the inability of American authorities to maintain order in Texas, he proposed that they should be allowed to take over the task of maintaining it on the other side of the border. On May 20 he instructed the minister in Mexico, as a means of checking raids, to suggest the military occupation of a tract of Mexican territory, disclaiming any purpose of annexation. Both this proposal and a further one for allowing American troops to cross the border "in close pursuit" of raiders were unhesitatingly rejected. When fresh revolutionary movements of 1876 in the border states of Mexico led to the introduction in Congress of a joint resolution authorizing such expeditions, there was a violent outcry in the Mexican press. The resolution was passed by the House, but held up by amendments in the Senate and not finally acted upon.

Before the close of the year matters had taken a new turn with the success of the revolution and the establishment of Porfirio Diaz as Provisional President. All other questions at once grouped themselves round that of his recognition. Appreciating the importance of the attitude of the United States, Diaz appropriated the greater part of a loan raised in Mexico City upon his accession to meet a payment of $300,000 due on awards made by the Mixed Claims Commission created in 1868. The gesture placed Fish in the awkward situation of having to pass at once on the question of recognition before payment could be received. In an instruction of January 19, 1877, Fish left the matter of recognition to the discretion of the minister in Mexico. He also directed the minister to express regret at the effect upon American interests of Diaz's annulment of various contracts made by President Lerdo, but not to treat the policy as an international question. The issue of recognition was postponed by a decision to send the money to Washington for payment through the Mexican legation there. That issue and the question of border raids, which Diaz showed no immediate signs of being able to check, were left to be dealt with by Fish's successor.[68]

IV

Fish's term of office was marked by important progress in the reorganization of the Department of State. Possessing a natural aptitude for administrative detail and the supervision of subordinates, he applied himself from the first to improving the machine through which the foreign relations of the country are directed. Regulations issued in October 1869 put the department's conduct on a businesslike basis, fixing the hours and conditions of the work of its employés. A more systematic assignment to their duties was likewise effected in the following year, by a reapportionment of functions among the departmental bureaus, which were first definitely recognized by law in 1873. Conscientious efforts were made by Fish to improve the quality of the personnel under his direction by applying the new Civil Service rules and the order of 1866 for examination of candidates for consular appointments. Himself free from political ambitions, he had no personal interest in the spoils system, but his efforts to stand out against it were largely neutralized by the influences which succeeded in annulling the Civil Service Act of March 3, 1871. So far as lay within his power, however, Fish's appointments and promotions were based upon recognition of merit, and his fairness won the confidence and loyalty of his subordinates. Greater efficiency was maintained for some time without increasing the force of some twenty-five clerks which had manned the department since the Civil War, but more liberal appropriations and installation in adequate quarters made possible, by 1876, the expansion to forty-five called for by the growing importance of the country's international relations. In the summer of 1875 the Department of State had ended its forlorn sojourn in the Washington Orphan Asylum and moved into its quarters in the south wing of the "grand Renaissance building" dear to guide-books, which it shared with the War and Navy

Departments. Here it was possible to augment and make more accessible the material equipment and instruments of work which were as important to the efficient operation of the department as its personnel.

The new Secretary had at once grasped the need of bringing into better order the papers embodying both the current business of his department and the precedents by which its daily acts and decisions were so largely guided. He found these in part uncertainly classified and difficult to keep track of and consult, owing to the lack of any general index. A system was introduced in 1870 of recording all correspondence in a central set of index volumes, replacing the practice of indexing each volume of papers separately. The archives were systematized by classifying and binding quantities of miscellaneous papers. In 1874, by one of the most important readjustments of the departmental organization of 1870, all this work was concentrated in a new Bureau of Indexes and Archives. These accomplishments, which have greatly facilitated research in the records of the department, also placed on a higher plane the effectiveness of the conduct of America's foreign relations.[69]

V

When Grant's second term drew to a close, Fish was glad enough to lay down the duties of the office he had filled during eight years. There had been some talk of bringing his name before the Republican National Convention as a possible candidate for the presidency, and Grant had even written, advising his nomination, a letter designed to be produced in case the dead-lock between Blaine and Conkling became hopeless. The project was abandoned, to Fish's own relief. He was approaching his seventieth year and looked forward to spending the rest of his life in undisturbed enjoyment of the leisure he had so long denied himself out of feelings of loyalty and duty. His remaining years, until his death, on September 6, 1893, were devoted to his home life, his private affairs, and his religious and philanthropic interests.

His retirement left in abeyance few of the important affairs he had dealt with. Only the problem of relations with Mexico called urgently for solution. The Cuban insurrection still smouldered, but the risk of complications had been practically eliminated. A tedious discussion with Great Britain over extradition remained to be concluded, and the commission had yet to render its award under Article XXIII of the Treaty of Washington. But a record of solid achievement had been built up, of which that treaty was the outstanding item, marking a turning-point in relations with Great Britain and an important precedent in international arbitration. It is a record less spectacular than that of Fish's predecessor, Seward, but it ranks high among those of the long list of Secretaries of State. The period in which Fish served was one of transition from war-time hysteria to the normal processes of peaceful development. Under his sober guidance the transition in the diplomatic field was effected without misadventure, and he left the country's foreign relations on an even keel of general friendliness and peace.

WILLIAM M. EVARTS

SECRETARY OF STATE

MARCH 12, 1877, TO MARCH 3, 1881

BY

CLAUDE G. BOWERS

ASSOCIATE EDITOR, NEW YORK *EVENING WORLD*

AND

HELEN DWIGHT REID

ASSISTANT PROFESSOR OF POLITICAL SCIENCE
UNIVERSITY OF BUFFALO

WILLIAM M. EVARTS

Wm. M. Evarts

WILLIAM M. EVARTS

CHAPTER I

THE FIRST PLACE IN THE CABINET

LONG before the contested election of 1876 was decided, Rutherford B. Hayes, communing with himself and a few intimate advisers in the rambling old house in the grove at Fremont, was framing his Cabinet as though assured of inauguration. The close contest had signalized a crisis for his party. It had signalized the passing of the tyranny of sectional fanaticism and had shown the need of purging the party and the country of the flamboyant corruption which shamed the Grant Administration. Hayes was having some difficulty in satisfying the contending factions, and he moved with caution in determining the personnel of his Cabinet. Quite early he realized that he was not entirely a free agent; had not Senator Morton already protested against an appointment for Benjamin Harrison? There was, however, one appointment on which he was irrevocably set. He wrote in his diary, January 17, 1877: "My thoughts rest on Evarts for the first place." [1]

At this time William Maxwell Evarts was representing Hayes's interests before the Electoral Commission, and Hayes felt some delicacy about approaching him while the issue was pending. Commissioning Senator

John Sherman to confer with Evarts whenever the former thought the time ripe, he awaited the outcome. A week before the inauguration there had been no formal offer of the post, but the plan was unchanged. "For State, I hope to have Evarts," Hayes wrote Carl Schurz, "but have not consulted him." [2]

Meanwhile he was left in no doubt as to the unpopularity of the choice in important quarters. Evarts had not been a politician after the heart of the professionals who for ten years had been making the public service a stench in the nostrils of decent men. It had been his devastating logic and eloquence that had saved Andrew Johnson from the impeachment that partisan intolerance demanded. Even his loyalty to Seward was no longer to his advantage. At no time had he participated in the petty intrigues of the bosses, and such was his independence that he had publicly denounced the Grant Administration for its insufferable use of the army and navy in the interests of the looters of Louisiana. Hayes was given to understand that the selection would be distasteful to the party organization in New York. Roscoe Conkling, arrogant and egotistic, frowned ominously on the suggestion, partly because he had not been consulted, primarily because he ardently desired to have his friend Tom Platt at the President's elbow. Platt was powerful.

It was Platt who, in the midst of the campaign a few months before, had assailed Evarts in a bitter letter to Hayes: "I do not hesitate to express the opinion that if the Hon. George William Curtis's favorite candidate, Mr. Evarts, had been nominated [for governor of New York] he would have been defeated beyond peradventure. The working Republicans of the State would not have supported a man who had never shown his faith by his works, who had received wealth and honor from an Administration he has publicly abused and vilified, and whose record as a Republican has been more than doubtful."[3]

Even so, the man in the grove at Fremont was unshaken. Hostility from the clique which had dimmed the record of the party of Lincoln only strengthened his resolve. His regime was pledged to a change, not a continuance. In due time the post was offered and accepted, and the nomination sent to the Senate for confirmation. There it fell like a bomb-shell among the old-guard leaders. Alone it would have been affront enough; accompanied by the nomination of Carl Schurz as Secretary of the Interior, it was like a declaration of war. Instantly the challenge was accepted, with Don Cameron, chairman of the Foreign Relations Committee, leading the opposition. When a motion was made to confirm the nomination of Evarts, Senator Cameron objected, and Senator Blaine moved to refer it to the committee of that uninspiring boss. But the machine politicians of New York and Pennsylvania failed to prevent confirmation, to the disgust of Cameron, who resigned his seat in the Senate. It was good to have one of Evarts's character and intellectual capacity in the Cabinet, and to be rid of Cameron in the Senate was itself an advantage.

Evarts was at this time the acknowledged leader of the American bar. No other American lawyer, save John Marshall on the bench, had been associated with so many cases tending to the determination of the course of government and the destiny of the people. As a young man he had sat at the feet of Greenleaf and Story at Cambridge, and had been associated with Daniel Lord, leading lawyer of New York, of whose methods he took note. At twenty-four his leadership at the bar had been predicted by John J. Crittenden, and Rufus Choate had conveyed to him the thanks of Daniel Webster for articles defending the Expounder's retention of his post in Tyler's Cabinet. He had led the fight for his intimate friend William H. Seward in the National Convention of 1860, where Blaine thought his speeches surpassed anything in the range of political oratory.

As early as 1853 his brilliant work in the celebrated Lemmon slave case had attracted national attention by its masterful exposition of the law where it operated to the slave's advantage; and very soon thereafter he electrified an audience at Castle Garden with a defence of the constitutionality of the fugitive-slave law. During the Civil War Lincoln summoned him to a service as essential to victory as that of the soldier in the field. Important legal principles had to be established in the courts. That accomplished, he was sent abroad in a professional as well as semi-diplomatic capacity to argue out the legal points involved in the building of Confederate cruisers in British waters. Then came his noble service as the defender of Andrew Johnson in the great impeachment trial, where his brilliant management, his finesse in the reclamation of the faltering, his lofty eloquence, his revealing wit and sarcasm, did much to save the nation from the fatal precedent of mobbing a President to serve a party end. A few months later we find him defending the constitutionality of the Legal Tender Act before the Supreme Court, and soon thereafter as the American colossus at Geneva in the case of the *Alabama* claims, where the brilliancy of his oral reply to the carefully written British argument gave him something of the glamour of an old-time knight of the tournament. His sallies of wit and his eloquence in the trial of Henry Ward Beecher had been read for months at breakfast-tables from sea to sea, and he had just emerged triumphant from the Electoral Commission.

These professional engagements, like Curran's in Great Britain, had made him one of the most impressive political figures of his time, yet he had been uniformly unfortunate in his political aspirations. Had Seward attained the presidency in 1860, Evarts was destined to the succession. Horace Greeley's ambition prevented Evarts's election to the Senate in 1861. When Chief Justice Taney died, powerful elements were at work to make the young man a successor of John Marshall. There can be no doubt that the Chief Justiceship allured him. How else explain the letter of Ebenezer Rockwood Hoar: "I had hardly read your parting words about the Chief Justiceship when the telegraph brought the disgusting intelligence, 'Chief Justice Taney is better'"?[4] Not without his knowledge was Hoar getting the unanimous recommendation of the Massachusetts Supreme Court in his favour, and negotiating with Charles Sumner for his influence, and with Eliot.[5] But the exigencies of politics interposed, although the ambition persisted. When Chase died, Hoar worked again for Evarts, writing: "I think he [Grant] will appoint you. . . . If fitness governs you will be the foremost."[6] But the defender of Johnson was not popular with Grant, and the place went to Waite, Evarts's class-mate at Yale.

His party eagerly made use of Evarts's genius as orator, advocate, and adviser, without rewarding him politically. But he who had been destined by powerful forces for the presidency and the Chief Justiceship, and who held undisputed leadership of the bar, sat by right of merit at the head of the Cabinet.

CHAPTER II

A PICTURE OF THE MAN

THEY who look for distinction in physical weight
or pompous pose would scarcely have noticed
Evarts in a crowd. Thin to attenuation, a slight student's stoop to his sloping shoulders, he had the facial
characteristics of the ascetic, though he was nothing of
the sort. The massive head, indicating something of his
intellectual power, seemed all too heavy for the slender
body. His keen, penetrating eyes, his pallor, his thin,
forceful lips, suggested the orator. "A thin, sharp-
featured, keen-faced man," wrote a fellow guest at
Blaine's dinner-table.[7] Delicate though he seemed physically, he fairly throbbed with nervous energy. Not without reason does the bronze medallion of Cicero in the
Yale Library bear a striking resemblance to Evarts,
who possessed so many of the temperamental traits of
the great Roman. The student of physiognomy would
have labelled him at once as that rare combination, the
assiduous worker and the artist.

In the realization of his lofty ambitions he was his
own unsparing taskmaster. Taking Cicero as his model,
he imposed upon himself the mastery of the art of speech
as a preliminary to the study of law. "Cicero, I think it
is," he said in the defence of Johnson, "who says that a
lawyer should know everything, for sooner or later there
is no fact in history, in science, or of human knowledge
that will not come into play in his arguments." Thus he

enriched his mind in literature and history and through careful observations of the great men of his time. He who had cultivated his style in youth by writing, and sharpened his wits in the debates of the Literary Club at Yale, never afterwards in his long professional and political career permitted himself to fall beneath the high standards of speech he had set himself.

He early took high rank as an orator, and this contributed largely to his success. He had a genius for clarity of statement. His special-occasion orations were prepared with meticulous care, and enriched with illustrations drawn from the literature of all ages and countries. He saturated himself with his subject and then spoke out of a mind full and running over. Wit and kindly humour, satire and sarcasm, logic aflame, eloquence of the sort that borrows nothing from the unworthy passions—such were his weapons.

It was in his great arguments in causes of far-reaching consequence that he was at his best, and here the influence of Cicero is most in evidence. Because of his high professional ideals he approached all these cases in a broad way, as deeply concerned with underlying principles as with facts. He viewed a controversy from every possible angle, looking with unerring eye through all the non-essentials to find the pivotal point, often to his opponent's discomfiture. His five-day argument in the case of Tilton *v.* Beecher ranks with the finest exhibitions of forensic eloquence; his speeches and writings on international controversies are veritable treatises on the history and theory of international law.

Though not yet an old man—he was born in Boston, February 6, 1818—he had enjoyed contacts with the moulders of the nation. His maternal grandfather, Roger Sherman, had sat with Jefferson in the committee which framed the Declaration of Independence. He himself could boast: "I am a contemporary of Lafayette," and recall a conversation with that hero in 1825, when the little boy had been warmly greeted as a descendant of the signer.

Albeit a man of refined tastes and sensibilities, he was simple in dress to the point of being plain and old-fashioned, and he wore a "shocking bad hat" on the crown of his head to the delight of the cartoonists. He bore himself with a natural dignity that repelled familiarity in the casual acquaintance, though he unbent in the company of friends. When young Henry Adams, fresh from England, went to Washington with high hopes of public service, the only warm spot he found was in the bosom of Evarts's family. "Generous by nature," writes Adams, "prodigal in hospitality, fond of young people, and a born man of the world, Evarts gave and took liberally without scruple, accepted the world without fearing or abusing it. He laughed where he could; he joked if a joke was possible; he was true to his friends and never lost his temper or became ill-natured."[8] This friendship proved valuable to Adams as a historian, for Secretary of State Evarts allowed him "unrestricted access to the archives of the United States, and especially to those of the State Department," and did his best to obtain for him similar privileges in the archives of France, England, and Holland.[9]

Even in controversy he was ever the pink of courtesy. He was a diplomat by nature. Moving familiarly through life, among men of commanding genius and ability, matching wits with many in arenas where nations were spectators, conscious of his powers, he never felt the need of a supercilious manner to advertise his own merits. "Man of the world" he was, a gentleman always.

In social relations he was particularly attractive, for he fairly scintillated at the dinner-table, and his witticisms gave his generation many a chuckle. "Professor," he once asked solemnly of a noted but too serious scientist at a dinner-party, "why is it that the liquid at the bottom of a bottle is more intoxicating than the liquor at the top?" "Well, I never had my attention called to the fact. Are you sure it is a fact?" "Yes," said Evarts, "I know men who have found by actual experience that it is so."

To the Englishman's serious question as to whether Washington actually threw a dollar across the Potomac, Evarts replied with a remark that was either old then or has since had time to age: "He might have performed that feat, for he once threw a sovereign over the sea." At a dinner where he was seated between an Englishman and a Frenchman he remarked: "It is a question whether an Englishman or a Frenchman is the pick of humanity, but for myself I prefer something between the two." On another occasion the toastmaster introduced him with a joking reference to his long sentences. "In this country," Evarts thereupon explained to the English guest of honour, "the only people who object to long sentences are the criminal classes."

It was inevitable that one so facile of speech, and so witty, should have been a favourite after-dinner speaker. A famous editor who often heard him wrote: "His was the wit, diamond-pointed, that sparkled without wounding. His was the humor as debonair as dry, and as genial as subtle. His was the power of epigram, antithesis, or characterization. His was the anecdotal power that united the finality of culture with the simplicity of experience, and . . . gilded conversation with the sheen of gold." [10] The United States has never had a Secretary of State better qualified by temperament and social gifts for the lighter side of diplomacy.

CHAPTER III

FENIANS AND FISHERIES

FOR the most part his career as Secretary of State was to be without dramatic international controversies. Its even tenor was disappointing to many who expected the spectacular from a Secretary of such brilliance. He sought the ways of conservatism and conciliation, and though sternly insistent on American rights, it was without bluster or brag. With the diplomats in Washington he enjoyed the most pleasant social and official relations. No one could be more courtly; no old-world diplomat more thoroughly appreciated the diplomacy of the dinner-table—yet it was here that he ran counter to the Administration for the first and only time. It was a strange defeat, in which he found infinite amusement. Evarts, by virtue of his position, made arrangements for entertaining a visiting diplomatic mission at a White House dinner. Knowing Mrs. Hayes's rule that no wines would be served at her table, he sought a concession for diplomatic dinners on the ground that they were State functions, not personal affairs, and that the customs of the guests should be respected. Mrs. Hayes remained adamant; but, much to her consternation, wine was served to the visiting mission. It was the last time. "After that," Evarts once said with a sly smile, "at all White House dinners water flowed like champagne."

He was soon confronted with more important problems. An American, caught in the Fenian movement in Ireland, had been sentenced to penal servitude for life. The traditional American sympathy with Irish struggles flamed, Irish organizations in this country stirred, the politician ever mindful of the Irish vote responded. Washington was deluged with petitions and demands. Hoping to prevent intemperate congressional action, Evarts instructed the American minister in London to call the attention of the Foreign Office to the extremity of the sentence, and to seek clemency. But England was in no mood to make concessions to the Fenians or their sympathizers, and nothing was done.

Then Congress took the field with a resolution reciting alleged facts challenging the fairness of the trial and asking the President to insist that a new one be granted. Evarts dispatched an agent to England to investigate and report to the American minister, instructing the latter to lay these findings before the British Government if they indicated Condon's innocence, with an expression of confidence that its sense of justice would require no suggestions; otherwise to renew his efforts for clemency, but in no circumstances to manifest a disposition to interfere with the domestic judicial administration of another state. Meanwhile the minister had an informal conversation with Lord Salisbury, and within a week the assurance was received that the Cabinet would recommend to the Queen the remission of the sentence. The Queen acquiesced. Some correspondence relative to the expense of returning Condon to the United States followed, ending with the British Government's agreeing to defray it. Thus, without offending Great Britain, the Fenian sympathizers in the

United States were satisfied, the politicians mollified, and a question charged with political dynamite was happily closed.[11]

More important and significant was the controversy during the same year over the Halifax fishery award. A commission appointed the year before to arbitrate the British claim for recompense for fishing privileges in Canadian waters had granted Great Britain $5,500,000. The award was denounced by American publicists and press as out of all proportion to the benefits received by American fishermen, and not in conformity with the terms of submission agreed to in the Treaty of Washington.[12] Evarts took the position that the proposition on which the award was based had transcended the commission's powers. He was not disposed to repudiate the result of the arbitration, but he wished to make it a matter of record that if the arbitrators had gone beyond the scope of the treaty, such action could not constitute a precedent. He protested that "the United States still maintains its interpretation of the privileges secured by the Convention of 1818, and protests against any implication from the magnitude of the award . . . or otherwise from its [the commission's] proceedings under the treaty of Washington, that the United States have sanctioned or acquiesced in any lesser measure of the privileges secured to the United States under the Convention of 1818, than . . . they have always insisted upon."

With precision and vigour he reviewed the record of the understandings between the two countries relative to fishery privileges, attacked the award as absurdly large in the light of these understandings, and left the way open for voluntary reopening of the case by Great

Britain. In all this there was not the slightest suggestion of repudiation. That would have done violence to his conception of the nation's obligations. We had submitted the dispute to arbitration. We had presented our case in court, and, the decision going against us, we were in honour bound to respect it. Demagogue politicians talked recklessly of refusing to pay; a few members of Congress of refusing to appropriate. The high-toned, dignified attitude of Evarts reflected the views of the responsible statesmen and journalists, and the force of the protest did much to moderate the ire of the more bitter. The money was appropriated, and paid, on Great Britain's refusal to reopen the case, "on the ground that the Government of the United States desires to place the maintenance of good faith in treaties and the value and security of arbitration between nations above all question in its relations with her Britannic Majesty's Government as with all other Governments."

CHAPTER IV

MEDIATION AND THE MONROE DOCTRINE

EVARTS was a strong advocate of international arbitration, although cautious in its application. He felt that "the United States is not prepared at present to adopt a general measure" submitting to arbitration all disputes arising under a particular treaty.[13] When China requested our intervention in her dispute with Japan over possession of the Loo Choo Islands, Evarts replied that in such a question our good offices could be tendered only "on the certain assurance that it would be agreeable to both parties." Of this he was hopeful:

"Standing as we do, by precept and example, as the prominent advocates of arbitration as a means of preventing calamitous wars between great peoples as well as small, it is not unlikely that the wise counsellors who guide the destinies of the two nations, if really disposed to seek a peaceful agreement, would naturally turn to this country and solicit its good offices jointly, in order to do away with the cause of the present tension, by resorting to a means of settlement at once honorable to both, and in accordance with the humane and enlightened spirit of the present age.

"You will, therefore, without making such obvious tender of the good offices of this government as might be in disparagement of the national dignity of

Japan . . . leave no doubt of the perfect readiness of the President to accept the gratifying position of mediator, should his action in that capacity be unmistakably agreeable to, or be formally solicited by, both Japan and China." [14]

Shortly thereafter he wrote to Seward, who had been "giving counsel, as a friend of China, looking to the building up of the case of its government and strengthening its position as against that of Japan":

"The government of the United States, if it expects to be looked up to as a proper mediator, or as an arbitrator perhaps, must occupy a position of unquestioned impartiality, leaning neither to the one side nor to the other. . . . This government, as friendly to China as to Japan, and . . . bound to each and both by the highest ties of friendship, would not wish to limit either in having recourse to the aid of our citizens, of whatever station; but in a question like this it is impossible that they should be supposed to speak in its name, or that, in event of the higher walk of mediation or arbitration being opened, their utterances could be appealed to in prejudice of the impartial liberty of action of this government." [15]

When Colombia and Chile made a treaty providing for the arbitration by the President of the United States of such disputes as might arise between them, Evarts expressed his gratification at their action "as indicating not merely concurrence with the great principle of arbitration which this country has so signally and practically maintained but as evincing also that confidence in the impartial amity of this government for the sister Republics of the American Continent which it has always been our proud privilege to welcome ... and to strengthen by our own example of good will and kindly interest in their welfare." [16]

There were numerous occasions during Evarts's secretaryship when such "good will and kindly interest" found expression. American good offices were exerted in behalf of Venezuela in re-establishing its relations with the Netherlands; [17] and in aid of Nicaragua both at the time of her difficulties with Germany in 1877 [18] and in the Mosquito arbitration. Austria was the arbitrating power in the latter case, and our minister there was instructed that the United States "is equally the friend of the two Powers. With this reserve, you can give any aid in your power, in assuring to Nicaragua the proper reception for its case and the proofs therein." Copies of important documents from the State Department files were accordingly given to the Nicaraguan agents to assist their case. [19]

During the war between Chile, Peru, and Bolivia, Evarts used considerable pressure to prevent European intervention, and repeatedly expressed our Government's "willingness to act as peacemaker if assured by all the parties to the struggle that its peaceable intervention would be acceptable, and unhampered by any conditions in disparagement of belligerent rights." [20]

Guatemalan inquiries as to our attitude in its controversy with Great Britain over the latter's encroachments on Belize brought an instruction to the American minister in London to "give him [Earl Derby] to understand that it is a cardinal policy of this government not to acquiesce in the establishment of new European colonies in this hemisphere or in the extension of those already established, by trespass from them on adjacent territory. It is believed that this policy is sanctioned by the public here, which would submit to sacrifice for its success." [21] Similarly, acquisition by England of the Bay Islands would violate both the Monroe Doctrine and the Clayton-Bulwer Treaty,[22] and rumours of the possible sale of the Danish West Indies to either England or France made Evarts urge upon our ministers abroad "cautious watchfulness respecting any movement affecting those Islands." [23]

On the other hand, the possibility that the Netherlands might be willing to transfer Curaçao to Venezuela elicited an instruction that "if the cession of the Island be well founded, and likely to be effected, this government could not look with disfavour on the conveyance of even a small possession from European rule to the control of an American State."[24]

CHAPTER V

THE PANAMA CANAL

IN the summer of 1879 M. de Lesseps, having succeeded at Suez, planned the building of a canal across the Isthmus of Panama under authority of a contract between L. N. B. Wyse and the Colombian Government. Under the provisions of our treaty of 1846 with New Granada we had acquired the right to use any such canal which might be constructed under authority of the Colombian Government. The de Lesseps project thoroughly aroused the American people. Questions arose as to its control if built under European auspices, as to the protection of its neutrality (which we had guaranteed), and as to possible conflicts with the Monroe Doctrine. The tone of the press was hostile. Both House and Senate passed resolutions warning the nations of Europe that a canal under their protection would be considered an unfriendly act, violating the Monroe Doctrine. Meanwhile Evarts was not inactive. Under his instructions our minister at Bogotá was impressing upon that Government the political embarrassments that would arise under the Wyse contract and urging that the de Lesseps project be discouraged. "This Government," wrote Evarts, "cannot consider itself excluded, by any arrangements between other powers or individuals to which it is not a party, from a direct interest, and if necessary a positive supervision and interposition in the execution of any project which, by completing an interoceanic connection through the Isthmus, would materially affect its commercial interests, change the territorial relations of its own sovereignty, and impose upon it the necessity of a foreign policy, which, whether in its feature of warlike preparation or entangling alliance, has been hitherto sedulously avoided."[25] With regard to a rumour that the British Government was seeking a naval station on Gonzales Island, he wrote:

"It is . . . deemed prudent to instruct you, with all needful reserve and discretion, to intimate to the Colombian Government that any concession to Great Britain or any other foreign power, looking to the surveillance and possible strategic control of a highway of whose neutrality we are the guarantors, would be looked upon by the Government of the United States as introducing interests not compatible with the treaty relations which we maintain with Colombia."[26]

In 1880, in compliance with a Senate resolution, the famous Evarts report on Isthmian canal policy was submitted, accompanied by a presidential message to the effect that "the policy of this country is a canal under American control."[27] In this report Evarts covered the entire course of negotiations prior to his own term of office with characteristic thoroughness, and outlined American policy in a style at once vigorous and inoffensive. The purport of it was that "no contract or negotiations could ever be entered into between private projectors and the Government of Colombia except in contemplation of the position of the United States under the treaty [of 1846], and of the necessity that both the private interests and the public engagements involved, in reliance upon the faith and power of this government for their protection, must be conformed to its rightful participation and control in any arrangements that may seriously affect the discharge of its stipulated responsibilities."

This positive and definitive declaration of policy was notice to the world. The American press was delighted, France impressed. In numerous interviews with the French minister at Washington Evarts was assured that the French Government had no interest in the project, an assurance which was reduced to writing at his request.[28] That France kept faith was evident in the reports Evarts received from Colombia, where the French minister was instructed "on no account to commit his government to the support of the project"; and the action of the French consul at Panama in referring to the "interest of the French people and Government" in his address of welcome to de Lesseps was rebuked and officially disavowed.[29]

The Secretary's earnest efforts to obtain a protocol providing that the United States alone should guarantee the neutrality of the canal did not suceed;[30] nor did the attempt to negotiate with Nicaragua and Costa Rica for a canal via Lake Nicaragua.[31] But in his report Evarts had rendered a distinct service to the country.[32]

CHAPTER VI

MEXICO

THROUGHOUT the greater part of the Hayes Administration Evarts found much to test his patience in our relations with Mexico. Diaz had seized control in November 1876, and though recognition was for a time withheld, official relations were resumed on March 23, 1878. Evarts was soon forced to take a strong stand in defence of American rights. The express exclusion of our citizens from settlement on the island of Ciare called forth vigorous protest as a direct violation of the treaty (of 1831) which could not be acquiesced in.

"The Mexican law forbidding United States citizens from holding real estate in that country, while that privilege is open to other aliens, may also be regarded as incompatible if not with the letter, certainly with the spirit of the treaty, the obvious purpose of which was to provide for equality generally between our citizens and other foreigners in that Republic. These injurious discriminations cannot fail to occasion distrust of the friendly disposition of the Mexican government in respect to the government and citizens of the United States."[33]

Meanwhile more disturbing questions threatened. The strong hand of Diaz had not yet awed the factions into peace, nor established order along the border.

Incursions across the Rio Grande were causing constant turmoil and friction. Because of the evident inability of Diaz to stop the depredations Evarts determined upon vigorous measures. On June 1, 1877 General Ord was directed, whenever necessary, to cross the Rio Grande and "overtake and punish" the marauders, retaking any stolen property. The momentary effect was electrical. The Mexicans blazed with indignation. Diaz, with a gesture to maintain his prestige, announced that he would meet force with force. On second thought he sent a Cabinet minister with his troops to the border, where a friendly arrangement was effected, providing for co-operative pursuit.

If this satisfied the Mexican Government, it did not conciliate an element in the United States. The American press teemed with editorial comments, some defending Evarts's course, many bitterly attacking it as high-handed and intolerable. We were overstepping our rights and making an imperialistic gesture. The Administration was seeking war to divert attention from domestic conditions. We were planning annexation, cried the suspicious. Did the Administration disclaim any such intent? No matter—the press knew better. Better still some of the politicians. Best of all James G. Blaine, who, with the ears of the country open to him, publicly met the official disavowal with a sneer. "As a comforting and consolatory addendum to the whole scheme, we are kindly assured that in no event shall any Mexican territory be acquired or annexed to the United States. As in many cases of similar design and movement, the most important feature may be that which is especially disavowed"—a charge that became peculiarly sinister in view of the delicacy of the situation. But the Plumed Knight knew his Machiavelli better than he knew the downright Evarts, who smilingly dismissed the accusation with the assurance that he was in the habit of telling the truth on all occasions— which carried its sting. He maintained his policy unafraid, and lowered his tone not one whit.

The conditions along the Rio Grande did not improve rapidly. It was not even clear that a serious attempt had been made. No doubt Diaz wished to meet his international obligations, but his inability was apparent, and the duty of the United States was clear. "The first duty of a government," Evarts wrote, "is to protect life and property. This is a paramount obligation. For this, governments are instituted, and governments neglecting or failing to perform it become worse than useless. This duty the Government of the United States has determined to perform." We were not solicitous as to the methods. "Protection in fact to American lives and property is the sole point on which the United States are tenacious." Was it complained that American troops "invaded" Mexico? "Mexican cattle thieves invade Texas; Mexican revolutionists, in violation of our laws, invade Mexico from this side of the Rio Grande according to the exigencies of their desultory warfare. But no American force ever goes over the Rio Grande except in pursuit of 'invaders' who have already 'invaded' the soil of the United States and are escaping with their booty."[34] Of course American sufferers would ask reclamation; and "some satisfactory recognition of the obligation of the Mexican Government to amply provide for such contingencies . . . might perhaps afford greater facility to the future adjustment of these cases," but promise of pecuniary redress is insufficient. The outrages must be stopped.[35] With biting sarcasm Evarts wrote:

"I share in Señor Nuñez's regret that it should be necessary to take an isolated case ... as a gauge of the disposition and ability of the Mexican Government to prevent and punish marauders on the territory of a friendly neighboring state. If the instances of wrong doing complained of were as isolated as the cases in which the offenders are brought to justice, or if the examples of prompt and severe punishment were as numerous as the cases of wrong, the isolated selection to which Señor Nuñez Ortega takes exception would most assuredly not have taken place. Should Señor Nuñez still be in office when this reaches you, you may find a convenient occasion to hint as much to him."[36]

These stiff, uncompromising notes made their impression. Slowly but steadily Diaz was getting a grip on the country, but Evarts was in no hurry to moderate his tone or his demands. He instructed Foster, December 2, 1878, to "continue by all proper means in your power to seek to bring the Mexican Government to realize the responsibilities which rest upon it, in the maintenance of international good will and the observance of its moral and legal obligations."[37] The next February, when American business men visiting Mexico were graciously received, he was unimpressed, and the following month he reiterated his position:

"It has been the hope and belief of this government that the checking of predatory raids and the decrease of hostile feeling upon the Rio Grande taken in connection with an apparently growing disposition to cultivate mutual good understanding and to develop international trade, were indications that all the points of difference between the two governments might be soon and happily disposed of. But the action or rather the inaction of the Mexican government . . . and its seeming indifference . . . to a class of demands which all civilized countries are wont to regard as worthy of prompt and earnest attention, cannot but tend to dissipate the hope thus entertained. Assuredly, the citizens of the United States will hesitate to embark in commercial enterprises in any region where life and property are insecure. They must naturally look to their own government to lend them such protection as may be within its power and to the Mexican Government for such co-operation in that protection as is customary among friendly nations. Above and beyond the mere question of the development of international trade, however, is the paramount obligation of every government to protect the lives and property of its people. This duty the government of the United States cannot neglect or relinquish." [38]

Thus, unrelenting as long as the outrages continued, he held the troops on the border until something of stability and order had been established. The famous order of June 1, 1877 was revoked on February 24, 1880, General Ord having stated in his annual report that it was no longer necessary. Evarts wrote: "It has afforded much satisfaction to the President to find in the actual situation upon the border, in the undisturbed security against violence that has for some time been maintained there, in the spirit and conduct of the military efforts made by Mexico its determination to observe its international obligations in preventing invasions of our territory." [39]

The United States thus entered upon a period of peaceful relations with its sister republic, due in large measure to the vigorous insistence of Evarts upon the protection of the lives and property of Americans. And fifty years later, when we found ourselves again in diplomatic controversy with our southern neighbour, Evarts's words were officially used to set forth the policy of the United States.

CHAPTER VII

LIBERTY AND JUSTICE FOR ALL

INSISTENCE upon strict and impartial justice was the keynote of Evarts's policy, whether as between nations or individuals, finding important expression in a strict neutrality throughout the wars and revolutions that occurred during his regime. He refused to permit the arming in our ports of Russian war-vessels built in Philadelphia, so long as the Russo-Turkish War continued;[40] and although "the unfortunate condition of unprotected foreigners in the Ottoman dominions is appreciated by the Department," our minister at Constantinople was not to extend his protection to Russian subjects, as "in the present emergency it is more incumbent on the United States than in ordinary times that the government should strictly adhere to the long established policy of non-interference with the affairs of two nations unfortunately at war with each other, and equally friendly to the United States. Our freedom from all complications with the Powers interested in affairs now transpiring in Europe must be preserved, and the best efforts of our representatives abroad should be directed to that end. . . . It seems proper that this protection should be extended by the Great Powers of Europe . . . rather than by the United States."[41]

It was particularly necessary for us to be cautious in regard to Latin America, for the filibusters of earlier days had somewhat damaged our reputation. Cuba was, as always, a particularly sore point, but rigid enforcement of our neutrality laws was maintained.[42]

In Venezuela our minister was instructed that "the complicated political situation ... calls for the utmost prudence on your part to avoid committing this Government by any specific act ... preserving meanwhile a discreet attitude, and concerning yourself chiefly with the proper protection of any American interests which may be menaced."[43] Accusation by the German chargé in Guatemala, at a diplomatic banquet, "that the United States purposed to absorb the Central American States" naturally elicited an earnest request for explanation, and a prompt disavowal by the German Government.[44]

The dissensions prevailing in Samoa and the activities of Colonel Steinberger, former American consul there, drew upon us some suspicion of partiality, which Evarts indignantly repelled as "without foundation." "The course pursued by this government," he wrote, "is in accordance with its long established policy of strict non-interference with the political affairs of other nations and peoples," and had consistently been "absolute non-interference with the domestic politics and government of the Samoan Islands."[45]

As we have already seen in the case of Mexican land-laws, Evarts would allow no discrimination against American citizens. Our minister at St. Petersburg was instructed: "If ... the invidious partiality now shown to other Consulates in regard to the immunity from search extended to their mails, shall be continued, and still denied to our Consulate, it should form a subject for your strong remonstrance. It is not the system which can properly be attacked, but the partiality shown in its application." [46]

American Jews in Russia were frequently running foul of the intolerant laws, and Evarts earnestly urged their right to protection under our treaty. Following a plot against the Tsar in 1880, in which Jews were implicated, an American citizen not accused of complicity was ordered out of the country. Evarts protested vigorously and served notice that if his expulsion was solely on religious grounds "he would be justly entitled to make reclamation for the damage and loss to which he might thereby be subjected." [47] His intervention was effective and Pinkos, the citizen in question, was not molested. Almost immediately another case arose involving an American, and Evarts instructed Foster to seek a definite understanding. He challenged Russia's right to discriminate against an American on the grounds of religion, but if it insisted upon that, he wanted at least some general rule of action to guide American merchants. The Russian Ministers joined in lamenting the "necessity" of intolerant laws because of "abnormal conditions," but the best that Foster could secure was the promise of special treatment for Jews of American citizenship.

Wherever persecution might be moderated by persuasion, Evarts urged toleration. Thus he commends the consul at Tangiers for his representations to the Sultan of Morocco, expressing the hope that "this disinterested appeal in behalf of an oppressed race, made by the representative of a country which has ever stood foremost as the advocate of the cause of liberty of conscience, will have a beneficial effect." [48] During the discussions regarding the establishment of official relations with Roumania, our minister at Vienna was instructed to remind the Prince that "this government has ever felt a deep interest in the welfare of the Hebrew race in foreign countries, and has viewed with abhorrence the wrongs to which they have at various periods been subjected by the followers of other creeds in the East." [49]

To the delicate question of the administration of justice in foreign lands, Evarts brought all his legal acumen and power of persuasive argument, and the rules he laid down have not been essentially modified since. "The intervention of this Government is not to be successfully invoked on all occasions in behalf of such of its citizens as may incur the penalty fixed by foreign law for public offences"; but when an American was sentenced to a year's imprisonment for speaking disrespectfully of the Kaiser, Evarts wrote that "in view of . . . the fact that a German, in like circumstances, in the United States, would incur no penalty for the free expression of his political views, even though overstepping the bounds of prudent speech, it is thought that the severity of the sentence . . . may, perhaps, warrant discreet representation." [50]

Turkey was trying to abrogate the capitulations indirectly by new and narrower interpretations of foreign rights, but Evarts met every such attempt with firm insistence upon treaty obligations. This is not the place for an elaborate discussion of our Turkish treaty, nor even of Evarts's share in the long diplomatic controversy as to the meaning of Article IV. It was primarily a legal debate, in which Evarts's argumentative skill was fully displayed. He surrendered an untenable position by formally admitting the inaccuracy of the official English version, *as a translation* of the Turkish, but took his stand on surer ground by insisting that it was a true expression of the intention of the negotiators and the practice of the times. Again, when Aristarchi Bey refused to consider any translation authentic, Evarts replied that "an international act wholly in a foreign tongue can only be incorporated into our domestic system through the medium of a translation," and that the acceptance of some translation by both parties must be the first step towards settling the controversy.[51] Ten years later the Turks finally complied with that request; meanwhile Evarts's logical exposition of the law and the facts had done much to clarify the issues involved.

In 1880 the famous Mirzan murder case tested the foundations of consular jurisdiction in Egypt. In view of the gravity of the offence, Evarts instructed our minister to Turkey to act as judge instead of the consul, giving him explicit directions as to the law and procedure to be applied. Only an expert criminal lawyer could have given instructions at once so concise and so comprehensive. He closes by laying down a principle often overlooked in extra-territorial courts: "In the administration of criminal justice the forms of law become of the substance, and none of them should be considered so trivial as to be unworthy of strict observance."[52]

Not only in Egypt and Turkey, but in Madagascar, Morocco, China, and Japan important judicial questions arose; some, like the Ross case in Japan, involving a conflict of jurisdiction with a third power.[53]

When an American missionary asked "whether it

would be possible for an American citizen, by surrendering his right of exterritoriality and placing himself under Japanese law, to acquire the right of residence in the interior of Japan," Evarts wrote: "It is not seen how that gentleman can expect official sanction to his proposition to occupy a non-descript position in Japan as to his rights of citizenship. He must be either an American citizen or a Japanese subject, and if he remains an American citizen, this Government has no authority to countenance any scheme by which his rights would be traded away. If he desires to relinquish his 'exterritoriality' and reside in the interior of the country, the right of expatriation and change of allegiance, common to all citizens, will probably furnish him with a practical means of accomplishing his purpose."[54]

In 1877 he wrote: "The rate of progress towards a higher civilization and a more liberal form of government in Japan, indicates that it will, before many years, reach a point where the administration of justice can be safely trusted to its courts by foreigners," but "it is certainly not the intention of this government to surrender that power at present."[55] As for China: "This Government is disposed to treat with the greatest respect the desire of the Chinese Government to meet, if possible, the divergence between the Chinese and American systems of jurisprudence and procedure by some judicial establishment which will be more observant than the present of the principle that territory and jurisdiction are and should be co-extensive."[56]

CHAPTER VIII

CHINESE IMMIGRATION

MEANWHILE Evarts was occupied with the readjustment of our relations with China, trying to substitute friendly diplomacy for the mob methods popularly advocated. The fifth and sixth articles of the Burlingame treaty, of 1868, had become embarrassing; the first recognizing "the inherent and inalienable right of man to change his home and allegiance, and also the mutual advantage of . . . free migration . . . from the one country to the other for purposes of curiosity, of trade, or as permanent residents," and "reprobating" involuntary emigration; the other granting "most-favoured-nation" treatment. Soon after the ratification of the treaty the influx of Chinese labourers created a problem of paramount importance in California. Since 1868 the Chinese resident there had increased from a few hundred to 116,000, most of them common labourers, dangerous competitors of Americans in that field.

As early as 1871 race prejudice had been fanned to a flame. Ever and anon a white mob would descend upon the Chinese quarters. In San Francisco and Los Angeles, assassinations; in the latter a veritable massacre. A mob of twenty thousand armed with knives, guns, and ropes marched upon the Chinese section, overpowered the police, and indiscriminately hanged twenty-two orientals. There was never again such a flaming of racial hate, but it was smouldering and by 1875 had taken the form of a grim determination that "the Chinese must go." Merchants headed their advertisements with the magic words. They constituted a resolution introduced in the Constitutional Convention. A popular San Francisco saloon-keeper solicited trade with a verse:

"His drinks are A 1, and his prices are low,
    His motto is always, 'The Chinese must go,'
So call on your friends, workingmen, if you please,
    Take a good solid drink and drive out the Chinese!"[57]

It was this appeal to the working-men, competing with coolie labour, that gave political significance to the crisis. The labourer broadcast his appeal for national action, looking to exclusion and expulsion. The canny politician was impressed, and both major parties inserted in their platforms demands for restrictive legislation. Dennis Kearney, the father of "sand-lot oratory," a strange, picturesque figure of fine audacity and rough eloquence, caught the ear of labour from coast to coast and set California on fire. He put the fear of the toiler into the heart of the politician—and the California election of 1879 was approaching. The combination was too much for human nature to withstand. Statesmanship yielded to politics, and in the closing days of the Forty-fifth Congress a bill reached the Senate from the House prohibiting ships from bringing more than fifteen Chinese a trip, and the Senate instructed the President to serve immediate notice of the abrogation of Articles V and VI of the treaty with China of 1868. Leaders of both parties, competing for the labour vote, made no effort to spare the sensibilities of a friendly nation.

James G. Blaine, his eye on the presidency, stooped to conquer, and warmly supported the bill. Senator Hamlin denounced it as an unmannerly method and a breach of international goodwill. The Chinese could not vote, labour could, and so could the Irish, under the militant leadership of Kearney. The press defended and attacked. The nation rocked with excitement—and the California election was approaching.

The debate had been followed anxiously in the executive branch of the federal Government. President Hayes had no doubt as to his duty regarding the measure. He wrote in his diary: "Our treaty with China forbids me to give it my approval. The treaty was of our asking."[58] Evarts, who was watching the turmoil with something of cynicism and amusement, not unmixed with down-right indignation, prepared a veto message, which Hayes accepted in its entirety and sent to Congress as his own.

This message bears the unmistakable impress of the Evarts mind and method. Did Congress wish to denounce the treaty as a whole? Evidently not, and it ought not to do so without the most impelling reasons. "A denunciation of a treaty by any Government is confessedly justifiable only upon some reason both of the highest justice and of the highest necessity." Only once had Congress gone to this extremity, in 1798, when it abrogated the French treaty—and then it set forth adequate reasons. Moreover, Congress now sought the impossible, for "a denunciation of a part of a treaty not made by the terms of the treaty itself separable from the rest is a denunciation of the whole treaty," and "as the other high contracting party has entered into no treaty obligations except such as include the part denounced, the denunciation by one party of the part, necessarily liberates the other party from the whole treaty." Did Congress intend "an exposure of our citizens in China, merchants or missionaries, to the consequences of so sudden an abrogation of their treaty protection"? Conditions had arisen requiring a modification of the existing treaty, but were these so pressing that they could not await the ordinary processes of diplomatic negotiations? Why outrage an ancient government, "ruling a polite and sensitive people, distinguished by a high sense of national pride"? Why proceed in a way that does not "maintain the public duty and the public honor"?

Whatever its effect on the politicians, this Evarts statement, sponsored by the President, made a profound impression on the thoughtful, and there was a very perceptible moderating of the heat and a disposition to seek readjustment through more conventional methods. The attempt to pass the act over the veto failed, and Evarts entered upon direct negotiations. As early as April 23, 1879 he had paved the way by instructing Seward:

"It is believed that inquiries may be made in China which will elicit the facts in regard to the immigration of contract laborers ... and means devised in concert with the Chinese government to prevent the departure of such persons for our shores. Your first duty will be to set on foot such an inquiry and report thereafter the facts which may be ascertained and the measures which the Chinese government may be willing to undertake in pursuance of existing treaty stipulations. . . .

"While conducting this negotiation, it is desirable that you should explain to the Ministers of the Foreign Office the disorders and difficulties which over immigration of their people into this country has occasioned, and that it is in the interest of our general relations and of their own people that judicious provision should be introduced into our treaty relations to correct the mischiefs of excessive immigration.

"As it is impossible to foresee the course of immigration, as our relations with China are peculiar and our people resident there enjoy many extraordinary privileges, and as it is desirable to work out all desired results without disturbing the good feeling now existing between the two countries and without impairing the opportunities and prospects which inure to us under existing treaty stipulations, it is considered desirable first to ascertain with precision the disposition of the Chinese government. . . .

"It is the wish of the President to conduct this negotiation in view of the general interests of our people, both at home and in China . . . so conduct these immediate negotiations as to avoid or allay irritation."[59]

In the summer of 1880 he sent a special mission to negotiate a new treaty. They were instructed thus:

"In treating with the Imperial Government on the urgent question of the principles and methods upon which a continued hospitality to a true and permanent removal of its subjects to become members of our society, can be regulated, suitably to the interests and sentiments of the two nations, you will take care to sever that discussion from all considerations bearing upon the rights and privileges of the Chinese population already transferred to our territory. . . . This population has and will continue to have, all the guarantees and protection . . . that the institutions of the country provide for immigrants from other foreign countries and for our own population. While no extra-territorial jurisdiction . . . is permissible in our policy, yet this neither springs from nor occasions any adverse discrimination to the disadvantage of the Chinese in our midst."[60]

The manly action of Hayes and Evarts had done much to soothe the sensibilities of the Chinese statesmen, and negotiations proceeded rapidly and satisfactorily. In November 1880 two treaties were signed and soon ratified by both parties, one commercial, the other modifying the Burlingame treaty so as to permit us to regulate, limit, or suspend the immigration of Chinese labourers. It was one of the great triumphs of Evarts's career.

Another treaty revision of outstanding importance was carried on by Evarts with the Japanese minister in Washington. The negotiation of the treaty of 1878 was a distinct modification of the co-operative policy in the Far East, and as such resented by some of the other powers, although it was not to become operative until they concluded similar agreements. This condition was never fulfilled, but Evarts's willingness to give Japan control of her own tariff, by independent action if necessary, gave welcome proof of American friendliness.[61]

In most of Evarts's negotiations (and they were numerous) the lawyer dominated the statesman. He particularly encouraged the conclusion of extradition treaties, displaying an exhaustive knowledge of the intricacies of criminal procedure and a clear appreciation of the interrelation of constitutional and international law. He gave similar careful attention to the protection of trade-marks abroad and the negotiation of consular conventions. In dealing with these technical questions he was always alert to prevent the careless creation of difficulties, so that his treaties have proved extraordinarily practicable.[62]

CHAPTER IX

LATER YEARS

BEFORE leaving office Evarts instructed Noyes to carry on "confidential and unofficial" negotiations through the American consul-general at Paris regarding an international monetary conference. As a result France and the United States issued a joint call for a conference on bimetallic standards, to meet in Paris, April 19, 1881, to which President Garfield appointed Evarts a delegate.

The conference over, Evarts returned to the practice of his profession, as the acknowledged leader of the American bar. He was elected to the United States Senate in 1885, but sixty-seven years of toil and achievement had chilled the fires of his ambition, and while he delivered several notable speeches, routine duties bored him. His eyes began to trouble him, and from 1893 until his death he seldom emerged from retirement. His keen mind lost nothing of its brilliance, as was shown on the rare occasions of his emergence to make a speech. Summers found him usually at Runnymede, his country home of several hundred acres at Windsor, Vermont, which he maintained not only as a delightful retreat, but as a practical farming enterprise. His town house in New York City was a fine old mansion on Second Avenue, in a section long abandoned by the fashionable, but he lingered there among its memories to the end. There, on his eighty-third birthday, February 6, 1901, he died; and at Windsor he was buried.

For sheer intellectual greatness he has had few peers among the servants of the Republic. While he directed the State Department, respect for the law of nations and of this nation was the guiding principle in American foreign policy.

JAMES GILLESPIE BLAINE

SECRETARY OF STATE

MARCH 7, 1881, TO DECEMBER 18, 1881
(FIRST TERM)

BY

JOSEPH B. LOCKEY, Ph.D.

ASSOCIATE PROFESSOR OF HISTORY
THE UNIVERSITY OF CALIFORNIA AT LOS ANGELES

JAMES G. BLAINE

James G. Blaine

JAMES GILLESPIE BLAINE

CHAPTER I

THE YEARS OF PREPARATION

JAMES GILLESPIE BLAINE served as Secretary of State under three presidents. He first assumed the duties of the office on March 7, 1881, in the Cabinet of James A. Garfield. A brief four months later Garfield was struck down by an assassin's bullet and for some weeks lingered between life and death. The fatal end came on September 19, and Chester A. Arthur succeeded to the presidency. Blaine immediately offered his resignation. By request of the President he remained at his post for three months longer and then retired to private life. He was next called to the Department of State by Benjamin Harrison at the beginning of his Administration, in 1889, and this time served until the summer of 1892, when, broken in health, he again resigned. This proved to be the end of his public career.

Garfield's choice of the ranking member of his Cabinet was in a measure predetermined by the conspicuous position which Blaine occupied in the Republican party, and by personal and political consideration of the most compelling sort. The two men had entered Congress at the same time, and through the vicissitudes of long association in public life they had come to regard each other with confidence and esteem. The events connected with the campaign of 1880 strengthened their friendship and put Garfield under deep obligations to Blaine. In the Republican National Convention of that year Blaine and General Grant were the leading candidates for the presidential nomination. So evenly divided were their partisans that a dead-lock arose, which was broken by the choice of Garfield as a compromise. To this result Blaine contributed by sanctioning and encouraging the break in Garfield's favour, and in the campaign which followed he supported the nominee with energy and enthusiasm.

In forming his Cabinet, therefore, Garfield turned first to Blaine, offering him a choice of posts. Blaine preferred the Secretaryship of State. In accepting it he wrote: "I shall give all that I am and all that I can hope to be freely and joyfully to your service. . . . However I might admire you as a statesman I could not enter your Cabinet, if I did not believe in you as a man and love you as a friend."[1]

Blaine did not rise to distinction from an obscure ancestry. James Blaine, his great-great-grandfather, emigrated from the north of Ireland towards the middle of the eighteenth century and settled in western Pennsylvania. In him were combined thrift, energy, and public spirit. By wise investments in lands he laid the foundation of wealth for his descendants, and by active and meritorious service to the community in which he lived, he set an example which the Blaines of succeeding generations were prone to emulate. His eldest son, Ephraim, played a conspicuous part in the Revolutionary War, as one of Washington's trusted officers. Ephraim's son, James, the grandfather of James Gillespie Blaine, after receiving a liberal education, which was broadened by a prolonged period of travel and study in Europe, devoted his energies to important business enterprises. The next in the line of descent, Ephraim Lyon Blaine, the father of the Secretary of State, was educated at Washington College, travelled abroad, studied law, and was admitted to the bar; but did not actively practise the profession. He was a personage of local distinction. He loved display and practised a lavish hospitality, which resulted in greatly exhausting the family fortune.

James Gillespie Blaine was born at West Brownsville, in the south-western part of Pennsylvania, on January 31, 1830. His mother was Maria Louise Gillespie, also of Scotch-Irish descent. Until he was about ten years of age, James Gillespie was educated at home. He was then sent to relatives in Ohio, and there had the good fortune to begin preparation for college under an excellent instructor, William Lyons, an uncle of the Lord Lyons who was during the Civil War British minister at Washington. After returning to West Brownsville to finish his preparatory studies, he entered Washington College at the age of thirteen. Four years later he was graduated, the youngest of a class of thirty odd, and one of the three among whom the first honours were divided.

The next half-dozen years the precocious youth devoted to teaching. For two or three years he was an instructor in the Western Military Institute, near Lexington, Kentucky. He then went to Philadelphia and began the study of law, but, being compelled to earn a livelihood, put aside his legal studies and accepted a position as teacher in the Pennsylvania Institute for the Blind.

In Kentucky he had met Harriet Stanwood of Augusta, Maine, to whom he was married at the age of twenty. This was for him the beginning of a happy and altogether admirable family life, which ended only with his death, forty-three years later. Through assistance furnished by his brothers-in-law in Maine, he was able to acquire an interest in the *Kennebec Journal*, a weekly Whig newspaper published at Augusta. In 1854 he abandoned teaching and assumed the editorship of this journal.

As an editor he was fortunate from the beginning. The time was propitious. Old party associations were being dissolved or readjusted, and a fresh, vigorous organization, soon to gain control of the national Government, was being formed. He became a member of this new party, just beginning to be designated by the term Republican, and shared in its victories. He was successful not merely because of his party connexions. He owed much to his talents and industry. A facile writer, endowed by nature with a keen, alert mind, which he applied assiduously to the study of national as well as state affairs, he soon won a place of leadership. After serving his party in various capacities he was in 1862 elected a member of the lower house of the national legislature.

In Congress he did not long remain in the background. He took an active part in the important legislation which a successful prosecution of the war demanded, and, rapidly becoming one of the most formidable debaters of his time, he made his influence strongly felt in the measures of reconstruction which engrossed the attention of Congress after the war. Successively reelected to the House of Representatives, he was in 1869 chosen as Speaker, in which post he continued to serve until 1875. In that year the Democratic majority in the House elected the Speaker, and Blaine resumed his place on the floor as leader of the minority.

At the close of his six years as Speaker of the House he occupied a conspicuous place among his contemporaries. He seemed destined for higher honours. Already his enthusiastic followers were laying plans to secure for him the party nomination for President. But suddenly his progress was checked by scandal. His personal integrity was questioned. In the spring of 1876 vague rumours were circulated, and then specific charges were set forth in the public press, accusing him of having engaged, some years back, in corrupt transactions in railway securities. A denial which he made on the floor of the House was without avail. The accusations were persisted in, and the House Judiciary Committee was instructed to make an investigation.

By the first week in June the inquiry was well under way. A week or ten days later the Republican National Convention was to meet at Cincinnati. It was believed that in the mean time the testimony of two witnesses, Warren Fisher, Jr., and James Mulligan, who had come to Washington to appear before the committee, would utterly destroy Blaine's chances for the nomination. Fisher had been a business partner of Eben C. Stanwood, a brother of Mrs. Blaine, and Mulligan had served as the confidential secretary of another brother, Jacob Stanwood. With Fisher, Blaine also had had business dealings, and a considerable correspondence concerning the transactions later alleged to be corrupt had been carried on between them. But as these various associations had given rise to friction, the connexions with each had been severed. Mulligan was now an employé of Fisher and both were hostile to Blaine.

When Mulligan began his testimony, it became known that he had in his possession the letters from Blaine to Fisher and intended to lay them before the committee. Before this was done, Blaine, through one of the members of the committee, secured an adjournment. Some hours later he called on Mulligan at his hotel and managed to get the documents into his own hands. He then refused to return them to their custodian, whom he regarded as having no right to them, and, on the advice of counsel, declined also to yield them to the committee. Instead he took them to the House, rose to a question of privilege, and, in one of the most dramatic scenes ever witnessed in that body, read them to his astonished colleagues.

Beginning with a recital of the circumstances leading up to the action that he was about to take and accompanying the reading with comments and explanations, he concluded by saying: "I have now read these fifteen letters, the whole of them. The House and the country now know all there is in them. They are dated and they correspond precisely with Mulligan's memorandum, which I have here. I keep this memorandum as a protection for myself; for it is very valuable as showing the identity of the letters in every respect."

Upon being asked whether he would allow the memorandum to be made public, he replied in the affirmative, first explaining that two other papers, which he had not read, were listed in the memorandum. "That makes eighteen papers," he said. "I will put them all in; let them all go." At this point Hale of Maine inquired: "Does the exhibit which the gentleman has made cover every paper of every kind whatever that came from Mulligan?" And Blaine replied: "Every solitary scrap and 'scrimption' as the children say."[2]

Captivated by Blaine's audacity and convinced by his arguments, the great majority of his audience, in the gallery as well as on the floor, expressed their approval in vigorous applause. In the press he was widely acclaimed and the impression prevailed, among his friends at least, that he had been completely vindicated. When the Republican convention met, eight days later, his popularity seemed to be but little if at all impaired. On the first ballot his vote was far in excess of that of his nearest competitor and but little short of the required majority. This position he held until the seventh ballot, when all the opposing elements combined against him and succeeded in nominating Rutherford B. Hayes.

After all, Blaine's defeat must be attributed to lingering doubts as to his rectitude. The irregularities with which his name was associated followed close upon the heels of other scandals involving men in high places. The public conscience had been aroused and no one, however eminent, was above suspicion. In the circumstances it is not surprising that a small but influential minority of the Republican party were unconvinced by his explanations and continued to distrust him. Whether or not this distrust was justified, the historian cannot yet say with complete assurance; for the facts have never been fully elicited. The investigation in the House collapsed after his sensational coup, and the evidence, the so-called Mulligan letters, upon which the accusers chiefly rested their case, remained in the hands of the accused. It has been charged that Blaine did not read all the letters and that he suppressed parts of some of them. Against these charges stands his own solemn declaration. A careful comparison of the originals with the versions published in the *Congressional Record* can alone settle this question. Even then the case would not be removed from the realm of controversy. Nor is it likely ever to be so removed. That Blaine failed to avoid the appearance of evil is about all that one may confidently assert. For that failure he paid the penalty.

A few weeks after the events which have just been chronicled, Blaine was elevated to the Senate, and there he remained until he was called to the Department of State.

What were Blaine's qualifications for the office of Secretary of State? Some of his predecessors—Jefferson, Madison, Adams, Calhoun—were profound students of history, government, and public law. Blaine was not a scholar in politics. Others—Randolph, Marshall, Webster, Marcy, Evarts—were great lawyers. Blaine was not a lawyer. Others—about half of those who preceded him—were practised in the technique of diplomacy. Jefferson had spent five years at the Court of France; Monroe had gone on various diplomatic missions; J. Q. Adams had been reared, as it were, in the diplomatic service; Clay had served as one of the commissioners to negotiate the treaty of peace at Ghent, and then had joined with Adams and Gallatin in concluding a commercial convention with England; and McLane, Everett, Forsyth, Buchanan, and Cass had been ministers abroad. Blaine took his post without diplomatic experience.

Nevertheless he possessed eminent qualifications for the office of Secretary of State. His gracious, dynamic personality; his resourceful, comprehensive mind, quick to grasp new situations and bold to conceive new plans; his large and devoted following; and his thorough acquaintance with the problems and tendencies of the nation—these were considerations that went far towards making good any shortcomings that might have been urged against him.

He had spent a quarter of a century in the public service, nearly eighteen years of which he had sat in Congress, where he could sense every pulsation of national and international life. For the greater part of his career, to be sure, questions of domestic political interest had entirely absorbed his energies. From early childhood, indeed, he had been steeped in them. His earliest recollections were of the comings and goings of the national heroes along the Cumberland Road. His college days were filled with discussions and debates on national issues. His youthful letters from Kentucky were concerned with such questions as slavery and the tariff. In Lexington he heard Henry Clay speak on the Mexican War and could quote years afterwards his opening sentence: "The day is dark and gloomy, unsettled and uncertain like the changing destinies of human and national life."[3] No sign as yet of an international outlook. The Mexican War interested him, as it interested Clay, because of its bearing on national life. And for the next two decades it was the life of the nation which wholly engaged him. As newspaper editor and party leader in Maine, he faced the greatest of national crises; and as a member of Congress during the war and for some years afterwards, he found no time for the expansive conceptions of international statesmanship.

It is to the period of the Civil War that one must go for the origin of the ideas and preconceptions which dominated Blaine as Secretary of State. Incidents of those years make intelligible, if they do not wholly justify, the distrust which, it must be confessed, he entertained in some degree towards certain of the Old World powers, particularly Great Britain, France, and Spain. His Anglophobia, if such it may be termed, was inspired by what he believed to be British partiality for the Southern cause.[4] This aroused in him a feeling of resentment, which fortunately time and the friendly settlement of the *Alabama* claims largely removed.

France and Spain had likewise given cause for offence in Blaine's eyes. They had taken advantage of the preoccupation of the United States to flout the Monroe Doctrine—an offence which a good American finds it difficult to condone. Under French protection the Second Empire had been established in Mexico, and Maximilian, Archduke of Austria, induced to ascend the throne, where he was maintained by French bayonets. Spain, disappointed in the part which it hoped to play in the intervention in Mexico, sought compensation by reincorporating Santo Domingo in its national territory, and on a flimsy pretext went to war with the Pacific states of South America in the hope, doubtless, of making further conquests in that quarter. To the disillusionment of the Spanish-American countries England had complacently looked on.[5]

These aggressions the United States was unable to prevent. Its resources were being expended in a colossal effort to thwart a dissolution of the Union. It protested, but mildly; it declined to recognize Maximilian, but without hostile gestures; it continued to deal with the patriot Government of Juárez, but without ostentatious partiality. It bided its time, and when the Civil War was over, it succeeded by a diplomacy which had force in the background in hastening, if not compelling, the withdrawal of the French troops from Mexican soil. Maximilian speedily fell and the Government of Mexico was recovered by its people. Spain also turned back. The sovereignty of the Dominican Republic was restored, and the war in the Pacific came to a futile end.

The moment was opportune for reviving the fraternal spirit which had prevailed among the states of the New World during the second and third decades of the century, and which later had been all but destroyed by the aggressive tendencies of the United States temporarily under the obsession of manifest destiny. Much of the fear and distrust aroused during that exuberant period had been removed by the outcome of the Civil War; for to the slave states had been attributed the imperialistic trend of the nation. With slavery gone and the Union restored, Latin America looked again to the United States as a friendly protector against European encroachments. On our side we had been chastened by our sufferings. The arrogant, impatient attitude that we had assumed towards our turbulent neighbours had yielded to a measure of sympathy and understanding. Had we not shed more blood in four years to settle internal difficulties than they in forty years? Did we not owe them gratitude for the unmistakable evidence which they had given of their desire for the preservation of the

Union? Under these changed conditions it was possible to begin building anew on just and lasting foundations a permanent structure of international American goodwill. That Blaine saw and made use of this opportunity is his chief title to lasting fame.

CHAPTER II

IN Blaine's own words the foreign policy of the Garfield Administration had two objects: "First, to bring about peace and prevent future wars in North and South America; second, to cultivate such friendly, commercial relations with all American countries as would lead to a large increase in the export trade of the United States, by supplying fabrics in which we are abundantly able to compete with the manufacturing nations of Europe."[6] The attainment of the first object was a prerequisite to the accomplishment of the second. Blaine's idea was to cease depending on partial measures—friendly interventions, patched-up treaties, ineffectual truces. Permanent peace, he believed, could be attained only by means of a comprehensive plan, and to this end he proposed to enlist the goodwill and active co-operation of all the states of the Western hemisphere in a general congress to be held at Washington. He did not immediately extend invitations to the congress, for there were difficulties in the way. A war involving Chile, Peru, and Bolivia was raging in South America, and nearer at hand hostilities threatened between Mexico and Guatemala. Concord among these states must first be restored.

The Mexico-Guatemala dispute was of long standing. It grew out of conflicting claims to the province of Chiapas, which in colonial times had been attached to the captaincy-general of Guatemala. In 1821 both Guatemala and Chiapas, acting separately, joined Mexico. On the fall of Iturbide, in 1823, Guatemala withdrew, with Mexican consent, to unite with Honduras, Salvador, Nicaragua, and Costa Rica in the short-lived Republic of Central America. Chiapas elected to remain a part of Mexico. The Guatemalan contention was that the province had been coerced; Mexico took the position that its choice had been free. In the mean time the province remained under Mexican control.

In his desire to contribute to a friendly adjustment of the dispute Blaine was influenced in a measure doubtless by a chivalric regard for the weaker contestant. He disclaimed partiality, it is true. Yet he was pleased to have Guatemala make formal application to the United States, "as the natural protector of Central American integrity," to use its good offices to bring about a peaceable settlement; and he gave heed to information received from Central American sources to the effect that Mexico was plotting to precipitate hostilities with a view to extend its borders far beyond the territory in dispute. Blaine feared that in a war so unequal, successful resistance on the part of Guatemala would be impossible, and that the other Central American states would become involved, which would result in their defeat and eventual absorption in the Mexican federal system. Thus we should have on this continent "another lamentable demonstration of the so-called right of conquest," which would postpone indefinitely "that sympathy of feeling, that community of purpose, and that unity of interest upon the development of which depends the future prosperity of these countries."[7]

Not only did Blaine wish to avoid the evils that would follow in the train of conquest, but he desired also to prevent the complications that would inevitably arise if some European power should intervene in the quarrel, as he had reason to believe would occur if Guatemala was driven to extremities. He accordingly urged that the conflict be averted by diplomatic means, or, these failing, by resort to arbitration. The Mexican Government did not receive his suggestion with favour. It believed that he had been instigated to interfere by Guatemala, and that he had therefore prejudged the case. Undiscouraged, he returned to the charge with new arguments and more urgent appeals, but without avail. Insistence served only to irritate. His proposal of arbitration, at first politely declined, was now indignantly rejected as officious interference. Blaine truly had cause to be exasperated, but he remained calm and conciliatory. In his last dispatch on the subject he expressed deep regret that Mexico should be unwilling to join the United States in establishing the principle of friendly arbitration of international differences on the American continent.[8]

When Blaine left the State Department, this dispute stood about as he found it. His successor did not press the matter, and Guatemala, no longer feeling that it had the support of a powerful friend, entered into direct negotiations with Mexico, as a result of which a settlement was arrived at some months later substantially in accordance with the Mexican contention.[9]

Simultaneously with his endeavour to effect a settlement between Mexico and Guatemala, Blaine was striving zealously to restore peace between the belligerents in South America. Here likewise he failed to attain his immediate aim, and the conflict, already in its second year, dragged on for three years longer. The heritage of bitter hatreds, and of angry bickerings over still unsettled questions growing out of this war, abundantly justifies the efforts which Blaine so persistently made to interpose his good offices in the interest of a just and lasting peace.

The War of the Pacific grew out of a territorial dispute. When the Spanish-American colonies began their revolt from the mother country, they tacitly adopted a rule which was intended to preclude conflicting territorial claims. This was a rule based on the Roman principle of law known as the *uti possidetis*. It provided that the new states should conform to the limits of the major administrative divisions existing in 1810, the year when Spain ceased to exercise over its American possessions full and undisputed authority.[10] The rule was generally observed; but in some regions the boundaries were so indefinite that disputes inevitably arose. This was the case in the desert of Atacama. There had never been in colonial times any necessity for determining exact lines of demarcation in that uninhabited and barren waste. Peru ended vaguely on its northern borders, and Chile began no less vaguely on its southern limits. In between, Upper Peru, destined to become later the Republic of Bolivia, thrust a strip of uncertain width to the Pacific. These haphazard frontiers the three republics inherited, and for some years no occasion arose to give them clearer definition.

Towards the middle of the century interest in the

neglected region was awakened, for it was found to be rich in mineral resources, chief among which was nitrate of soda. Boundaries were no longer a matter of indifference. The *uti possidetis* of 1810 acquired a new interest for the possessors of this storehouse of wealth. Old documents were brought forth and re-examined in support of the varying claims. On the north, Peru and Bolivia were able to agree on a dividing line marked by the Loa River, which flows into the Pacific at about 21 degrees 30 minutes south latitude. Farther down the coast, the claims of Bolivia and Chile overlapped. By treaty in 1866 the two countries set the boundary conditionally at latitude 24 degrees south. In 1874 this boundary was confirmed by a second treaty, which stipulated that neither party would impose within the territory formerly in dispute any taxes in excess of those already fixed by law. Claiming that Bolivia had violated the agreement, Chile seized, in February 1879, the Bolivian port of Antofagasta. Bolivia immediately replied with a declaration of war against Chile. In consequence of a secret treaty of alliance, which it had concluded with Bolivia in 1873, Peru soon became involved in the war.[11]

The outcome of the contest was dependent on sea-power. Bolivia had no navy, and its population was concentrated in the high plateau beyond the Andes, at a great distance from the scene of conflict. Difficulties of transportation alone put the country at a tremendous disadvantage. It could neither save its coast provinces nor render effective assistance to its ally. Peru, after the first few months of the war, confronted Chile alone. Its cruisers for a time held the enemy in check, but finally succumbed to the growing power of the Chilean Navy, and the whole Peruvian coast lay open to attack. First Tarapacá, richest of the nitrate fields, then Tacna and Arica, yielded to the vigorous Chilean onslaught. Progressively the operations moved up the coast. A well-equipped army was concentrated about Lima and in January 1881 forced it to surrender. Except for desultory fighting, the war was at an end.

At the moment of its defeat Peru had no government with which the victor would treat. In the midst of the war the constitutional regime had been set aside and Nicolas de Pierola had been proclaimed dictator. On the fall of Lima he escaped with a remnant of his forces to the interior, whence he made various ineffectual attempts to open peace negotiations with the Chileans. An effort to end this anomalous situation resulted in the establishment, under Chilean protection, of a provisional Government with Francisco García Calderón as President. This Government was recognized by the United States in the hope of facilitating peace negotiations.[12] Chile, however, never fully recognized it; indeed, later the Chilean authorities became hostile to Calderón and took him away a prisoner to Santiago.

Thus matters stood when Blaine assumed the duties of Secretary of State. The opportunity for the peacemaker was an alluring one. If the United States could find the means of re-establishing harmonious relations between the belligerents, its prestige as the friend and counsellor of the American nations would be greatly enhanced, and the way to the adoption of a comprehensive peace plan would be made relatively easy. As in the Mexico-Guatemala dispute, Blaine's chief concern was to prevent annexation of territory by conquest. He had reason for anxiety, as the Chilean Government had officially declared that the cession of Antofagasta and Tarapacá as a reimbursement for the expenses of the war was an indispensable condition to the negotiation of peace.[13] From this demand Chile showed no signs of receding, though it stoutly contended that the war was not one of conquest.

In writing his first full instructions on the subject, Blaine recognized the *fait accompli*. The United States, he said, could not refuse to acknowledge the rights which the Chilean Government had acquired by the successes of the war. Annexation of territory might be the necessary price to be paid for peace; but it should be made as a result of negotiations, not of conquest. It would be injudicious therefore for Peru to declare that it would in no circumstances cede a part of its national domains, and he hoped that Chile, since it had distinctly repudiated the idea that the war was one of conquest, would not demand the cession of territory as a condition precedent to peace negotiations. A meeting of minds on this basis would be possible. The points at issue would then be a proper indemnity to Chile, and suitable guaranties for the maintenance of peace in the future. Whether Peru would be able to make any arrangement at home or abroad that would furnish the necessary indemnity or supply the required guaranties was uncertain; but if it could do so without sacrificing the integrity of its territory, the United States would tender its good offices for the execution of such a project. If no plan could be devised for meeting the reasonable conditions of Chile, the exaction of territory as a prerequisite to peace would become a fair subject of consideration.[14]

The recipients of these instructions were Stephen A. Hurlbut and Hugh Judson Kilpatrick. Both were veterans of the Civil War, in which both attained the rank of major-general; both had served for a time immediately after the war as ministers to South American countries, and both had recently been called back to the service and were proceeding on their missions as ministers to Peru and Chile respectively. Unfortunately the parallel does not end here. Both became partisans of the countries to which they were accredited; both muddled their instructions, destroying all hope of an early peace; and, finally, both died at their posts, Kilpatrick two weeks before Blaine's resignation, Hurlbut three months afterwards. Their appointments were both unfortunate. The ministers whom they superseded, Thomas A. Osborn in Chile and Isaac P. Christiancy in Peru, had been on the ground from the beginning of the conflict, were thoroughly familiar with all its details, had kept the Department of State well informed of the course of events, and had generally performed their duties with ability and discretion. If they had not been recalled, the unhappy complications which ensued might have been avoided.

The ill success of his ministers induced Blaine to try a new plan. The whole matter of the peace negotiations he now entrusted to William H. Trescot, a highly accomplished professional diplomatist, who was appointed as special envoy, with the rank of minister plenipotentiary, to the republics of Peru, Bolivia, and Chile. In his instructions to Trescot, Blaine left much to the envoy's discretion. There were two points, however, upon which he spoke positively. First, in regard to the extinction of the Calderón Government, if Trescot should find that the Chilean Government had been moved to that act by resentment towards the United States for its continued recognition of Calderón, he was to say that the United States regarded the proceeding as an "intentional and unwarranted offense"—"an act of such unfriendly import as to require the immediate suspension of all diplomatic intercourse." Secondly, if Chile refused to allow the formation of any government in Peru which did not pledge its consent to the cession of territory, Trescot was to express "in language as strong as is consistent with the respect due an independent power" the disappointment and dissatisfaction felt by the United States at such a "deplorable policy." Indemnity and guaranties, he repeated, Chile had a right to claim, but annexation as a condition precedent to negotiations would be conquest and dangerous to the best interests of all the republics of this continent.[15]

Trescot's mission was doomed to fail. Before he reached his destination, an inauspicious change took place in Washington. Frelinghuysen succeeded Blaine at the State Department. Unwilling to follow the vigorous course traced by his predecessor, he began curtailing Trescot's powers by new instructions. When the Senate called for the correspondence relating to the attempt to bring about a peace, Frelinghuysen sent everything, including the instructions to Trescot and other communications of the most confidential sort. It is difficult to escape the conviction that the object was to expose Blaine—to discredit him before the American people.

Shamelessly the peace and welfare of sister republics were thrown into the balance of partisan politics. The correspondence was republished in Chile, with the editorial comments of newspapers in the United States hostile to Blaine, and the impression was created that his policy had excited among his countrymen a strong popular opposition, that the Government was now engaged in explaining away what was deemed objectionable.[16] In these circumstances Trescot's presence in South America was worse than useless.

What Trescot might have accomplished if he had not been rendered powerless by Frelinghuysen is a matter of speculation. Given his diplomatic ability and the moral support of a great nation behind him, it is not too much to suppose that he would have brought about a negotiated adjustment far more satisfactory to all parties concerned than the dictated and unstable peace which was finally made. Indeed, Trescot met with an initial success which held out great promise for his mission. Arriving in Chile some three or four weeks before Frelinghuysen's countermanding orders reached him, he began negotiations under his original instructions. Upon his assurance that the United States had no "intention to suggest any solution which would compromise the honor, endanger the true interest, or wound the susceptibilities of either of the belligerents," diplomatic discussions were begun under conditions of the greatest cordiality. The Chilean Government disclaimed intentional offence to the United States in the arrest of Calderón, accepted the good offices that Trescot was authorized to extend, promised to facilitate communication with the provisional Government of

Peru, and proposed conditions of peace. The conditions were hard, but Trescot thought they might be modified by the earnest remonstrance of the United States. At this point came the hampering instructions of Freling-huysen, and Peru and Bolivia were left to their fate. For this phase of the question the reader is referred to the sketch of Frelinghuysen in the next volume.

On still another point Blaine was reversed. His plans for assembling a Pan-American Congress at Washington were rudely set aside. Three weeks before his resignation he had extended the invitations, with President Arthur's concurrence. The harmony that was thought to be a prerequisite to such a conference had not been attained, but the date was set sufficiently far in advance to allow for the adjustment of pending differences. The single purpose of the Congress—to consider methods of preventing war between the nations of America—made a strong appeal, and acceptances soon began to arrive in Washington. Then Frelinghuysen, in a dispatch which was published, forecast the abandonment of the project. He doubted whether "partial confidence," extended to "selected friendly nationalities," would conduce to peace.[17] Blaine was greatly exasperated and addressed to the President a public letter of remonstrance, in which he protested that if the Congress was renounced on the ground that it would offend the powers of Europe for the nations of America to meet to discuss their own affairs, the United States would be deeply humiliated, would lose the friendship of its neighbours, and would add nothing to its prestige in the European world. He begged the President, therefore, not to permit the Government to assume a position so contrary to our traditions and so derogatory to our self-respect. The President was unmoved. After submitting the proposal to Congress, without evoking an expression of views, he instructed Frelinghuysen to withdraw the invitations.

Hostility to Blaine did not end with the reversal of his foreign policy. Once more he was harassed by having his personal integrity questioned. Shortly after the publication of the Chile-Peruvian correspondence, charges were made that one or more ministers who served under Blaine were improperly connected with business transactions in which the intervention of the United States was being sought. The House Committee on Foreign Affairs was ordered to make an investigation. It was clear enough that the chief, no less than the subordinates, was on trial. When called before the committee, Blaine submitted cheerfully to examination, and answered all questions fully. Numerous other witnesses were summoned, and hundreds of pages of testimony were taken. Having failed, after six months of minute inquiry, to uncover any official wrongdoing, the committee made its report. As Blaine was not technically under investigation, no reference was made to him by name; but it was declared that there had not been the "slightest intimation or even hinted suspicion" that any officer in the Department of State had at any time been personally interested in any of the transactions.[18]

In his testimony before the committee Blaine had an opportunity to bring to public view one of the strongest motives for his interest in the War of the Pacific; namely, his desire to prevent European interference. The nationals of England, France, and other continental powers had important financial interests in the belligerent countries, and Blaine feared that unless the conflict was brought to a speedy conclusion, one or more of those powers would find occasion to intervene. The war had its origin, he believed, in the machinations of these private interests, particularly the British. "It is a perfect mistake," he said, slightly off his diplomatic guard, "to speak of this as a Chilean war on Peru. It is an English war on Peru, and I take the responsibility of that assertion. Chile would never have gone into the war one inch but for her backing by English capital." Outside influences caused the war, and outside pressure would be necessary to bring it to an end. "I think it will be demonstrated in the very near future," he declared, "that the United States will have to assume a much more decided tone in South America than the one which I took and which was rescinded, or else it will have to back out of it, and say that it is a domain that does not belong to us, and we surrender it to Europe." In concluding his testimony Blaine said that if there was any chapter in his life of which he was proud, and of the complete and absolute vindication of which in history he felt sure, it was that in connexion with the policy laid down by the Administration of President Garfield with respect to the South American states.[19]

CHAPTER III

CORRESPONDENCE WITH GREAT
BRITAIN

AMERICAN affairs were by no means Blaine's only
concern. His attention was in good part devoted
to European questions, some of which he inherited from
his predecessor, and others of which he himself initiated.
Whatever the issue, he dealt with it vigorously and in
the spirit of intense Americanism which characterized
his whole administration of the State Department.

With England he found the Fortune Bay claims
under discussion. These were claims of American fishermen who had been prevented by the inhabitants of Newfoundland from exercising fishing-rights guaranteed to
them by the Treaty of Washington. After some preliminary correspondence the matter was referred to Blaine
and the British minister at Washington, Sir Edward
Thornton. They promptly reached an agreement by
which Great Britain paid the claims;[20] but unfortunately
the causes which gave rise to them were not removed,
and the fisheries question remained as long as Blaine
was in office—indeed, for years afterwards—to vex the
relations between the two countries.

The Irish question, always capable of producing friction between the United States and England, became
acute about the time Blaine assumed office as Secretary
of State. Trouble arose over the execution in Ireland of

the so-called Coercion Act. This was an exceptional and arbitrary measure, the chief object of which was to authorize the arrest and the detention without trial of persons suspected of being guilty of certain enumerated crimes or other acts tending to interfere with the maintenance of law and order. Under its provisions a number of American citizens of Irish extraction, or pretended citizens, who were travelling or residing in the land of their birth, were from time to time arrested and thrown into prison. They claimed the protection of the United States, and the Secretary of State directed the diplomatic and consular officers to investigate the cases and report the results to the department.

In dealing with the situation, Blaine behaved with singular dignity and restraint. His detractors call him a blusterer. Why he did not on this occasion play the part, they do not explain. He had an excellent opportunity to pose as the champion of American rights against British "aggressions"; but he did not take advantage of it. In his instructions to the American minister at London, James Russell Lowell, he disclaimed any desire on the part of his Government to shield its citizens from the legal consequences of their acts while within British jurisdiction, or to interfere in the administration of the local or general municipal laws of Great Britain. Dispassionately and justly he characterized the act as "repugnant to the principles of civil liberty and personal rights which are the common glory of British and American jurisprudence"; and he declared that whatever the necessity for its enforcement in Ireland, the United States could not view with unconcern its application to American citizens of Irish origin.[21] If it should be so applied, he would insist on a speedy trial, or if no specific charges were brought, he would demand a prompt release. He instructed Lowell to make such representations as would in his judgment conduce to the attainment of these ends.

Lowell's task was not without its difficulties. On the one hand, it was desirable that he should do everything possible to assist Americans in the assertion of their personal rights, and, on the other, it was equally desirable that he should be on his guard against introducing any avoidable element of discord between the two countries. Following the spirit rather than the letter of his instructions, he declined to intercede in behalf of the majority of the prisoners; for upon investigation he found that after being naturalized in the United States they had returned to Ireland and settled down there as permanent residents. They engaged in business, voted, held office, and in general conducted themselves as British subjects. They had misconceived, Lowell thought, the process through which they had passed in assuming American citizenship. They looked upon themselves as Irishmen who had acquired a right to American protection, rather than as Americans who had renounced the claim to Irish nationality. They put off or put on citizenship as seemed most convenient. Moreover, the professed object of some of them was to involve the United States in war with England in the interest of Ireland.[22] In the circumstances Lowell's course was prudent, and it met with the commendation of his chief.

So quietly had the negotiations been conducted that the public remained in ignorance of the matter until after Blaine had left the State Department. Then began a clamour which doubtless had an eye more to the disparagement of Blaine and the conciliation of the Irish vote than to the release of the prisoners. Heated discussions appeared in the newspapers, and the House of Representatives, taking note of the angry outcry, called on the executive for information regarding the arrests. Again Blaine was treated ungraciously by the Administration that he had done his best to serve. Frelinghuysen asserted that the former Secretary had told the President nothing about the arrests, that his own attention was not called to them when he entered upon the duties of his office, and that he had not learned the "real facts" until some weeks afterwards from friends of the prisoners.[23] The implication was obvious: Blaine was guilty of a dereliction of duty. By skilful manipulation it was made to appear that a radically different procedure had been adopted after the "real facts" were known, and to the uninitiated this was made more plausible some months later when most of the prisoners were released. But they were not released through any change of policy at the State Department. From beginning to end the Administration followed the course marked out by Blaine. In justice he should have been rewarded with praise, not blame.

More important than the fisheries claims or the protection of naturalized Americans in Ireland was the interoceanic canal question. This was not a novel issue between the United States and Great Britain, but for some years it had remained in the background. By his famous instructions to Lowell of June 24, 1881, Blaine brought it once more within the field of discussion. Identical instructions were sent to the United States ministers in other European countries. The occasion for this communication was a rumour that the great powers of Europe were considering a joint guaranty of the neutrality of the canal, the construction of which was about to begin under the Wyse and de Lesseps contract. Blaine recognized the necessity for a proper guaranty, but, he averred, that necessity had been foreseen and abundantly provided for in the treaty of 1846 between the United States and the Republic of New Granada. The provisions of this treaty, according to his view, required no "reinforcement, or accession, or assent from any other power."[24]

Blaine's letter elicited no reply from Lord Granville, the British Foreign Secretary, until four months later. Lord Granville then wrote a brief note in which he merely pointed out that the position of Great Britain and the United States with reference to the canal was determined by the convention of April 19, 1850, commonly known as the Clayton-Bulwer Treaty, upon the observance of which Her Majesty's Government would rely with confidence.

By Article I of this treaty the United States and Great Britain agreed that neither would ever obtain exclusive control over a ship-canal by the Nicaragua route; by Article III they engaged to protect the persons and property of parties undertaking to build such a canal; and by Article VIII they further agreed to "extend their protection by treaty stipulations" to the Tehuantepec and Panama routes. This last provision, which Blaine regarded merely as an "inchoate agreement to agree," had not been perfected by the required treaty stipulations; that is, the rights and privileges of the

United States under the prior agreement with Colombia remained unimpaired. Blaine did not deem it necessary, therefore, in a communication dealing exclusively with the Panama route, to mention the Clayton-Bulwer Treaty.

The scope of the discussion soon broadened. The policy of the Administration was a canal under American control—a policy which could not be carried into effect, particularly by the Nicaragua route, unless the Clayton-Bulwer Treaty was radically modified. With a view to obtaining British consent to such a modification Blaine wrote a dispatch to Lowell, dated November 19, 1881, in which he specified the desired changes and set forth at length his arguments in support of them. A week later Lord Granville's note reached Washington, and Blaine wrote again in reply to this. The Secretary of State's arguments were met by Lord Granville in two lengthy dispatches, which were not received at the State Department until January 1882. It fell to Frelinghuysen's lot to continue the correspondence, and for once he did not reverse Blaine.

Unfortunately space will not permit an analysis of this correspondence. Often reprinted, it has been the subject of varied comments, which have generally been derogatory to Blaine.

Blaine's first letter, it has been said, was ignored for four months. Lord Granville himself declared that the delay was "mainly caused by the suspense which so long existed as to the termination of the sad tragedy of the 2d of July"; and that in the mean while the letter received all the consideration which its importance demanded.[25] By some writers the omission of any reference to the Clayton-Bulwer Treaty in Blaine's dispatch of

June 24 has been mildly described as a surprising over-sight; and by others it has been more severely charac-terized as a serious blunder, due possibly to ignorance. The omission may have been singular, but there is no ground for supposing that it was due to an oversight or to ignorance; for the letter was carefully prepared and it received consideration in a full Cabinet meeting ten days before it was sent.[26] The animadversions to which it has given rise had their origin partly, perhaps, in the false assumption that it was a rash performance, for which Blaine alone was responsible, and partly, no doubt, in the equally erroneous belief that he first had his atten-tion called to the treaty of 1850 by Lord Granville. Blaine's position was not without precedent. Webster and Evarts, notably, had contended as Blaine did that the provisions of the Clayton-Bulwer Treaty had not been extended to the Isthmus of Panama.[27]

It has generally been held that Blaine suffered an ignominious rout in his debate with Lord Granville, and for his failure he has been mercilessly reproached. His arguments, it has been said, lacked logical consistency and moral force. Viewing the contest purely as a matter of polemics, some such conclusion may be justified. But Blaine had embarked on no mere academic controversy. He was contending for a policy—a policy which no rea-soning at the moment, however solid, could have brought England to accept. Time and a changing world alone could do this. It is hardly conceivable that posterity will hold Blaine culpable for a failure to accomplish the im-possible. The futility of his efforts to achieve a desirable object should be forgotten; his clear comprehension of the object itself should be remembered.

The diplomatic exchanges between the United States and Great Britain during Blaine's first brief incumbency of the office of Secretary of State were not all controversial in nature. On the contrary, much of the correspondence evinced the most cordial friendship between the two nations. The murderous attack on Garfield, fofowed by his lingering illness and death, brought from all parts of the British Empire a mighty outpouring of sympathy. Kindred peoples were bowed under a common grief. The spectacle, said Blaine, was a touching and memorable one. It bore "eloquent testimony to the closeness with which the two nations are united, as members of a common family, with a common history, a common interest, and a common glory of successful achievement in the path of progress."[28] The evidences of goodwill on the one side were met by a graceful compliment on the other. On the occasion of the celebration of the centennial of the battle of Yorktown the President ordered the forces of the army and navy to salute the British flag. The British promptly reciprocated by assigning to the American flag the most conspicuous place in a notable procession in London. Multitudes cheered along the route, and the flag was given the unique distinction of being carried within the sacred precincts of Palace Yard, where it was grounded opposite the entrance to Westminster Hall, while bands of music played "The Star Spangled Banner."[29]

With the other powers of Europe no issues deserving extended notice engaged the attention of Blaine at this time. The dispatch on the neutralization of the Panama Canal, when communicated to them, drew no controversial replies. The correspondence of the State

Department was largely routine relating to such matters as trade, immigration, and the protection of naturalized Americans. The traditional policy of non-participation in the political affairs of Europe, with its correlative principles of non-interference of European powers in American affairs, was strictly maintained. In his efforts to protect American Jews in Russia, however, Blaine contemplated a procedure which on the surface implies a departure from the traditional policy. He proposed that the United States and Great Britain act conjointly in protecting their nationals of the Jewish faith in Russia, and that the two Governments initiate a movement with other powers to the end that Russia might be influenced by their united representations to ameliorate the conditions of its whole Hebrew population in consonance with the spirit of the age.[30] Nothing came of the proposal, but even if it had been acted upon, no abandonment of the time-honoured policy would have resulted. For the aim was humanitarian, not political; the method one of persuasion, not of force.

In his correspondence with France, Blaine had occasion to take a positive stand on the non-interference principle. He rejected a suggestion of President Grévy that the United States join France and Great Britain in an effort to bring the War of the Pacific to an end, and he used his good offices to prevent French intervention in Venezuela. A dispute had arisen out of the non-payment of sums due to French creditors, and France had broken off diplomatic relations with Venezuela. Forcible collection, involving the occupation of Venezuelan territory, seemed imminent. As other powers, including the United States, had claims against Venezuela, the

Venezuelan authorities appealed to the Government at Washington to act as trustee in the interest of all the creditor nations.[31] Blaine accepted the plan in principle and proposed a general convention whereby the United States should place an agent at Caracas, with power to take the necessary funds from the custom-houses at La Guayra and Puerto Cabello, in case of default. The arrangement was not carried out, yet it is of interest. It foreshadows the financial interventions of a later day.

On driving by the State Department some months after his resignation, Blaine said: "Here I fully expected to raise my Ebenezer for eight years." He spoke without regret, for with the passing of Garfield no hope of achievement remained. With a sense of relief he had put aside the cares of office to wait until opportunity should again knock at his door. How he grasped that opportunity we shall see when we take up, in the next volume in this series, Blaine's second term in office as Secretary of State.

APPENDICES

APPENDIX
TO SKETCH OF SEWARD

BIBLIOGRAPHICAL NOTE

For this study of Seward's work as Secretary of State, use has been made of the volumes from 1861 to 1869 of the official publication, *Diplomatic Correspondence of the United States* (cited as *Dip. Corr.*), and of manuscripts in the archives of the Department of State which contain unpublished portions of the correspondence of the Department of State for the same years. These have been examined in the light of letters and diaries of Seward and his associates and contemporaries, together with biographies and histories covering the eight years of his service. The literature of the period is abundant, and most of the vital source-material has been worked over by competent historians.

The best biography of Seward is Frederick Bancroft's *The Life of William H. Seward* (2 vols., New York, 1900). Among other valuable sources used, besides those mentioned in the footnotes, are the following: *The Life and Works of William H. Seward* (5 vols., Boston, 1883), by George E. Baker (cited as Seward, *Works*); *William H. Seward, an Autobiography, with a Memoir of His Life and Selections from His Letters* (3 vols., New York, 1891), by his son, Frederick W. Seward; *William H. Seward's Travels around the World* (New York, 1873), by his adopted daughter, Olive R. Seward; *William Henry Seward* (Boston, 1899), by T. K. Lothrop in the American Statesmen Series; *The Life of Thurlow Weed* (Vol. I, autobiography, edited by his daughter, Harriet A. Weed; Vol. II, memoirs, edited by his grandson, Thurlow Weed Barnes); *Diary of Gideon Welles*, Secretary of the Navy; *Abraham Lincoln, a*

History (10 vols.), by Nicolay and Hay (cited as Nicolay and Hay); *The Complete Works of Abraham Lincoln* (12 vols.), edited by Nicolay and Hay (cited as Lincoln, *Works*); *Letters of John Hay, and Extracts from His Diary* (printed, but not published); *Evolution of Seward's Mexican Policy* (West Va. Univ. Studies, Series I, Nos. 4, 5, and 6), by J. M. Callahan. Especially valuable for its study of unpublished British records is *Great Britain and the American Civil War* (2 vols., New York and London, 1925), by Ephraim Douglass Adams.

When direct quotation has been made from these works, or others used in preparing this sketch, reference to the source is given in the footnotes.

FOOTNOTES

[1] *Reminiscences of Carl Schurz*, II, 34.

[2] New York *Tribune*, editorial, November 9, 1860.

[3] Seward to Weed, December 4, 1860, *Life of Thurlow Weed*, II, 308.

[4] Lincoln to Seward, December 8, 1860, Lincoln, *Works*, I, 657.

[5] Seward to Weed, December 13, 1860, F. W. Seward, *Seward at Washington*, II, 481.

[6] Swett to Weed, December 10, 1860, *Life of Thurlow Weed*, II, 301.

[7] Davis to Weed, same date, *Ibid.*

[8] Seward to Lincoln, December 16, 1860, Nicolay and Hay, III, 216.

[9] Weed, *Autobiography*, 603–606.

[10] For this proposition see Frederick Bancroft, *Seward*, II, 10, note 2.

[11] Seward to Lincoln, December 26, 1860, Nicolay and Hay, III, 262.

[12] *Ibid.*

[13] Lincoln to Weed, December 17, 1860, *Life of Thurlow Weed*, II, 310.

[14] Lincoln to Gilmer, December 15, 1860, Lincoln, *Works*, VI, 80.

[15] Seward to Lincoln, January 27, 1861, Nicolay and Hay, III, 365.

[16] Seward to Lincoln, December 29 (?), 1860, Frederick W. Seward, *Seward at Washington*, II, 488.

[17] Seward MSS., quoted by Bancroft, Seward, *Works*, II, 497.

[18] Frederick W. Seward, *Seward at Washington*, II, 497.

[19] *Ibid.*, 490.

[20] *Ibid.*, 497.

[21] Lincoln to Seward, January 3, 1861, *Ibid.*, 492.

[22] *Seward at Washington*, II, 505.

[23] Rhodes, *History of the United States from the Compromise of 1850 to the Final Restoration of Home Rule at the South in 1877*, II, 493.

[24] Bigelow, *Retrospections of a Busy Life*, I, 366.

[25] Schleiden to his Government, February 18, 1861, quoted by E. D. Adams, *Great Britain and the American Civil War*, I, 116 (hereinafter cited as E. D. Adams).

[26] Gilmer to Seward, March 12, 1861, Bancroft, *Seward*, II, 547.

[27] Lincoln's remarks, April 13, 1861, to a committee from the Virginia Convention, *Speeches and Presidential Addresses by Abraham Lincoln* (New York, 1907), 149.

[28] Bancroft, *Seward*, Appendix, II, 544, for memorandum of Samuel Ward.

[29] Campbell to Seward, Seward MSS., quoted by Bancroft, *Seward*, II, 115.

[30] Seward's letter of March 8, 1861, Seward, *Works*, II, 518.

[31] Opinion on Sumter, March 15, 1861, *Ibid.*, V, 606, *et seq.*

[32] R. H. Lutz, "Rudolf Schleiden and the visit to Richmond," *Annual Report*, Am. Hist. Assoc., 1915, 210.

[33] E. D. Adams, I, 60.

[34] Helms to Seward, March 24, 1861 (marked "Received March 31"), Department of State, *Consular Letters from Cuba, Havana*, XLI.

[35] McLane to Cass, March 30, 1860, No. 72, and later dispatches; and Cass to McLane, September 20, 1860, Department of State, *Instructions, Mexico*, XVII, 306.

[36] Seward to Tassara, April 2, 1861, *Ibid., Notes to Spanish Legation*, VII, 200.

[37] Nicolay and Hay, III, 436.

[38] *Ibid.*, 438.

[39] *Naval Records of the Rebellion*, IV, 108.

[40] *Ibid.*, 107, 108.

[41] Lincoln, *Works*, VI, 239.

[42] Bancroft, *Seward*, II, 134.

[43] The order, and comments by Welles, may be found in his article in the *Galaxy* for November 1870, page 624. I do not find the order in *Naval Records of the Rebellion*, possibly because Lincoln authorized Welles to disregard it.

[44] E. D. Adams, II, 157, and note.

[45] Seward's circular letter to diplomatic representatives abroad, April 24, 1861, *Dip. Corr.*, *1861*, 18, *et seq.*, and *Digest of International Law*, VII, 573.

[46] Russell to Lyons, May 18, 1861, quoted by E. D. Adams, I, 161.

[47] Russell to Palmerston, August 26, 1861, *Ibid.*, I, 168.

[48] C. F. Adams, *The Life of Charles Francis Adams*, 209.

[49] Adams to Seward, May 21, 1861, No. 2, Department of State, *Dispatches, Great Britain*, LXXVII, 77.

[50] Adams to Seward, July 19, 1861, *Dip. Corr.*, *1861*, 98.

[51] Dayton to Seward, May 30, 1861, *Ibid.*, 200.

[52] Seward to Dayton, June 17, and July 6, *Ibid.*, 210, 216.

[53] Lyons to Russell, March 26, 1861, E. D. Adams, I, 65.

[54] Lyons to Russell, April 23, 1861, *Ibid.*, I, 245.

[55] Dallas to Seward, May 2, 1861, *Dip. Corr.*, *1861*, 84.

[56] Seward's letter home, May 17, 1861, Seward, *Works*, II, 557.

[57] Nicolay and Hay, IV, 276.

[58] Virginia, April 17; Arkansas, May 4; and North Carolina, May 20.

[59] Seward to Adams, April 10, 1861, *Dip. Corr.*, *1861*, 60.

[60] Adams to Seward, June 14, 1861, *Ibid.*, 104.

[61] Bancroft, *Seward*, II, 210.

[62] E. D. Adams, I, 129.

[63] Newcastle to Sir Edmund Head, June 5, 1861, quoted by C. F. Adams in Mass. Hist. Soc. *Proceedings* for November 1911, 65, note.

[64] See Palmerston's letter to Delane, November 11, 1861, *Ibid.*, 54.

[65] London *Times*, leading article, November 28.

[66] *Ibid.*, November 30.

[67] Weed to Seward, several letters, dated December 2, 4, and 6, quoted in Bancroft, *Seward*, II, 231, note.

[68] Bancroft, *Seward*, II, 234.

[69] William H. Russell's letters in the London *Times* of December 3 and 10.

[70] *Life of Thurlow Weed*, I, 640.

[71] Bancroft, *Seward*, II, 243.

[72] Seward to Mrs. Seward, March 13, 1862, F. W. Seward, *Seward at Washington*, III, 72.

[73] *Ibid.*, II, 590.

[74] Welles, *Diary*, I, 195.

[75] *Ibid.*, 196.

[76] Rhodes, *History of the Civil War*, 191.

[77] Lyons to Russell, December 22, 1862; Russell to Lyons, January 3, 1863; E. D. Adams, II, 72.

[78] McMaster, *History of the People of the United States during Lincoln's Administration*, 113.

[79] Russell to Palmerston, October 17, 1861, Spencer Walpole, *Life of Lord John Russell*, II, 344.

[80] Palmerston to Russell, October 18, 1861, Ashley, *Life of Palmerston*, II, 218.

[81] Lyons to Russell, November 29, 1861, E. D. Adams, I, 254.

[82] E. D. Adams, I, 289–292.

[83] Bancroft, *Seward*, II, 290.

[84] Seward to Dayton, July 10, 1862, *Dip. Corr., 1862*, 372.

[85] Seward to Adams, July 28, 1862, *Dip. Corr., 1862*, 157.

[86] Seward to Adams, August 2, 1862, Bancroft, *Seward*, II, 294–296.

[87] Palmerston to Russell, September 14, 1862, Walpole, *Russell*, II, 360.

[88] Russell to Palmerston, September 17, 1862, *Ibid.*, II, 361.

[89] Palmerston to Russell, September 23, 1862, *Ibid.*, II, 362.

[90] C. F. Adams, *Life of Charles Francis Adams*, 321.

[91] Russell to Lyons, March 28, 1863, Lord Newton, *Life of Lord Lyons*, I, 99.

[92] Lyons to Russell, February 24, 1863, E. D. Adams, II, 126.

[93] Lyons to Russell, March 10, 1863, *Ibid.*

[94] Rhodes, *History of the United States*, IV, 366, 367.

[95] Russell to Lyons, March 24, 1863, E. D. Adams, II, 127.

[96] "A vessel sailing from a neutral port with intent to violate a blockade is liable to capture and condemnation as prize from the time of sailing." The Circassian. U. S. Supreme Court Reports, 2 Wallace, 135.

Such capture was valid, however, only while the blockade was effectively maintained at the port. Therefore I cannot agree with Professor Adams when he says (E. D. Adams, II, 137): "There remained but one reasonable supposition as to the intended use of privateers. If the Rams compelled the relaxation of the close blockade the only recourse of the North would be to establish a 'cruising squadron' blockade remote from the shores of the enemy." The right to capture "remote from the shores of the enemy" for breach of blockade was wholly dependent on the effective maintenance of the blockade at the port.

[97] Russell to Lyons, April 7, 1863, E. D. Adams, II, 136.

[98] Seward to Adams, July 11, 1863, H. Ex. Doc. 1, Part I, 38 Cong., 1 Sess., p. 356.

[99] C. F. Adams, *Life of Charles Francis Adams*, 339.

[100] Russell to Palmerston, September 3, 1863, *Later Correspondence of Lord John Russell*, II, 334; and Walpole, *Life of Lord John Russell*, 359, note. This letter is quoted by Professor Adams (E. D. Adams, II, 135, 136) and there erroneously said to have been written about April 3, and applied as tending to show that the "crisis of relations with regard to Southern ship-building in British yards" occurred in March–April 1863, though Adams again refers to the same letter (II, 145) and there gives it the correct date, September 3.

[101] McMaster, *op. cit.*, 300, 364.

[102] Benjamin to Slidell, June 22, 1863, Rhodes, *History of the United States*, IV, 386, note.

[103] Rhodes, *History of the United States*, V, 58, 59.

[104] Seward to Tassara, April 2, 1861, Department of State, *Notes to the Spanish Legation*, VII, 200.

[105] Seward to Bigelow, May 21, 1864, Bancroft, *Seward*, II, 430.

[106] Bancroft, *Seward*, II, 434.

[107] Oberholtzer, *History of the United States since the Civil War*, I, 511.

[108] Bancroft, *Seward*, II, 435.

[109] See C. A. Duniway, "Reasons for French Withdrawal from Mexico," *Annual Report*, Am. Hist. Assoc., 1902, I, 312.

[110] Rhodes, *History of the United States*, VI, 337. See also Bancroft, *Seward*, II, 494.

[111] Tyler Dennett, "Seward's Far Eastern Policy," in *Am. Hist. Review*, XXVIII, 47. For this subject see also the same author's *Americans in Eastern Asia*.

[112] Bancroft, *Seward*, II, 474–475.

[113] F. W. Seward, *Reminiscences of a Wartime Statesman and Diplomat*, 360.

[114] Bancroft, *Seward*, II, 470–479.

[115] Seward, *Travels*, 778.

APPENDIX

TO SKETCH OF WASHBURNE

BIBLIOGRAPHICAL NOTE

Owing to the brevity of Washburne's tenure of office and his lack of influence on American foreign policy, no sources need be cited for the period of his secretaryship. No volume of *Foreign Relations* was published for the year including that period, and no important State papers bear his signature. Information concerning his earlier career and the circumstances of his appointment and resignation has been gathered from secondary works, such as the histories of Rhodes, Channing, and Oberholtzer, from James G. Blaine's *Twenty Years of Congress* (2 vols., Norwich, Conn., 1884–1886) and George S. Boutwell's *Reminiscences of Sixty Years in Public Affairs* (2 vols., New York, 1912). For the period of his diplomatic service, covered by his own *Recollections of a Minister to France* (2 vols., New York, 1887), besides the papers published in *Foreign Relations*, his correspondence relating to the most important incidents was specially communicated and published, in response to a Senate Resolution, under the title *Franco-German War and Insurrection of the Commune* (Washington, Government Printing Office, 1878).

APPENDIX

TO SKETCH OF FISH

BIBLIOGRAPHICAL NOTE

The published American sources for the study of Hamilton Fish's diplomacy are reasonably adequate, though scattered. *Foreign Relations* is especially defective in that no volume was published for the year 1869. The official papers relating to the important affairs of that year, however, have mostly been printed in Senate and House Documents, as have those relating to negotiations of later years, such as the correspondence regarding Cuba initiated by Fish's instruction of November 5, 1876, which were excluded from *Foreign Relations*. These numerous documents are referred to in the footnotes. Examination of the files of the Department of State has resulted in the addition of but little significant unpublished material.

For the most important episode of Fish's secretaryship, the negotiations concerning the *Alabama* claims, the diplomatic documents themselves are inadequate, since the preliminary exchanges of views were conducted mainly through informal conversations not officially recorded. Source material relating to these is to be found in several secondary works. The paper on "The Treaty of Washington: Before and After" by Charles Francis Adams, Jr., published in his *Lee at Appomatox and Other Papers* (New York, 1903), is based largely on Fish's diary, from which numerous extracts are given. J. C. Bancroft Davis, who was Assistant Secretary of State at the time, has incorporated much first-hand material in his *Mr. Fish and the Alabama Claims* (New York, 1893). Extracts from Davis's manuscript journal are printed in the chapter entitled "The Geneva Arbitration" in Vol. I of John Bassett Moore's *History and Digest of the International Arbitrations to which the United States Has Been a Party* (Washington, Government Printing Office, 1898), which gives also a full but succinct account of the proceedings of the high commission which concluded the Treaty of Washington. The most significant contribution to the British side of these informal negotiations is contained in the first volume of Lucien Wolf's *Life of the First Marquess of Ripon* (London, 1921). Indispensable material bearing on both the *Alabama* claims and the Dominican question is found in Vol. IV of E. L. Pierce's *Memoir and Letters of Charles Sumner* (Boston, 1893). Some light is thrown on the latter question in the article of J. D. Cox, Secretary of the Interior at the time, "How Judge Hoar Ceased to be Attorney General," in the *Atlantic Monthly* for August 1895.

There are as yet no edition of Fish's papers and no biography based upon them. Brief sketches are given in the memorial address delivered before the legislature of the state of New York by Senator George F. Edmunds of Vermont, April 5, 1894 (*Proceedings*, published by J. B. Lyon, Albany), and in the hundred-page monograph, *Hamilton Fish*, by A. Elwood Corning (New York, 1918).

FOOTNOTES

[1] E. L. Pierce, *Memoir and Letters of Charles Sumner*, IV, 388, 410, 413. C. F. Adams, Jr., "The Treaty of Washington" in *Lee at Appomatox and other Papers*, 103–104, 150–155.

[2] Sen. Ex. Doc. 11, 41 Cong., 3 Sess., pp. 2–5. The instructions are dated May 15, 1869.

[3] Sumner to Motley, June 11, Pierce, IV, 409–410.

[4] Sen. Ex. Doc. 11, 41 Cong., 3 Sess., pp. 5–11; Adams, 117.

[5] J. C. B. Davis, *Mr. Fish and the Alabama Claims*, 45–46.

[6] Adams, 125–126.

[7] *Foreign Relations, 1873*, III, 329–336.

[8] Pierce, IV, 414; Adams, 156–157.

[9] H. Ex. Doc. 160, 41 Cong., 2 Sess., pp. 75–83.

[10] *Ibid.*, 13–17, 22–27.

[11] Quoted from Fish's diary, Adams, 119.

[12] H. Ex. Doc. 160, 41 Cong., 2 Sess., pp. 69–70.

[13] Sen. Ex. Doc. 34, 41 Cong., 3 Sess., pp. 2–3.

[14] Babcock's testimony before a special committee, June 9, 1870, *Sen. Report* 234, 41 Cong., 2 Sess., pp. 34–36, 189.

[15] Sen. Ex. Doc. 34, 41 Cong., 3 Sess., p. 6.

[16] *Sen. Report* 234, 41 Cong., 2 Sess., pp. 188–189.

[17] J. D. Cox, "How Judge Hoar Ceased to be Attorney General," *Atlantic Monthly*, August 1895, 167–168.

[18] Sen. Ex. Doc. 17, 41 Cong., 3 Sess., pp. 80–86, 94–95, 105–108.

[19] Pierce, IV, 434–435; Adams, 228.

[20] Adams, 218; Cox, 168–171.

[21] Pierce, IV, 443.

[22] Adams, 222–223.

[23] *Ibid.*, 216–217.

[24] *Congressional Globe*, 41 Cong., 2 Sess., 4506–4507. The statement that the resolution simply "passed the House," made in Latané's *Diplomatic Relations of the United States and Spanish America* (p. 151), and in Chadwick's *The Relations of the United States and Spain* (p. 311), is misleading as to the effect of this action.

[25] Department of State, *Instructions. Spain*, XVI, 125–129.

[26] *Foreign Relations, 1871*, 697–773.

[27] *Foreign Relations, 1870*, 195; *1871*, 291.

[28] *Foreign Relations, 1870*, 68–69, 116.

[29] *Ibid.*, 193–194.

[30] *Ibid.*, 303, 305.

[31] *Ibid.*, 396, 398.

[32] Adams, 158–159.

[33] *Foreign Relations, 1870*, 433.

[34] Adams, 137, 140; Pierce, IV, 444; Sen. Ex. Doc. 11, 41 Cong., 3 Sess., pp. 15–16.

[35] Adams, 160.

[36] *Ibid.*, 162.

[37] Sen. Ex. Doc. 11, 41 Cong., 3 Sess., pp. 16–37.

[38] Adams, 162.

[39] J. B. Moore, *International Arbitrations*, I, 523–525; Davis, 59–64. The plan of procedure is shown to have been adopted by the British Cabinet on the suggestion of Lord Tenterden in Lucien Wolf's *Life of the First Marquess of Ripon*, I, 239.

[40] Moore, I, 525–526.

[41] Adams, 169.

[42] Moore, I, 526–531. The memorandum and notes made by Davis on the conversation are quoted in full. The notes exchanged with Sir Edward Thornton are printed in *Foreign Relations, 1871*, 496–498.

[43] Davis, 77; April 23, 1872, Department of State, *Instructions, Great Britain*, XXIII, 110, No. 184.

[44] Moore, I, 541–544, 629–637.

[45] *Ibid.*, 716–719. The provision for reference to a commission is contained in Article XXIII.

[46] Fish to Schenck, telegram, March 1, 1872, Department of State, *Instructions, Great Britain*, XXIII, 42. With this exception, the papers connected with the Geneva arbitration are printed in *Papers Relating to the Treaty of Washington*, included as Part II of *Foreign Relations, 1872*. An authoritative summary is given by Moore.

[47] *Foreign Relations, 1872*, Part I, 580–584.

[48] *Foreign Relations, 1873*, Part I, 842–843.

[49] *Ibid.*, 932–933.

[50] Nos. 323, 345, 366, Department of State, *Instructions, Spain*, XVI, 442–449, 474–480, 494–502.

[51] Nos. 391, 395, *Ibid.*, 518, 520–525, 527–528.

[52] The correspondence relating to the *Virginius* incident is printed in *Foreign Relations, 1874.*

[53] Department of State, *Instructions, Spain*, XVI, 534.

[54] *Foreign Relations, 1874*, 859–863 (with omissions); Department of State, *Instructions, Spain*, XVII, 13.

[55] Telegram, February 6, 1874, Department of State, *Instructions, Spain*, XVII, 177.

[56] *Foreign Relations, 1875*, 1115.

[57] Nos. 182, 242, 246, Department of State, *Instructions, Spain*, XVII, 251, 315–317, 322.

[58] This instruction, with a certain amount of accompanying correspondence, was first printed in H. Ex. Doc. 90, 44 Cong., 1 Sess. The practically complete correspondence was published in Sen. Ex. Doc. 213, 54 Cong., 1 Sess. (reprinted in Sen. Ex. Doc. 885, 55 Cong., 2 Sess.).

[59] Telegram to Schenck for transmission, Department of State, *Instructions, Great Britain*, XXIV, 154–155.

[60] H. Ex. Doc. 160, 41 Cong., 2 Sess., pp. 69–70; *Foreign Relations, passim.*

[61] Latané, *Diplomatic Relations of the United States and Spanish America*, 173.

[62] H. Ex. Docs. 90, 100, 44 Cong., 1 Sess.

[63] *Foreign Relations, 1877*, 496.

[64] Sen. Ex. Doc. 26, 45 Cong., 3 Sess., pp. 76, 80.

[65] Fish to Thornton, August 21, 1873, Sen. Ex. Doc. 44, 45 Cong., 2 Sess.

[66] The papers referred to in this section are printed in *Correspondence in Relation to the Proposed Interoceanic Canal between the Atlantic and Pacific Oceans, the Clayton-Bulwer Treaty and the Monroe Doctrine* (Washington, Government Printing Office, 1885).

[67] Senator Edmunds, in his memorial address (p. 59) states: "During the last administration of President Grant, Mr. Fish was engaged in important correspondence with the British government on the subject of the Clayton-Bulwer

treaty, in which he maintained . . . that the United States were no longer bound by its provisions." The statement is repeated by Corning (p. 56) and appears in a different form in W. F. Johnson's *Four Centuries of the Panama Canal* (p. 75). An examination of the files in the Department of State for the entire second Administration has revealed no trace of any such correspondence.

[68] *Foreign Relations, passim.*

[69] For reorganization of the Department of State, see Gaillard Hunt, *The Department of State* (New Haven, 1914).

APPENDIX

TO SKETCH OF EVARTS

BIBLIOGRAPHICAL NOTE

There is no biography of William Maxwell Evarts. We are informed that the material collected by Mr. Sherman Evarts for a life of his father contains nothing not now in print on the period of Evarts's secretaryship. The material from which this sketch was prepared consists principally of the official correspondence of the department during his incumbency. Much important material has been printed in the appropriate volumes of *Papers Relating to the Foreign Relations of the United States* (Washington, 1861—), but an examination of the unprinted files of the State Department revealed matter of considerable significance hitherto unpublished.

Moore's *Digest of International Law* (8 vols., Washington, 1906) is invaluable for brief discussions of the international issues of the period, often with important excerpts from Evarts's official writings. His legal career, but not his diplomacy, is reflected in *Arguments and Speeches of William Maxwell Evarts* (3 vols., New York, 1919), edited by his son.

Among the books dealing with the Hayes Administration the most valuable is C. R. Williams, *Life of Rutherford Birchard Hayes* (2 vols., New York, 1914). J. W. Burgess, *The Administration of President Hayes* (New York, 1916), presents a calm survey of the politics of the time. The supplementary eighth volume of James Ford Rhodes's well-known *History of the United States* (New York, 1919) deals very little with the foreign affairs handled by Evarts, except for the excellent chapter on the Chinese immigration question, based on a thesis prepared for the late historian by David M. Matteson, the indexer of the publication now in the reader's hands. James G. Blaine's *Twenty Years of Congress, 1860–1880* (2 vols., Norwich, Conn., 1884–1886), is a brilliant review of the political history of those decades seen through partisan eyes. Anything that the author of that unique book *The Education of Henry Adams* has to say is always worth reading. The *Biography of James G. Blaine*, by Gail Hamilton (Norwich, 1895), is informative, but not definitive. Senator George H. Hoar's *Autobiography of Seventy Years* (2 vols., New York, 1903) is the best political autobiography for the period. The volume *Ebenezer Rockwood Hoar, A Memoir* (New York, 1911), prepared by Moorfield Storey and E. W. Emerson, contains some letters exchanged by Hoar and Evarts on the Chief Justiceship.

FOOTNOTES

[1] C. R. Williams, *Life of Rutherford Birchard Hayes*, II, 17.

[2] *Ibid.*, II, 19.

[3] *Ibid.*, II, 24.

[4] *Ebenezer Rockwood Hoar, A Memoir*, 138.

[5] *Ibid.*, 141–143.

[6] *Ibid.*, 235.

[7] G. Hamilton, *Biography of James G. Blaine*, V, 303.

[8] *Education of Henry Adams*, 245.

[9] Department of State, *Instructions, Great Britain*, XXV, 397; *France*, XX, 46; *Netherlands*, XV, 347; *Notes to the French Legation*, IX, 360.

[10] St. Clair McKelway in the *Brooklyn Eagle*.

[11] Case of Edward O'M. Condon, *Foreign Relations, 1878*, 258, 278, 280.

[12] Article XVIII of the Treaty of Washington allowed citizens of the United States to take fish in common with British subjects in certain specified territorial waters of British North America, for ten years, with provision for continuation after that time if not denounced. Article XIX

gave British subjects the right to take fish in common with American citizens in territorial waters of the United States on the eastern coast north of the thirty-ninth parallel of north latitude; and Article XXI provided reciprocity of importation between the United States and Canada, including Prince Edward Island, of ocean fish and fish oil. Article XXII stipulated that "inasmuch as it is asserted by the Government of Her Britannic Majesty that the privileges accorded by Article XVIII to the citizens of the United States are of greater value than those accorded by Articles XIX and XXI of this treaty to the subjects of Her Britannic Majesty, and this assertion is not admitted by the Government of the United States," a mixed commission should determine this question and the amount of any compensation which in its opinion ought to be paid to the British Government.

For this phase of the Treaty of Washington, see sketch of Hamilton Fish, *ante*, p. 170 and p. 171.

[13] Note to the Italian minister, J. B. Moore, *Digest of International Law*, VII, 75.

[14] Evarts to Bingham, Department of State, October 25, 1879, *Instructions, Japan*, II, 543–544.

[15] *Ibid., Instructions, China*, III, 70–71.

[16] *Ibid., Instructions, Colombia*, XVII, 192.

[17] *Ibid., Instructions, Netherlands*, XV, 314, 317, 354; *Notes to the Venezuelan Legation*, I, 172, 180, 182.

[18] *Ibid., Instructions, Costa Rica*, XVII, 322, 342, 352, 369, 370, 392.

[19] *Ibid., Instructions, Austria*, III, 105, also pp. 54, 55, 73, 78, 90, 118; and *Credences*, V, 370.

[20] *Ibid., Instructions, Chile*, XVI, 273. See also Sen. Ex. Doc. 26, 46 Cong., 3 Sess., Vol. I, for correspondence in regard to American efforts to bring about peace.

[21] *Ibid., Instructions, Great Britain*, XXV, 9; also *Credences*, V, 236, for Evarts's note to the Guatemalan Minister of Foreign Affairs.

[22] Moore, *Digest*, VI, 432.

[23] Department of State, *Instructions, Denmark*, XV, 224; *Instructions, France*, XX, 62, 181; *Instructions, Great Britain*, XXV, 536.

[24] *Ibid., Instructions, Netherlands*, XV, 346. A similar confidential instruction was sent to the United States minister to Venezuela, *Instructions, Venezuela*, III, 76.

[25] Moore, *Digest*, III, 15.

[26] Evarts to Dichman, July 31, 1880, *Ibid.*, III, 16. For Evarts's careful distinction between the guaranteed neutrality of any canal route across the Isthmus in Colombian territory and "the rules of neutrality which Colombia, as a sovereign state, may feel called upon to enforce in all her territory as towards other nations who may be at war," see *Ibid.*, III, 27.

[27] Sen. Ex. Doc. 112, 46 Cong., 2 Sess., Vol. IV.

[28] Outrey to Evarts, *Foreign Relations, 1880*, 385.

[29] Dichman to Evarts, November 6, 1880, *Ibid., 1881*, 337.

[30] Moore, *Digest*, III, 23–24.

[31] Department of State, *Instructions, Costa Rica*, XVII, 366, 379, 383.

[32] For reference to important House and Senate documents regarding canal policy, see Moore, *Digest*, III, 15–17.

[33] Evarts to Foster, March 26, 1879, Department of State, *Instructions, Mexico*, XIX, 548; cf. XX, 1–4.

[34] Evarts to Foster, August 13, 1878, *Foreign Relations, 1878*, 572.

[35] Evarts to Foster, September 20, 1878, *Foreign Relations, 1878*, 612.

[36] Evarts to Foster, April 24, 1879, Department of State, *Instructions, Mexico*, XIX, 580.

[37] *Ibid.*, 483.

[38] *Ibid.*, 567.

[39] Evarts to Foster, *Foreign Relations, 1880*, 781. Most of the correspondence with Mexico with regard to the Ord order

and its repeal is printed in the appropriate volumes of *Foreign Relations*.

[40] Department of State, *Notes to Russian Legation*, VII, 259.

[41] *Ibid., Instructions, Turkey*, III, 247.

[42] There are innumerable notes on the question, between Evarts and the Spanish minister in Washington, most of them unpublished. See *Ibid., Notes to Spanish Legation*, IX, 496, *et seq.*, and X, 72, 90, 96, 101, 105, 114. Steps were taken also to prevent attacks upon Mexico from the American side of the border. See *Instructions, Mexico*, XIX, 348, 362, 388, 422; XX, 155, 176, 189; and *Notes to Mexican Legation*, VIII, 97, 102, 107, 218.

[43] *Ibid., Instructions, Venezuela*, III, 54.

[44] *Ibid., Instructions, Germany*, XV, 594.

[45] *Ibid., Notes to German Legation*, IX, 328; Moore, *Digest*, I, 538–539, gives a very brief summary of the situation in Evarts's time. See also *Instructions, Great Britain*, XXV, 405, 453; *Notes to British Legation*, XVII, 388, 417, 421, 427; *Notes to German Legation*, IX, 331; X, 61.

[46] Department of State, *Instructions, Russia*, XVI, 137. See also *Ibid.*, 128, 139.

[47] *Foreign Relations, 1880,* 875.

[48] *Ibid.*, 804.

[49] *Ibid.*, 35.

[50] Department of State, *Instructions, Germany*, VI, 414.

[51] Moore, *Digest*, II, 681; Department of State, *Notes to Turkish Legation*, I, 218, March 30, 1878.

[52] Department of State, *Instructions, Turkey*, III, 336. A masterly statement of the significance of extra-territorial status to the individual is contained in an instruction from Evarts to Maynard, April 17, 1877, *Ibid.*, 235–238.

[53] *Ibid., Instructions, Japan*, II, 589; III, 2, 3, 13, 26; *Notes to British Legation*, XVIII, 419, 547. See also the case of Cheers, where an English naval officer refused to surrender

a' deserting American seaman in Yokohama. Evarts wrote that such practices would be "most offensive to the sentiments of our people as savouring too much of the historical claim of the right of search, in regard to which the citizens of this country are properly sensitive." *Instructions, Great Britain*, XXV, 624. For the facts, see Moore, *Digest* II, 643.

[54] *Ibid., Instructions, Japan*, II, 493.

[55] *Ibid.*, 408.

[56] *Ibid., Instructions, China*, III, 120.

In Madagascar the refusal of the French and English consuls to hear complaints brought by Americans against their respective subjects drew an earnest protest from Evarts. *Ibid., Instructions, France*, XIX, 523, and *Instructions, Great Britain*, XXV, 81. Of the Moroccan question there is an excellent summary in Moore, *Digest*, II, 747, but there is a considerable amount of unpublished material in the files of the Department of State.

[57] For conditions in California see C. Chapman, *A History of California; the American Period*, 415–421; J. F. Rhodes, *History of the United States*, VIII, 180–196.

[58] Williams, *op. cit.*, II, 214.

[59] Department of State, *Instructions, China*, III, 20–23.

[60] *Ibid.*, 126. See also *Ibid.*, 121, 148, 154, 189.

[61] For negotiations see *Ibid., Notes to Japanese Legation*, I, 143, 179; *Notes from Japanese Legation*, II, III, and *Instructions, Japan*, II, 396–585; *Instructions, Great Britain*, XXV, 340; *Notes to British Legation*, XVIII, 25, 42; *Notes to German Legation*, IX, 458. Moore, *Digest*, V, 752–753, has a very brief discussion.

[62] The data on Evarts's treaty negotiations are almost entirely unpublished. Of course, where they were conducted personally in Washington there is very little record even in the State Department archives; notes to and from the foreign legation in question and occasional memoranda of interviews, sometimes supplemented by a survey sent to the American

minister accredited to the government concerned, are all we can expect to find there. When negotiations were carried on at a foreign capital, the instructions to our representative there are exceedingly interesting as indicative of Evarts's legalistic attitude.

In regard to extradition, negotiations were conducted with Colombia, Great Britain, Greece, Denmark, and the Netherlands. See Department of State, *Notes to Netherlands Legation*, VII, 470–566 VIII 1–7 (this last a particularly valuable note for one who would see Evarts at work on a legal problem), 13–20; *Instructions, Denmark*, XV, 206; *Instructions, Greece*, I, 185, 187; *Notes to British Legation*, XVII, 389–455; *Instructions, Colombia*, XVII, 68, 79, 81, 120, 138, 236; and *Foreign Relations* for 1877, 1878, 1879, 1880.

For discussion of special extradition problems, see *Instructions, Portugal*, XV, 188; *Notes to Mexican Legation*, VIII, 133; *Instructions, Colombia*, XVII, 142; *Instructions, Great Britain*, XXV, 314; and instructions of March 5, 1879 to Lowell in Spain, *Foreign Relations, 1879*.

New consular conventions were concluded with Belgium, the Netherlands, and Italy. See *Notes to Belgian Legation*, VII, 117–238; *Notes to Netherlands Legation*, VII, 475–555; *Instructions, Netherlands*, XV, 312–349; *Notes to Italian Legation*, VII, 359–398.

Conventions regarding trade-marks were made with Brazil and Great Britain, and discussed with Italy. See *Instructions, Brazil*, XVII, 92–119; *Notes to Italian Legation*, VII, 442, 462. There were negotiations for a commercial treaty with Roumania, *Instructions, Roumania*, I, 16; and *Foreign Relations* for 1878 and 1879. A treaty of somewhat different nature was the one signed by Evarts with the Samoan special envoy, January 17, 1878. The only correspondence on it is in *Notes from Other States*, II.

APPENDIX

TO SKETCH OF BLAINE

BIBLIOGRAPHICAL NOTE

The sketch of Blaine, published partly in this volume and partly in the next, is based mainly on the *Foreign Relations of the United States* for the years 1879–1882 and 1888–1892. Additional primary material is found in special reports of the United States Senate and House of Representatives. Sen. Ex. Doc. 26, 46 Cong., 3 Sess.; Sen. Ex. Doc. 79, 47 Cong., 1 Sess.; and *H. Rept.* 1790, 47 Cong., 1 Sess., relate to Blaine's efforts to make peace between Chile, Peru, and Bolivia; Sen. Ex. Doc. 106, 50 Cong., 2 Sess., and *H. Rept.* 3885, 50 Cong., 2 Sess., relate to the Bering Sea controversy; and various similar documents elucidate the Samoan question. H. Ex. Doc. 91, 52 Cong., 1 Sess., contains not only the diplomatic correspondence relating to the Chilean imbroglio, but also the correspondence with naval officials and the report of the commissioners appointed to make an inquiry into the *Baltimore* affair. The documentary material concerning the first Pan-American conference is found in *International American Conference, 1889–1890, Minutes of the Conference* (Washington, 1890), and in *International American Conference, 1889–1890, Reports of Committees and Discussions thereon* (4 vols., Washington, 1890). The published documents here enumerated provide abundant sources for the history of the foreign relations of the United States during Blaine's incumbency. Furthermore, the manuscript materials in the Bureau of Indexes and Archives at Washington were accessible to the author, and from this source he was able to obtain new light on certain moot points of Blaine's diplomacy.

Among the more important secondary sources are the

following: John B. Henderson's *American Diplomatic Questions* (New York, 1901); John W. Foster's *A Century of American Diplomacy* (Boston, 1901) and *American Diplomacy in the Orient* (Boston, 1903); Freeman Snow's *Treaties and Topics in American Diplomacy* (Boston, 1894); Ira D. Travis's *The History of the Clayton-Bulwer Treaty* (Ann Arbor, Mich., 1900); A. B. Hart's *Foundations of American Diplomacy* (New York, 1901); D. R. Dewey's *National Problems* (New York, 1905); A. C. Coolidge's *The United States as a World Power* (New York, 1908); C. R. Fish's *American Diplomacy* (New York, 1919); J. B. Moore's *Principles of American Diplomacy* (New York, 1918); W. F. Johnson's *America's Foreign Relations* (2 vols., New York, 1921); John H. Latané's *America as a World Power* (New York, 1905) and *The United States and Latin-America* (New York, 1920); and Graham H. Stuart's *Latin-America and the United States* (New York, 1922). Works on the War of the Pacific are numerous. The following are representative: Sir Clements Markham's *The War Between Peru and Chile* (London, 1882); M. F. Paz Soldán's *Guerra de Chile contra el Perú y Bolivia* (Buenos Aires, 1884); Victor M. Maúrtua's *The Question of the Pacific* (Philadelphia, 1901); V. A. Belaunde's *Nuestra Cuestión con Chile* (Lima, 1919); A. V. Hancock's *A History of Chile* (Chicago, 1893); Diego Barros Arana's *Histoire de la guerre du Pacifique* (2 vols., Paris, 1881); and Gonzalo Búlnes's *La Guerra del Pacífico* (3 vols., Valparaiso, 1912–1919).

Of a half-dozen or more lives of Blaine, Edward Stanwood's *James Gillespie Blaine* (New York, 1905), in the American Statesmen series, is by far the best. A volume by Gail Hamilton (Abigail Dodge) entitled *Biography of James G. Blaine* (Norwich, Conn., 1895) is fuller and in some respects more informing, though less objective, than the book by Stanwood. The rest, published while Blaine was still alive or soon after his death, are of little value except for an occasional bit of information not easily obtainable elsewhere. The *Letters of*

Mrs. James G. Blaine (2 vols., New York, 1908), edited by Harriet S. Blaine Beale, present a captivating view of Blaine's family life and at the same time throw light upon his public career. Much interesting information can be gleaned from the biographies and memoirs of his contemporaries. Among these T. C. Smith's *The Life and Letters of James Abram Garfield* (2 vols., New Haven, 1925) is particularly enlightening.

FOOTNOTES

[1] T. C. Smith, *The Life and Letters of James Abram Garfield*, II, 1052.

[2] *Congressional Record*, June 5, 1876, 44 Cong., 1 Sess., Vol. IV, pp. 3604–3609.

[3] Gail Hamilton (Mary Abigail Dodge), *Biography of James Gillespie Blaine*, 85.

[4] James G. Blaine, *Twenty Years of Congress*, I, 572; II, 484.

[5] J. V. Lastarria, *Obras*, V, 373.

[6] James G. Blaine, *Political Discussions*, 411.

[7] Blaine to Morgan, June 16, 1881, *Foreign Relations, 1881*, 768.

[8] Blaine to Morgan, November 28, 1881, *Foreign Relations, 1881*, 815.

[9] See *Bulletin of the American Geographical Society*, Vol. XXIX, Nos. 2 and 3, for articles by Matías Romero on the Mexico-Guatemala boundary question.

[10] Diego Barros Arana, *Histoire de la guerre du Pacifique*, *première partie*, 1, 15.

[11] Osborn to Evarts, April 3, 1879, *Foreign Relations, 1879*, 160.

[12] Blaine to Christiancy, May 9, 1881, *Foreign Relations, 1881*, 909.

[13] Diego Barros Arana, *op. cit.*, *deuxième partie*, 112; Osborn to Evarts, March 5, 1880, MSS., Department of State.

[14] Blaine to Hurlbut, June 15, 1881, *Foreign Relations, 1881*, 914; Blaine to Kilpatrick, June 15, 1881, *Ibid.*, 131.

[15] Blaine to Trescot, November 30, 1881, *Foreign Relations, 1881*, 142.

[16] Trescot to Blaine, January 27, 1882, *Ibid.*, *1882*, 63.

[17] Frelinghuysen to Trescot, January 9, 1882, *Ibid.*, 58.

[18] *Chile-Peruvian Investigation, H. Rept.* 1790, p. 21.

[19] *Ibid.*, 217, 353.

[20] Blaine to Sir Edward Thornton, May 6, 1881, May 28, 1881, *Foreign Relations, 1881*, 586, 589.

[21] Blaine to Lowell, May 26, 1881, June 2, 1881, *Ibid.*, 530–532.

[22] *Ibid.*, 206, 504, 882; Lowell to Blaine, June 4, 1881, No. 562, Department of State, *Dispatches, Great Britain*, CXLVI.

[23] Frelinghuysen to Lowell, April 25, 1882, *Foreign Relations, 1882*, 232.

[24] *Foreign Relations, 1881*, 537.

[25] Hoppin to Blaine, November 11, 1881, *Foreign Relations, 1881*, 549.

[26] T. C. Smith, *The Life and Letters of James Abram Garfield*, II, 1167.

[27] J. B. Moore, *Digest*, III, 11, 14.

[28] Blaine to Lowell, November 14, 1881, Department of State, *Instructions, Great Britain*, XXVI.

[29] *Foreign Relations, 1881*, 550.

[30] Blaine to Lowell, November 22, 1881, Department of State, *Instructions, Great Britain*, XXVI.

[31] Camacho to Blaine, August 13, 1881, *Foreign Relations, 1881*, 1219.

INDEX

Prepared by DAVID M. MATTESON

THE
AMERICAN SECRETARIES OF STATE
AND THEIR DIPLOMACY

VOLUME VIII

THE AMERICAN SECRETARIES OF STATE AND THEIR DIPLOMACY

SAMUEL FLAGG BEMIS

EDITOR

J. FRANKLIN JAMESON
H. BARRETT LEARNED
JAMES BROWN SCOTT

ADVISORY BOARD

NEW YORK
COOPER SQUARE PUBLISHERS, INC.
1963

MANUFACTURED IN THE UNITED STATES OF AMERICA
NOBLE OFFSET PRINTERS, INC., 400 LAFAYETTE ST., NEW YORK, N. Y.

VOLUME VIII

TABLE OF CONTENTS

EDITOR'S PREFACE

TO VOLUME VIII

THE feud in the Republican party which arose out of President Hayes's dismissal of the spoilsman Chester A. Arthur from the collectorship of the port of New York led by way of revenge of the "Stalwarts" to the nomination of Arthur as candidate of the party for Vice-President in the campaign of 1880, and to his subsequent elevation to the position of Acting-President of the United States after the assassination of Garfield. The advent of Arthur in succession to Garfield really meant as much of a political overturn, as far as the Department of State was concerned, as would have followed a change of parties. The brilliant if not always stable Blaine was succeeded by Frederick T. Frelinghuysen, a man without experience in diplomacy or in large affairs. The confused situation brought about by the changes in instructions by the new Secretary to the ministers in Chile and Peru, for example, shows the Department of State functioning at its lowest grade of efficiency. It has been the task of Professor Brown to sketch the diplomacy of Acting-President Arthur's Secretary of State.

Frelinghuysen and his successors to 1897 had fewer important foreign questions to deal with than have confronted the Department of State in any other equal stretch of years. American diplomacy from 1881 to 1897 was really at its most passive period. The attention of the country during those years was engrossed with problems of political and social legislation arising out of the settlement and exploitation of the Far West and the new economic revolution which was rapidly transforming life in the United States from the traditional agrarian to a new urban and industrial character.

Fortunate is the country whose foreign relations are devoid of spectacular incidents or pressing international issues. The quiet of peace, blessed and profound peace, characterized the administration of the Department of State in the days of Thomas F. Bayard, whose career and whose routine diplomatic problems have been placed before the reader by Professor Shippee.

Blaine was a man who was bound to produce colourful happenings in our foreign relations in even the quietest of times. Professor Lockey here resumes his study of Blaine as Secretary of State, during that statesman's second tenure of the Department, under President Harrison. In the principal episodes of Blaine's second term, the Bering Sea controversy, and the meeting of the first Pan-American Conference, the reader follows through the remainder of his interesting career as a diplomatist. The failure of the American contention in the Bering Sea dispute was offset by Blaine's success in achieving a beginning of the International American Conferences which have been such a conspicuous part of American foreign affairs in our generation.

John W. Foster is the only Secretary of State sketched in this volume who came into the office with a wealth of diplomatic experience behind him. Mr. Castle, whose knowledge of our foreign affairs is illuminated by practical experience in the administration of the Department, has presented Secretary Foster at work, among his other tasks, in the hopeless Bering Sea case, and in nursing the Hawaiian situation toward annexation, an aim which was frustrated temporarily by the return of President Cleveland to power in 1893.

Cleveland's second Administration brought two more Secretaries of State who had had no special training nor experience for the management of foreign affairs. The first of them, Walter Q. Gresham, handled the diplomatic business of the Government with dignity and integrity, but left no mark on American policy. He was a negative character whose dealings, under Cleveland's superior direction, with the Hawaiian problem — the only important one which confronted him — would not generally receive the plaudits of students of our history who are privileged to look back at it from the vantage-point of a third of a century.

In treating of the diplomacy of Richard Olney, Mr. Schuyler has a far more positive and aggressive personality than the politician Gresham. Olney's comparatively brief tenure of office gave him at the outset a paramount issue. His decisive championing of the Monroe Doctrine, with Cleveland's guidance, impressed his country more than had any Secretary of State between Seward and Hay. The Olney note to Great Britain on the Venezuela boundary controversy was a trumpet-blast to the world which announced the approach of a new era for American affairs — the imminent rise of the United States as a world power. It was a dramatic close to a dull but happy period of American diplomacy recorded in the activities of the Secretaries included in this volume.

S. F. B.

FREDERICK THEODORE FRELINGHUYSEN

SECRETARY OF STATE

DECEMBER 19, 1881, to MARCH 5, 1885

BY

PHILIP MARSHALL BROWN, A.M., LL.D.

PROFESSOR OF INTERNATIONAL LAW
IN PRINCETON UNIVERSITY

FREDERICK T. FRELINGHUYSEN

FROM AN ENGRAVING BY H. B. HALL & SONS

Fred^k T. Frelinghuysen

FREDERICK THEODORE
FRELINGHUYSEN

CHAPTER I

A "STALWART" REPUBLICAN
SECRETARY

WHEN the nomination of James G.
Blaine's successor was sent to the
Senate by President Arthur on
December 12, 1881, the Springfield
Republican observed: "Mr. Freling-
huysen is understood to hold that the American eagle
should not strain his naturally fine voice by shrill and
prolonged screaming on small occasions." And the *Nation* expressed the belief that "Mr. Frelinghuysen was
a public man of large experience and a conservative
spirit, likely to take us safely through the muddles in
which we have recently become involved."

These opinions would seem to reflect general public
sentiment, which had been growing more and more res-
tive regarding Blaine's conduct of the Department of
State. His method of approach to Great Britain on the
subject of the revision of the Clayton-Bulwer Treaty,
and also his attempts at mediation in the "War of the
Pacific," had aroused much adverse criticism, which
was increased when Blaine gave out some of the diplomatic correspondence in these matters shortly before

leaving office. There were utterly baseless, though ugly insinuations concerning sinister financial interests involved in American efforts at mediation. It was alleged that Blaine was supporting doubtful claims of pseudo-American citizens, and that he was in alliance with the *Société Générale de Crédit Industriel et Commercial*, a "dollar diplomacy" scheme for intervention to end the war and safeguard foreign investments.[1]

American public opinion was frankly distrustful of Blaine and sympathetic towards Frelinghuysen. Furthermore, it must be remembered that, whatever may have been Blaine's talents, and the merits of his foreign policy, he was not a typical Secretary of State; while Frelinghuysen conformed absolutely to the type to which the American people had been accustomed. This contrast was well brought out by Edward Stanwood in his biography of Mr. Blaine:

"A study of the diplomatic history of the United States will convince any candid mind that the policy of every Secretary of State before Mr. Blaine may be truly described as a waiting policy. It was almost as a necessary consequence of the voluntary isolation of the country. Foreign enterprise was unknown in our diplomacy. The State Department took up, discussed, and settled the questions brought before it, as they arose, whether the matter were a grievance of the government, or a claim against it, a boundary dispute, or a proposition looking toward improved commercial relations. Every such question was dealt with individually, in accordance with the well-established and traditional policy. Unless a situation developed which required the government to assert its rights as against some other government which it held to be encroaching upon them, there was almost nothing of self-assertion and initiative upon the part of the United States. . . .

"The explanation of the absence of general initiative on the part of Secretaries of State from Jefferson to Evarts—a roll of great men—is not that they lacked power, energy, and boldness, or breadth of conception, or patriotism. The country of set purpose chose to hold itself aloof from world-politics, engaged in warmly-worded diplomatic controversies only when its interests were directly at stake, suppressed its opinion upon the internal and international difficulties of other nations save only when it observed a people endeavoring to overthrow an effete monarchy."[2]

If Blaine chose to venture on a policy of "foreign enterprise," Frelinghuysen clearly chose a "waiting policy" which was in harmony with the rigid traditions of the Department of State as well as with his own conservative temperament. It must be remembered, moreover, that Frelinghuysen belonged to that section of the Republican party called "Stalwarts," to which President Arthur and Senator Conkling belonged, the "regulars" or "standpatters" of the present day. These Republicans had little liking for the Republicans of the type of Blaine and Garfield, whom they contemptuously called "Half-breeds." The contrast between Frelinghuysen and Blaine in temperament and in methods was most significant. In seeking an explanation for the

action of Secretary Frelinghuysen in reversing certain of
the policies adopted with passionate conviction by Secretary Blaine, it is not necessary, therefore, to adduce
personal motives of a vindictive nature, as intimated by
Mrs. Blaine.³ Let it suffice to emphasize the fact that,
while Blaine was a departure from type, his successor
conformed most naturally and willingly to the traditions of the Department of State, whose guiding principles would seem ever to have been: "Never anticipate
trouble," and "In case of doubt, do nothing."

By inheritance and training, Frelinghuysen was essentially conservative, of solid Dutch ancestry, a member of the Dutch Reformed Church, a lawyer identified
with property interests, a statesman concerned primarily with the conservation of existing institutions.
Twice he served as United States Senator from New
Jersey, once by appointment at the hands of his personal friend Governor Olden, from 1866-1869, and once
by election by the legislature of his native state, from
1871-1877. He was a member of the Senate committees
on naval affairs, on the judiciary and on claims. In the
proceedings against President Johnson he took a vigorous stand in favour of impeachment. He was a member
of the electoral commission which declared President
Hayes lawfully elected. He represented New Jersey
with Governor Olden at the peace congress, held in
Washington in 1861 at the instance of Virginia, to seek
to avert the outbreak of hostilities between the North
and the South. He served as Attorney General of New
Jersey from 1861 to 1866. President Grant nominated
him in July 1870 to be minister to Great Britain, an
honour which he declined with alacrity. As a lawyer and

an orator he attained high distinction. Among his clients were the New Jersey Central Railroad and the Morris Canal and Banking Company.

The grandfather of Secretary Frelinghuysen, Frederick Frelinghuysen, served in action during the Revolutionary War, represented New Jersey in the Continental Congress, and was elected senator from New Jersey in 1793. Theodore Frelinghuysen, the uncle of the future Secretary of State — whom he adopted at the age of three, on the death of the boy's father, Frederick Frelinghuysen — was a candidate for Vice-President on the Whig ticket with Henry Clay in 1844, and also was elected senator from New Jersey in 1826.

From this summary it may be seen that, by reason of his family inheritance and traditions, by the influence of his surroundings and education from the day of his birth in Millstone, New Jersey, August 4, 1817, and by his record as a student in Rutgers College of the class of 1836, Frederick Theodore Frelinghuysen was destined to a life of useful service of the finest quality, and to a position of conservative influence in the nation, as well as in his own immediate community.

When Frelinghuysen became Secretary of State, on December 19, 1881, it was not to be expected that his conduct of the foreign relations of the United States would be dramatic or spectacular. There were plenty of thorny problems, however, that called for good sense and diplomatic skill, notably the controversy with Great Britain concerning the construction of an interoceanic canal, and the mediation of the United States in the War of the Pacific. Other questions of considerable interest dealt with by Frelinghuysen were the

Berlin Congo Conference in 1884, the opening of Korea, the boundary dispute between Mexico and Guatemala, the arrest of American naturalized citizens in Ireland suspected of Fenian sympathies, and many disputes with Spain concerning Cuba.

CHAPTER II

THE question of the War of the Pacific, which subsequently developed into the Tacna-Arica question,
was the most embarrassing problem confronting Frelinghuysen on assuming control of the Department of State.
His predecessors, Evarts and Blaine, had wrestled with
it in vain. The former arranged a peace conference of
the three belligerents, Chile, Peru, and Bolivia, aboard
the U.S.S. *Lackawanna* in the harbour of Arica, Peru,
in October 1880. Nothing but friction having resulted
from this, Blaine next undertook to intervene in the dispute, with lamentable consequences to all concerned.
Various European powers interested in the vast nitrate
and guano deposits in the territory at stake in this war,
or guided by other political or financial motives, repeatedly offered their mediation.[4] Peru, towards the end of
her struggle against the heavy demands of Chile, threatened to appeal for European intervention.[5] The menace of European intrigues and interference caused the
American Government great anxiety. To appreciate
properly the embarrassing situation which Frelinghuysen
had to face, it should be observed that his predecessor
had gone to great lengths in endeavouring to persuade
Chile to moderate her claims against Peru. He had
threatened to break off diplomatic relations over the

action of Chile in arresting Francisco García Calderón, President of the provisional Government in Lima, which had been rather hastily recognized by the United States against the good judgment of the American minister to Peru. Blaine was disposed to infer that this action was taken in resentment of American recognition and support of the Calderón Government.[6]

The reader has already noted in the preceding sketch of Blaine's first incumbency of the Department of State, in Volume VII of this series, that Secretary's final attempt—after the failure of the missions of Hurlbut and Kilpatrick and the deaths of those ministers at their posts in Chile and Peru—to settle the Pacific imbroglio by the special mission of the veteran and experienced diplomatist William H. Trescot. With Trescot was associated Blaine's son, the Third Assistant Secretary of State, Walker Blaine.

In his instructions of December 1, 1881 to Trescot, Blaine not only threatened to break off diplomatic relations with Chile over the arrest of Calderón, but threatened also that, if the good offices of the United States in behalf of peace should be rejected, and the "policy of the absorption of an independent state should be persisted in, this government [American] will consider itself discharged from any further obligation to be influenced in its action by the position which Chile has assumed, and will hold itself free to appeal to the other republics of this continent to join it in an effort to avert consequences which cannot be confined to Chile and Peru, but which threaten with extremest danger the political institutions, the peaceful progress and the liberal civilization of all America."[7]

Such was the situation confronting Secretary Freling-huysen. The whole imbroglio had become a matter of public discussion with charges not merely of ineptitude, but also of corrupt influences[8] at work to bring about active intervention by the United States. It can be imagined that to a man essentially of an irenic disposition and averse to extreme measures, this situation must have been most distasteful and embarrassing. Secretary Frelinghuysen's first telegraphic instructions of January 3 and 4, 1882 to Trescot were to the effect that he should exert peaceful good offices and avoid "every issue which might lead to offence." In his written instructions of January 9, the Secretary disclaimed any intention on the part of the United States to intervene by force in South American affairs, and definitely revoked that portion of Secretary Blaine's instructions to Trescot, already cited, concerning the suspension of diplomatic intercourse with Chile over the Calderón incident. It appears that Secretary Frelinghuysen had already accepted on January 7 the explanation of Mr. Martínez, the Chilian minister in Washington, to the effect that the arrest and imprisonment of President Calderón was not to be interpreted as due to resentment towards the United States for its recognition of the provisional Government. In these instructions to Trescot, Frelinghuysen wrote: "Believing that a prolific cause of contention between nations is an irritability which is too readily offended, the President prefers that he shall himself determine after report has been made to him whether there is or is not cause for offence." Most unfortunately, Trescot only learned of the revocation of his original instructions in the course of an important interview with the Chilian Minister for Foreign Affairs, Señor Balmaceda, January 31, 1882! The latter had received a full cabled version of Secretary Frelinghuysen's instructions of January 9, before they had reached Trescot, the official correspondence having been published on January 27, in response to a resolution of Congress. The humiliation and embarrassment caused this admirable diplomat may be imagined. The satisfaction felt by Chile in realizing that the Blaine policy had been definitely reversed may also be imagined, as well as the effect on the Peruvians, who saw that they could no longer count on the support of the United States in resisting the demands of Chile. The task of Trescot and Walker Blaine was hardly made any easier by further instructions from Secretary Frelinghuysen dated February 4, to the effect that, while the United States would not impose its good offices on Chile, it would in no event take part in negotiations based on the surrender of the Peruvian province of Tarapacá and a further indemnity of twenty millions, as such a demand was considered "exorbitant." And again on February 21, 1882, Frelinghuysen telegraphed that: "should Chile persist in her demands for such cession, the creditors of Peru might possibly maintain that the revenues of Tarapacá had been already hypothecated." The President, he said, desired to urge "moderation on the part of Chile." These telegraphic instructions were confirmed on February 24 by detailed written instructions in which Frelinghuysen stated that the President "is not willing to become the medium for a proposal, which in his judgment, is so onerous that it cannot be entertained by Peru." He also added that, "should Chile occupy and absorb without the consent of Peru, territory whose productions are pledged to creditors of that power, this could not be done without raising grave question in the future of Chile, which the United States, as a friend of that energetic and industrious people would wish to avoid." Frelinghuysen further added that the United States did not wish to impose its wishes upon the belligerents or to act as an arbitrator or umpire, "unless moved to it by the wishes of the parties or by controlling interests of our own."[9]

It may be seen, in the light of these bewildering instructions, how delicate were the negotiations of Trescot with the Government of Chile. After securing what he deemed to be considerable concessions, which he brought confidentially to the notice of the provisional Government of Peru, Trescot was recalled to Washington with his colleague, Walker Blaine. Another stage in the negotiations was opened by the appointment of a new minister to Chile, Cornelius A. Logan, a man well versed in South American affairs. His instructions from Secretary Frelinghuysen, dated June 26, 1882, were singularly contradictory and inconclusive. They were to the effect that the United States would continue to use its efforts for an impartial mediation "until they are crowned with success or until they result in pronounced failure." Frelinghuysen alluded somewhat cryptically to the possibility of active intervention in the case of the intrusion of European powers in the conflict. He stigmatized the action of Chile in disorganizing the Government of Peru, in paralysing its financial interests, and in disastrously affecting the pecuniary and other interests of the citizens of neutral states. While disclaiming again any intention to dictate conditions of peace, Frelinghuysen actually authorized the breaking off of diplomatic relations "should Chile refuse to moderate her demands to a point to which you may be willing to commit the United States as a mediatory power. . . ." But in his instructions of the same date to Minister Partridge in Peru, Frelinghuysen served warning that the Peruvians must not count on the support of the United States in resisting the "reasonable demands" of Chile!

Under these bewildering conditions, Logan proceeded to reopen peace negotiations between the Chilian Government and the political factions of Peru. These negotiations were carried on laboriously over a long period of time with rare diplomatic skill, and resulted in the signing, in May 1883, of a peace protocol by Señor Lavalle, representing the political faction of General Iglesias in Peru, and Señor Novoa, the Chilian representative in Lima. This protocol, which contained the actual solution proposed originally by Minister Logan, was embodied in the famous treaty of Ancón, signed on October 20, 1883, whereby Peru consented to the occupation of the provinces of Tacna and Arica for the period of ten years, at the end of which time a plebiscite was to be held to determine their eventual disposition, upon the payment of ten million *pesos* by the country retaining permanent possession. (The phrase in article two of this treaty that occasioned most of the subsequent controversies concerning the plebiscite reads in Spanish as follows: *Expirado este plazo un plebiscito decidirá, en votación popular, si el territorio de las provincias referidas queda definitivamente del dominio y sobe-*

*ranía de Chile, ó si continúa siendo parte del territorio
peruano.* Peru argued that the phrase *expirado este plazo*
should be interpreted as meaning that the plebiscite
should have been held immediately at the close of the
ten-year period of occupation by Chile, while the latter
insisted that it could be held at any subsequent time,
a point of view sustained by the arbitral decision of
President Coolidge.)

The part played by Secretary Frelinghuysen in these
negotiations was of minor significance. In a telegram to
Logan dated January 5, 1883, the Secretary left it to
Peru to decide whether it could agree to the cession of
Tarapacá, Tacna and Arica. In a laboured review of the
entire dispute dated March 23, 1883 Frelinghuysen disclosed that he had endeavoured, in separate discussions
with diplomatic representatives of Peru and Chile in
Washington, to secure an "impartial arbitration of the
question whether any additional territory shall be ceded,
and if so, how much and on what terms." In a dispatch
dated August 25, 1883, addressed to Phelps, the American representative in Lima, Frelinghuysen expressed
apprehension lest the interests of American citizens
should not be adequately protected in the articles of the
treaty between Chile and Peru relating to the foreign
debt of Peru, adding that "the President would see
with regret any insistence by Chile upon the policy
which would impose upon Peru heavier burdens than
she has been disposed to impose during the past negotiations." The Secretary closed this melancholy record
of American intervention with the following comment,
in a dispatch to Phelps dated November 15, 1883:

"Of the terms of the treaty itself I cannot at present speak. You are already acquainted with the views of this Government upon the main points involved. It remains to be seen whether the people of Peru, in the expression of their national sovereignty, are disposed to accept the terms proposed to them. With this the Government of the United States has no desire to interfere. It respects the independence of Peru as a commonwealth entitled to settle its own affairs in its own way. It recognizes too keenly the calamities of protracted strife, or the alternative calamity of prolonged military occupation by an enemy's forces, to seek, by anything it may say or do, to influence an adverse decision of the popular representatives of Peru. And a due respect for their sovereign independence forbids the United States from seeming to exert any positive or indirect pressure upon these representatives to influence their course."[10]

Thus ended the attempt to protect Peru from the aggressions of Chile, an attempt which was bound to result ingloriously, so long as the United States was unwilling to employ force. Whether Secretary Blaine would have been willing to employ force to coerce Chile is a matter of conjecture. It is quite clear that Secretary Frelinghuysen never contemplated anything more than the exertion of moral suasion, except possibly in the event of the intervention of European powers, of whose aims and policies he maintained a vigorous distrust. Such a conservative policy, if followed consistently from the beginning, might have had fortunate results. The unpleasant fact to be noted, however, is that the influence of American diplomacy in this dispute must be recognized to have been lamentable. Chile retained a vivid resentment against the United States for having opposed what she chose to regard as her legitimate claims, while Peru naturally felt that her interests had been sacrificed, after every indication of hearty support on the part of the United States. Nor have later developments, namely, the arbitration of this dispute by the President of the United States and the complete fiasco of the attempt to hold a plebiscite in accordance with that arbitration in the provinces of Tacna and Arica, in 1926, served to improve American prestige as a friendly arbitrator on this continent. In spite of the generous disinterested purposes of the United States, and the conciliatory disposition of Secretary Frelinghuysen, the history of this controversy can only be regarded with the deepest regret.

CHAPTER III

FRELINGHUYSEN FROWNS ON THE
PROPOSED PAN-AMERICAN
CONFERENCE

NO Secretary of State seems ever to have shared the
enthusiasm of Blaine for an energetic, comprehensive Pan-American policy. It would appear to be a tradition of the Department of State to preserve the utmost
freedom of action on the part of the United States with
reference to the other nations of this hemisphere. On
November 29, 1881, three weeks before his retirement,
Secretary Blaine, with the evident approval of President
Arthur, sent out invitations for a conference of American nations to assemble in Washington on November 24,
1882.[11] Its purpose was stated to be: "to seek a way of
permanently averting the horrors of cruel and bloody
combat between countries, oftenest of one blood and
speech, or even the worst calamity of internal commotion and civil strife." Blaine protested that the United
States did not assume "to counsel any determinate solution of existing questions which now divide any of the
countries of America," and that it would "enter the deliberations of the Congress on the same footing as the
other powers represented."

Trescot counselled against presenting this invitation
to the three countries then at war, namely, Peru, Chile
and Bolivia, particularly as his instructions apparently
contemplated the exertion of pressure on Chile to mod-

erate its plans of conquest.[12] The premature presentation of this invitation to Peru by the American minister
compelled Trescot to hasten its transmission to Chile,
in the interview above referred to, when he learned, to
his consternation, from the Chilian Minister for Foreign
Affairs that his original instructions from Secretary
Blaine had been revoked by Secretary Frelinghuysen.[13]
In the instructions from Frelinghuysen of January 9,
already cited, occurred the following reference to the
projected congress:

"The United States is at peace with all the nations
of the earth, and the President wishes hereafter to
determine whether it will conduce to their general
peace which he would cherish and promote, for this
government to enter into negotiations and consultation for the promotion of peace with selected friendly
nationalities, without extending a like confidence to
other peoples with whom the United States is on
equally friendly terms.

"If such partial confidence would create jealousy
and ill-will, peace, the object sought by such consultation, would not be promoted.

"The principles controlling the relations of the
republics of this hemisphere with each other and
with other nationalities may, on investigation, be
found to be so well established that little will be
gained at this time by reopening a subject which is
not novel. The President at all events prefers time
for deliberation."

Upon the publication of these instructions on January 27, 1882, Blaine felt compelled to address an open

protest to President Arthur.[14] He pointed out that the invitation for a conference of American nations had been approved by both President Garfield and President Arthur, and he recapitulated the arguments in its favour. Blaine bitterly resented Secretary Frelinghuysen's inference that such a congress—to use Blaine's paraphrase—"would create jealousy and ill-will on the part of monarchistic governments in Europe." This letter evoked a statement from the White House that the President had not recalled the invitation to the congress; and that Mr. Frelinghuysen's instructions did not refer to Europe, but merely meant that it was not thought desirable that Mr. Trescot should visit Brazil and Argentina and thus consult only two out of all the friendly powers of this continent. It was also announced that the whole question would be put up to Congress then in session.[15] President Arthur said in a special message on April 28, 1882:

"I am glad to have it in my power to refer to the Congress of the United States the propriety of convening the suggested international congress, that I may thus be informed of its views which it will be my pleasure to carry out."

Congress having taken no action whatever in this matter, as was to have been expected, the invitation for the proposed conference was withdrawn in August, 1882. This was done on the grounds that the continuation of the conflict between Chile and Peru and Bolivia rendered it impossible to assemble the congress. Secretary Frelinghuysen expressed the belief that "the fact that such a Congress having been called has not been without benefit, it having directed the attention of the people of the United States as well as of the republics of South America, to the importance of having a more defined policy, to be satisfactory to all, governing the international relations of the republic."[16]

While Secretary Frelinghuysen was clearly opposed in principle to the proposed conference, he would seem to have been on sound grounds in distrusting a conference of this character held at a time when conditions in both Central and South America were most unfavourable for the discussion of plans for permanent peace. Furthermore, despite President Arthur's attempt to attach a restricted meaning to the language employed by Secretary Frelinghuysen in his instructions of January 9 to Trescot, it was quite evident that he was constantly in dread of provoking an intervention by European powers in the War of the Pacific. There was reason to believe, moreover, that public sentiment in Brazil had been aroused against the proposed congress, by European influences insinuating that such a congress would offer to the United States an opportunity to assert a predominant and arbitrary control in the affairs of these republics. The Chileans, likewise, had been led to fear that such a conference might prove the means of bringing pressure upon Chile to sacrifice its conquests from Peru. Frelinghuysen would seem to have been fully justified, therefore, in regarding the whole idea as inopportune, to say the least.[17]

The need of "a more defined policy" on the part of the United States toward its American neighbours was becoming more and more evident. Frelinghuysen expressed himself in favour of a cautious policy of encouraging closer commercial relationships between the United States and the South American republics as the basis of closer political relations and friendship. In a letter to Senator John F. Miller, chairman of the Senate Committee on Foreign Relations, Frelinghuysen opposed a revived plan for a conference of American nations, on the ground that a preliminary agreement on its agenda and "on some definite assurances of general accord" was necessary.[18] He also objected in principle to any conference where the United States might be embarrassed by the demands of smaller states for protection in case of attack. He held that: "the smallest states would have a voice equal to that of the United States, and while we need not necessarily be bound by the conclusions reached, it would weaken rather than strengthen our influence with these countries if we should feel forced to reject measures adopted by the conference." Frelinghuysen therefore proposed to accomplish American aims by a series of reciprocity treaties with the states of Central and South America. He advocated the appointment of a commission "to carefully consider what the best interests of North and South America and the Isthmus require; to send, if found advisable, delegates to confer with the other countries, and, after this commission has made its report upon the most feasible means of carrying out measures of mutual advantage, then empowering the President if he sees proper, to call a convention." The views of Secretary Frelinghuysen on the subject of a Pan-American policy were set forth more fully in his instructions to the commissioners whose appointment was authorized by an act of Congress approved July 7, 1884.[19]

"This government cannot assume any control or authoritative influence over those countries. It would regard it as the part of wisdom, and due to the interests of its own people, to avoid such relationship toward them as might imply responsibility for their acts, either as among themselves or as toward foreign powers. But it cannot overlook the concurrent interest of all the American states in avoiding and averting all pretext for foreign interference in the affairs of the American continent. It would unhesitatingly favor any common understanding whereby the evils of war among them might be securely warded off by a resort to peaceable arbitration of differences not adjustable by diplomatic means. We would gladly guarantee the exertion of our good offices, in whatever quarter our counsel may be solicited. This government might even be prepared to consider the practicability of instituting a consultative council of representatives from the several states of the continental family, whose views as to international questions among them might have respectful heed. Beyond this necessarily inconclusive expression of general views we cannot at present go."

A practical test of this policy occurred in the boundary dispute between Great Britain and Venezuela, which later on, during the second Cleveland Administration, was destined to create an alarming crisis in the relations between the United States and Great Britain. The apparent intention of the latter to extend the boundaries of British Guiana right up to the mouth of the Orinoco River led Secretary Frelinghuysen to suggest that

Venezuela should propose to Great Britain that the controversy be arbitrated by the United States. He then said that: "the United States, whilst advocating strongly the recourse of arbitration for the adjustment of international disputes affecting the states of America, does not seek to put itself forward as their arbitrator; that, viewing all such questions impartially and with no intent or desire to prejudge their merit, the United States will not refuse its arbitration if asked by both parties, and that regarding all such questions as essentially and distinctively American, the United States would always prefer to see such contentions adjusted through the arbitrament of an American rather than a European power."[20] Upon the refusal of Great Britain to arbitrate through the United States, Frelinghuysen stated to Ex-President Blanco of Venezuela:

> "The moral position of the United States in these matters was well-known through the enunciation of the Monroe Doctrine, but formal action in the direction of applying that doctrine to a speculative case affecting Venezuela seemed to me to be inopportune, and I could not advise Venezuela to arouse the discussion of the point."[21]

An added reason for Secretary Frelinghuysen's disinclination for a conference of the American republics was the controversy raging between Mexico and Guatemala over their common boundary, together with the further complication of the attempt of President Barrios of Guatemala to bring about, by force of arms, the union of Central America. Such differences naturally did not provide the proper atmosphere for a general peace conference. Guatemala early made appeal for the good offices of the United States in its dispute with Mexico, alleging that the presence of numerous Mexican troops along the boundary was a threat against its independence. Secretary Blaine immediately responded on June 16, 1881, by instructing Morgan, the American diplomatic representative in Mexico, to urge upon the Mexican Government the importance of protecting the interests of the Central American republics and the other republics of this continent against European intrigues and aggressions. Blaine stated that the President would regard "as an unfriendly act toward the cherished plan of upbuilding strong republican governments in Spanish America, if Mexico . . . shall seek or permit any misunderstanding with Guatemala, when the path toward a pacific avoidance of trouble is at once so easy and so imperative an international duty." This was followed up by a still more vigorous instruction of June 21 to Morgan, to call upon Mexico for a disavowal of a policy of conquest and aggrandizement. Referring again, on November 28 of the same year, to Blaine's desire for the union of the Central American republics under one federal government, the Secretary expressed regret over the apparent hostility of Mexico to this project, adding that: "this country will continue its policy of peace, even if it cannot have the great aid which the cooperation of Mexico would assure." There is little doubt that the situation was one which might not only lead to war between Mexico and Guatemala, but also, as in the case of the War of the Pacific, to the intervention of European powers. It was feared, even, that Guatemala might go to the length of ceding a portion of the disputed territory to a foreign nation. Here again Secretary Frelinghuysen displayed his natural aversion to extreme measures and exerted his influence in favour of a peaceful adjustment of the controversy, without allowing the United States, as again in the case of the War of the Pacific, to appear as the advocate or the antagonist of either party. The results of his policy were most satisfactory, in that both of the disputants were able to come together, and by the treaty of September 27, 1882, completely to put an end to a controversy which threatened gravely the peace of Central America.[22]

CHAPTER IV

FRELINGHUYSEN'S ISTHMIAN ARGUMENTS

THAT Mr. Frelinghuysen's apprehensions concerning the danger of European intrigues in the affairs of the American continents were justified was illustrated in the problem of the interoceanic canal, which greatly interested him and enlisted his exceptional legal talents. The construction of the Suez Canal in 1869; the granting of the Panama concession to de Lesseps in 1878; the difficulties the United States experienced in fulfilling its obligations under the treaty of 1846 with New Granada to protect transit across the Isthmus of Panama; the apparent purpose of Great Britain to continue to interfere in Central Amercan affairs under the pretext of its duty to protect the rights of its protégés, the Mosquito Indians in Nicaragua; all these factors stimulated the liveliest interest and apprehension in the United States concerning the fate of a ship canal across Central America. The failure of negotiations with Colombia to secure to the United States the practical control of any canal across the Isthmus of Panama, and the belief that Colombia was on the point of inviting the powers of Europe to unite in a joint guaranty of its sovereignty over the Isthmus, as well as of the neutralization of the canal, served to bring American public opinion to the realization that any interoceanic canal connecting the Atlantic with the Pacific must be controlled exclusively by the United

States.[23] This opinion had already found expression in the declaration of President Hayes on March 8, 1880, that "the policy of this country is a canal under American control. The United States cannot consent to the surrender of this control to any European powers or any combination of European powers." It was reaffirmed by President Garfield in his inaugural address on March 4, 1881. Secretary Blaine undertook to convey to the European powers this declaration of independence in his circular letter of June 24, 1881, to the diplomatic representatives of the United States in Europe.

It is a singular fact that Blaine had completely ignored the Clayton-Bulwer Treaty of 1850, whereby Great Britain believed it had secured a privileged position with respect to any interoceanic canal across Central America. Before the protest of Lord Granville, British Secretary for Foreign Affairs, reserving all British rights under this treaty, was received in Washington, Blaine sent special instructions to James Russell Lowell, American minister in London, to the effect that the Clayton-Bulwer Treaty required modification. The most striking statement of these instructions was that the United States "will not consent to perpetuate any treaty that impeaches our rightful and long established claim to priority on the American continent."[24]

It was at this point that Secretary Frelinghuysen brought his great legal acumen to bear on the extremely complicated and highly technical debate that had been set on foot by Blaine. Frelinghuysen's argument took a somewhat different trend, urging the complete abrogation of the Clayton-Bulwer Treaty as being no longer applicable to changed conditions, whereas Blaine had argued for its modification. Frelinghuysen's argument may be summarized as follows: (1) The safety of the United States requires the absolute control of an interoceanic canal; (2) a joint European guaranty would be in direct opposition to the Monroe Doctrine, which was originally suggested and approved by Great Britain; (3) the primary object of the Clayton-Bulwer Treaty was the construction of the Nicaraguan canal by aid of British capital; as this had not been secured the treaty was no longer binding; (4) another main object of the treaty "was to dispossess Great Britain of settlements in Central America whether under cover of Indian sovereignty or otherwise"; Great Britain not having observed this agreement, the treaty was voidable; (5) the provisions of the treaty were only to apply to other canal projects by special "treaty stipulations"; as no agreements of this kind have been entered into, Frelinghuysen held that the special guaranty of the United States under the treaty of 1846 with New Granada to maintain "a perfect neutrality of the Isthmus" could not be superseded by the intervention of any other state. Great Britain was therefore excluded from the Panama Canal route. Secretary Frelinghuysen consequently insisted that the United States could not consent to the proposal of Lord Granville that the United States should take the initiative in an invitation to other powers to enter into a joint guaranty of the neutrality of an interoceanic canal across Central America.[25]

It is hardly necessary here to do more than advert to the extremely able arguments of Lord Granville in reply to the arguments presented by Secretary Frelinghuysen. Nor is it necessary to venture an opinion on the rights of the case. Suffice it to say that the contentions of both sides were sustained with vigour and good feeling. The position of the United States may be summed up in the phrase employed by Frelinghuysen in his instructions of May 5, 1883 to Lowell:

"You will remember that my No. 368 to you [of May 8, 1882] showed that the first seven articles of the treaty related to a particular canal then in contemplation, to aid the construction of which the treaty was signed; that the United States, being then without the means to build the canal, for which they had secured an exclusive grant from Nicaragua, naturally turned to England for capital, to secure which they were willing to surrender some of their exclusive privileges, and that the canal never having been built, the reason for the surrender of privilege has ceased and the treaty with Great Britain is voidable, being without consideration or [sic] any object to which it is applicable."26

England, however, rested on the wording of the Clayton-Bulwer Treaty, and would not admit this new interpretation of it. That Government could not be induced to meet even in a conciliatory spirit the reasonable exigencies of the situation from the point of view of the United States, which were subsequently recognized in the Hay-Pauncefote Treaty of 1903—but in a different age and in a different international situation. Firm in the belief in the absolute justice of the rights of the United States, and actuated by a robust patriotism, Frelinghuysen proceeded to negotiate a treaty in 1884 with Nicaragua, whereby the United States was granted exclusive rights in the construction and control of any canal to be built across that country, in open derogation of the claims of Great Britain under the Clayton-Bulwer Treaty.[27] This treaty was not ratified by the Senate. It was later withdrawn by President Cleveland and never was submitted again. A diplomatic impasse existed which could not be removed by legal arguments of the kind advanced by Secretary Frelinghuysen. He could rest satisfied, however, in the realization that he had done all in his power to defend the legitimate interests of his country in the construction, operation, and protection of the interoceanic canal which ultimately should bind the Atlantic and Pacific coast lines together.

A N important decision involving a departure from the traditional policy of the United States was the acceptance of Bismarck's invitation to participate in the Berlin Congo Conference of 1884. The purpose of this conference was stated by the German Government to be of a threefold nature: (1) freedom of commerce in the basin of the Congo; (2) freedom of navigation of the Congo and the Niger Rivers; (3) definition of formalities to be observed regarding new acquisitions of territory in Africa. After consultation by telegraph with Kasson, American minister in Berlin, Secretary Frelinghuysen came to the conclusion that it would be proper for the United States, because of its sympathy for Liberia, its recognition of the International Association of the Congo, and its material interests in that region, to participate in the proposed conference, particularly as it would be merely a *conference* and not a *congress* to reach final decisions. In accepting the invitation, Frelinghuysen stated to Baron von Alvensleben, the German minister in Washington, that "the object of the conference being simply discussion and accord the Government of the United States, in taking part therein, reserves the right to decline to accept the conclusions of the conference." And in his instructions of October 17, 1884 to Kasson, Frelinghuysen said: "You will take care that no act of yours may seem to pledge the United

States to any course or conclusions contrary to its well known policy, and that the freest liberty of action upon the conclusions of the conference will be reserved to this government."

The Conference met in Berlin from November 15, 1884, to February 26, 1885, and agreed upon a series of declarations embodied in a "General Act," which was subject to a subsequent ratification by the powers signing the protocol. This form of agreement was chosen in order to meet the objections of the United States to any joint commitments. The final act of ratification took place in Berlin on April 19, 1886, the United States having declined, in the words of Secretary Bayard, "to join in the responsible political engagements in so remote and undefined a region as that of the Congo Basin, which the general act imposes on the signatories." Kasson, ably supported by the associated delegate, Henry S. Sanford, former American minister to Belgium and a director of the International Association of the Congo, and by the great African explorer, Henry M. Stanley, played a most important and—it may be accurately asserted — a decisive role in the deliberations of the Berlin Conference.[28] It was largely through the influence of the American delegation that the conference agreed to insure freedom of trade and intercourse in Central Africa, the abolition of the slave traffic, and the neutralization of this region in time of war. Unfortunately, they were unable to obtain the suppression of the liquor traffic among the African natives. The influence of the United States in this conference may thus be held to have justified its participation, although President Arthur's Administration incurred violent criticism, both inside and outside of Congress, for having violated, as it was charged, the traditional American policy of non-interference in European political matters.

Secretary Frelinghuysen, while proceeding with his accustomed caution in this matter, did not fail to see the great interests involved in this conference, and had the courage to exert American influence in behalf of humanity and civilization, as well as of the material interests of the United States.[29]

Secretary Blaine, in his glowing conception of an aggressive American policy, included, as had Seward, in the sweep of his vision, the mastery of the United States in the northern Pacific, at least with respect to the Hawaiian Islands, which he considered as the outpost of an interoceanic canal. He was much concerned over British attempts to secure a voice in the affairs of the islands through the introduction of Indian coolies, who—it was proposed—were to enjoy extraterritorial privileges under the jurisdiction of British consuls.[30] Secretary Frelinghuysen did not seem to feel the alarm on this subject which had animated Blaine, but he did negotiate for an American naval base in Pearl Harbour. When Great Britain and other European powers were annexing some of the islands of Polynesia, much to the disturbance of the Hawaiian Government, Secretary Frelinghuysen merely said that the matter was not one calling for the interposition of the United States, though he added: "While we could not view with complacency any movement tending to the extinction of the national life of the intimately connected commonwealths of the Northern Pacific, the attitude of this Government toward the distant outlying groups of Polynesia is necessarily different."[31] Frelinghuysen believed that the immediate interests of the United States would best be served—as in the case of South America—through improved commercial relations, and he signed a convention with Hawaii on December 6, 1884 for the extension for seven years of the reciprocity convention of 1874, whereby the United States had gained valuable commercial privileges not extended to other nations under the most-favoured-nation clause. It also secured the right to use Pearl Harbour as a naval base.

With reference to American policy in the Far East, there is no evidence that Secretary Frelinghuysen contemplated anything more than the passive traditional policy of the "Open Door." The opening up of Japan by Commodore Perry had greatly impressed American imagination, and another American naval officer, Commodore R. W. Shufeldt, was moved to emulate this achievement in the opening up of Korea, the "Hermit Kingdom."[32] Our Government had no desire to concern itself, as did Great Britain, in the intricacies of Far Eastern politics. We instinctively sympathized with the policy advocated by General Grant after his memorable visit to the Far East, namely, to favour the independence and the upbuilding of the nations of Asia in order to counterbalance European intrigues and aggressions. Our Far Eastern policy was extremely simple and was not preoccupied with diplomatic details or methods, though individual American officials, such as James Russell Young in Peking—a personal friend of Grant —Commodore Shufeldt, and George C. Foulk in Korea, displayed great interest and intelligence in mastering the intricate maze of politics in the Orient.

When Commodore Shufeldt, who had had considerable experience in the Far East, undertook to negotiate
a treaty for the opening up of Korea, the project met
with the hearty approval of the Department of State,
though the means by which this was to be done seemed
to give it little concern. Japan, however, was keenly interested, having secured a privileged position by its
treaty of 1876 with Korea. This had greatly disturbed
China, which laid claim to Korea as a tributary state.
Japan, though consenting at first to be an intermediary
for the negotiation of a treaty between Korea and the
United States, apparently was unwilling, as a matter of
fact, to have Korea enter into diplomatic relations with
any other power.[33] Thereupon, Li Hung Chang, the
powerful statesman then in the ascendancy in China,
offered to serve as an intermediary between the United
States and Korea in order to vindicate the claims of
China as overlord of Korea. When Li Hung Chang
sought to include in the proposed treaty a clause expressly acknowledging the dependence of Korea on
China, Commodore Shufeldt strongly demurred, on the
ground that this would virtually amount to a joint guaranty by China and the United States.[34] He endeavoured
to secure from the Department of State explicit instructions on this most important point, but Secretary Frelinghuysen failed to reply to his request. After waiting
some time for instructions, Commodore Shufeldt on his
own responsibility proceeded to sign the treaty with
Korea, on May 22, 1882, minus the provision concerning the dependence of Korea on China. Two days later,
Commodore Shufeldt received from the King of Korea
a letter addressed to President Arthur stating that: "the

Chou Hsien country is a dependency of China, but the management of her governmental affairs, home and foreign has always been vested in the sovereign."

This treaty was much more comprehensive in scope than any of the other treaties with China and Japan. It did not conform, moreover, to the instructions from Secretary Frelinghuysen to Commodore Shufeldt that his mission was restricted to negotiating a treaty for the protection of shipwrecked sailors and that he should not attempt to secure too many or too great advantages. Among its important provisions were those opening up certain ports for trade, the granting of extraterritorial privileges, and the fixing of tariff rates. A most singular provision, to which too great significance has undoubtedly been attached, was that of Article I:

"If other powers deal unjustly or oppressively with either government, the other will exert their good offices, on being informed of the case to bring about an amicable arrangement, thus showing their friendly feelings."

Such a provision would seem prima facie to amount only to a pledge of friendly mediation and conciliation, although President Arthur—presumably on the suggestion of Secretary Frelinghuysen—made use of the following language in his third annual message to Congress, on December 4, 1883:

"Korea, as yet unacquainted with the methods of western civilization, now invites the attention of those interested in the advancement of our foreign trade, as it needs the implements and products which the United States are ready to supply. We seek no monopoly of its commerce and no advantages over other nations, but as the Chosenese, in reaching for a higher civilization, have confided in this republic, we cannot regard with indifference any encroachment on their rights."

This interpretation of our treaty obligations to Korea would seem to imply that the United States intended to support the independence of Korea from both China and Japan. Nevertheless, it is difficult to perceive that the American Government had any very definite conception of its policy in the Far East nor any clear realization of its commitments.[35] It does not seem to have recognized that Korea, in a like situation to that of Belgium in Europe, was destined to be the cockpit of oriental rivalries.[36] The failure of Secretary Frelinghuysen to instruct Commodore Shufeldt on the important point of Korean independence may have been due to his embarrassment on finding the United States embroiled in the maze of oriental intrigues. The archives of the Department of State afford no positive evidence on this point. A significant clew, however, is found in the special memorandum dated May 1, 1882, from Philadelphia, by John Russell Young, American minister to China, in response to a verbal request from Frelinghuysen, evidently only a few days after receiving the cable from Commodore Shufeldt, asking for instructions concerning the question of Korea's relation to China. Mr. Young, after a brief survey of Korea's relations to other powers, revealed his own indecision regarding the wisest course for the

United States to pursue in the conclusion that: "It is difficult for any Western power to determine the delicate and hazy conditions pertaining to the independence of Asiatic powers."

It may readily be conceived that Frelinghuysen, on receiving the opinion of the best expert on Far Eastern matters then at hand, believed it safer to refrain from committing the United States to any definite line of action. He therefore allowed Commodore Shufeldt to assume the entire onus of the decision concerning the demand of Li Hung Chang that the treaty with Korea should contain a recognition of its dependence on China.

Whether a policy of favouring Chinese domination over Korea in opposition to the aggressive aims of Japan would have achieved better results would seem unprofitable speculation. This much would appear certain, however, that Korea was bound, sooner or later, to enter into closer relations with the rest of the world and to become the bone of contention among Japan, China, and Russia. The assertion of a fictitious dependence on China, or of an equally fictitious independence of both Japan and China would seem to have been futile in the light of the actual course of events. Only a vigorous aggressive policy on the part of the United States for the maintenance of the *status quo* would have been of any possible avail, and this, too, is mere speculation. Secretary Frelinghuysen probably followed the only course warranted by our traditional policy and by the actual situation in the Far East.

Among the numerous other diplomatic controversies which occasioned great annoyance and trying negotiations were disputes with Spain concerning commercial relations with the Spanish Antilles, and the inevitable difficulties experienced by the United States in enforcing its laws against filibustering expeditions. Feeling ran high at times, notably in Key West, where threats against the life of the Spanish consul were made by Cuban sympathizers. These matters were all handled by Secretary Frelinghuysen with the greatest good sense and consideration. His efforts were especially directed to the negotiation of a convention for commercial reciprocity between .the United States and the Spanish Antilles. This convention was submitted to the Senate by President Arthur on December 10, 1884, but encountered the bitter opposition of various commercial interests, even before the treaty was made public. It was withdrawn later on by President Cleveland.

Another question causing the Department of State very great annoyance and much diplomatic correspondence was the embargo placed by France, Germany, and Turkey on the importation of American pork products, which were alleged to be infected with trichinosis.

A difficulty calling for great tact and good judgment was the necessity of making repeated representations to the British Government on behalf of various American naturalized citizens of Irish origin who were imprisoned, on returning to Ireland, under the provisions of the Coercion Act. The most famous and most typical case was that of Daniel McSweeney, who was long detained in prison without trial. Frelinghuysen, while conceding to every sovereign power the right to prescribe its own code of crimes and its own mode of trying offenders, insisted on the reciprocal courtesy accorded to Great Britain during the Civil War to intercede in behalf of

British imprisoned in the United States for various causes relating to the conduct of the war. He asserted the following general principle:

"American citizenship is a great privilege not to be lightly put on or unworthily worn. Its assumption implies the promise and the obligation to observe our laws at home, and peaceably as good citizens to assist in maintaining our faith abroad, without efforts to entangle us in internal troubles or civil discord with which we have not and do not wish to have anything to do. When an American citizen thus conducts himself, whether at home or abroad, he is entitled to the confidence of his government and the active support of all its officials. If business interests or the ties of affection take him into lands where from any cause the laws which will protect him from arrest and imprisonment do not exist, his government claims the right to interpose its own shield to take the place of the protection which is denied by local laws."[37]

McSweeney was subsequently released after having refused to accept the condition that he should at once leave Ireland.

A most pleasing incident in the course of Anglo-American relations at this time was the action of the British Government in presenting to the American Government the Arctic exploration ship *Alert* to aid in the rescue of Lieutenant A. W. Greeley and his companions in their scientific expedition to Lady Franklin Bay.[38] Another event which gave Frelinghuysen great satisfaction was the return to Japan on March 21, 1883, of the portion of the indemnity fund ($785,000.87) which had been received by the United States for its participation in the joint naval expedition with Great Britain, France, and Holland in 1864 for the purpose of opening up the Straits of Shimonoseki. The return of this money had been long urged by him before he had became Secretary of State, mainly on the grounds that the nature of American help in this expedition did not warrant any compensation.[39]

Public office had exacted too heavy a toll of his strength, and on relinquishing office to his Democratic successor, Secretary Bayard, on March 4, 1885, Frelinghuysen returned to his home in Newark too weak even to receive the honours and the warm welcome which his fellow townsmen were so eager to give him. There he quietly ended his days on May 20, 1885, survived by his widow and six children.

Mrs. Frelinghuysen (Matilda E. Griswold) was a gracious hostess and of great help in enabling the Secretary to uphold the best traditions of his high office. Their home at 1731 I Street in Washington was the scene of many brilliant receptions and entertainments. Everything was done on a generous scale and with dignity.

Frelinghuysen was a man of exceptionally fine physique and handsome features. In carriage he was stately. His manners were most courtly and dignified. No one ventured to presume in his relations and dealings with the Secretary. His subordinates in the Department of State could always count, however, on the utmost courtesy and consideration. A deeply religious man—at the time of his death president of the American Bible Society—he had the greatest reverence for the sanctity of the individual, and was earnestly solicitous concerning the religious affiliations and observances of those of his immediate household.

It is difficult to appraise properly Mr. Frelinghuysen's services as Secretary of State. His natural conservatism, together with a sensitive regard for the feelings of others, was reflected in his conduct of the foreign relations of the United States. There was little that was striking, and nothing dramatic. He was intensely American in his sentiments, and inclined to be distrustful of the attitude and policies of certain of the European nations. It cannot be said, however, that he in any way failed to safeguard the essential interests of his country. But in defending American rights he was ever solicitous for the rights and the sensibilities of other nations. His fellow countrymen could well be proud to have been able to command the services of a Christian gentleman who had none of the arts and the guile of a professional politician, and who laboured devotedly to serve what he believed to be the highest interests of America and of all mankind.

THOMAS FRANCIS BAYARD

SECRETARY OF STATE

MARCH 6, 1885, TO MARCH 4, 1889

BY

LESTER B. SHIPPEE, Ph.D.

PROFESSOR OF AMERICAN HISTORY
UNIVERSITY OF MINNESOTA

THOMAS F. BAYARD

FROM A CONTEMPORARY PHOTOGRAPH

THOMAS FRANCIS BAYARD

CHAPTER 1

CLEVELAND'S FIRST SECRETARY
OF STATE

FTER the election of Cleveland there was
naturally much speculation about his Cabinet. Cleveland himself permitted the dis-
semination of information as to men he had
under consideration in order to get the reaction of the public and of political leaders. In most
combinations which arose in Cleveland's mind or which
others proposed appeared the name of Thomas Francis
Bayard—a Cabinet without Bayard was unthinkable.[1]
Bayard was one of a family which had already furnished three United States Senators from Delaware.
Destined for a business career, on the death of an older
brother, Thomas Francis Bayard was dedicated to the
public service for which he was in part prepared by
studying law with his distinguished father. A year as
federal district attorney in Delaware and a brief sojourn
in Philadelphia preceded his settling down in Wilmington in law partnership with William Shippen in 1857.
Thomas F. Bayard like his father was a peace Democrat during the Civil War; he opposed secession and he
opposed the war, but in doing so he unquestionably represented the majority opinion of his state, for when his

father resigned his seat in the Senate in 1869, he was chosen to succeed him. Bayard served on the Electoral Commission and was a minority member, except for one Congress, of a few important committees, although not of the Committee on Foreign Relations. While he participated in discussion and exhibited an intelligent comprehension of many questions which came up, he displayed no particular interest in matters of foreign policy. If he entered the Department of State with no special training he was like many of his predecessors. His senatorial training, however, coupled with his native ability, gave him a broad grasp of policy. Withal he carried into office a sense of fair play and of courtesy; his legal experience gave him the fundamental background of many of the problems presented to him; his dignified bearing and innate courtliness fitted him for the amenities of his position.

When the new Administration took office one of the things most eagerly watched was its attitude toward the letter and spirit of civil service reform. It was to be expected that Cleveland, as a Democrat, would desire to be represented abroad eventually by men sympathetic with him and his party. There was, however, "no indecent haste about such proper changes," as one contemporary put it. When changes came, most of the appointments received commendation even from vigilant and critical civil service reformers. Edward J. Phelps, an outstanding member of the American bar who had been elected President of the American Bar Association in 1881 and who, at the time of his appointment, was Kent Professor of Law at Yale University, was selected to represent the United States near the Court of St. James's.

George H. Pendleton was chosen for the position of minister at Berlin; Pendleton was a well-known figure in American political life, for he had been both Representative and Senator from Ohio, had sponsored the civil service measure of 1883, and was the vice-presidential candidate on the Democratic ticket in 1868. To France went Robert M. McLane of Maryland. McLane, educated in part in France, had graduated from West Point and served in the army of the United States until 1843, when he took up the profession of law. He had been commissioner from the United States to China, Japan, Siam, Korea and Cochin China, later minister to Mexico, and from 1879 to 1883 a member of Congress from Maryland. Other major diplomatic appointments were generally of the same high character. In the consular service there was no clean sweep, as many Republicans feared and some Democrats hoped there would be; there were fewer changes than there had been when Garfield succeeded Hayes. Such generally satisfactory appointments, approved, when not suggested, by Bayard, did not avert criticism of some unfortunate selections.

An example of the less fortunate choices was Anthony M. Keiley, of Virginia, who was appointed minister to Italy. The Italian Government objected to Keiley on account of some remarks made fourteen years earlier at a meeting called by the Bishop of Richmond to protest against the incorporation of Rome in the Italian kingdom. Keiley saved the Administration from embarrassment by resigning, but he was solaced by being offered the mission to Austria-Hungary. As soon as this was known in Vienna, Count Kalnoky instructed Baron Schaefer, the Austro-Hungarian minister in Washington, to say that his Government, like the Italian, had scruples against his reception, for, among other things, the position of a foreign envoy wedded to a Jewess "would be untenable and even impossible in Vienna." Bayard told Schaefer that such a reason could "not be assented to by the Executive of the Government of the American people, but is and must be emphatically denied." After some fencing Schaefer came out definitely and said: "Our objections to Mr. Keiley's appointment as minister of the United States to the Imperial Court are founded upon want of tact evinced on his part on a former occasion, in consequence of which a friendly power has declined to receive him; and upon the certainty that his domestic relations preclude that reception of him by Vienna society which we judge desirable for the representative of the United States, with which power we wish to continue the friendly relations existing between the two governments." Despite this definite statement and Minister Francis's guarded communications from Vienna, the Administration persisted in its stand until word came that Keiley would not be received. There was nothing to do but accept his resignation, for Cleveland would not recall him, and the incident was closed.[2] As an indication that the President was not pleased, the Vienna legation was left in the hands of a chargé d'affaires for two years.

There were, of course, some weak appointments. The minister selected late in 1885 to replace William L. Scruggs at Bogotá was wholly inexperienced in diplomacy and had to be instructed minutely in the very elements of his duties. He showed his incompetence by exceeding his instructions and had been at his post scarcely six months when he was recalled to Washington and persuaded to resign. Later it was found that he had taken from the legation archives some of the official correspondence and the Department was put to considerable trouble to recover it.[3]

CHAPTER II

THE NORTHEAST FISHERIES

DURING Bayard's tenure it was with Great Britain that, on the whole, arose the most important issues as well as the most extensive diplomatic correspondence, for the relations of the United States with Great Britain were more intimately interwoven than with those of any other foreign country. Some of these questions were of long standing. None was older, nor, at this juncture, more irritating than the hoary problem of the northeast fisheries, which, dating from the treaty of 1783, had been a perennial source of disputes. When Cleveland entered office the fisheries question was in a particularly awkward stage, because certain clauses concerning it in the treaty of Washington were about to terminate.[4] For various reasons—the feeling that too large a pecuniary indemnity had been awarded, the desire of New England fishermen to keep out Canadian fish, a general tendency toward protection in the country, the irritation remaining from the Civil War period—there was a determination to abrogate this article at the earliest possible moment. By act of Congress the special privileges enjoyed for the past twelve years were to cease on July 1, when the provisions of the convention of 1818 would revive. Because July was in the middle of the fishing season and Yankee fishermen might be expected to exercise their prerogatives to the last moment, thus inviting misunderstanding and probable friction, Bayard and Sir Lionel Sackville-West, the British minister at Washington, worked out a temporary agreement to hold for the season, in the expectation that a permanent arrangement could be reached before the next spring.

By this *modus vivendi*, which was incorporated not in a formal convention but in a series of notes, the special privileges of the treaty of 1871 were to continue for the rest of the year, on the understanding that the President would ask Congress for authority to appoint American members of a joint commission to thresh out the whole thing, and to refund duties paid on Canadian fish and fish products in American ports after July 1. Lord Granville directed Sackville-West to emphasize the fact that the understanding was temporary, that it did not prejudice any claims that might later be advanced for a more satisfactory equivalent, and that it did not minimize the value of the inshore fisheries of the Dominion and of Newfoundland.[5]

Cleveland, in his annual message, did bring the matter before Congress and urge legislation. Congress pointedly refused to accede to his wishes. In the light of discussions in both houses it is not difficult to conclude that the preponderant motive, particularly in the Senate, was political. By a small majority the Republicans controlled the upper house, and this majority showed conclusively that it did not intend to facilitate the program of a Democratic Administration. In addition to motives arising from the exigencies of party politics, those which had brought the abrogation of the fisheries article in the treaty of Washington played a part.

To re-establish the restrictions of the convention of 1818 was to create a difficult situation for the American fisherman, provided he attempted to conform to the law. If, as was frequently the case, little heed was paid to Canadian regulations there was bound to be trouble. According to the terms of the old agreement Americans could take fish in specified territorial waters of Labrador and Newfoundland, and could land on unoccupied shores to cure and dry fish. They were allowed to enter harbours and ports to get water and wood, make repairs and seek shelter. Because of the way the fisheries had developed during the previous half century these privileges had come to be of little practical value. Their small worth was accentuated when contrasted with the privileges enjoyed during the past dozen years. The Canadians knew just how galling the old restrictions were and they intended to enforce them in order to get something in payment for relaxation. They wanted the removal or reduction of customs duties on many Canadian products, something secured in part by the treaty of Washington, for they believed that reciprocal trade relations with the United States were well-nigh indispensable to their economic well-being. The people of the United States, in spite of a drift toward a protective policy, had elected a Democratic president pledged to lower tariff schedules, and the time seemed opportune to exert pressure. The logic of the Canadian position is obvious.

Emphasis has been laid on Canadian rather than British policy, for the British Government was relatively indifferent to the whole matter and quite openly accorded the initiative to the colonials. Whether or not direct intercourse with the Canadian Government would have made it possible for Bayard to reach a definitive and amicable adjustment at this time is open to question; nevertheless, the lack of such intercourse caused delays and increased exasperation. Whenever a fisheries complaint went from Washington to London it was submitted to the Secretary of State for Foreign Affairs; this Minister called it to the attention of the Colonial Secretary who communicated with the Governor-General of Canada, who, in turn, laid it before his Government. The reply returned over the same roundabout route necessitating weeks and sometimes months to settle even trivial matters. Bayard, of course, knew the reasons for delay and was inclined to take them into consideration, but the man who got his information from the daily papers considered it another example of British high-handedness and indifference to the rights of others.

Almost as soon as fishing craft reached northern waters in the season of 1886 complaints began to pour into Washington.[6] Some of them on investigation proved to be results of attempts to evade legitimate Canadian regulations. Others demonstrated that Canadian and Newfoundland officials were not only authorized to enforce the treaty strictly but sometimes in their zeal went farther than the letter of the law allowed. In May, taking as a theme the seizure of two fishing schooners, Bayard protested that, as deep-sea fishing had not been comprehended in the terms of the convention of 1818 and as bait was used only for this fishing, "therefore to prevent the purchase of bait or any other supply needed in deep-sea fishing, under color of exercising the provisions of the treaty of 1818, would be to expand that convention to objects wholly beyond its purpose, scope and intent, and give to it an effect never contemplated by either party, and accompanied by insults unjust and injurious to the citizens of the United States." He complained that while Canadian fishermen could enter American ports to purchase supplies, make repairs, ship crews, and the like, every American in a Canadian port ran the risk of a fine if he tried to do the same things. A few days later he called Sackville-West's attention to a bill, then under consideration by the Canadian Parliament, which, if enacted, would subject to seizure and forfeiture any American fishing vessel found within territorial waters for a purpose not sanctioned by the law of nations, a treaty or a law of Canada or Great Britain. These are but illustrations from a voluminous correspondence carried on throughout the season and occasioned by hundreds of complaints from irate Yankees.

While Bayard did what he could to defend American rights under the treaty he was conscious that it was, as applied to fishing in the eighties, very narrow. Canadians, on the other hand, were determined to use every legal quibble technically possible. Realizing this, Bayard framed what seemed to him an equitable basis for a permanent understanding, after the mackerel season of 1886 ended, for the consideration of the British Government.[7] It contemplated the appointment of a mixed commission to agree upon lines separating exclusive from common fishing waters in conformity with the spirit of the convention of 1818, except that in bays ten miles or less in width the "distance of 3 marine miles from such bays and harbors [should] be measured from a straight line drawn across the bay or harbor, in the part nearest the entrance, at the first point where the width [did] not exceed 10 miles." Other proposals included a definition of American privileges under the treaty, an agreement on penalties and procedure in trials, the right to purchase bait and supplies for deep-sea fishing similar to that enjoyed by Canadians in American ports, the release of vessels then being detained, and determination by a commission of the amount of damages resulting from seizures. While the British Government welcomed any kind of a solution which would appease the United States and not offend Canada, before anything could be done it had to consult the Dominion Government.[8] Then the Earl of Iddesleigh, the Foreign Minister, died and it was some time before Lord Salisbury, who took over the duties of his department, could take under serious consideration what was, from the British point of view, a decidedly minor issue.

In the interval Congress had been busy. Both houses had started inquiries and the Senate Committee on Foreign Relations, acting under the direction of a resolution, on January 19, 1887, submitted a voluminous report with which was included an historical survey of the question and a mass of testimony obtained at hearings.[9] The committee concluded that British pretensions to jurisdiction over arms of the sea more than six miles wide were unfounded. Without discovering any real ground for criticism of Canadian and British laws enforcing the treaty, nevertheless "when it comes to the matter of just and reasonable judicial determination of any question arising, the committee does think that the methods and limitation of procedure were harsh and unjust, and beyond the right of the British Government to provide, under its authority by the treaty to make only such restrictions as should be necessary to prevent the abuse by the American fishermen of this right to enter non-fishing waters." The committee recommended that the President be given authority, when he should be satisfied that the conduct of British and Canadians was unfair, to refuse them such privileges in American waters as he might deem advisable. Knowledge that negotiations for an adjustment were going on did not prevent the passage of a retaliatory act in harmony with this recommendation, and the President signed the bill, although he could use discretion about enforcing it.

Retaliation did not commend itself to the Secretary of State. While the House Committee on Foreign Affairs had the bill under consideration he telegraphed Phelps about it and added: "The situation difficult by absence of reply to our proposition of settlement. I strongly deprecate entrance upon policy of retaliation which acceptance of proposition would avert. Prompt action essential."[10]

The fishing season of 1887, then, opened with a prospect of a repetition of the previous year's experience. Fishing interests hoped the President would use the retaliatory power. Among the Cleveland Papers is a letter written by a Boston commission merchant reporting a rumour that a Gloucester boat was about to be sent to Nova Scotia so that it might be seized. It was also whispered about that "they would force the President to issue a proclamation prohibiting the importation of Canadian fish, adding that there would be a seizure soon. . . . There is a good deal under the surface of this Fisheries dispute which, owing to the persistent misrepresentations of some of the advocates of the New England fishermen, is not generally known."

Salisbury's reply to Bayard's proposal reached the Department on April 6, 1887. Some of the American assertions, said the British Minister, seemed well founded, but others were of a nature to "give rise to endless and unprofitable discussion . . . inasmuch as they appear . . . to be based upon the assumption that upon the most important points in the controversy the views entertained by Her Majesty's Government and that of Canada are wrong, and those of the United States are right, and to imply an admission by Her Majesty's Government and that of Canada that such assumption is well founded." Salisbury did not fall in with the ten-mile proposition, pointing out that the United States repudiated this doctrine as to Delaware Bay. Nevertheless he welcomed the note as a possible basis for discussion and adjustment. Meantime he suggested, understanding that one of the principal reasons for abrogating the fisheries article of the treaty of 1871 was dissatisfaction about the money award, that for the ensuing season and perhaps longer they might return "to the condition of things existing under the treaty of Washington, without any suggestion of pecuniary indemnity."

Before Bayard made a formal reply there was a new development. Recognizing that the real negotiations must take place with Canada, in April he intimated to its Government through Erastus Wiman, a Canadian-born business man of New York, that he would be glad to confer either with the Premier, Sir John MacDonald, or with Sir Charles Tupper, Minister of Finance and High Commissioner to England.[11] Accordingly Tupper in May saw Bayard, who met him with this declaration: "Well, Sir Charles, the confederation of Canada and the construction of the Canadian Pacific Railway have brought us face to face with a nation, and we may as well discuss public questions from that point of view." Since the commercial relations of the two countries were too great to be hampered by the eternal "triangular duel," and the fisheries question especially needed to be settled, Tupper's suggestion for a conference in Washington was approved by both Bayard and the President, who agreed to designate persons to meet with "authorized agents" of Great Britain to draw up proposals for a temporary and a permanent adjustment. Phelps was instructed to propose this to the British Government and to suggest the discussion of a mode of settlement of all matters affecting the relations between the United States and the British possessions in North America.[12]

The British Government cordially welcomed the proposal and before the end of August had selected as their representatives Joseph Chamberlain, Sir Charles Tupper and Sir Lionel Sackville-West. Bayard, Dr. James B. Angell, then President of the University of Michigan, and Judge William L. Putnam, a prominent Portland lawyer, were chosen to represent the United States. After the exchange of full powers on November 22, 1887, the conferences began. At Bayard's suggestion no full written minutes were kept, since he believed an agreement could be more easily reached if there was no formal record of proposal and counter-proposal. On December 10 the meetings were adjourned to allow Chamberlain and Tupper to go to Canada to consult with the Government there. When the sittings were resumed on January 9 a change in the attitude of the American delegates was observable; whereas previously they had been willing to discuss with open minds all the outstanding points of difference with Canada, now they seemed averse to treat of anything except the fisheries question and even with that there was lacking that spirit of conciliation so conspicuous earlier. Tupper and Chamberlain had been able to persuade Sir John MacDonald to yield on some points in return for American concessions, but it appeared now that the United States would concede nothing and demand everything. The negotiation appeared to be about to end in failure. Sackville-West told Bayard that Chamberlain was convinced that nothing could be done and intended to return to England, whereupon at the next joint meeting a new spirit seemed to prevail and both a treaty and a *modus vivendi* were soon shaped on lines suggested at the previous conferences.[13]

The treaty, completed on February 10, 1888, and accepted by the President five days later, provided for a joint commission to ascertain and designate the territorial waters of Canada and Newfoundland as to which by the treaty of 1818 the United States renounced the right to take, dry and cure fish. In laying these down on admiralty charts the three-mile limit was to be measured from low-water mark except that as to a limited number of indentations specific bounds were stated in the treaty. Elsewhere "such three marine miles shall be measured seaward from a straight line drawn across the bay, creek, or harbor, in the part nearest the entrance at the first point where the width does not exceed ten miles." The Strait of Canso was to be open to the free navigation of American fishing vessels. In bays closed to fishing, vessels need not enter and clear when seeking shelter or repairs, nor, outside regular ports of entry, when after wood or water, and they were not liable for compulsory pilotage, harbour and other dues. By securing licenses Americans might purchase casual provisions or supplies necessary for a homeward voyage. The fifteenth article stipulated that whenever Congress should remove the duties from fish and fish oils similar American products would be duty-free in Canada, and, moreover, Americans might purchase bait, ice, seines, lines and other supplies, transship fish for forwarding by any means of transportation, and ship crews in Canadian and Newfoundland ports.

The *modus vivendi*, which was to be in force for two years or until the treaty was ratified, permitted entry into Canadian ports to purchase supplies of all kinds on payment of an annual fee of $1.50 per ton by each vessel securing a license. They could also transship their cargoes and receive and discharge crews. At any time when Congress might remove the duties in American ports, these privileges could be had without paying the fee. More liberal regulations were provided for vessels entering Canadian and Newfoundland ports for purposes enumerated in the convention of 1818.

On the day he signed the treaty the President transmitted it to the Senate with a voluminous mass of correspondence and an urgent plea for its ratification.[14] Disinterested comment agreed that it was a fair compromise, that the United States gained at least as much as was conceded, and that it promised to stop bickering over the fisheries problem. Nevertheless it was doomed to defeat. This was a presidential year and, as a Republican Senator told Tupper at one time during the negotiation: "We cannot allow the Democrats to take credit for settling so important a dispute." Much direct criticism of the treaty was made, in particular because of its failure to contain any provisions for adjusting the complaints of American fishermen arising from seizures, although it was explained that the point had not been forgotten and would continue to be the subject of negotiations. Opponents of the treaty said that it contained nothing more than could be legitimately claimed under the convention of 1818. It was not a case of *quid pro quo* but of *quid pro nullo*. But, taking into consideration all the arguments raised against it, the fact remains that the principal cause of its defeat was political.[15]

CHAPTER III

BRITISH AND CANADIAN ISSUES

AMONG the matters "affecting the relations between the United States and the British possessions in North America" were the questions of the Alaskan boundary and that of regulating the north Pacific fur-seal fisheries. One of the principal fur-seal herds of the world made the Pribilof Islands, just north of the Aleutian chain in the Bering Sea, its summer home and breeding place. During the summer months these seals were accustomed to make excursions far out to sea, twenty, fifty, sixty or more miles from their rookeries, and it was then that sealers from various parts of the world indiscriminately slaughtered them. Since it was impossible to distinguish the males from the females, the old from the young, this pelagic sealing was making deep inroads into the herd and was steadily decreasing its size, because the young females, upon whose existence the perpetuation of the herd depended, were being killed in ever increasing numbers. The American Government could restrain its own citizens and prevent their engaging in pelagic sealing, just as it could protect the seal on land and within the three-mile jurisdictional limit from the depredations of sealers of any nationality. When it came, however, to attempting to prevent pelagic sealing by Japanese, Russians or Canadians, it was altogether a different question, although the statutes of the United States seemed to contemplate some sort of jurisdiction over this portion of the high seas.

Sir Lionel, in September, 1885, acquainted Bayard with a cause of friction which had arisen from the seizure by an American revenue cutter of three British-Columbian sealing schooners. Ascertaining that the vessels had been taken while "engaged in killing fur-seal within the limits of Alaska Territory and in the waters thereof in violation of section 1956 of the Revised Statutes of the United States," Bayard secured from the Treasury Department their release but "without conclusion at this time of any questions which may be involved in these cases of seizure." In 1887 six more vessels were taken and declared to be forfeited by Federal District Judge Dawson, who, in rendering his opinion, announced that Bering Sea was *mare clausum.* Thereupon Sackville-West was directed to make representations to the Department and to "reserve all rights to compensation on behalf of the owners and crews."

Bayard now took a step calculated both to stop pelagic sealing and to avert further complications. In an identic instruction of August 19, 1887, to the representatives of the United States in Germany, Norway and Sweden, Japan, Great Britain, France and Russia, he stated that recent occurrences had drawn his attention to "the necessity of taking steps for the better protection of the fur-seal fisheries in Behring Sea"; hence, "without raising any question as to the exceptional measures which the peculiar character of the property in question might justify this Government in taking, and without reference to any exceptional marine jurisdiction that might properly be claimed for that end, it is deemed advisable—and I am instructed by the President to inform you—to attain the desired ends by international co-operation." The ministers were instructed to invite the governments to which they were accredited to enter into "such an arrangement with the Government of the United States as will prevent the citizens of either country from killing seal in Behring Sea at such times and places, and by such methods as at present are pursued, and which threaten the speedy extermination of those animals and consequent serious loss to mankind."

A favourable reception to this overture was accorded by each of the governments. It appeared that everything pointed to an amicable and equitable adjustment. An obstacle, however, arose later in the year in the attitude of Canada. Lord Salisbury, acknowledging the propriety and importance of trying to save the industry, told Phelps that "the Canadian Government objected to any such restrictions, and until its consent could be obtained, Her Majesty's Government were not willing to enter into the convention; that time would be requisite to bring about this end and meantime the convention must wait." Phelps, when he reported the conversation, advised Bayard to take strong measures. Since "a colony which has for three years harrassed the fisheries of our country with constant captures of vessels engaged in no violation of treaty or legal rights" had no regard for international comity, why should the United States hesitate "to put an end to a pursuit of the seal by Canadian ships which is unjustifiable and illegitimate?" He was convinced that a resolute stand would end the difficulty. Bayard, however, was unwilling to force the issue in this way, and the question went over to the next Administration with no hampering commitments.[16]

Shortly after assuming office local conditions in the northwest directed Bayard's attention to the fact that not only was the water boundary between Alaska and British North America in doubt in certain quarters, "although not in doubt so far as this Government is concerned," but that the land boundary "which is supposed to follow a mountain range, an impracticable one to survey, if not a geographical impossibility," was in question. "I am not aware," he wrote Phelps, "that any question concerning the true location of the line so stipulated ever arose at any time between Great Britain and Russia prior to the cession of Alaska to the United States. . . . It is certain that no question has arisen since 1867 between the Government of the United States and Great Britain in regard to this boundary." But, since the line was a theoretical one, difficulties might be avoided in the future by "appointing an international commission at the earliest practicable day to fix upon a conventional boundary which, while in substantial accord with the presumed intent of the negotiators of the Anglo-Russian convention of 1825, shall be fixed and readily determinable in whole or in part under the ordinary conditions of astronomical and topographical surveys."

Lord Salisbury, wholly agreeable to the proposal, as usual had to ascertain the views of the Dominion Government, which thought, on account of the difference in expense, that "a preliminary survey, such as was suggested in the President's message to Congress," was preferable to a formal joint commission. As no real progress in fixing the boundary was made during Cleveland's Administration the only significance of the correspondence attaches to Bayard's statement, not denied or refuted by Salisbury, that no question about the boundary as laid down in the treaty of 1825 and incorporated into that of 1867 had previously arisen.[17]

Another question bequeathed Bayard was that of a new extradition treaty with Great Britain, negotiations for which were already in progress when Frelinghuysen left the Department. The end sought was an amendment of the provisions of the Webster-Ashburton Treaty so that several crimes or misdemeanours not enumerated therein would be made extraditable. On June 25, 1886, Phelps and Lord Rosebery signed a convention which made subject to extradition those charged with manslaughter, embezzlement or larceny where fifty dollars or more was involved, burglary and malicious injury to property where the life of a person was endangered. This convention encountered especial opposition from Irish-Americans, and it met the fate which had overtaken the fisheries treaty.[18]

Toward the close of Bayard's career as Secretary of State there came an episode in which his policy appears to run counter to the conciliatory course he had hitherto consistently pursued. Lord Sackville, for Sir Lionel had been raised to the peerage, allowed himself to fall into a clever political trap when he intimated, in reply to a letter purporting to have come from a naturalized Englishman named Murchison, that Cleveland's continuance in office as a result of the election of 1888 would be best for British interests. The letters were published just before the election. They created a tremendous furor, and Sackville was denounced for having attempted to interfere in the domestic affairs of the United States. Republican papers were filled with denunciations of Cleveland as a tool of England; they linked the affair up with the fisheries treaty, the Fenian troubles, and generally what was called "truckling" to Great Britain, the "arch-enemy" of the United States.

Just how much Bayard was personally sympathetic with and responsible for what followed is difficult to say. As one familiar with questions of diplomatic etiquette and with the difference between issues of real importance and those of no moment, he realized the intrinsic triviality of the affair, although he deplored Sackville's blunder. As a politician he knew the havoc the letter might create. Whatever may have been his personal feelings he had to take a strong course. On October 26 he telegraphed Phelps: "Sackville, in his correspondence and in frequent interviews intended to be published, has impugned the motives of the President and the Senate in regard to Canadian questions, and . . . his usefulness in this country is at an end. A strong public sentiment has been aroused, and Lord Salisbury should be permitted as speedily as possible to understand the necessity of immediate action."

Four days later Phelps was informed that Sackville's "continuance in his present official position in the United States is no longer acceptable to this Government" and that he had been given a passport to "facilitate his withdrawal." After an interview with Salisbury the American minister reported him as saying that, as the letter had been a private one, it "did not itself afford ground for any action by Her Majesty's Government";

he could not act until he had been "apprized of the language used by Lord Sackville, and giving him an opportunity for explanation or disavowal." After explanations had been received he wrote Phelps: "It is, of course, open to any Government on its own responsibility, suddenly to terminate its diplomatic relations with any other state or with any particular minister of any other state. But it has no claim to demand that the other state shall make itself the instrument of that proceeding, or concur in it, unless satisfied by the reasons, duly produced, of the justice of the grounds on which the demands were made." As a private communication, he maintained, the Murchison letter could not be a legitimate basis on which to recall Sackville.

The whole situation, except in an academic sense, was terminated by the dismissal of the British minister; nevertheless the correspondence continued till toward the close of January and ended with an instruction to Phelps wherein Bayard summed up and justified the course of his Government. This note, which displayed a tinge of pique absent from most of the previous correspondence, was intended to leave on record so indubitable a repudiation of the imputation that the Democratic party was in any way subservient to a foreign nation that the ghost of such an accusation could never rise to confront it. Altogether the episode was regrettable, for the British Government and the British public felt that Lord Sackville had been sacrificed in the game of American politics. The growing cordiality in diplomatic relations was marred, and the century-old bug-bear of traditional British hostility to the United States was galvanized into greater liveliness.[19]

CHAPTER IV

SAMOA

MANY of the more important international issues brought to Bayard's attention involved Great Britain in one way or another. One critical problem introduced that power only in a secondary way, so far as the United States was concerned. This was the Samoan issue. Down in the South Seas, centring about a group of islands aggregating scarcely a thousand square miles of land in a vast waste of ocean, were the elements of an international drama which for at least two years was a major interest in Washington, a matter of considerable concern in Berlin, and in London a pawn in a greater game of international colonial politics.

Bayard, when he entered office, found this situation: in 1878 the United States had secured the right to establish a naval station at Pago-Pago, the best harbour in the Samoas and one of the best in the southern Pacific, as well as most-favoured-nation treatment in the islands. The Samoan envoy who negotiated the treaty had sought at least American protection but what he obtained in return for his concessions was this promise, at the time a pious gesture: "If, unhappily, any differences should have arisen or shall arise between the Samoan Government and any other government in amity with the United States, the government of the latter will employ its good offices for the purpose of adjusting those differences upon a satisfactory and solid foundation." Years of internal rivalry and disorder, in part stimulated by the consuls of the United States, Great Britain and Germany, each working for the interests of his countrymen, culminated, in 1879, in several acts designed to produce a reign of peace. England and Germany secured treaties which gave them, and particularly Germany, considerable powers of intervention in native affairs; a general agreement between the Samoan Government and the consuls created the district of Apia, the principal port, a neutral zone and placed its government under a municipal board consisting of the consuls. This agreement the Government of the United States never formally ratified, but the American consul was permitted to act with his colleagues. In an attempt to allay strife between rival native factions an agreement was made on board the U.S.S. *Lackawanna* by which Malietoa Laupepa was recognized as king of Samoa and Tupua Tamasese, vice-king, a position created to placate the party in opposition to Malietoa.

In 1884 the Germans, whose material interests in Samoa considerably exceeded those of the Americans and British combined, were becoming uneasy. New Zealand wanted to annex the islands, and the Samoans, especially those of the Malietoa faction, were sympathetic with the idea, the more so because their repeated appeals to Great Britain and to the United States for protection, annexation—almost anything to escape German domination—had been vain. The general international situation had an influence on the Samoan problem. In 1884 came the Berlin conference on the Congo;[20] the Egyptian snarl was disturbing England;

and Germany had definitely entered upon a policy of acquiring colonies. In the delicate balance between France and Great Britain over Egypt, Germany could tip the scales, and Bismarck, in return for a benevolent passivity in equatorial Africa and in the South Seas, was willing to tip them for the British.[21] So, while Bayard at the outset unquestionably expected that Great Britain and the United States would stand together to resist German encroachment on Samoan autonomy, Great Britain followed Germany's lead throughout the whole affair.

Just before Frelinghuysen retired he received from the German minister in Washington a communication transmitting a copy of a treaty lately concluded between the German consul and Malietoa and Tamasese. This agreement, which Malietoa asserted had been obtained under duress, provided for a German-Samoan administration which virtually made the government of Samoa a German affair. Bayard adopted a waiting policy, especially when assured that American treaty rights would not be molested and that the German Government disavowed their consul's act in raising the German flag at Apia. Throughout 1885 affairs appeared to remain *in statu quo* although the information received from Consul Greenebaum was disquieting. Greenebaum himself was told that since the United States had not ratified the municipal agreement it was "an open question whether our tacit acceptance of that convention and the entrance *de facto* of our consul into the municipal council of Apia give us any right to resent supposed interference therewith." Nevertheless, "the moral interests of the United States with respect to the islands of the Pacific, necessarily dependent in greater or less degree on our American system of commonwealths, would counsel us to look with concern on any movement by which the independence of those Pacific nationalities might be extinguished by their passage under the domination of the foreign state; and this would be equally true of possible English as well as possible German protection." This was Bayard's "open door" policy.

Word was received in January, 1886, that the German consul at Apia had hauled down the Samoan and raised the German flag. Immediate inquiry was made in Berlin as to the significance of the act,[22] and Pendleton reported that Count Herbert Bismarck, the son of the illustrious Chancellor and Minister of Foreign Affairs, assured him that Germany intended "to maintain the status as it has heretofore existed." Reports from the islands, however, did not seem to bear out this assertion; from everything that reached Washington it appeared that Samoan autonomy was a thing of the past or was rapidly disappearing. Consequently on March 19, Bayard, in an instruction to Pendleton, commented on the "recent astonishing proceedings of German officials in Samoa" and said that their course was "so inconsistent with the independence and autonomy of Samoa as to be a matter of very grave concern to the Government." Pendleton was directed to make known the views of his Government at the earliest possible moment and to consult his British colleague in an informal way.[23]

Consul Greenebaum interpreted his instructions with extreme liberality, for, on an appeal from Malietoa for assistance under the terms of the treaty of 1878, he raised the American flag and announced that his Government would protect the Samoans and preserve order. Bayard's disavowal of this act afforded him an occasion again to state the position of the United States and to propose that the British and German ministers in Washington be authorized to confer with him in order to come to an agreement whereby Samoan order would be restored and autonomy maintained. It was his idea that the natives should select a new chief who would be upheld by the powers, new consuls be appointed, a war vessel stationed in Samoan waters for two years, and the three powers by joint declaration make known their stand against annexation or a protectorate. Bismarck's suggestion that each Government, before the conference, send an agent to Samoa to investigate and report was approved.

After each Government had received its representative's report[24] the conference took place in Washington in the summer of 1887. At the first session Bayard submitted a plan which included the recognition of Malietoa as king, the appointment of a council composed of the king, the vice-king and three foreigners selected by the treaty powers, an assembly elected by the natives, and the submission of the confused land titles to a court. Von Alvensleben, the German minister, proposed the recognition of Tamasese as king to rule with the assistance of an adviser appointed for five years by the power with the largest material interests in Samoa; after the expiration of this period there should be another selection in accordance with the same principle. He desired a special commission to pass upon land claims. Sackville-West, for Great Britain, generally agreed with the German proposal, although he suggested some modification in details. The American and German proposals were so far apart that, although each yielded on some minor points and agreed to recognize the king chosen by the natives, there was little hope of complete agreement.[25] At this impasse Bayard proposed an adjournment until the autumn so that each Government might come to a definite conclusion as to its policy.

In assenting to the postponement Bismarck instructed von Alvensleben to state that His Majesty's Government could not "renounce an immediate reparation for the insults against His Majesty the Emperor and the national honor committed by partisans of Malietoa . . . on the occasion of His Majesty's birthday, by the ill-treatment of German citizens in Samoa and by violence inflicted upon them." Then came in rapid succession the driving of Malietoa from Apia, German recognition of Tamasese as king, the surrender and exile of Malietoa, and the appearance in Apia of one Brandeis, who became Tamasese's principal adviser. Thus informally the German proposal was put into effect. For something like a year the Government of Samoa, still nominally native, actually was the Government of the German Brandeis acting in close co-operation with Consul Becker and a German naval force. Americans complained that their rights were ignored and the British were none too well pleased. There was almost constant friction between Consul Sewall, who had replaced Greenebaum early in 1887, and Becker or the Brandeis-Tamasese Government. What with the small number of foreigners implicated and the triviality of many of the causes of discord, the whole thing presents something of the appearance of *opéra-bouffe*, but to the Samoans, part of whom steadily opposed the Brandeis-Tamasese régime, it was an affair of deadly seriousness.

On October 11, 1887, Bayard telegraphed Phelps and Pendleton that, while the consul-general reported most distressing conditions in the islands, he had been instructed to preserve the strictest neutrality. However, in light of the situation, the United States Government was anxious, pursuant to the treaty of 1878, to urge a peaceful adjustment and considerate treatment of the Samoans, hence it proposed an immediate election of a new king and vice-king in accordance with the decision reached by the conference. Pendleton reported that Count Bismarck said that a new king *had* been elected, and produced telegrams showing that Tamasese was recognized as king in September, and "that quiet reigned on the island; that there were no more disorders." The assumption that Tamasese's selection had been an act of the natives stirred Bayard deeply. Still believing that the British would with him resent the course taken by the Germans in Samoa with every appearance of support from their Government, on November 11 he sent an instruction to Phelps in which he quoted from the protocols of the conference the understanding about a free and unhampered election: "It is not practicable at the present time to tell how far American interests may have been affected by the recent German action in Samoa, nor is it intended to enter in this instruction, into a general discussion of the subject. All I desire now to say is that the German action . . . was a most unaccountable proceeding; and especially so as all the

alleged causes for it, as stated to me by the German minister, existed anterior and some of them long anterior—
to the meeting of the Conference, at none of whose sessions were they even mentioned." Phelps was directed
to ascertain the views of Lord Salisbury about the German action and its probable effect on the course of his
Government, for "it can hardly be supposed that either
Her Majesty's Government or that of the United States
will be inclined to pass without notice or protest the
sudden disregard and frustration of their efforts at
friendly co-operation, and resume, without condition,
a conference which, while held with the express object
of securing peace and a native autonomy in Samoa,
may at any moment be defeated by the forcible deposi-
tion by one of the parties to the pending conference of
the titular Head of the native government and the setting up, under the protection of the arms of the same
party, of another Head."[26]

This instruction, consistent with his earlier statements, gives the key to the course Bayard pursued
during the next year. To the German Government he
expressed the same sentiments in answer to a somewhat
querulous note from Prince Bismarck. He outlined the
situation at length and denied Bismarck's implication
that the course of the American consul, acting either
under instructions or on his own initiative, had made
restoration and maintenance of peace more difficult.

"These general observations are made because,
notwithstanding the efforts of the Government to
state its views in respect to Samoa in a spirit of entire
frankness, it has sometimes seemed that they had

not been fully apprehended; or else that the Governments of the United States and Germany, while
agreeing to the same general principles, differed as
to their relative importance and the order in which
they should be applied. . . . To Germany the primary
object has seemed to be the establishment of a
stronger government. To the United States the object
first in importance has seemed to be the preservation
of native independence and autonomy. And so regarding the matter this Government, while not questioning Germany's assurances of the absence of any
intention on her part to annex or establish a protectorate over the islands, has been compelled to dissent
from propositions which seemed to subordinate all
other considerations to the strengthening of German
commercial and landed interests in the islands, and
correspondingly to diminish, if not entirely to destroy, the probability of the establishment of a Samoan Government, and of the neutralization of the
group, at least in respect to the powers now immediately concerned."[27]

Throughout 1888 disorder increased in Samoa. German war vessels upheld the power of Tamasese and
assisted in overawing the opposing native faction.
Discontent ripened into open revolt under Mataafa,
whom the members of the old Malietoa faction declared
their king in September, and thereafter Tamasese had
the support of few besides the Germans. This gave Bayard an opportunity to cable Pendleton, in Berlin, that,
as Mataafa appeared to have been selected by a majority of the Samoans, the Government of the United

States intended to respect this choice and assumed that "the other treaty powers, in pursuance of their joint understanding, would do the same." Councillor Holstein of the German Foreign Office told Pendleton that "it was not a matter of importance to Germany who was king of Samoa, provided German interests were not allowed to suffer." Apparently, however, they did suffer, for reports which came from Apia showed that not only was the German squadron augmented but that it was used in operations against Mataafa, and finally a state of war was declared to exist.[28]

When this news came, Admiral Kimberly, then at Honolulu, was ordered to Apia to reinforce the vessel or two of the United States Navy already there and aid in protecting American lives and property, as well as to "protest against the subjugation and displacement of the native government by Germany." This was a significant gesture especially when the Department knew that American naval officers had already interposed in behalf of Samoans against German operations. Shortly after, Cleveland transmitted to Congress the latest correspondence on the Samoan question and pointed out what the course of the Administration had been. Congress responded by appropriating half a million dollars to protect American interests and a hundred thousand to develop a naval station at Pago-Pago, where nothing had been done for the past ten years.

By this time the affair began to look really serious, and Bismarck was faced with the question whether the game was worth the candle, or, perhaps, whether the desired end might not be accomplished in some other way. A war with the United States over Samoa was not to be contemplated. Accordingly on February 4 Count von Arco Valley, who had replaced von Alvensleben not long before, read to Bayard Bismarck's instruction where he said that it was the duty of the three powers to stop the war in Samoa; the best method of doing this seemed by a resumption of the conferences, and the German Government invited Great Britain and the United States to resume negotiations in Berlin. "I am also instructed to declare," announced the German minister, "that any supposition that Germany would not feel satisfied with a neutral position in the Samoan islands is unfounded, as we have already declared in the last conference (of 1887) it is neither our intention to put in question the independence of the island group nor the equal rights of the treaty powers." The next day Bayard told Arco Valley that the President accepted the invitation, and suggested that instructions be sent immediately to suspend hostilities pending the result of the conference.[29] While the Berlin conference did not meet until after Bayard was out of office, his diplomacy had been successful; the nominal autonomy of Samoa was maintained and there was no annexation or establishment of a protectorate. Whether this was the best solution the following years were to demonstrate.

CHAPTER V

THE PACIFIC AND THE ORIENT

FARTHER north in the Pacific the Hawaiian Islands presented quite another problem for the United States. Just before the close of the Arthur Administration the treaty of reciprocity of 1875 had been renewed but it was not ratified by the Senate until January 20, 1887. In ratifying it the Senate added an article whereby the United States was to have the exclusive right to enter the harbour of Pearl River and there establish and maintain a naval coaling and repair station. This cession was not only a form of payment for the reciprocal trade privileges desired by Hawaiian sugar planters, it was an indication of a peculiar interest of the United States in that strategically located group. What this interest was finds an expression in many of Bayard's instructions. When Minister Merrill wrote from the islands about the discontent which had produced the new constitution of 1887, Bayard replied:

"Whilst regretting deeply the existence of domestic disorders in Hawaii, and with no disposition whatever to interfere therein or to obtrude counsel unasked, yet the consequences which may possibly result to the interest of American citizens which have grown up under the extension of the commerce between that country and the United States, under the guarantees of the existing treaty, must not be jeopardized by internal confusion in the government of those islands, and it is the duty of the United States to see that these interests are not imperilled or injured, and to do all things necessary for their protection. . . .

"As is well known, no intent is cherished or policy entertained by the United States which is otherwise than friendly to the autonomical control and independence of Hawaii, and no other of the family of nations has so great and immediate interest in the welfare of Hawaii on such a basis as this Republic. . . ."

At another time, in the course of the correspondence over Samoa, a comment of Bismarck's about American action in Hawaii being a precedent for German conduct in Samoa brought an even stronger expression from Bayard:

"In respect to this it needs only to be observed that the treaty was one of special reciprocity which both the contracting parties were alone competent to make, and that the United States has at no time, since the convention was concluded, sought to use it to control the native government of the islands or to regulate their internal affairs against the wishes of the inhabitants, although the geographical and historical relations of the group to the United States necessarily give this Government an interest in the future such as no foreign Government can possibly possess."

The peculiar interest of the United States was also emphasized when, after the acquisition of Pearl Harbour, the Government of Great Britain proposed that "the United States Government should, with England and Germany, guaranty the neutrality and equal accessibility of the islands and their harbors to the ships of all nations without preference." Bayard replied that there was nothing in the Hawaiian-American treaties to impair the sovereignty of the island, that, furthermore, they created "special and important reciprocities . . . and by one of the articles the cession of any part of the Hawaiian territory to any other government without the consent of the United States is inhibited." Under the circumstances it did "not seem needful for the United States to join with other governments in their guaranties to secure the neutrality of Hawaiian territory."[30]

In the Far East during these years there arose no issue of pre-eminence. A treaty negotiated with the Chinese minister was intended to smooth out difficulties in administering the exclusion acts and, in return, not only provide indemnity for loss of Chinese lives and property in the United States, but assure China that her subjects legally in this country would be given the protection extended to nationals of the most-favoured nations. This agreement, with some amendment not fundamental, was ratified by the Senate, but the Tsung li Yamen refused to confirm it without further discussion. The threat of a drastic exclusion act, placed before the President for his signature while the Chinese Government was considering the treaty, and failure of the Congress to provide legislation adequate to prevent indirect participation of Americans in the opium trade in China, as well as the treatment which had been accorded individual Chinese in some parts of the United States, played a part in its rejection.

Korea, nominally a dependency of China, presented to Bayard an interesting problem growing out of the treaty of 1882. Article I of this convention contained these words: "If other powers deal unjustly or oppressively with either Government, the other will exert their good offices, on being informed of the case, to bring about an amicable arrangement, thus showing their friendly feelings." A protest against Great Britain's occupation of Port Hamilton was made by Korea, the Government of which, relying on the literal application of the words of the treaty, besought the United States to use their good offices "to bring about an amicable arrangement." The request was refused and at the same time Phelps was instructed to explain to the British Government the relations of the United States and Korea, and to state that his Government did not construe the treaty "as empowering us to decide and maintain that the acts in respect to which good offices were desired are in fact *unjust* or *oppressive*." The policy of the United States forbade the slightest appearance of intervention on behalf of either party to an international dispute of this character.[31]

Bayard either ignored or was unaware of the contest going on between China and Japan over Korea. In any case, however, his attitude was in harmony with his oft-emphasized policy of non-intervention in the *political* concerns of foreign nations. When China, on grounds of Korea's vassalage, objected to her sending a diplomatic representative to the United States, he instructed Denby to express his great surprise, especially since there had been no objection to Korea's making the treaty—no question of her vassalage having been raised as to the conduct of her internal affairs or her foreign relations. He agreed, however, with Denby that agitation of China's claim to suzerainty was neither desirable nor beneficial, and it was not necessary to raise the question unless some affirmative act occurred. The position of the United States simply required the observance of treaty rights: "The interest of this Government is not political. It seeks merely the protection of American citizens where such protection is possible."

Japan presented a set of issues in some respects similar to those afforded by her neighbours, Korea and China.[31a] There was, however, an outstanding difference; Japan had been rapidly adjusting herself to western ways, and for a decade or more had been seeking to shake off the two symbols of international inferiority: restrictions upon her customs administration and the extraterritorial jurisdiction of foreign nations.

Reverting to the policy of Secretary Evarts, President Cleveland and Secretary Bayard were agreed that "the chief object of the United States is to secure to Japan, as far as practicable, complete autonomy." Accordingly, when a conference of foreign representatives was set for 1886, Bayard instructed the American minister at Tokio, Richard B. Hubbard, to attend the meetings and to work for a revision of the treaties whereby "the regulation by Japan of her foreign commerce and of her domestic affairs [would] follow as an attribute of sovereignty, to be restrained only so far as she may deem it expedient by independent treaties." He intimated that if "the work of revision should fail to secure to Japan, now or within the near future, the measure of autonomy to which we think she is entitled, it [would] remain for this government to determine its course and consider whether the desired result [might] be otherwise reached by independent negotiations between the United States and Japan, on more practical and more immediately applicable bases than are found in the separate treaty of 1878."

The results of the conference were negative, for the concessions which Count Inouye, Premier and Minister of Foreign Affairs, was disposed to yield did not meet with the approval of the Japanese people and he was forced from office. Count Okuma, Inouye's successor, turned to the policy of the negotiation of separate treaties, and Hubbard was instructed to enter upon a negotiation which would bring about "improvements . . . in the jurisdictional system as respects foreigners in Japan, and relief . . . to that country from the present undue and repressive foreign control in matters of commerce," as President Cleveland put it in his annual message of 1888. The convention, which was signed by Hubbard and Okuma on February 20, 1889, was calculated in part to accomplish the emancipation of Japan from foreign control of her internal policy so far as the United States was concerned. Americans were to be accorded rights of residence and travel in Japan, although there were temporary restrictions upon their acquisition of land; outside the treaty ports of Yokohama, Kobe, Hakodate, Tokio, Osaka and Nagasaki, American citizens were to be subject to the jurisdiction of Japanese courts, and even in these places American extraterritorial privileges were to cease at the expiration of five years from the proclamation of the treaty, although during this period American judges were to sit upon the bench of the Japanese supreme court in cases involving their countrymen; Japanese control of customs was increased, although complete autonomy in this respect was not stipulated. The new convention did not reach Washington until the Cleveland Administration was out of office. It was, therefore, subjected to the criticisms of another President and of Secretary Blaine, who was not altogether sympathetic with the somewhat radical changes, and was never submitted to the Senate for ratification.

It is noticeable that in the question of the revision of the Japanese treaties, both President Cleveland and his Secretary of State adhered to the policy which had characterized their course in relations with other countries; namely, an insistence, so far as it was within the power of the United States, upon the principle of autonomy. It is possible that neither Secretary Bayard nor Minister Hubbard had a complete understanding of all the questions involved in the Japanese issue, and that they were inclined to advance too rapidly; nevertheless one can grasp the point of view of the Department, especially in the light of other issues with which it had to deal.

CHAPTER VI

THE ISTHMIAN TRANSIT AND
LATIN AMERICA

EVERY Secretary of State expected to have a considerable portion of his time and energy consumed
by questions which grew out of Latin-American relations whether or not the Monroe Doctrine was invoked,
and Bayard was no exception to the rule. Here, as with
most of the problems already considered, no outstanding issue of pre-eminence gave an opportunity for
brilliant diplomacy or an international *coup;* it was
rather a case of pursuing a steady and consistent course
amid a number of irritating and potentially dangerous
events. With the nearest of the Latin neighbours,
Mexico, little except routine matters came to the surface. The killing of Captain Crawford of the United
States Army when he was in pursuit of bandits across
the border gave rise to a long correspondence, but there
was no fundamental issue involved and the matter was
adjusted. Disorders in several states of South America
elicited Bayard's formula of maintenance of treaty
rights without intervention.

With some of the countries about the Caribbean,
however, there arose questions of more than passing
interest centring around the proposed isthmian transit.
Here Bayard's policy was one of non-interference and
avoidance of the kind of co-operation which had the
least tinge of "entanglement." Such a policy of friendly

help and maintenance of legitimate American interests, divorced from any suggestion of intervention, necessitated careful treading. Not only was there an obligation to prevent foreign encroachment upon territorial rights and sovereignty of these mercurial nations and, incidentally, promote peaceful relations among them, but the way must be kept clear for an interoceanic canal, neutralized and open to the commerce of the world.

It is quite beyond the scope of this sketch to attempt even an outline of the happenings about the Caribbean during these four years; as ever, since their separation from Spain, the course of events there presents kaleidoscopic annals rather than history. Boundary disputes between Nicaragua and Costa Rica, as well as between the latter and Colombia, a revolution in Panama, an attempt by the President of Gautemala to force Central American states into a federal union, a revived controversy between Nicaragua and Great Britain over the sovereignty of the Mosquito Coast—these were some of the things which animated Bayard's Latin-American diplomacy.

Among the questions demanding immediate attention when the Cleveland Administration assumed office was the Frelinghuysen-Zavala canal treaty, a convention which President Arthur and his Secretary of State had worked hard to have Nicaragua ratify, but which was still hanging fire in the United States. It propounded a rather vital question: should the new Administration endorse the plan of a canal built, operated and preponderantly controlled by the United States and continue the attempt to abrogate the Clayton-Bulwer

Treaty, or should it revert to the older idea of a waterway constructed by private capital? Cleveland's answer
to this question was given when he withdrew the treaty
from the Senate and when, later, in his first annual message, he said: "Maintaining, as I do, the tenets of a line
of precedents from Washington's day, which proscribe
entangling alliances with foreign states, I do not favor
a policy of acquisition of new and distant territory or
the incorporation of remote interests with our own."
He indicated his friendliness to any practicable kind of
transit, "removed from the chance of domination by
any single power," and pledged the efforts of his Administration in behalf of its realization, "ever bearing
in mind the principles on which it must rest, and which
were declared in no uncertain tones by Mr. Cass, who,
while Secretary of State, in 1858, announced that
'What the United States want in Central America,
next to the happiness of its people, is the security and
neutrality of the interoceanic routes which lead through
it.'"

Bayard must, then, watch closely anything which
threatened to interfere with the "security and neutrality of the interoceanic routes" existing or in prospect.
The alarm which the Panama operations of the de
Lesseps Company had excited earlier was subsiding,
for their probable failure at no distant time was anticipated.[32] When it was rumoured that efforts were being
made by private parties to purchase an island in Fon-
seca Bay for a French coaling station, the United States
minister in Central America was instructed to watch
diligently "any transactions of this class from whatever quarter they may be reported."[33] Upon receiving

information from the Nicaraguan minister in Washington that Colombia had designs upon Corn Island, Bayard considered it a "matter . . . of considerable importance to this Government in view of the strategic value of the island with reference to the Atlantic mouth of the projected Nicaraguan canal," and expressed his gratification when he learned that the apprehension of its seizure was dispelled. When there were intimations that the Government of Costa Rica had granted a railroad concession to an English company he was anxious to find out whether "an international canal concession from Nicaragua" was also being sought.

In harmony with Cleveland's message Bayard did not, like his immediate predecessors, seek to get England to modify or denounce the Clayton-Bulwer Treaty. Nevertheless, it was not his intention to allow to pass unnoticed any act which threatened the political adjustment of Central America and which might have a bearing on a future canal. On September 10, 1888, J. P. H. Gastrell, the British minister in Central America, addressed a note to the Nicaraguan Foreign Minister calling to his attention several things which, in the opinion of the British Government, contravened the "provisions and spirit" of the treaty of Managua of 1860 and its interpretation in the award of the Austrian Emperor in 1881 in respect to the Mosquito Coast. The Nicaraguan envoy in Washington promptly apprized Bayard of the fact and the latter, on November 23, addressed an instruction to Phelps. He adverted to the long-continued and voluminous correspondence between Great Britain and the United States on the question of the Mosquito Reservation and traced the course of events to the award of 1881, which he analysed in the light of the alleged infractions by Nicaragua. He refused to admit that either the treaty or the award gave Great Britain "a right to interfere in every dispute that, may arise between the Mosquito Indians and their sovereign [Nicaragua]," for "the stipulations of the treaty of Managua relative to the privileges to be accorded to the Mosquito Indians were not for the benefit of Great Britain, and are not enforceable by her. . . . The President can not but regard the continued exercise of the claim on the part of Great Britain to interfere . . . as the assertion of a British protectorate in another form. . . . Whether the interference of the British Government be regarded as a breach of existing treaty engagements, or whether it be looked upon simply as an effort, not prohibited by express agreement, to extend her influence in this continent—in either case the Government of the United States can not look upon such acts without concern."[34]

When questions of disputed boundaries arose Bayard's first thought was of the possible effect upon treaty rights of the United States. Years before, Colombia and Costa Rica had agreed to submit to arbitration a claim of the former to territory well up toward the San Juan River, but the plan had been halted when Blaine served notice that the United States would not be bound by any decision which might affect American rights. The issue was to the fore again with the renewed agitation over a canal site. Bayard modified the position taken in 1881 by letting it be known that his Government would be satisfied if both Colombia and Costa Rica gave prior assurance that, no matter what the award was, the legitimate rights of the United States secured by treaty would remain intact.[35] When Nicaragua ratified the Frelinghuysen-Zavala treaty the Costa Rican Government was much perturbed, for under it the United States appeared to be about to receive from Nicaragua rights which touched the question of Costa Rican territory and sovereignty. Both Frelinghuysen and Bayard, however, assured the Costa Rican minister that it had "never been the intention of the United States to ignore any right which Costa Rica might have along the proposed line of the canal, or to invade her territory without her previous consent."[36]

When the canal treaty was withdrawn from the Senate by President Cleveland there was no longer any question of possible infraction of Costa Rican rights, but the boundary controversy itself remained alive. It was stimulated anew when the prospect of a canal constructed by private capital was agitated again and promoters of the scheme sought concessions from Nicaragua. Through the good offices of Guatemala, Costa Rican and Nicaraguan envoys were brought together to conclude a treaty. They sought the advice of the American minister whom Bayard permitted to be present as the personal friend of both Governments, "if requested by both, but any diplomatic intervention in behalf of either is incompatible with our attitude when this Government is called upon to arbitrate." A treaty was concluded but the Nicaraguan Congress refused to ratify it. Thereupon both Governments had recourse to the arbitration of President Cleveland in accordance with an understanding which had been reached when there were indications that direct negotiations would fail. Both the President and the Secretary of State, however, refused to extend the functions of an arbitrator to include the settling of questions which grew out of the award; hence, on Nicaragua's complaint that Costa Rica's grant of a railroad concession violated the terms of the award, Bayard telegraphed Hall: "We have no authority in regard to contract, but are only concerned in promoting good relations between Nicaragua and Costa Rica."[37]

At the very moment Bayard assumed his duties as Secretary there was awaiting his attention an isthmian problem. Late in 1884 a revolution started in some of the Colombian states, and in January it reached Panama. On April 2 Minister Becerra intimated to Bayard "that sufficient American forces on board of vessels of war stationed at Panama and Colón should be there, within sight of events, ready and competent to give to persons and property of American citizens that effective protection and shelter" that the Colombian Government was, unfortunately, unable to afford at the moment. Two days later Señor Becerra incorporated in a memorandum to Bayard his understanding of the attitude of the United States: he said the American Secretary of State had declared that reinforcements were sent to the Isthmus "solely in order that the duty might be fulfilled which is rendered incumbent on the United States by the treaty of 1846." Minister Scruggs at Bogotá was instructed to state the same thing to the Colombian Foreign Minister and to emphasize the fact that there was no intention of intervening in the domestic struggle. Again when Cleveland gave an account of the affair in his annual message, he said that he had complied with the stipulations of the treaty without any idea of intervention.

Out of the Colombian revolution came one episode in dealing with which Bayard displayed something of his Latin-American policy and incidentally his interpretation of the Monroe Doctrine. One Cerruti, an Italian subject, was arrested for complicity in the insurrection and was subsequently rescued by Italians and placed on a war vessel. The Colombian Government tried to institute legal proceedings but Italy denied their jurisdiction and demanded an indemnity for Cerruti's arrest. This the Colombians refused to pay, whereupon the Italian minister demanded his passports and left Bogotá announcing that war vessels would visit Atlantic and Pacific ports of Colombia to enforce the payment. As soon as Bayard knew about the affair he sought the co-operation of Great Britain and France in urging upon Italy and Colombia the submission of the controversy to the arbitration of Spain, and said that "the United States can not view with indifference a resort to armed force by a European Power upon a government with whom as to a part of its territory we have a special convention guaranteeing neutrality, which means freedom from obstruction."[38] When the two countries consented to submit the issue to Spain's arbitrament, Bayard reiterated this sentiment in an instruction to the minister at Bogotá: "We are sincerely glad of a mode of settlement which will not excite the serious concern of the United States, were a European Power to resort to force against a Sister Republic of this Hemisphere, as to the sovereign and uninterrupted use of a part of whose territory we are guarantors, under the solemn faith of a treaty."[39] It was not upon abstract principles of the Monroe Doctrine but because of specific treaty engagements that he feared possible Italian intervention.

Another situation containing disconcerting possibilities grew out of an attempt of President Barrios of Guatemala to effect by force a federal union of the Central American states. Just before the close of the Arthur Administration Barrios issued a proclamation to this effect, declaring traitors all persons hostile to the union and announcing that treaties concluded by any one of the states thereafter would be void. This pronouncement about treaties particularly disturbed Bayard, for the Frelinghuysen-Zavala convention had not yet been disposed of by the Administration. But Barrios, if it had been his intention to get rid of this treaty for some reason or other, soon saw the danger of the proposal and in a subsequent decree stated that there was no intention of molesting engagements already entered upon.

Nicaragua and Costa Rica opposed the Barrios scheme from the first, and while Honduras and Salvador at the beginning fell in with the idea, President Zaldivar of Salvador later reconsidered his position and made ready to resist any attempt to hold him in line. Barrios found himself in an embarrassing situation. He persisted, nevertheless, in trying to carry it through, in the face of the hostility of three Central American states and the disapproval of Mexico and the United States, until his army was defeated and he himself killed in an encounter with the Salvadoreans. The good offices of the United States, as well as those of other countries which had diplomatic representatives in Central America, aided in getting the opponents together and patching up a temporary peace. Within a week President Zaldivar attempted to initiate a project which had all the outward appearance of Barrios's scheme, but he, too, lacked the co-operation of all Salvador's neighbours except Honduras. Some rather inconclusive fighting took place, Guatemala protested against Nicaragua's attempt to interfere in the domestic affairs of Salvador, and once more the good offices of foreign powers, including the United States, brought about an adjustment.

From time to time during the next three years schemes for uniting these five republics were proposed. Each time Bayard took the same position he had in 1885: "The progress of the Central American States toward some more concentrated expression of their geographical association and their common and compatible interests, is watched with much solicitude and interest. The five States undoubtedly possess a quasi-national relation, if not among themselves as a federation, at least collectively as regards the rest of the world. The attitude of Salvador, the most progressive and populous of the States, can not fail to effect the material solution of the problem."[40] Bayard, however, set his face against union by force and disapproved the action of the states in intermeddling with each other's affairs. "We strongly reprobate such plotting against each other's peace by Central American States. You can express our positive disapproval of all such schemes": this was the essence of a cable instruction to Hall in July, 1885.[41]

One incidental result of the attempt to force union

upon Central America raised a delicate though not a lasting question. Mexico watched closely what Barrios was doing and, at one time, by a concentration of forces on the frontier for the ostensible purpose of maintaining order roused apprehension in Guatemala and concern in Washington. Mexican intervention in Guatemala, with whom Mexico had a long-standing boundary quarrel, promised to bring about a situation fraught with danger for all Central America as well as for the United States. Bayard's method of procedure had in mind Mexico as well as Guatemala, as a letter he wrote to the President intimates: "From the enclosed telegram you will see that Barrios is likely to receive a check from Mexico—and I believe the telegram denouncing coercion and demanding peace and unity which I sent to our Agent in Central America day before yesterday may save much trouble and assist in restoring order."[42]

Another topic, entirely disconnected with the question of an isthmian transit, had already been brought to the attention of the Department before Bayard became Secretary and was to come up from time to time until its solution was reached in Cleveland's second Administration. This was the dispute over the boundary between Venezuela and British Guiana. Bayard had been in office less than a month when Señor Soteldo, the Venezuelan envoy, wrote him that he hoped soon to present information about "the recent attempts of the British authorities to consummate the usurpation of a great part of Venezuelan Guiana in order to control the mouth of the Orinoco." A month later came a summary of correspondence with Frelinghuysen and a request for Secretary Bayard to turn his attention to the problem. No definite invitation for the United States to take positive action was made, for the Government of Venezuela hoped that nothing would occur that might "disqualify that Republic from arbitrating with absolute independence in the matter." After carefully going through the earlier correspondence Bayard sent Phelps a "compendious report" on July 20, 1885, and instructed him to ascertain from General Guzman, then in London on this business, what progress was being made. After sketching the course of the conversations with Soteldo he said:

"The proposals of Venezuela to this Government for an alliance, in return for certain exclusive privileges in the navigation of the Orinoco and other Venezuelan waters, has never assumed a definite form and has not been renewed; and it is adverted to here as in the last instruction to Mr. Lowell, simply for your confidential guidance in any conversation you may have with General Guzman, or with the Venezuelan minister. The Venezuelan Government, as you will perceive from the correspondence, has never definitely stated what course it desires this Government to pursue; but on the contrary has expressed a desire to be guided by our counsel, indulging, perhaps, in the hope that we will ultimately act in its behalf to establish its claim against Great Britain."[43]

The affair moved slowly until the latter part of 1886. Great Britain continued to maintain her previous position that the whole question could be settled by direct negotiation and that there was no need for an arbitration. The Venezuelan Government, however, steadily became more irritated until in December the situation looked so dubious that Phelps was instructed to tender "to Her Majesty's Government the good offices of the United States to promote an amicable settlement of the respective claims of Great Britain in the premises," and at the same time to offer American arbitration if acceptable to both sides. Bayard called attention to the fact that this offer had never before been made, primarily because of the reluctance of Venezuela to have the United States do anything that would disqualify that Government as an arbitrator. But Venezuela was now agreeable to the plan and let it be known that if no reply or an unfavourable response should be received before the convening of her Congress, diplomatic relations with Great Britain would be broken. The British Government, taking this as a threat, informed Phelps that, although fully appreciating the friendly feelings prompting the action of his Government, they were precluded from submitting the question to a third power then; they had already refused a similar offer from Spain. Consequently on February 12, 1887, diplomatic relations were "suspended" although not "severed" and on March 12 the British minister left Caracas.

Interruption of diplomatic relations was not followed by any more serious results, although war vessels were stationed in Venezuelan waters to care for the interests of British subjects. Nevertheless, the situation was delicate and Bayard was not at ease about it. In the middle of May, 1887, he telegraphed Phelps to inquire if then the good offices of the United States "could be availed of to effect a renewal of formal relations." It appeared that an adjustment was not out of the question but the return, shortly after, of British war craft in response to a complaint from British ship-owners that they were being mulcted by the Venezuelans under colour of legal process, the alleged assertion of a claim to jurisdiction over the gold-mining region of Caratal by the legislature of Demarara, and the reported decree of the Governor of British Guiana denying the validity of a Venezuelan railroad grant on the ground that its line would pass through British territory, these events threw things back where they were.

All this was disquieting information if it was well authenticated. On February 17, 1888, Bayard wrote Phelps in a confidential dispatch: "The claim now stated to have been put forth by the authorities of British Guiana necessarily gives rise to great disquietude, and creates an apprehension that the territorial claim does not follow historical traditions or evidence, but is apparently indefinite." Pointing out the lack of agreement between the maps in successive issues of the British colonial office lists he went on:

"It may be well for you to express anew to Lord Salisbury the great gratification it would afford this Government to see the Venezuelan dispute amicably and honorably settled, by arbitration or otherwise, and our readiness to do anything we properly can to assist to that end.

"In the course of your conversation you may refer to the publication of the London Financier of January 24 . . . and express apprehension lest the widening pretensions of British Guiana to possess territory over which Venezuelan jurisdiction has never here-tofore been disputed may not diminish the chances for a practical settlement.

"If, indeed, it should appear that there is not a fixed limit to the British boundary claim, our good disposition to aid in a settlement might not only be defeated, but be obliged to give place to a feeling of grave concern."[44]

Subsequent intelligence made Bayard doubt a little whether some of the Venezuelan suspicions were well founded. Furthermore he suspected all along that the Government of Venezuela was quite willing to have the United States assume a principal role, a position which did not comport either with Bayard's sense of fitness or with his policy of non-intervention. "This Govern-ment can not, of course," he wrote Phelps in April, 1888, "assume in any way to act as negotiator for Venezuela, and the Department takes it for granted that Mr. Blanco concurs in this view of the subject."[45] Moreover, it was evident that Venezuela was unwilling to admit that any portion of the disputed area could possibly belong to Great Britain. In spite of everything, how-ever, Bayard felt that a peaceable adjustment was far from being out of the question, but the first step in its direction must come through a resumption of diplo-matic relations and in this Venezuela had to take the initiative. But no further progress was made before the Administration went out of office and the issue remained unsettled until Cleveland became Presi-dent again and Bayard American ambassador near the Court of St. James's.

Throughout the four years of Bayard's secretaryship there were numerous issues which consumed time and led to what seemed, in some cases, endless correspondence. Questions arising from the shipping act of 1884, from the exclusion of American pork from certain European countries, questions of naturalization and the treatment of naturalized Americans in their native lands, old spoliation claims, passport regulations, rights under treaties—all these had to be handled with patience and good humour, but none of them brought up particularly important, certainly not critical problems.

Thomas F. Bayard took into office with him a seriousness of purpose observable through all his career. His was a traditional policy—avoidance of entangling cooperation with foreign countries. Maintenance of such a policy was becoming more and more difficult as one Secretary succeeded another, for the fight against those forces which drew America into closer touch with the rest of the world was ever being waged against greater odds. It would have taken merely acquiescence in many a case to plunge the United States into the midst of *Weltpolitik*, but Bayard was not passive. He fought against all those insidious tendencies with a consistency almost unparalleled. His rule of conduct which he was constantly impressing upon American representatives abroad may be summed up in the words from an instruction to a Central American chargé:

"The United States does not act in combination or alliance with any foreign state in its relations to any third power. Good faith and fair dealing directly with the Government to which he is accredited is the measure of the duty of an American envoy and abstention from taking sides between parties in domestic questions and local disputes is a prime and essential rule of conduct."[46]

When the Cleveland Administration left office Mr. Bayard retired to private life and resumed his law practice in Wilmington. Four years later he was drawn again into public service by accepting the position as ambassador of the United States near the Court of St. James's. This acceptance placed in London a worthy successor to a long line of distinquished envoys of ministerial rank, where he sustained the high traditions which attached to that particular position by his urbanity, his dignity and his knowledge of American foreign relations. He adopted, as he had while Secretary of State, a policy of conciliation far removed from the truculent aggressiveness which would have appealed to a large section of his countrymen, some of whom were of his own political party. The diplomacy of the United States during Bayard's sojourn in Great Britain belongs properly in the sketches, which follow in this series, of Secretaries Gresham and Olney. This, however, may be the place to mention certain facts which were connected more with Bayard personally than with the broader field of diplomatic policy.

On several occasions as ambassador, Bayard had an opportunity to make public addresses which were characterized by both candour and good feeling. In November, 1895, speaking to an Edinburgh audience on "Individual freedom: the germ of national progress and permanence," he paid his respects to autocracy on the one hand and to socialism on the other, and, in the course of his remarks, made this statement:

"In my own country I have witnessed the insatiable growth of that form of state socialism styled 'protection,' which, I believe, has done more to foster class legislation and create inequality of fortune, to corrupt public life, to banish men of independent mind and character from public councils, to lower the tone of national representation, blunt public conscience, create false standards in the popular mind to familiarize it with reliance upon state aid and guardianship in private affairs, divorce ethics from politics, and place politics upon the low level of a mercenary scramble than any other single cause."

This speech, when reported in the United States, created a commotion which was not wholly submerged by the publication of the correspondence over the Venezuela boundary, and gave rise in Congress to much acrimonious discussion. In the House of Representatives a proposal to impeach the ambassador was brought forward, and resolutions of censure were adopted by that body after a discussion which reached the low political level adverted to by Bayard in his address.

Upon the expiration of Cleveland's second term, in 1897, Mr. Bayard returned to his home in Delaware, but he did not take up his active professional life, for his health was failing. In the summer of 1898, while on a visit to his daughter, Mrs. Samuel D. Warren, at Dedham, Massachusetts, he was fatally stricken and died on September 28.

JAMES GILLESPIE BLAINE

SECRETARY OF STATE

MARCH 5, 1889, TO JUNE 4, 1892

(SECOND TERM)

BY

JOSEPH B. LOCKEY

ASSOCIATE PROFESSOR OF AMERICAN HISTORY
UNIVERSITY OF CALIFORNIA AT LOS ANGELES

JAMES G. BLAINE

FROM A PHOTOGRAPH BY L. C. HANDY

JAMES GILLESPIE BLAINE

CHAPTER I

PRIVATE CITIZEN

AS we have seen in the previous volume, James Gillespie Blaine's first tenure of the office of Secretary of State came to a premature close in December, 1881, following the death of President Garfield. Retiring to private life he enjoyed for the first time in more than twenty years freedom from the cares of office. A part of his leisure he devoted to the happy associations of family and friends, and a part he employed in the congenial task of writing. The chief product of his literary labours was his *Twenty Years of Congress*, which appeared in two volumes, the first in 1884, and the second two years later. "The book puts you easily and securely in the front rank of American men of letters,"[1] wrote John Hay, after he had read the first volume. Hay's encomium was perhaps a bit hasty. Though the second volume proved to be in no way inferior to the first, the work hardly gives Blaine an eminent position among American writers. It has merit and as it was widely read at the time of its publication, it enhanced the fame of its author. Nearly half the first volume is devoted to a review of the events leading up to the Civil War. The rest of this volume, together with the second, consists of a circumstantial account of the two decades from the beginning of Lincoln's Presidency to that of Garfield. The emphasis, in harmony with the title, is on the doings of Congress; and as Blaine sat in the House and Senate during the greater part of the period, he brought to the performance of his task an exceptional knowledge of the events of which he was the chronicler. For this reason and because of the author's enlivening and penetrating comments on the men and measures of the time, the work will long remain a source of peculiar enlightenment to the student of that momentous epoch.

Blaine was no recluse, intent in the absorption of intellectual pursuits. Essentially a man of action, he must have chafed under his enforced retirement. He must have yearned for the vindication of his foreign policy, which had been ruthlessly cast aside by his successor at the State Department. Activity such as would satisfy him and vindication such as he hoped for could only come with the return to power of his own section of the party. In this event, he himself might be the fortunate occupant of the White House, or else he would again be given an opportunity to renew his labours as Secretary of State. Without impatience he calmly awaited the turn of events. In March, 1883, Mrs. Blaine wrote to one of her daughters: "Your father is as little a candidate as though he had succeeded in '76 and '80. The one thing he perhaps does desire is to be once more Secretary of State."[2] A year later, as the time for the nominating convention approached, his attitude had suffered no apparent change. He did nothing to encourage the idea that he was a candidate. He seemed positively disinclined to have his name used, but he made no effort to check a movement begun in his favour by his friends; and when the convention met, his supporters were in the ascendancy. They gave him the nomination on the fourth ballot.

In his letter of acceptance, Blaine reverted to his much criticized views on foreign affairs. He forecast a return to the policy of the Garfield Administration with its emphasis on the promotion of peace and commerce in the new world. He proposed to advance peace by inviting the other American countries to join the United States in an agreement to adjust all their differences with one another by amicable means; he hoped that the accomplishment of this object in the western hemisphere would favourably affect the nations beyond the sea, and thus powerfully contribute to the universal acceptance of the philanthropic and Christian principle of arbitration. Adverting to the unsatisfactory state of our commerce with our friends and neighbours of this continent, he averred that we received from them vastly more than we sent them in exchange, the balance going not to them but to European manufacturers, for whom we were but paymasters. This condition he hoped to change by enlarging the Latin-American market for our goods. In his opinion, no field promised so much and none had been so little cultivated. He concluded his letter by declaring that "Our foreign policy should be an American policy in its broadest and most comprehensive sense—a policy of peace, of friendship, of commercial enlargement."[3]

Blaine entered the campaign only to be defeated. Of the several causes which produced this result, the most important was a serious defection from the ranks of the

Republican party. The followers of President Arthur were held in line, but a considerable group, known as the Reformers, broke away and enlisted under the banner of the Democratic nominee, Grover Cleveland. Among this intransigent element were some of the great journalists, who used the powerful influence of their newspapers to defeat Blaine; and among them also were some of the most highly respected leaders of the party, in whose train thousands of voters doubtless followed. This opposition was based in the main on the old charges concerning the candidate's personal integrity, and to a less degree on the belief that his foreign policy would embroil the United States in conflict with other nations.

An incident which occurred in New York City toward the close of the contest was one of the minor causes of Blaine's defeat. The candidate was there visited by numerous delegations, and the spokesman of one of them, a certain Reverend Mr. Burchard, in an address distinguished for its impropriety, characterized the Democratic party as the party of "Rum, Romanism and Rebellion." Blaine apparently did not notice the obnoxious phrase and said nothing in his reply to rebuke what was a manifest attempt to introduce a sectarian issue.[4] The absurd alliteration was instantly caught up and attributed to Blaine himself. When, a day or two later, he tried to correct the false report, it was too late. The harm could not be undone. He lost New York, and with it the Presidency, by a little more than one thousand votes.

Deeply disappointed in the outcome of the election, Blaine sought consolation in a return to his writing.

When he had finished his *Twenty Years of Congress*, he made a collection of his speeches, articles, and diplomatic correspondence, which he published under the title of *Political Discussions*. In the summer of 1887, he sailed for Europe, where he remained travelling in the British Isles and on the Continent for more than a year. He was in Paris the following December, when Cleveland sent his famous message to Congress on tariff reform. Instantly seizing the opportunity to controvert the President, Blaine dictated an interview which was cabled to New York and published close upon the heels of the message. His spirited rejoinder served as a rallying cry to his party, and the tariff became the issue of the approaching campaign. The once defeated candidate seemed destined to be again the Republican standard-bearer. He proved unwilling to allow his name to go before the convention unless he were "called upon by the practically unanimous judgment and wish of the party." Such unanimity Blaine knew could not be attained.[5] He remained abroad and his friends withheld his name. Their support, at Blaine's request, was turned to Benjamin Harrison, who was nominated and elected.

For the second time Blaine had been in effect a president-maker, and for the second time public opinion designated him as Secretary of State. About the middle of January, 1889, he received the formal tender of the office, and with it a personal note from the President-elect.[6] In this confidential communication, Harrison assured Blaine that the offer was made in a spirit of the most perfect cordiality and confidence, and then he indicated summarily what he conceived should be the foreign policy of the Administration. "I am especially interested," he said, "in the improvement of our relations with the Central and South American States. We must win their confidence by deserving it. It will not come on demand. Only men of experience, of high character and of broad views, should be sent even to the least important of these states. In all this, I am sure you will be a most willing coadjutor, for your early suggestions and earnest advocacy have directed public attention to the subject." Turning then to our relations with the European governments, Harrison expressed the belief that they would be easy of management. There were certain pending questions which would require early and discreet attention; but he was convinced that Blaine's familiarity with the origin and progress of these differences, and indeed with the whole history of our diplomacy, would give him great advantage in dealing with them.

Finding the views thus briefly outlined in accord with his own, Blaine had no hesitation in accepting the appointment. Thus he resumed the task which the assassination of Garfield had so grievously interrupted. He was now, in some respects at least, better qualified for the post. Leisure, well-spent, had deepened his knowledge. Travel had broadened his outlook on life, and experience had ripened him. He was physically old beyond his years, but his intellectual powers were as yet unimpaired. Entering upon his duties with enthusiasm, he devoted himself assiduously to the tasks which were presented to him at the State Department.

THE settlement of the Oregon question and the acquisition of California, shortly before the middle of the century, had strongly attracted the attention of the American people toward the Pacific. Blaine, then growing to manhood, seems to have shared the conviction of many of his countrymen, that the rounding out of our continental area would be followed by further annexations in the ocean beyond. What might have been the outcome if sectional issues and a great civil conflict had not diverted the energies of the nation temporarily into other channels, no one can say. But the preoccupations of the time did not entirely destroy the hunger for territory. In the closing years of the war negotiations for the purchase of the Danish West Indies were begun, and when they proved ineffectual, various schemes were set on foot under Seward's secretaryship looking to other acquisitions in the region of the Caribbean. As the Senate, backed perhaps by public opinion, frowned upon expansion in that direction, the negotiations all resulted in failure. No territory once ardently desired by the slave interests was to be acquired. With Alaska the case was different. It was purchased in 1867, and in the same year Midway Island, more than a thousand miles west of Hawaii, was formally occupied by an officer of the American

Navy. Thus were established new contacts with the Pacific.

Blaine took no stand either officially or unofficially on any of these specific issues. When the bill appropriating funds for the purchase of Alaska came before the lower house, he did not speak, and abstained from voting. A little later, however, in the interval between the election of Grant and his assumption of the Presidency, Blaine set forth his views in general and rather inflated terms, forecasting an era of expansion and national self-assertion. With the change of administration would come, he predicted, a "higher standard of American citizenship — with more character and dignity to the name abroad." Our diplomacy would be rescued from the "subservient tone" by which we had been humiliated, and our true position as the "first nation of the earth in rank and prestige" would be asserted. Every exigency, he maintained, whether of financial embarrassment, or domestic trouble, or misunderstandings with foreign nations, or peaceful "expansion of our flag and our sovereignty over insular or continental possessions, north or south," would be met with "the courage, the ability, and the conscience which American nationality and Christian Civilization demand."[7]

By the time Blaine first became Secretary of State, his idea of expansion had suffered a radical change. His Pan-American policy had taken definite shape in his mind, and territorial aggrandizement at the expense of the neighbours, whose friendship was essential to the success of that policy, was no longer to be thought of. He accordingly took advantage of every opportunity to assure these states of his most scrupulous regard for their independence and territorial integrity. To Mexico, he expressed himself unequivocally. "At this late day," he said, "it needs no disclaimer on our part of the existence of even the faintest desire in the United States for territorial expansion south of the Rio Grande. The boundaries of the two republics have been long settled in conformity with the best jurisdictional interests of both. The line of demarcation is not conventional merely. It is more than that. It separates a Spanish-American people from a Saxon-American people. It divides one great nation from another with distinct and natural finality."[8]

Against expansion in other directions, he had no scruples. Whatever may have been his early attitude toward the purchase of Alaska, he later came to look upon the territory as a valuable possession. He had long favoured the annexation of Hawaii.[9] A definite proposal to that end had been made by the Hawaiian Government in 1854, but as it was accompanied by demands unacceptable to the American Government, it was rejected. Shortly after the Civil War, on the initiative of Secretary Seward, the project was revived, likewise without result. As an alternative, various attempts were made in the meantime to negotiate a reciprocity treaty, and at last, in 1875, such an agreement was concluded. By its terms, virtual free trade was established between the ports of the islands and those of the United States. The advantages which the United States thus secured were made exclusive by a stipulation binding the Hawaiian Government not to grant similar privileges to any other power. The arrangement proved of great material benefit to both parties. The sugar industry was prodigiously increased in the islands, resulting in a corresponding increase in commercial interchange with the United States.[10] Annexation projects were no longer agitated. Accordingly, it fell to Blaine's lot as Secretary of State, not to promote schemes of acquisition, but to defend the arrangement of 1875.

As soon as the treaty went into effect complications arose, due to claims which Great Britain and Germany made against the Hawaiian Government. The German claims, being based on general grounds and having no support in treaty rights, were soon abandoned. This was not the case with the British claims. A trade convention which was in force between Great Britain and Hawaii, and which contained the most-favoured-nation clause, gave the British Government a more plausible basis for complaint. In effect, the British contention was for equality of trade privileges. The United States was an interested observer of the dispute, for if Hawaii had acceded to the British demands, the result would have been practical nullification of our treaty of 1875. As the negotiations proceeded, the United States did everything in its power to strengthen the hands of its Pacific protégé. The matter was still pending in 1881. Blaine took no new ground, but with his usual vigour he re-stated the position of his Government: namely, the traditional American principle that the advantages conceded to the United States under the treaty were an equivalent for certain reciprocal concessions to Hawaii, and could not as a matter of right be claimed by another nation under the most-favoured-nation clause. He warned Hawaii against yielding, and assured it of support in the event undue pressure should be brought to persuade or compel action in derogation of the treaty. With this the incident was closed. Perhaps Great Britain was unwilling to press the matter further, through fear of precipitating a new movement for American annexation.

Another Hawaiian matter came before Blaine's attention during his first administration of the office of Secretary of State. This was the subject of coolie immigration. The astonishing agricultural development in the islands, together with the rapid decline of the native population, had created an unusual demand for labour, which certain interests, supposedly hostile to the United States, wished to satisfy by bringing in workers from India. The idea seems to have been to build up a countervailing influence against the ever-growing power of the United States, by introducing into the islands a mass of British subjects who would form in time, perhaps, a majority of the population. A convention was discussed under the terms of which it was proposed that the labourers brought in should be subject to a British protector, and not to the courts of the country. Blaine pointed out that extraterritorial privileges of this sort would violate the treaty rights of the United States, and he admonished the Hawaiian Government in no uncertain terms against entering into such an agreement.[11] Nothing more was heard of the proposal; but it is fair to say that it may not have had at any time the serious backing of the British Government.

These were, after all, small matters. Blaine's comprehensive mind did not linger with them. It swept on to issues far more weighty. He was concerned not alone with Hawaii, but with the immense area of the Pacific. More than that, he was concerned with the maritime and commercial supremacy of the United States among the nations of the earth. Hawaii merely served him as a point of departure for the expression of a new conception of manifest destiny. "Taking San Francisco," he said, "as the commercial center on the western slope, a line drawn northwesterly to the Aleutian group, marks our Pacific border almost to the confines of Asia. A corresponding line drawn southwesterly from San Francisco to Honolulu, marks the natural limit of the ocean belt within which our trade with the oriental countries must flow, and is, moreover, the direct line of communication between the United States and Australasia. Within this line lies the commercial domain of our western coast."[12]

The Pacific policy of the United States Blaine regarded as the natural complement of its Atlantic policy. The extension of commercial empire westward was a vitally important factor in the development of the states fronting the Pacific Ocean; but no less important was free communication between the western and the eastern coasts through an isthmian channel under American control. The Atlantic coast we had been able to guard against foreign interference, without extending our territorial possessions beyond the mainland. Cuba was a case in point. We had prevented the intervention of France and England in the island, and though it remained in the hands of Spain, it formed a part of the American commercial system. In the meantime, we had acquired in the north Pacific a dominant influence which we could never consent to see decreased by hostile intrusion. Hawaii on the one side occupied a position similar to that of Cuba on the other. One was the key to the maritime dominion of the Pacific states, the other the key to the Gulf trade. The material possession of Hawaii was no more desired than was that of Cuba. But under no circumstances, declared Blaine, could we permit either to be cut adrift from the American system, to which both indispensably belong.[13]

Such was Blaine's Pacific policy in 1881, and such essentially was to be his policy seven or eight years later, when he assumed for the second time the Secretaryship of State. The situation in some respects by then had changed. The international rivalries which in the earlier period revolved about Hawaii had been attracted to a more distant centre in the island group of Samoa. It so happened that of all the matters pressing for the attention of the Department of State, upon the accession of Harrison to the Presidency, a dispute arising out of a conflict of interests between the United States, Germany, and Great Britain in Samoa was the most urgent.

The history of the dispute cannot be again rehearsed here. The reader is referred to earlier pages of this volume for a summary of our relations with the people of Samoa and their rulers. An absorbingly interesting chronicle of the rivalries of England, Germany and the United States from 1875 to 1889 may be found in Robert Louis Stevenson's *A Footnote to History*. Explaining his title, Stevenson said that an affair worthy of a note of a few lines in any general history had been expanded to the size of a volume. It is a brief note rather than a volume which will serve our purpose. The subject may be dismissed by saying that commercial rivalry between the foreign interests in the islands was at the bottom of all the disturbances. What the Governments at Washington and London and Berlin did to restrain their eager nationals in the midst of the Pacific is of more interest, and deserves more space in the history of American diplomacy.

As the United States was under obligations by the terms of the treaty of 1878 to use its good offices in behalf of Samoa, Secretary of State Bayard suggested a conference of the three powers. His suggestion was favourably received and the conference was held at Washington in the summer of 1887.[14] After lengthy discussion, agreement was found to be impossible, and the conference adjourned to meet at a later date, with the understanding that in the meantime the *status quo* should be maintained. Unfortunately, as soon as news of the failure at Washington reached the islands, a fresh outbreak occurred. On some pretext, Germany declared war on the native King, Malietoa, dethroned and deported him, and set up a certain Tamasese in his stead.[15] As these proceedings went on, the American and British consuls, supported by their countrymen and backed by warships, ranged themselves on the side of Mataafa, leader of the native element hostile to the Germans. The relations between the Americans and Germans had by this time become very tense, and armed conflict was feared. In this state of affairs, Prince Bismarck proposed, in January, 1889, a renewal of the conference in Berlin. President Cleveland accepted the proposal, but as the end of his Administration was approaching, left the appointment of commissioners to his successor.

Of these arrangements Blaine was aware, and, in anticipation of the duties in connection with the conference, he began at once the study of the Samoan question. On February 10, 1889, Mrs. Blaine, who invariably reflected her husband's interests, wrote: "Now your father is reading aloud Samoa to Walker [Blaine's son, and Assistant Secretary of State], and my thoughts diverge to Malietoa," and a day later: "Your father is now looking up Samoa on the map. It would be worth your while, if you have not already done so, to read up Samoa."[16] Indeed, Blaine took the matter seriously, and when he set about writing the instructions to the commissioners to the Berlin conference, he had a thorough grasp of every detail of the question. Whether he had a solution for the difficulties remains to be seen.

The American commissioners were John A. Kasson, William Walter Phelps and George H. Bates. Harold M. Sewall accompanied them as secretary. Kasson was a diplomatist of ability and of varied experience. Phelps was a distinguished lawyer, who had served creditably as a member of Congress and for a brief period as minister to Austria. Bates and Sewall furnished expert knowledge. Bates had been sent by the preceding Administration to investigate and report upon conditions in the islands, and Sewall had performed for some time the duties of United States consul at Apia. Thus the commission was well constituted, and it had need to be, for the German representation headed by Prince Bismarck, and the British by Sir Edward Malet, would otherwise have placed the Americans at too great a disadvantage.

Blaine's instructions to the commission maintained the two principles upon which his predecessor had based his negotiations.[17] These were: first, that the independence of the native Samoan Government should be respected; and, secondly, that the three treaty powers should enjoy perfect equality of commercial rights and privileges in the islands. These principles, Blaine thought, provided a sound and sufficient basis for cooperative action. But previous discussions had developed what seemed to be an irreconcilable difference. Germany had proposed a plan whereby the power having preponderating interests in the islands should appoint, with the concurrence of the other powers concerned, an adviser to the Government of Samoa, who, as mandatary, should be charged with the duty of maintaining public order and the security of property. As Germany's interests were admittedly preponderant, the adoption of such a plan would have given that power control of the islands. International equality would have been destroyed and Samoan independence violated. It would have been better frankly to deliver the islands to Germany as a colonial possession. The United States could not permit such an arrangement, for it was under obligations to protect the rights and interests of its citizens resident in the south Pacific. Without desiring to dominate, it had every wish to develop a stable and just government in Samoa, but to convert the assumed supremacy of one of the powers into a legalized government, promised no relief.

There were other reasons, averred Blaine, why the United States could not accept a scheme of subordination. Its interests required the possession of a naval station in the remote parts of the Pacific, and by treaty we had obtained such a station. We could not consent, therefore, to any form of government in Samoa which in contingencies of the future might check or control development of this American right. Nor could we forget that our interests in the Pacific were steadily increasing; that our commerce with the East was rapidly developing; and that the certainty of an early opening of an isthmian canal under American control must create changes in which no power could be more directly interested than the United States. Consequently, the United States could not accept even temporary subordination in any question involving the present and future relations in the Pacific. To do so would be inconsistent with that international consideration and dignity to which this country by continental position and expanding interests must always be entitled.

These were the general considerations of Blaine's Samoan policy. Specifically he had little to suggest. The scheme advocated by Secretary of State Bayard, in the previous conference, providing for the appointment by the treaty powers of three secretaries to form, with the king and vice-king, the executive government of Samoa, he did not find acceptable. Such an arrangement, he maintained, would be in effect a joint protectorate, to which there were grave and obvious objections. Under the limitations set forth, the elaboration of a plan was the proper work of the conference, and weighty consideration would be given to any solution it might propose.

The conference met late in April, 1889, and after a number of formal sessions extending over a period of six weeks, reached an agreement which was drawn up in the form of a general act, declaratory of the views and purposes of the three powers. In due course, the instrument was ratified by the signatory powers, and with the assent of Samoa, it went into effect. Blaine regarded the plan as substantially in accord with the American position, and he entertained the hope that it would be conducive to "the good government of Samoa under native autonomy." He believed, moreover, that it would settle the vexed questions which had agitated the three powers in their complex relations in the islands.[18] Apparently he did not perceive the true purport of the act. It did not conform to American ideals, nor was it destined to give the results desired. It assured the observance of only one of the principles for which our Government had stood. It safeguarded the equality of the United States, but failed to guarantee the autonomy of the Samoan Government. It set up a supreme court with wide jurisdiction over natives and foreigners and it provided that the one judge of the court should be named by the signatory powers, or, failing their agreement, by the King of Norway and Sweden. It contained provisions giving the foreigners control of municipal government, land titles, taxation, and other matters. In effect, the natives were left with nothing but the shadow of self-government. Not even the promised right of electing their own king was real; for it was provided that Malietoa, the deposed ruler, should be restored, that Mataafa should not be eligible, and that in case of dispute over future elections, the supreme court should decide the issue.[19]

With the establishment of the tripartite agreement,

Blaine's part in the Samoan affair ended. He had failed to solve the difficulty. The dissensions which the agreement was intended to quell soon broke out afresh, involving the American Government in troubles no less serious than those from which it had momentarily escaped. As soon as the failure of the agreement became apparent, it was denounced as a flagrant departure from our time-honoured custom of non-participation in the political arrangements between other governments. The situation illustrated, in the words of President Cleveland, "the impolicy of entangling alliances with foreign powers." These criticisms were not without justification. But it should be remembered that the entanglement began before Blaine assumed the duties of Secretary of State in 1889. It existed in an aggravated form during Cleveland's first Administration, and it was not made worse by the Berlin act. Indeed, this agreement seems to have been a necessary step toward the disentanglement which was effected some years later.

CHAPTER III

THE BERING SEA CONTROVERSY

THE Harrison Administration fell heir to a trouble-some controversy with Great Britain over the fur-seal fisheries in Bering Sea. Two main points were at issue: whether the United States had any right to exclusive jurisdiction in Bering Sea; and whether it had any right of protection or property in the fur seals outside the ordinary three-mile limit.

Claims to certain exclusive rights and privileges in the northwestern part of America and in the surrounding waters as far south as the fifty-fifth degree of latitude were made by Russia as early as 1799. By ukase of Emperor Alexander I in 1821 more extensive claims were made. Upon the remonstrance of the United States and Great Britain, Russia receded somewhat from these claims and concluded with the two powers in 1824 and 1825, respectively, nearly identical conventions, by the terms of which it was agreed that American citizens and British subjects should not be interfered with while navigating or fishing in "any part of the Great Ocean, commonly called the Pacific Ocean, or South Sea." The parallel of fifty-four degrees and forty minutes of north latitude was agreed upon as the southern limit of the Russian possessions on the "Northwest Coast of America." With slight changes, these stipulations remained in force until Alaska was transferred to the United States in 1867. In the meanwhile, the Americans and the British took little advantage of the right which they may have had under the treaties, or under international law, to share in the very remunerative industry of fur-seal fishing. That industry remained in effect a Russian monopoly.

Upon taking possession of the country, the United States succeeded to this virtual monopoly. Laws were immediately enacted prohibiting the killing of fur-bearing animals "within the limits of Alaska Territory, or in the waters thereof," except under authorization of the Secretary of the Treasury.[20] Among the fur-bearing animals thus protected the seal was the most important. Fur seals had formerly thrived in the seas of both hemispheres, but they had been nearly exterminated everywhere except in the North Pacific. Here three herds were left, two of which, known as the Asiatic herds, frequented the waters of Asia, and the third and most important, called the American herd, inhabited during the breeding season the islands of St. Paul and St. George in the Pribilof group in Bering Sea. In 1870, the United States leased the privilege of taking fur seals at the breeding places, called rookeries, to the Alaska Commercial Company. Stringent regulations intended to preserve the herd were put into force. Under this régime the industry became exceedingly lucrative and foreign vessels, particularly Canadian, were attracted to it. As these newcomers were not permitted to catch seals on the islands or within the three-mile limit, they confined their operations to slaughter in the open sea. The seals were innocent of the three-mile limit. The open sea operations of foreign hunters threatened the destruction of the herd, and the Americans engaged in the industry complained; but complaints proved ineffectual and more energetic measures were adopted.

In the summer of 1886, three Canadian schooners, while fishing at distances varying from 70 to 115 miles from land, were seized by an American revenue cutter and taken before the circuit court at Sitka on a charge of infringing the law, which forbade the taking of seals, without proper authorization, within the limits of Alaska, or "in the waters thereof." The judge who tried the case gave the phrase, "in the waters thereof," a broad interpretation. In his charge to the jury he declared that all the waters comprised between the western boundary of Alaska, as set forth in the treaty of 1867, on the one side, and the Aleutian Islands on the other—that is, nearly the whole of Bering Sea—were to be considered as the waters of Alaska, and that the prescribed penalties must attach against any violation of the law within these limits. The jury thus charged found the prisoners guilty, and the penalties of fine and imprisonment for themselves and confiscation for their vessels and cargoes were enforced against them. The trial judge, it appears, acted under the advice of the Attorney General at Washington. In part the action of the court seems to have been based on the theory that Bering Sea was *mare clausum*.[21]

Before the official reports of the trials reached Washington, the British Government protested against the seizures; and the President ordered the discontinuance of all pending proceedings. He directed moreover that the vessels should be discharged and that the prisoners should be released. But the next summer other arrests were made, which led to the spirited diplomatic exchanges between the Marquis of Salisbury and Secretary of State Bayard, already noticed in the preceding sketch of this series, and to Bayard's effort to settle the difficulty by international co-operation,[22] rather than by relying on a claim to jurisdiction over Bering Sea. The co-operative scheme was then reluctantly abandoned by the United States, after the British Government, on request of the Canadian authorities, withdrew from the proposed conference. Feeling in the United States was aroused. The press generally favoured drastic action, and Congress discussed with more or less heat every phase of the question. The House of Representatives proposed to solve the difficulty by declaring Bering Sea to be under the jurisdiction of the United States, and a bill to this effect was passed; but it was defeated in the Senate on the ground that it "involved serious matters of international law."

When Blaine assumed the duties of Secretary of State, the outlook for an adjustment of the dispute was far from promising. Owing to the refractory attitude of Canada a settlement by friendly agreement seemed remote. Negotiations had reached a stalemate. On the one side there was unwillingness to give up the right to take seals in the open sea, and on the other unwillingness to forgo the seizures until some provision should be made to protect the seal herd from indiscriminate killing. Accordingly, in the summer of 1889, the United States revenue cutters were again instructed to prevent the sealing operations in Bering Sea, and a number of British vessels were seized. Renewed protests of the British Government were met by Blaine in a communication of January 22, 1890, in which he made an earnest, if not altogether effective attempt to justify the means employed to protect the seal fisheries.

In this dispatch, Blaine did not defend the doctrine of *mare clausum*. His principal argument was that "the Canadian vessels arrested and detained in Bering Sea were engaged in a pursuit that was in itself *contra bonos mores*, a pursuit which of necessity involves a serious and permanent injury to the rights of the Government and people of the United States."[23] The taking of seals in the open sea, he averred, rapidly leads to the extinction of the herd. This was not only the opinion of experts based on prolonged observation and investigation, but the fact was also demonstrated by the well-nigh total destruction of all seal fisheries, except those in Bering Sea, where the Government of the United States was striving to preserve the industry, not altogether for the use of the American people, but for the use of the world at large. The reason for the destructiveness of taking seals in the open sea was clear. It was impossible to distinguish between the sexes, and male and female, old and young, alike, were killed. Of the females slaughtered many had helpless young on the island and these were left to starve. Not more than one-fifth, perhaps, of the seals killed were recovered from the water. The remedy was to take these animals on land only. There the necessary discrimination could be made, and there the necessary governmental supervision could be exercised. "It would seem, then, by fair reasoning," said Blaine, "that nations not possessing the territory upon which seals can increase their numbers by natural growth, and thus afford an annual supply of skins for the use of mankind, should refrain from the slaughter in open sea, where the extinction of the species is sure and swift."

The British Government, he said, justified the course of the Canadian vessels on the ground that their acts were committed on the high seas. But he doubted whether the British Government would permit interference with certain of its own interests on the same ground. The pearl fisheries of Ceylon, which extended more than twenty miles from the shore line, had been enjoyed by England without molestation ever since their acquisition many years before. So well organized was British ownership of those fisheries that the British Government felt authorized to sell the pearl-fishing rights from year to year to the highest bidder. The fisheries of the Grand Banks afforded another illustration. It was not likely that Great Britain would consent to highly destructive methods of fishing in those waters on the plea that the vicious acts were committed beyond the three-mile limit. The Bering Sea case was parallel. The Canadian vessels, in exterminating the fur seal, were totally destroying an article useful to mankind, in order that temporary and immoral gain might be acquired by a few persons. Could it seriously be maintained that the law of nations is powerless to prevent such violation of the common rights of man? Were the supporters of justice to be declared incompetent to prevent wrongs so odious and so destructive? "The law of the sea is not lawlessness," he declared. Nor could it be perverted to justify acts which are immoral in themselves, and which inevitably tend to results against the interests and against the welfare of man. He could not conceive that the British Government could be less indifferent to these evil results than was the Government of the United States.

In support of his position, Blaine appealed also to the doctrine of prescription. Though he was unwilling to make the extreme claim of *mare clausum*, yet he contended that Russia, and after it the United States, had acquired through the long-continued acquiescence of all nations, certain rights in Bering Sea. Russia had enjoyed the exclusive control of the seal fisheries from their discovery to 1867, and a like undisturbed control had been exercised by the United States for a period of twenty years. There had been no interruption or intrusion from any source. Under the United States, the business had been conducted peacefully, lawfully, and profitably—profitably to the Government, profitably to the Alaskan Company, profitably to the Aleuts, and profitably to the large numbers of English labourers who prepared the skins for the markets of the world. "The precedents, customs and rights," he maintained, "had been enjoyed by Russia and the United States for nearly a century." Into this secluded field of labour certain Canadian vessels asserted their right to enter. "Whence did the ships of Canada derive the right," he asked, "to do that which they had refrained from doing for more than ninety years? Upon what grounds did Her Majesty's Government defend in the year 1886, a course of conduct in Bering Sea which she had carefully avoided ever since the discovery of that sea? By what reasoning did Her Majesty's Government conclude that an act may be committed with impunity against the rights of the United States, which had never been attempted against the same rights when held by the Russian Empire?"

In bringing his dispatch to a close Blaine struck a conciliatory note. The United States had been ready to concede much, he declared, in order to adjust all differences of view. It had already proposed a solution which was not only equitable but generous. As the British Government had thus far declined to accept that solution, the United States awaited with interest and solicitude any counter proposal which might be submitted for a reasonable settlement of the difficulty. The American Government had not abandoned the position which it had maintained against the Russian claims to exclusive jurisdiction, nor would it withhold from any nation the privileges which it then demanded for itself. On the other hand, it was not disposed to exercise in those possessions any less authority than it was formerly willing to yield to Russia. "The President is persuaded," he concluded, "that all friendly nations will concede to the United States, the same rights and privileges on the lands and in the waters of Alaska, which the same friendly nations conceded to the Empire of Russia."

While this note was receiving the careful consideration of Lord Salisbury, negotiations were going on in Washington between the Secretary of State on one side, and the British minister, Sir Julian Pauncefote, and Charles H. Tupper, Minister of Marine and Fisheries of Canada, on the other. As Russia was interested in protecting its own seal fisheries, the Russian minister joined in the discussion. But no progress was made. A memorandum prepared by the Canadian representative disclosed a wide divergence of view on an essential point. It was contended that injury to seal life came from the indiscriminate slaughter at the breeding places on land, and that no instance could be shown where any harm had been done by killing at sea only. This was the reverse of the American contention. In view of this difference of opinion, Sir Julian Pauncefote proposed the appointment of a mixed commission of experts, who should investigate and report within two years. If agreement should then be impossible, all differences were to be submitted to the arbitration of an impartial government. Meanwhile, provisional regulations restricting pelagic sealing were to be put in force. The United States rejected the proposal, on the ground that the suggested regulations were inadequate. It offered, however, to continue the negotiations, and proposed that British sealers be forbidden to enter Bering Sea during the ensuing season. This proposal was in turn rejected by Great Britain. Thus the summer of 1890 approached with every prospect of more serious disagreement between the two powers. As the revenue cutters were being dispatched with fresh orders to arrest intruding sealers, Sir Julian Pauncefote communicated to Blaine a formal protest concluding with the declaration "that Her Britannic Majesty's Government must hold the Government of the United States responsible for the consequences that may ensue from acts which are contrary to the established principles of international law."[24]

The legal rights involved were discussed by Lord Salisbury in his reply to Blaine's dispatch of January 22. The agreement that pelagic sealing was *contra bonos mores* involved, he contended, two questions: first, whether the killing of fur seals in certain parts of the open sea was, from the point of view of international morality, *contra bonos mores;* and secondly, whether, if such were the case, this fact justified the seizure and confiscation of the private vessels of a friendly nation. By a principle of international maritime law universally accepted by jurists, the seizure of vessels on the high seas in time of peace was only admissible in the case of piracy, or in pursuance of mutual agreement. The pursuit of seals in the open sea had never been considered as piracy by any civilized state. Not even in the case of the slave trade had any one government "been allowed that general control of morals in this respect which Mr. Blaine claims on behalf of the United States in regard to seal hunting." Fur seals, he maintained, are animals *feræ naturæ,* universally regarded by jurists as *res nullius* until they are caught. It required something more than a mere declaration that the Government and people of the United States were losers by a certain course of proceeding, to render that course an immoral one. If, however, injury should be proved, Her Majesty's Government would be ready to consider what measures could properly be taken for the remedy of such injury, but they would be unable on that ground to depart from a principle on which free commerce on the high seas depends.

Lord Salisbury next dealt with Blaine's argument that the seal fisheries had been exclusively controlled by Russia and the United States successively down to 1886. He denied that either power had enjoyed such a monopoly, and in support of his position quoted from the writings of John Quincy Adams to show that the United States did not admit any part of the exclusive claims made by Russia in 1821. Referring to the statement that the taking of seals in the open sea rapidly leads to their extinction, he declared that abundant evidence could be adduced on the other side. But as it had been proposed that this part of the question should be examined by a committee to be appointed by the two Governments, he did not deem it necessary to deal with it. Finally, he maintained that in the absence of any special international agreement there was no sufficient justification for the forcible action taken against the subjects of Her Majesty engaged in lawful operations on the high seas.[25]

Lord Salisbury's communication elicited from Blaine a lengthy reply,[26] devoted mainly to an argument to show that the United States and Great Britain had never questioned Russia's claim to jurisdiction over Bering Sea. The quotation which Lord Salisbury had taken from a letter of J. Q. Adams to prove the contrary was, Blaine contended, erroneous, defective and misleading, for Adams did not protest against the ukase of Alexander as a whole, but only against that part of it which extended the Russian claim of sovereignty southward to fifty-one degrees north latitude. Both the United States and Great Britain contended that Russia's southern limit should rest at sixty degrees. The whole dispute was over the territory known as the northwest coast intervening between these limits. The treaties of 1824 and 1825 settled the question by an almost equal division of the disputed area, fixing the boundary at fifty-four degrees forty minutes. Though the Aleutian Islands dipped below this line, Russia's title to them was never in doubt, Blaine asserted.

Thus, according to the Secretary's thesis, all the lands bordering on Bering Sea were Russian, and the claim of Russia to exclusive rights and privileges in that sea remained unimpaired. The rights of navigation and fishing which the United States and Great Britain had obtained by treaty in "any part of the Great Ocean called the Pacific Ocean, or South Sea," did not apply to Bering Sea, for it was not a part of the Pacific Ocean. Except as modified by treaty, the ukase of 1821 stood as law in the Russian possessions until their transfer to the United States. Blaine admitted that this law did not declare Bering Sea *mare clausum*. It merely declared that the waters within one hundred miles of the shores were reserved for Russian subjects, the object being to protect the fur trade. Both the United States and Great Britain recognized, respected, and obeyed this law. Whatever Great Britain agreed to do or to refrain from doing touching the Russian province of Alaska and Bering Sea was not changed by the mere fact of the transfer of sovereignty; for by the treaty of cession it was expressly declared that "all the rights, franchises and privileges" belonging to Russia were conveyed to the United States. It was for the British Government to show, said Blaine, by what law it gained rights in that sea after the transfer of sovereignty to the United States.

Finally, Blaine reaffirmed the assertion that no destructive intrusion by sealers into Bering Sea had begun until 1886. The cases submitted by Lord Salisbury to rebut this argument were few, vague, and unimportant. They formed just a sufficient number of exceptions to establish the truth of the American contention. They showed something more. Among the cases cited there was not a single instance of the intrusion of a British sealer into Bering Sea until after Alaska had been transferred to the United States. Blaine felt justified therefore in asking once more: "Whence did the ships of Canada derive the right to do, in 1886, that which they had refrained from doing for nearly ninety years?"

In replying to these arguments, Lord Salisbury referred in greater detail to the diplomatic correspondence, and carefully analysed the treaties and other pertinent documents, copies of which he enclosed, in an effort to show: first, that England refused to admit any part of the claim asserted by the ukase of 1821 to a maritime jurisdiction and exclusive right of fishing from Bering Straits to the fifty-first parallel; secondly, that the convention of 1825, between Great Britain and Russia, was regarded on both sides as a renunciation on the part of Russia of that claim in its entirety; and thirdly, that though Bering Straits was known and specifically provided for, Bering Sea was not known by the name, but was regarded as a part of the Pacific Ocean. The answer to Secretary Blaine's question, therefore, was that Her Majesty's Government had always claimed the right of fishing in the waters of Bering Sea. Whether the right had been exercised or not was immaterial, for a public right to fish, catch seals, or pursue any other lawful occupation on the high seas could not be held to be abandoned by a nation from the mere fact that for a certain number of years it had not suited the subjects of that nation to exercise it. In conclusion, Lord Salisbury proposed that if the United States after examining the evidence and arguments submitted, still differed from the British Government as to the legality of the seizures, the question, with the issues that depended upon it, should be referred to impartial arbitration.[27]

Blaine was unconvinced. Legal and diplomatic questions, he observed, are often found, after prolonged discussion, to depend on the settlement of a single point. Such was the case in the present controversy. If Great Britain could maintain her position that Bering Sea, at the time the treaties were made with Russia in 1824 and 1825, was included in the Pacific Ocean, the Government of the United States would have no well grounded complaint against her. If the contrary could be shown, then the case against Great Britain would be complete and undeniable. The dispute prominently involved the meaning of the phrase "northwest coast," the British view being that it included the whole of the coast as far north as Bering Straits, and the American understanding being that it embraced only that part south of the Alaskan Peninsula; that is, the part below sixty degrees north latitude. The point was important. The former interpretation supported the British contention that Russia had renounced its exclusive claims throughout the whole region as far north as Bering Straits; and the latter strengthened the position of the United States in its argument that that renunciation only applied to the more restricted area, exclusive of Bering Sea. If in all the correspondence there had been no reference to Bering Sea, as Lord Salisbury pointed out, the explanation was that the negotiation had reference only to the northwest coast and the waters of the Pacific adjacent thereto. That Bering Sea was regarded as a separate body of water and not merely as a part of the great South Sea, Blaine attempted to prove by submitting a list of one hundred and five maps published before 1825, on every one of which it was designated with a distinctive name, the most common being the Sea of Kamchatka. On a few it bore the name Bering Sea.

Turning to Lord Salisbury's renewed offer to submit the dispute to arbitration, Blaine declared that it would mean something tangible if Great Britain would consent to arbitrate the real issues under discussion. What these were he indicated by propounding a series of questions revolving about the two main points at issue; that is, the right of jurisdiction in Bering Sea, and the right of protection or property in the fur seals. In conclusion, he made it clear that the United States would not base its case upon the doctrine of *mare clausum*. "The Government," he asserted, "has never claimed it. It expressly disavows it." At the same time, he maintained that the United States did not lack authority for holding a small section of Bering Sea for the protection of fur seals. Controlling a comparatively restricted area of water for that specific purpose was by no means the equivalent of declaring the sea, or any part of it, *mare clausum*.[28]

This prolix and tedious discussion between Blaine and Lord Salisbury had now been going on for more than a year. The dispute itself had been in progress for more than four years. Another year was to pass before a definite agreement should be reached to submit the controversy to the decision of a court of arbitration; for neither contestant had yet completely exhausted his store of arguments. The meaning of "Pacific Ocean" was still to be debated. The right of protection and property in the fur seals was to be newly asserted and freshly denied. The exact form of the questions to be submitted to the arbitrators, the issues that would arise in case the decision should be in favour of Great Britain, the reference of the question of liability—the consideration of all these matters involved prolonged negotiation. Finally, a *modus vivendi*, thought to be necessary for the purpose of allaying temporarily the irritating differences, had to be arranged. At last all difficulties were overcome, and on February 29, 1892, a treaty was signed by which a tribunal, to sit at Paris, was invested with the power to decide the questions which had so long been the subject of controversy.

It was agreed that the following points should be submitted to the arbitrator. They are substantially in the form proposed by Blaine:

"1. What exclusive jurisdiction in the sea now known as the Behring's Sea, and what exclusive rights in the seal fisheries therein, did Russia assert and exercise prior and up to the time of the cession of Alaska to the United States?

"2. How far were these claims of jurisdiction as to the seal fisheries recognized and conceded by Great Britain?

"3. Was the body of water now known as the Behring's Sea included in the phrase 'Pacific Ocean,' as used in the Treaty of 1825 between Great Britain and Russia; and what rights, if any, in the Behring's Sea were held and exclusively exercised by Russia after said Treaty?

"4. Did not all the rights of Russia as to jurisdiction, and as to the seal fisheries in Behring's Sea east of the water boundary, in the treaty between the United States and Russia of the 30th March, 1867, pass unimpaired to the United States under that Treaty?

"5. Has the United States any right, and, if so, what right of protection or property in the fur seals frequenting the islands of the United States in Behring Sea when such seals are found outside the ordinary three-mile limit?"[29]

At this point, Blaine's part in the controversy ends. The reader may follow the controversy to its end in the following sketches of Secretaries Gresham and Olney. The tribunal of international arbitration, suffice it to say at this place, decided on every point of right against the United States. It also found the facts of seizures proposed by the British agent to be true, and compensation to the Canadian sealers, to the amount of nearly a half million dollars, was afterwards adjusted. The American case had been ably presented and there was no disposition to question the award. Thus the judges had rendered a decision on the debate between Blaine and Lord Salisbury. Blaine had gone down in defeat. But is there nothing to say in his defense?

When he entered Harrison's Cabinet in 1889, he found a situation from which he could not easily escape. The state of public opinion in the United States would hardly have supported an abandonment of either the jurisdictional claims, or the protection of the seals. The only course that seemed feasible was to remain firm on these points until an adjustment by arbitration could be agreed upon. Though the continued seizures of the vessels of a friendly power were without justification, yet that was a wrong for which there was reparation. Those who suffered loss were indemnified, and the freedom of the seas was vindicated by the decision of a high tribunal. On the other hand the seal herd once destroyed could never be restored. It was, in fact, all but destroyed, before Great Britain was induced some years later to accept the protective measures advocated by the United States. Under the arrangements at last adopted, the herd began rapidly to increase, and is now again approaching its former flourishing condition. If this result was too long delayed, not all the blame should rest upon the shoulders of James G. Blaine. Something should be charged to British obstinacy.

CHAPTER IV

MOB VIOLENCE AND INTERNATIONAL OBLIGATION

TWO manifestations of mob violence disturbed the diplomatic calm of Blaine's second administration of the State Department. The first of these lawless exhibitions occurred in March, 1891. It was a case of lynching perpetrated by American citizens on a number of persons of Italian origin in New Orleans, Louisiana. The second took place in October of the same year. It consisted in a fatal attack directed by the Chilean citizens against members of the crew of the U.S.S. *Baltimore* in the port of Valparaiso, Chile. Hence it is known as the *Baltimore* affair. In one case the Italian Government made complaint against an outrage committed upon Italian subjects in the United States. In the other the Government at Washington protested against the maltreatment of American citizens in Chile. In the first case the United States was on the defensive; in the second it was on the offensive. Together, the two incidents put to the test Blaine's diplomatic skill.

The immediate cause of the lynching at New Orleans was the failure of a jury to convict a number of persons who had been arrested and placed on trial for their supposed connection with the murder of David C. Hennessy, Chief of Police of that city. Primarily, the cause was a long series of similar miscarriages of justice. New Orleans had for a number of years been the scene of assassinations instigated, it was believed, by a secret society known as the Mafia. As a rule these brutal deeds were surrounded with mystery and bore evidence of having been the result of deliberate, concerted action. More often than otherwise the victims were Italians. Arrests were made, and though in many cases proof of guilt was of the strongest, the accused escaped punishment through perjury or by means of an alibi.[30]

Against this criminal element, Chief of Police Hennessy had waged relentless warfare. His death, it seems, was decreed as an act of revenge. The failure to punish the supposed murderers was deeply disappointing to the citizens of New Orleans. To the onlookers at the trial, the evidence of guilt, at least in some of the cases, appeared to be overwhelmingly convincing. The outcome of the trial was ascribed to the corrupting and terrorizing influence of the evil forces responsible for the crimes. Public indignation at last vented itself in mob action. A mass of citizens estimated at from 6,000 to 8,000 marched without interference from the local authorities upon the jail where the accused were still held, and put to death eleven of those charged with complicity in the murder of Hennessy. This occurred about mid-day on March 14.

Of the persons thus summarily executed, five had not been tried, three were awaiting a new trial, and the other three had been acquitted but not released. Three were Italian subjects. The rest were either naturalized citizens of the United States, or had made declaration of their intention to become citizens.

The Italian consul at New Orleans immediately reported the affair to Baron Fava, the Italian minister at

Washington. The consul expressed the fear that other acts of violence would occur, and declared that he himself was in great danger. The same day Marquis Rudini, the Italian Minister of Foreign Affairs, instructed Baron Fava to denounce the act of the mob, and to request the Government of the United States to take immediate and energetic steps for the protection of the Italian colony in New Orleans, and for the punishment of those guilty of murdering Italian subjects. In a note to Blaine the next day he repeated the request, and protested in the most solemn manner against the conduct of the local authorities, who had maintained a purely passive attitude while the murder of the Italians was going on in the prison. Reserving the right of his Government to demand any other reparation that it might think proper, he invoked the aid of the federal Government to the end that the regrettable incident might be brought to a speedy termination.[31]

In a telegram to Governor Nicholls of Louisiana, on March 15, Blaine called attention to the fact that a treaty between the United States and Italy guaranteed to Italian subjects domiciled in this country "the most constant protection and security for their persons and property." He expressed the deep regret of the President that the citizens of New Orleans had so disparaged the purity and adequacy of their own judicial tribunals as to transfer to the passionate judgment of a mob a question that should have been adjudged dispassionately and by settled rules of law, and he declared that the United States should give foreign subjects within its territory the same security it demands for our citizens abroad. It was the hope of the President, there-

fore, that Governor Nicholls would lend his co-operation in maintaining the obligations of the United States
towards the Italian subjects who might be within the
perils of the existing excitement, in order that further
bloodshed and violence might be prevented, and in order that all offenders against the law might be promptly
brought to justice. A copy of this telegram was sent to
Baron Fava, and its contents were cabled to the American minister, Porter, at Rome, to be delivered to the
Italian Foreign Office.[32] The next day Blaine received
a telegraphic reply from Governor Nicholls assuring
him that everything was quiet in New Orleans, that
no further trouble was anticipated, and that the recent
violence was directed against individuals, race or nationality not being a factor in the disturbance. By letter a
few days later, Governor Nicholls confirmed these statements, and added that the whole subject of the killing
of the men was under investigation by the grand jury.

The action of the United States was not sufficiently
"energetic" to satisfy the demands of the Italian Government. Six days after the lynching, Marquis Rudini
cabled Baron Fava as follows: "Necessary the United
States Government give us official communication that
the guilty of New Orleans massacres have been brought
to justice. Moreover, you are instructed to request indemnity, which, we trust, will be granted directly. A
simple declaration, though cordial and friendly, is not
sufficient; we want positive facts."[33] Baron Fava delivered this message at the State Department, accompanying it with a note further expressing the impatience of
his Government.

Blaine sent a prompt and curt rejoinder. He had

asked Marquis Imperiali, Secretary of the Italian legation, to furnish the names, circumstances, and conditions of the three Italian subjects who were said to have
been murdered in New Orleans. That information had
not yet been received. On March 24, Marquis Rudini
cabled that an immediate solution was indispensable.
The right of his Government to demand and obtain
punishment of the murderers and an indemnity for the
victims was, he declared, unquestionable.[34] Unless definite steps were taken at once the Italian Government
would find itself in the painful necessity of recalling its
minister from a country where justice could not be obtained. The next day Baron Fava furnished the desired
information regarding the murdered Italians. As Blaine
made no reply, Baron Fava, in conformity with orders
received from his Government, took his departure from
Washington on leave. Upon informing Blaine of this
action he stated again the demands of his Government,
which, as now expressed, required that the United States
(1) give official assurance that the guilty parties would
be brought to trial; and (2) recognize in principle that
an indemnity was due to the relatives of the victims.

The situation was not so serious in reality as it appeared to be. Much of the correspondence was meant
for home consumption. The recall of Baron Fava was
in part a diplomatic gesture intended rather to impress
the Italian people with a show of energy than to bring
pressure to bear upon the United States; for the Ministry of which Marquis Rudini was the head dreaded
adverse popular feeling, however temporary.[35] In part
the recall of Baron Fava was a mock attack, designed
to cover the abandonment of an untenable position.

From an impossible demand for immediate punishment and the instant payment of an indemnity, the Italian Government had retreated to a reasonable request that the guilty be brought to trial, and that an indemnity be recognized as due in principle.

Blaine took advantage of the Italian Government's show of weakness, to declare in a note to Marquis Imperiali that he had on various occasions impressed upon Baron Fava the utter inability of the United States to meet the demands which the Italian Government had first made; that even if the national Government had the entire jurisdiction over the alleged murderers, it could not give assurance to any foreign power that they should be punished; that inasmuch as the Constitution of the United States guarantees trial by an impartial jury, it needed no argument to prove that a jury could not be impartial if it were in any sense bound before the trial by any assurance which the President might venture to give to a foreign power; and that as the constitution of Louisiana, under whose jurisdiction the murderers would be tried, contained substantially the same provision, the Governor of that state would be as unable to give a pledge in advance as the President would be if the leaders of the mob were tried under the laws of the United States.

As to the second demand, the United States, so far from refusing, had distinctly recognized the principle of indemnity to those Italian subjects who might have been wronged by a violation of the rights secured to them by treaty. In conclusion, Blaine asserted that he had repeatedly assured Baron Fava that all the incidents connected with the unhappy tragedy at New Orleans would be thoroughly investigated. But in a matter of such gravity, the Government of the United States would not permit itself to be hurried; nor would it make answer to any demand until every fact essential to a correct judgment should have been ascertained through legal authority. "The impatience of the aggrieved may be natural," he said, "but its indulgence does not always secure the most substantial justice."[36] Perhaps there was something here also for home consumption.

In reply the Italian Government affirmed that it had asked nothing beyond the prompt institution of judicial proceedings through the regular channels, and it took note of the "declaration whereby the Federal Government recognizes that an indemnity is due to the families of the victims in virtue of the treaty in force between the two countries." The first assertion Blaine controverted. He gave at length his reasons for asserting that the demand had been at first for punishment, not trial. On the second point, he maintained that his language had been misinterpreted. He had not recognized that an indemnity was due. He had merely recognized the principle of indemnity under the treaty. This left unsettled the important question whether the treaty had been violated. The United States did not become by that treaty the insurer of the lives and property of Italian subjects resident within its territory. "No Government is able," said Blaine, "however high its civilization, however vigilant its police supervision, however severe its criminal code, and however prompt and inflexible its criminal administration, to secure its own citizens against violence promoted by individual malice or by sudden popular tumult. The foreign resident must be content in such cases to share the same redress that is offered by the law to the citizens, and has no just cause of complaint or right to ask the interposition of his country if the courts are equally open to him for the redress of his injuries."[37] This pronouncement Blaine was soon to have used against him in connection with the Chilean imbroglio.

The Secretary of State was well aware that the grand jury then investigating the affair in New Orleans might fail to present indictments. He promised, therefore, that if it should appear that among the victims of the mob there were Italian subjects, resident or domiciled in that city, and that the public officers charged with the duty of protecting life and property connived at the work of the mob, or, upon proper notice or information of the threatened danger, failed to take any steps to bring the guilty to trial, the President would under such circumstances feel that a case was established that should be submitted to the consideration of Congress with a view to the relief of the families of those who had lost their lives by lawless violence.

The perusal of Blaine's communication produced on Marquis Rudini, he declared in a telegram to Marquis Imperiali, "à most painful impression." He charged Blaine with a lack of conformity with diplomatic usages in making public his telegram of March 24, which, he claimed, had been communicated in strict confidence; he maintained that his words "punishment of the guilty" in the brevity of telegraphic language actually signified only that prosecution should be commenced; and he declared that the Italian Government was under the sad necessity of concluding that what to every other government would be the accomplishment of simple duty was impossible to the federal Government. "It is time to break off the bootless controversy," he said. "Public opinion, the sovereign judge, will know how to indicate an equitable solution of this grave problem. We have affirmed, and we again affirm, our right. Let the federal Government reflect upon its side if it is expedient to leave to the mercy of each State of the Union, irresponsible to foreign countries, the efficiency of treaties pledging its faith and honor to entire nations. The present dispatch is addressed to you exclusively, not to the federal Government."[38]

Marquis Rudini's dispatch was published by the Associated Press on May 4, 1891. Blaine took notice of only one point; namely, the charge of a breach of diplomatic etiquette. In a dispatch to United States Minister Porter at Rome, he declared that the intimation that the telegram in question was delivered in strict confidence was a total error. As the telegram expressed the demand of the Italian Government, it was impossible that Marquis Rudini could transmit it in confidence. It was delivered by Baron Fava, in person, written in English in his own handwriting, without a suggestion of privacy, and it bore not a single mark denoting a confidential character. To prove the error into which Marquis Rudini had fallen, facsimiles of the telegram were forwarded to Porter. Having had the last word, Blaine was willing that the "bootless controversy" should end.

A year passed and passions cooled. Then suddenly the incident was brought to a close on April 12, 1892. Blaine addressed a note to Marquis Imperiali admitting that the "lamentable massacre at New Orleans" was an injury for which it was the solemn duty of the United States to pay a satisfactory indemnity. He was instructed by the President, he said, to offer 125,000 francs to be distributed among the families of the victims. It was the hope of the President, he said further, that the transaction would efface all memory of the unhappy tragedy; that the old and friendly relations of the United States and Italy might be restored; and that nothing untoward might ever again occur to disturb their harmonious friendship. In the name of his Government Marquis Imperiali accepted the indemnity at once and declared that from that moment diplomatic relations between the two countries were fully re-established.[39]

The attack on the American sailors in Santiago, Chile, must now be briefly considered. This incident had a direct connection with the civil war, which broke out in 1891, between the executive and legislative branches of the Government of that republic. By the letter of the Chilean constitution, the Government was presidential rather than parliamentary in form; but by long-continued custom—the constitution had been in force since 1833—it had become parliamentary. Cabinets regularly resigned when their measures failed to receive the support of Congress. Not until the Administration of José Manuel Balmaceda, who was elected for the usual five-year term in 1886, was the practice seriously questioned. Balmaceda had an ambitious program of reform which he was at first able to promote in harmony with the legislative branch of the Government. In time some of his supporters deserted him and he was confronted with a hostile majority in Congress. His Cabinets were repeatedly overthrown. His Administration was embarrassed by the refusal of the legislative body to pass the necessary appropriation bills. He maintained that in such case both the constitution and precedent authorized him to extend the budget by decree. This he did on January 1, 1891,[40] whereupon the Congressionalists denounced him as a dictator, ruling in defiance of the constitution. The result was civil war.

The opponents of Balmaceda were able to win over to their cause the principal vessels of the Chilean fleet. They established themselves in the rich nitrate fields of the north, and after seven or eight months of preparation moved against Valparaiso. After desperate fighting the city fell into their hands on August 28, 1891. Feeling that his cause was lost, Balmaceda sought asylum in the Argentine legation and immediately published his resignation. A few days later the revolutionary junta set up a provisional government in Santiago with Admiral Jorge Montt as President. As this Government was generally accepted by the Chilean people, it was promptly recognized by foreign powers. But its success was not followed by oblivion of the past. There followed a persecution of Balmacedist leaders, many of whom found refuge in foreign legations or fled to foreign vessels. Balmaceda himself, scorning "vulgar escape," and being unwilling longer to embarrass the Argentine minister by his presence in the legation, committed suicide, in the vain hope that his death might relieve his friends from further punishment.[41] The provisional régime continued a few months longer, when, after an election, Montt was legally installed as President of the Republic.

The Baltimore affair occurred in the interval between the downfall of Balmaceda and the re-establishment of constitutional government in Chile. Upon the outbreak of the revolution the United States dispatched to the scene of conflict three naval vessels to protect American interests, one of which was the *Baltimore*, under the command of Captain W. S. Schley. On October 16, 1891, while the *Baltimore* was lying in the harbour of Valparaiso, Captain Schley gave shore leave to one hundred and seventeen petty officers and men of his crew. After they had been ashore a few hours they were attacked, toward six o'clock in the evening, in several localities of the city, by a numerous mob composed of Chilean sailors, longshoremen, and citizens. It was charged that some of the police also joined in the attack. One American was killed, another later died of wounds received in the mêlée, and still others were brutally stabbed and beaten. No Chileans were killed. None even received serious injury, for the Americans were unarmed and defenseless. It does not appear that the shore party had done anything to provoke so furious an onslaught. The police, who arrived tardily, arrested a number of American sailors, but they were later released; nor did the authorities after a thorough investigation bring any charges against Captain Schley's men.[42] The Government at Washington, duly informed of the affair, took the position that this was no mere sailors' brawl to be dealt with by the usual disciplinary measures. It was, according to the American view, a serious and premeditated assault, animated by hostility to the men as American sailors, and hence constituted an offense for which the United States was entitled to demand reparation.

At the time this incident occurred, Blaine was ill at his home in Maine. He did not return to Washington until a week or two later. On October 23, Acting Secretary of State Francis W. Wharton complained in a telegraphic communication to Patrick Egan, the American minister at Santiago, that though a week had passed since "this cruel work" took place, yet no expression of regret or of a purpose to institute proceedings against the guilty parties had been made to the United States. The Provisional Government gave assurance that the affair was being investigated, but as this was done in a communication offensive in tone, the Government at Washington resolved to postpone further discussion of the matter until after the inauguration of the Constitutional régime. In his annual message to Congress, however, in December, 1891, President Harrison promised to bring the subject to the attention of that body for such action as might be necessary, if the just expectations of the United States should be disappointed, or if further delay should intervene.[43]

The portion of the President's message referring to the incident, together with a report on the subject by the Secretary of the Navy, was immediately published in Chile. These publications greatly enraged the Chilean Minister of Foreign Affairs, and he vented his anger in a public letter in which he declared that there was no exactness or sincerity in what was said at Washington. This insult strained the relations between the two countries almost to the breaking point. For a time Minister Egan suspended intercourse with the Chilean Foreign

Office, and the surveillance to which the legation had for some time been subjected, because of the political refugees harboured there, became at last so intolerable that the Argentine minister, as dean of the diplomatic corps, was moved to protest.[44]

As was expected, the tenseness of the situation was relieved with the change of government in Chile, which occurred late in December, 1891. Events now moved rapidly, though not smoothly, toward a final adjustment of the controversy. The new Chilean Minister of Foreign Relations, Luis Pereira, expressed "very sincere regret for the unfortunate events" which occurred at Valparaiso, and he withdrew, with some qualifications, the offensive language of his predecessor. When Blaine insisted on a full and frank withdrawal, the Chilean Government countered by asking for the recall of Minister Egan, on the ground that he was *persona non grata.* These evasions Blaine met with peremptory demands. The President, he said, after giving careful consideration to everything submitted by the Chilean Government touching the assault on the crew of the *Baltimore,* was still of the opinion that the attack was directed against the uniform of the United States, and that the public authorities had flagrantly failed in their duty to protect our men. If the demands of the United States were not satisfied, therefore, the only course open would be to terminate diplomatic relations between the two countries. Concerning the recall of Minister Egan, that was a matter which could well await the Chilean reply, as it would then be known whether any correspondence could be maintained with that Government upon terms of mutual respect.[45]

Four days later, no response having been received from Chile, the President laid the whole matter before Congress. On the same day the Chilean reply was delivered to Minister Egan at Santiago, but not in time to forestall the President's message. Signed by the Minister of Foreign Affairs Pereira, it was an able, statesmanlike document, which at last met the just demands of the United States, in a straightforward and dignified manner. After reciting the substance of the American demands, Pereira set forth the views and decisions of his Government. He gave assurance that the people of Chile, far from entertaining a feeling of hostility toward the uniform of the United States, had esteemed and respected that uniform ever since the days of the glorious struggle when they saw it figuring honourably in the ranks of the sailors and soldiers who established Chilean independence. He admitted the gravity of the attack on the American sailors, again expressed regret for the occurrence, explained the cause of the delay in arriving at the facts in the case, and extenuated the ineffective action of the Chilean police. He urged that due allowance should be made for the disorganizing effects of the civil war which had just been brought to a close, and in further extenuation he recalled the words of Secretary of State Blaine, in which he contended that as no nation, however civilized, could guarantee its own citizens against violence growing out of individual malice or a sudden popular tumult, the foreign resident must be content in such cases to share the same redress offered by law to the citizen.

Nevertheless the Chilean Government did not hesitate to condemn, in vigorous terms, the act committed on

October 16, or to offer just reparation. For the purpose of determining the reparation due, Pereira suggested that the Supreme Court of the United States or a special tribunal of arbitration be designated. He deplored the employment of the offensive expressions by the former Minister of Foreign Relations, and in fulfillment of a high duty of courtesy and sincerity toward a friendly nation, he declared that they were absolutely withdrawn. This frank and explicit declaration, he hoped, would carry to the mind of President Harrison and of the American people the conviction that the Government and people of Chile were moved by a lively desire to maintain unalterable the good and cordial relations which had hitherto existed between the two countries. Finally, with regard to the suggested recall of the American minister at Santiago, Pereira stated that no action would be taken without the accord of the United States.[46]

This note of the Chilean minister brought the dispute to an honourable and happy conclusion. The amount of the reparation was later fixed by direct negotiation at $75,000. This sum Chile paid to the families of the men killed and to those who were injured. Referring to the settlement in his annual message the following December, President Harrison said that the reparation was accepted not only as an indemnity for a wrong done, but as a most gratifying evidence that the Government of Chile rightly appreciated the disposition of the United States to act in a spirit of fairness and friendliness in its intercourse with that brave people. Further evidence of the mutual respect and confidence existing between the two nations was furnished, said Harrison, by the fact that a convention submitting to arbitration the mutual claims of the citizens of the two republics had been agreed upon. Here we may add that that convention was negotiated in Santiago by Patrick Egan. He continued, as long as Harrison was President, to serve the United States as minister to Chile.

In connection with this incident, Blaine was subjected to much unjust criticism. His detractors explained the violent outburst of the Chileans against the American sailors as an expression of resentment due to Blaine's domineering attitude in 1881, and to his interference in the civil war in 1891. Much of the criticism revolved about Patrick Egan. It was charged that he owed his appointment to his influence with the Irish vote; that he was tactless and inexperienced; that he allied himself for personal reasons with the fortunes of Balmaceda, who was trying to suppress democratic institutions and establish a vulgar dictatorship; that because of this corrupt relationship, he did not report fully and impartially the course of events; that he needlessly antagonized the British and Germans in Chile; that he exceeded his authority in harbouring political refugees in the legation—such were the strictures of the time. Unfortunately the limitations of space forbid the examination of these charges in detail. This may be said: A careful weighing of the available evidence convinces the present writer that they are based upon misapprehensions and falsehoods. Blaine's conduct throughout was correct. Egan was not inept. He demonstrated unusual ability, and, far from being corrupt, he was singularly upright. Moreover, he was tactful, discreet, and courageous. He quite properly maintained friendly relations with the Balmacedist Government as long as it survived, and any resentment which the provisional authorities may have felt toward him for this reason, or because of his offer of asylum to the unfortunate adherents of Balmaceda, was wholly without justification.

CHAPTER V

THE INTERNATIONAL AMERICAN
CONFERENCE

IN a preceding volume of this series will be found a reference to the attempt which Blaine made, during his first administration of the office of Secretary of State, to bring about a conference of American nations. Though the scheme was abandoned after his retirement from the State Department, yet the idea survived. Impressed by the advocacy of the former Secretary of State and by the warm approbation of some of the Latin-American countries, various members of the Senate and House of Representatives introduced resolutions in Congress during the next two or three years proposing more or less extensive plans for Pan-American co-operation. But as the Administration of President Arthur frowned upon all these measures, none received the approval of both houses. In the last year of Arthur's Presidency, however, Congress, at the suggestion of Secretary of State Frelinghuysen, passed an act authorizing the appointment of a commission to visit Central and South America to collect information and to sound the various governments as to their attitude toward sending representatives to Washington to discuss matters of common interest. In due course the commission made its investigation and submitted reports, recommending a conference to promote commercial intercourse and to prepare a plan of arbitration. The

Democratic party, which had in the meantime succeeded to power, looked upon the suggestion with favour. Renewed agitation in Congress resulted finally in the enactment on May 10, 1888, of a law, which was approved by President Cleveland, authorizing a conference to be held at Washington during the following year.[47]

In accordance with the provisions of the act, Secretary of State Bayard dispatched, in July 1888, a circular letter of invitation to the eighteen Latin-American states. He designated October 2, 1889, as a suitable date for the assembly to convene. Within the next few months favourable replies came from the five Central American republics and from Uruguay and Argentina. After November, 1888, when Harrison was elected to the Presidency, no further acceptances were received until the following spring. The delays for the most part caused no concern; for they were occasioned either by the unwarranted expectation that the new Administration would announce a change of plans, or by misunderstandings of slight importance, which could easily be removed. But in the case of three of the republics, Chile, Peru, and Bolivia, silence was ominous; for the serious questions growing out of the War of the Pacific, which still divided these countries, might result, it was feared, in their abstention and, possibly, in the failure of the whole enterprise. Chile, being in possession of the spoils of the war, was reluctant to give other powers an opportunity to open the old questions or to interfere in the pending issues. Peru and Bolivia, on the other hand, though they had everything to gain and nothing to lose by joining in the Conference, were unwilling to participate unless Chile was brought, as it were, to the bar of justice. They were waiting to see what their adversary would do. Evidently Chile was the key to the situation.

With perfect propriety, Bayard might have left the solution of the difficulty to his successor; but he preferred to attempt an adjustment before the new Administration should come into power. For this purpose he entrusted, in January 1889, a confidential mission to John G. Walker, secretary of legation at Bogotá.[48] Arriving in Chile some weeks later, Walker was able to confirm, in an interview with the Minister of Foreign Relations, what was already believed; namely, that the real objection of the Chilean Government was its unwillingness to submit to arbitration questions growing out of the late war with Peru and Bolivia. Shortly afterward, the American commissioner was so far successful in convincing President Balmaceda that the Conference would not interfere in these matters that the President at once announced his acceptance of the invitation.[49] With this obstacle removed, general participation was assured, and all the states, with one exception, signified their intention to send delegates. The exception was Santo Domingo. This little republic had a grievance against the United States. A treaty of arbitration and commercial reciprocity, which had been concluded between the two republics in 1884, had remained during the intervening years without ratification by the United States. In view of this fact, the Dominican Government declared in its reply that it was not "at liberty to enter into a new discussion of the subjects already settled by the treaty of 1884."[50]

The Conference assembled on the date agreed upon.

Though most of the Latin-American countries sent one representative only, there were in all thirty-seven delegates.[51] Ten of these represented the United States. As it was agreed that the voting should be by states, this arrangement established no essential inequality. At the head of the United States delegation was John B. Henderson, with whom was associated the veteran diplomatist, William H. Trescot, and others of less note, including the captains of industry, Clement Studebaker and Andrew Carnegie. Among the foreign delegates, Roque Saenz Peña, representing Argentina, was easily one of the most distinguished and influential. Of equal importance was the Mexican, Matías Romero. His perfect command of English, his friendly attitude toward the United States, and his genuine enthusiasm for cooperation among the American countries, together with his unusual ability, made him one of the most valuable members of the Conference. Brazil sent three representatives, among whom Salvador de Mendonça was perhaps the ablest. It is worthy of note that while the Conference was in progress, Brazil accomplished the remarkable feat of converting its form of government, without bloodshed, from monarchy to republic. This revolution was accompanied by no change in the delegation at Washington, except the resignation of one of the three members. Other countries, including the lesser as well as the greater, were worthily represented. As a whole, indeed, the personnel was such as to give promise of earnest and thoughtful efforts to achieve results of a lasting and beneficial character.

Profoundly stimulated by the prospect, Blaine welcomed the delegates in a carefully prepared address in which he declared that their presence signified much to the whole of America and might signify far more in the days to come; for, he declared, no conference had ever assembled to consider the welfare of territorial possessions so vast, or to contemplate the possibilities of a future so great and so inspiring. He then indicated in general terms what the assembly might accomplish. It could do much to establish permanent relations of confidence, respect, and friendship between the nations of America. It could show the world a spectacle of eighteen independent powers meeting together on terms of absolute equality, without coercion and without secret understandings. It could proscribe conquest and cultivate an American sympathy as broad as the two continents. It would avoid, he predicted, the errors of conventional diplomacy. It would form no selfish alliance against the older nations from which we are proud to claim inheritance. It would, in fine, seek nothing, propose nothing, endure nothing, that was not, in the sense of all the delegates, timely, wise, and peaceful.

These remarks the speaker followed with a concise declaration, which may be regarded as his Pan-American creed. He said:

"We believe that we should be drawn together more closely by the highways of the sea, and that at no distant day the railway systems of the north and south will meet upon the isthmus and connect by land routes the political and commercial capitals of all America.

"We believe that hearty co-operation, based on hearty confidence, will save all American States from the burdens and evils which have long and cruelly afflicted the older nations of the world.

"We believe that a spirit of justice, of common and equal interest between the American States, will leave no room for an artificial balance of power like unto that which has led to wars abroad and drenched Europe in blood.

"We believe that friendship, avowed with candor and maintained with good faith, will remove from American States the necessity of guarding boundary lines between themselves with fortifications and military force.

"We believe that standing armies, beyond those which are needful for public order and the safety of internal administration, should be unknown on both American continents.

"We believe that friendship and not force, the spirit of just law and not the violence of the mob, should be the recognized rule of administration between American nations and in American nations."[52]

At the conclusion of his address, Secretary Blaine invited the delegates to be the guests of the nation on a visit to various parts of the country, in order that they might have the opportunity to observe conditions in the United States, and in order that our people might have "the privilege and pleasure of extending the warm welcome of Americans to Americans." The invitation was accepted. Accordingly, after completing its permanent organization, Blaine being elected as president, the Conference adjourned to reassemble on November 18, thus allowing about six weeks for the excursion.

Accompanied by a number of prominent American citizens, the delegates visited the manufacturing centres of New England, then turned westward, going to Buffalo and Niagara Falls, thence to Cleveland, Detroit, Chicago, St. Louis, and other middle-western cities, and finally ended their journey with visits to Pittsburgh, Philadelphia, Baltimore, and New York. In the meantime plans for the Conference were being elaborated.

When the sessions were renewed, the Conference devoted itself with commendable industry to the achievement of the tasks for which it had been assembled. The work was apportioned among fifteen different committees. The mere enumeration of the subjects with which these bodies had to deal will give some idea of the scope and purpose of the Conference. They were: customs union, communication on the Atlantic, communication on the Pacific, communication on the Gulf of Mexico and the Caribbean Sea, railway communication, customs regulations, port dues, weights and measures, sanitary regulations, patents and trade marks, extradition, monetary convention, banking, international law, and finally, general welfare.[53]

Within the next three or four months the committees brought in their reports, which were discussed and in most cases unanimously adopted. In two or three instances unanimity was not attained. As it happened, differences arose over matters in which Blaine was most concerned. One of these was the proposed customs union, on which both majority and minority reports were submitted. The majority treated the subject sympathetically, but believed that insuperable constitutional difficulties stood in the way of the establishment of a customs union, if by that term was meant the inclusion of several nations in a single customs territory with reciprocal free trade between the states concerned and with uniform tariff laws for the collection and apportionment of duties on foreign imports among the members. A union of a more restricted sort, limited to reciprocal free trade, without a joint administration of duties on goods of nations not members, they favoured in principle, but thought it impracticable on a continental scale. Such a union was an ideal, however, toward which the majority thought the nations of America should work, by the adoption of partial reciprocity treaties, which they regarded as alone feasible at the moment. They made recommendations in accordance with these views.

The report of the minority was brief and to the point. It recommended simply that the proposal of a customs union between the nations of America be rejected.

These reports gave rise to a long and spirited debate, which was led on the side of the minority by Saenz Peña, who, together with one of the Chilean delegates, signed the minority report. On the side of the majority, the argument was sustained mainly by Henderson and Romero, with whom were associated representatives of Brazil, Colombia, Nicaragua, and Venezuela. The Argentine delegate, who forced the issue, presented his views with brilliance and energy. Whoever reads the speeches on both sides will be driven to the conclusion that there was no substantial difference of opinion on the economic questions involved; for the majority and minority were agreed as to the impracticability of a customs union; and against reciprocity, which the majority favoured, the leader of the minority could say nothing except that the committee had no authority to report on that subject.[54] Though there was good ground for this contention, yet Saenz Peña was evidently moved by other and more powerful considerations. His real object seems to have been to contest the leadership of Blaine, with whose Pan-American aims he was not altogether in accord. This does not mean that the Argentine delegate was influenced by personal animosity toward Blaine, or by any unfriendly feeling toward the United States. He was merely acting in harmony with the traditions of his country, for Argentina from the beginning of its independence had pursued what was apparently an extremely individualistic foreign policy. It had declined to follow the lead of Colombia at Panama in 1825, and of other Latin-American countries subsequently. It was now loath to recognize the leadership of the United States.

While this debate was going on, Blaine presided over the meetings of the Conference, for which task something more than the skill of the practised parliamentarian was required. To avoid wounding national susceptibilities much tact and doubtless an occasional departure from strict parliamentary procedure was necessary. It would have been the height of folly if, for example, he had attempted to thwart the ill-disguised attack of Saenz Peña by the use of the arbitrary power of the presiding officer. An incident which occurred at the close of the debate will illustrate the good sense with which Blaine met the difficult situations which arose.

The report of the majority, when it was finally put

to a vote, was adopted. Three states, Argentina, Chile, and Bolivia, alone expressed disapproval. Paraguay abstained from voting, and on this ground as well as on the ground that the majority report had made no definite recommendation on the subject of a customs union, Saenz Peña moved that the minority report be voted on. Some discussion followed as to the propriety of taking up the minority report after that of the majority had been adopted. Henderson finally suggested that the correct procedure would be to reconsider the vote by which the majority report had been approved and to let that of the minority come up as a substitute. Blaine, who was in the chair, entertained a motion to this effect, and the roll-call was begun. It was soon interrupted, however, by Henderson, who asked unanimous consent to withdraw the motion, since he had discovered that a majority of the United States delegation was not in harmony with his views. There was objection and the roll-call continued, to be again interrupted—this time by Quintana, one of the Argentine delegates, who rose, in a spirit of banter, perhaps, to a question of order. He wished to know whether a delegate could, against the majority of his delegation, make a proposal. "That," said Blaine instantly, "is a point of metaphysics upon which the chair himself declines to rule. The roll-call will proceed."[55] Though the motion was defeated by a decisive vote, yet Saenz Peña stood his ground, and again moved a vote on the minority report. The chair entertained the motion and it was put; but it was defeated, the result being now five for and eleven against.

The Argentine Republic, it must be remarked, was not averse to all forms of American accord. It had been eager to assume leadership in a concert of a different sort from that proposed by Bolivar earlier in the century, and it was now no less desirous of pointing a way to the united action of the Latin-American states in opposition to the plans of Blaine. At the close of his first speech on the customs union, Saenz Peña seized upon the occasion to suggest vaguely what the nature of that action might be. Affirming his love for America, he declared that he did not lack confidence in, or gratitude toward, Europe. "I do not forget," he said, "that Spain, our mother, is there, contemplating with sincere rejoicings the development of her ancient territory through the energy of a generous and manly people who inherited her blood; that Italy, our friend, is there, and France, our sister, who illuminates with the effigy of a goddess, the harbor of New York. . . . Let the century of America, as the twentieth century is already called, behold our trade with all nations of the earth free, witnessing the noble duel of untrammeled labor, in which it has been truly said God measures the ground, equalizes the weapons and apportions the light. Let America be for mankind."[56]

The epigram "America for mankind," was subsequently adopted as a rallying cry, doubtless to the great satisfaction of Saenz Peña, by those who feared the United States and were engaged in efforts to check its influence in Latin America. Interpreting the simple statement of the Monroe Doctrine, "America for the Americans," as meaning America for the United States, the followers of Saenz Peña haughtily proclaimed the nobler conception—America for all mankind. Ignoring the real significance of the Monroe declaration, they

were wont to contrast the broad, humanitarian policy
of the Argentine Republic with the narrow, selfish aims
of the United States. Yet the Argentine statesman's
own aims were somewhat less generous than his senten-
tious phrase seems to indicate. It is significant that in
the speech from which we have quoted, none but Latin
nationalities were mentioned. Whatever may have been
Saenz Peña's ultimate object, his immediate aim was a
union of the Latin-American republics with the Latin
states of Europe as a balance of power against the encroachments of the English-speaking peoples. This he
revealed with the greatest frankness in an address which
he made some years later in Buenos Aires.

In Westminster Abbey and under the dome of the
capitol at Washington, said Saenz Peña, were heard
"strange rumors, threats against peoples, conflicts of
races." These were signs, he declared, announcing the
birth of an idea, which would not fail to be carried into
execution. In the presence of so great a danger he
believed it to be incumbent upon the people of Argentina to cultivate friendly relations with the nations of
Spanish America. "Let us respect the sovereignty of all
these states," he urged, "and let us found upon them
and for their benefit a single society with a common
destiny, with a view to the defense of this part of
America from dangers common to all. . . . The masterful audacity of James Blaine, who was undoubtedly
more intense than Roosevelt, though less fortunate in
the affections of the people, wished to make of America
a market, and of the sovereign States, tributaries. The
idea, economic in form, was in essence political. . . .
A brilliant and haughty spirit speaks and commands

one hemisphere in the name of the other hemisphere; gives orders to Europe in the name of our America; and ends by setting up a chancellory of the New World, without the authority of the rest of the States and without delegation of their powers, since they neither ask protection nor need it."[57]

Argentina and the United States did not work at cross-purposes as far as other issues before the Conference were concerned. They generally stood together. A notable example was afforded by their united efforts to secure the adoption of a plan of arbitration. The committee on general welfare, to which the subject had been referred for study, submitted the draft of a treaty which dealt with the matter in thoroughgoing fashion. By the terms of this convention, it was proposed to adopt arbitration as a principle of "American international law," and to make it obligatory in all questions, with the sole exception of those in which the independence of one of the parties might be imperilled. Unfortunately the plan did not meet with unanimous approval. The Chileans feared that their Government might be obligated, under its provisions, to reopen the old questions with Peru and Bolivia. Moreover, they were unwilling, they declared, "to entertain the illusion" that conflicts affecting the dignity or honour of a nation should be submitted to the decision of a third party.[58] They accordingly abstained from voting, and on like grounds the Mexican delegation withheld its vote. No argument could budge these recalcitrant representatives from their position. The rest approved the draft without a dissenting voice, after which a resolution was adopted expressing the wish that controversies between American nations and the powers of Europe might be settled in the same friendly manner. Mexico joined in approving this resolution. Chile, however, consistently held aloof.

Thus two of the measures which concerned Blaine most—namely, those looking to the extension of commerce by reciprocity and the promotion of peace by arbitration—were dealt with in a manner which he could hardly have regarded as entirely satisfactory. Another proposal, in which he had scarcely less interest, met with a somewhat better fate, due to the influence which he himself was able to wield in its favour. This was a resolution, complementary to the proposed arbitration treaty and bound up with it, on the subject of conquest. The form in which the proposal was presented gave rise to an extended and acrimonious debate, in which the United States delegation assumed the attitude of opposition to the views of the Latin-American delegates, who favoured the resolution. When it became evident that agreement on the proposal as it stood would be impossible, Andrew Carnegie, on one of the few occasions on which he intervened in the debate, secured the floor and moved a recess in order that the committee on general welfare, which had the matter in charge, should come together and attempt to solve the difficulty by consultation. The motion was carried and Blaine retired with the committee. An hour later all vital differences had been removed by a restatement of the resolution. Blaine himself took the floor and moved the new wording as a substitute. Without further debate the resolution was now unanimously adopted, Chile alone abstaining.[59]

The resolution recommended to the Governments

represented in the Conference the adoption of the following declarations:

"First: That the principle of conquest shall not, during the continuance of the treaty of arbitration, be recognized as admissible in American public law.

"Second: That all cessions of territory made during the continuance of the treaty of arbitration shall be void if made under threats of war or in the presence of an armed force.

"Third: Any nation from which such cessions shall be exacted may demand that the validity of the cessions so made shall be submitted to arbitration.

"Fourth: Any renunciation of the right of arbitration, made under the conditions named in the second section, shall be null and void."[60]

Not only did Blaine's favourite measures lack unanimous support in the Conference, but they failed to obtain even the partial application which might have been expected. Due to his efforts, a reciprocity provision was inserted in the McKinley act of 1890, under which, during the next two or three years, reciprocal trade arrangements were made with a number of countries; but before the scheme was fairly tested, the act was repealed by a hostile Congress. Nor did the plan of arbitration have the desired outcome. The Governments whose representatives adopted the treaty failed to give it their approval. The declaration against the acquisition of title by conquest being an integral part of the arbitral plan, was likewise left without the official sanction of the Governments concerned. These failures were more apparent than real. In the sequel the nations of the New World have been prone to adopt the trade policy which Blaine advocated; they have given unmistakable evidence of their predilection for amicable methods of settling international disputes; and they have in various ways expressed their aversion to wars of conquest. On this last point the two greatest powers, appropriately, have been most outspoken. Brazil, in 1891, adopted a constitution containing a provision which declared that the nation in no case should "engage in a war of Conquest, directly or indirectly, by itself or in alliance with any other nation";[61] and the United States has been repeatedly committed to the same principle by the public declarations of its Presidents and Secretaries of State. It is far from the truth, therefore, to maintain that in these matters the labours of the Conference were futile.

The Conference produced at least one concrete result of great importance. This was the establishment in Washington of a bureau of information as the agent, or permanent secretariat, of the International Union of American Republics. Regarded at the time as a minor achievement, it has developed into a unique and most useful organization. Its cumbersome name was subsequently changed to the Pan-American Union. Non-political in character, it aims to develop good understanding, friendly intercourse, commerce, and peace between the American nations. It is controlled by a Governing Board composed of the Secretary of State of the United States and the diplomatic representatives in Washington of the other republics. It is housed in a magnificent building in Washington, the gift of Andrew Carnegie, where the affairs of the Union are administered by a Director-General, assisted by a numerous staff of experts. At the laying of the corner-stone of this Pan-American building in 1908, the Brazilian ambassador, Joaquim Nabuco, declared that there had never been a parallel for the sight which that ceremony presented—"that of twenty-one nations of different languages, building together a house for their common deliberations."

The Pan-American Union is usually regarded as the only important result of the Conference. There is no justification for so contracted a view. Although the acts of the assembly did not eventuate, except in the one case, in any definite and immediate outcome, yet it is far from the truth to maintain that they were therefore of no importance. Indirect and distant consequences must be taken into account. It is not too much to claim that the Washington assembly was the progenitor of the four similar conferences since held successively at Mexico City, Rio de Janeiro, Buenos Aires, and Santiago de Chile. Each of these assemblies can boast of a modicum of achievement for which the first Conference should have a share of the credit. And the series goes on. Another Pan-American gathering, which bids fair to be more fruitful than all the rest, will take place in Havana, Cuba, in 1928. These conferences no longer find it possible to deal with all the matters which demand co-operative action. A multiplication of agencies has been found necessary. Financial and monetary matters, for example, are now discussed in special conferences, whose resolutions are carried into effect by a permanent High Commission. Questions of law are submitted to an international commission of jurists. Subjects such as commerce, highways, public health, labour, child-welfare, science, education, journalism, and other matters of common interest are considered in conferences *ad hoc*, and where necessary, appropriate machinery is created to promote continuous co-operation in these fields. All this must be taken into consideration in any just appraisal of the first International American Conference.

CHAPTER VI

LAST DAYS

IN a strangely abrupt manner Blaine resigned the office of Secretary of State on June 4, 1892. He had given no one the least intimation that he was contemplating such a step and the note in which he tendered his resignation contained no word of explanation; nor did it embody any of the usual expressions of regret. It was a cold, formal request for relief from duty, to which the President acceded, naturally enough, in a reply equally cold and formal. So brusque a severance of official relations between a Cabinet member and the chief executive was unprecedented. The fact that the Republican National Convention was to meet at Minneapolis three days later seemed to offer an explanation; for Blaine's excited interest in the proceedings of the convention, together with his manifest disappointment when he learned of the renomination of Harrison, gave colour to the surmise that he entertained the hope of being himself named once more as the candidate of his party. On the other hand he must have known, as his friends knew, that the precarious state of his health rendered his candidacy utterly impracticable.[62] Besides, not long before his resignation he expressed to his friends, apparently in all sincerity, his repugnance for the presidential office. It cannot be maintained with any degree of certainty that his attitude had changed; for he did not reveal to anyone, so far as is known, what was in his mind. The motives of his strange conduct will perhaps never be known.

He did not long survive his retirement from public life. Though he was but fifty-nine years of age when he accepted the post in Harrison's Cabinet, he had already entered upon his decline. A severe attack of illness in 1887 had deprived him of much of that physical buoyancy and vigour which characterized his younger manhood. Under the stress of his official duties he was again stricken, and as a result his strength was so impaired that he was compelled to remain away from the State Department from May 1891, until the following October. Thereafter he found it increasingly difficult to attend to the duties of his office. Frequently important papers were kept for days, or even weeks, awaiting his signature. Personal sorrows interrupted his work and hastened his physical decay. In January 1890, while the International American Conference was in session, and while the Bering Sea controversy was at its height, he suffered in the death of his eldest son, Walker, a bereavement from which he was never quite able to recover. Two or three weeks later death again invaded the family, removing his eldest daughter, Mrs. Coppinger. Of his older children a son, Emmons, alone remained, and when he too died, in the summer of 1892, Blaine's proud spirit succumbed. He could no longer withstand the wasting power of disease nor bear up under the sorrows which afflicted his household. After lingering a few months he breathed his last on January 27, 1893.

Though a full generation has passed since Blaine's public career came to an end, it is still too early to speak with assurance of his place among the forty-odd occupants of the high office which it was his distinction to fill for more than four years. From the time he became a personage of national importance, controversy raged about him. No American statesman was ever plagued by political enemies more bitter or more unrelenting, and none was ever supported by followers more ardent or more steadfast. He was seldom viewed dispassionately. Seen through the eyes of friend or foe he was either a hero of the noblest proportions or a villain of the deepest dye. He was in fact neither the one nor the other. He was neither the ideal, romantic, "plumed knight" of his admirers, nor the grotesque, sordid self-seeker imagined by his detractors. Of these two views of the man the former is no longer entertained, while the latter, somewhat softened by time, tends to persist. His defects are still harped upon. His alleged blunders and failures are inordinately magnified, while his great aims and his real achievements fail to receive the consideration which they deserve. In a true perspective this order will doubtless be reversed, and it may be predicted that posterity will assign to James G. Blaine his rightful place among the greatest of American Secretaries of State.

JOHN WATSON FOSTER

SECRETARY OF STATE

JUNE 29, 1892, TO FEBRUARY 23, 1893

BY

WILLIAM R. CASTLE, Jr.

ASSISTANT SECRETARY OF STATE

JOHN W. FOSTER

FROM A PHOTOGRAPH BY ALVEY A. ADEE

John W. Foster

JOHN WATSON FOSTER

CHAPTER I

DIPLOMATIC CAREER

W HEN, toward the end of his Administration, President Harrison appointed John Watson Foster Secretary of State, he chose a man of wide diplomatic experience and broad training in international law, a man who, in various capacities, had served his country almost continuously since boyhood. Foster wrote later:[1] "With the exception of Andrew Johnson, I have been honored by a commission and served my country under every President of the United States beginning with Abraham Lincoln and ending with Theodore Roosevelt."

He was born in Pike County, Indiana, on March 2, 1836. He entered the State University of Indiana, graduating as valedictorian of his class in 1855. He spent a year in the Harvard Law School, a year in a law office in Cincinnati, and was admitted to practice at the bar at the age of twenty-one. Anti-slavery was not popular along the Kentucky border but Foster was so keen in the cause that he was often called an abolitionist, an opprobrious epithet in those times and particularly in that section of the country. He took an active part in the campaign for the election of Lincoln and it was inevitable that when war was declared he should enlist. In

July, 1861, he was commissioned a major in the 25th Indiana Regiment and thereafter took part in many of the important engagements of the Civil War, retiring at the end as brigadier general. He came into contact with General Grant several times during the war and probably this acquaintance on the battle-field facilitated his appointment in 1873 as minister to Mexico. Senator Oliver P. Morton felt that to Foster was due in large measure the success of the Republican campaign of 1872 in the doubtful state of Indiana and promised to get him as reward whatever political office he wished. He asked to be made minister to Switzerland, but as this position was already promised he was given the far more important Mexican post. Foster doubted his own fitness but years afterward in reviewing his own career he wrote: "Had I begun my career after college graduation by appointment as a Secretary of Legation, for instance, and risen by long service and merit to the mission to Mexico, I would have been free from the misgivings and trepidation which marked my acceptance of the appointment, for I would have been thoroughly versed in the routine duties; but I might not have possessed that strength of character and ability to meet men in the discussion of weighty matters which I had acquired by the experiences through which I had passed."[2] He realized, however, that the practice of diplomacy was not, after all, so very different from that of any other profession and that success could come only through strict devotion to duty and through understanding of the matters in hand. It was just these qualities which gave distinction to Foster's diplomatic career.

The mission to Mexico, which lasted seven years, was successful in that the minister managed to preserve reasonably cordial relations between the two countries through difficult times and frequent misunderstandings. He had to protect American missionaries, to smooth over border disputes as best he might, to persuade his Government to recognize the Diaz régime, which he realized almost immediately was best for the country. He worked indefatigably and with some measure of success to build up the languishing trade between Mexico and its northern neighbour. He made himself popular by learning Spanish, by mixing socially with the Mexicans and by travelling extensively through the country.

President Hayes nominated Foster as minister to Russia in January 1880. He reached St. Petersburg in the early summer. In March of the next year Alexander II was murdered. There was much to report to the Department of State but little work to do otherwise, except to protest against Russian treatment of American citizens of Jewish blood. Foster found the life interesting but unsympathetic to a man of his democratic tastes. Also he found it almost impossible to live on his salary and therefore resigned in November 1881, with the intention of practising law in Washington. In regretfully accepting his resignation Secretary Blaine wrote: "Permit me to express the deep sense of satisfaction with which the Department looks back on its relations with you, and the unvarying approbation which your official actions have received at its hands during your incumbency of the responsible missions intrusted to you."[3]

President Arthur early in 1883 persuaded Foster once more to accept a diplomatic post, this time as minister to Spain with the express mission of negotiating, if possible, a treaty of commercial reciprocity for Cuba and Porto Rico. It seemed a propitious moment to advance such a proposition since a similar treaty with Mexico had aroused great interest in Spain and the Cuban sugar planters demanded that measures be taken to secure for Cuban sugar treatment equally advantageous with that granted Mexican sugar. In spite of this interest and all the favourable indications, Foster found that to deal with the Spaniards was only a repetition of what he had learned in Mexico, that to the Spanish mind the prompt dispatch of public business is something inconceivable. He succeeded almost immediately, it is true, in reaching an agreement which put an end to the shipping war between Cuba and the United States. He secured the abolition of an unjust tax collected by Spanish consuls under the guise of a fee on cattle exported from Florida to Cuba and the return of the money collected. He had very little success in procuring payment of the long-standing American claims against Cuba, but finally negotiated and signed on November 25, 1884 the wished-for treaty of commerical reciprocity. But it was too late. Cleveland had been elected President and his influence was strongly opposed to reciprocity. The Senate refused to consent to ratification.

The tariff was the principal issue of the campaign of 1888, in which Harrison defeated Cleveland and Congress proceeded immediately to the drafting of new tariff legislation. A large section of the Republican party wanted to put sugar on the free list, whereas an-

other section, led by Blaine, Secretary of State, wanted
to revive the reciprocity negotiations. A compromise
was finally reached. The McKinley tariff act of October 1, 1890 put sugar and other tropical products on
the free list but provided that if any country imposed
"duties or other exactions upon the agricultural or other
products of the United States" the President should
have the power "and it shall be his duty to suspend, by
proclamation to that effect, the provisions of this act
relating to the free introduction of such sugar, molasses,
etc." John W. Foster, as one of the leading exponents
of reciprocity, had been often consulted, and Blaine immediately requested him to take charge of the negotiations. He began with Brazil and signed a reciprocity
agreement with that country by the middle of January.
Cuba, as the principal producer of sugar, was the most
important country to bring into line, but Spain was still
irritated over American failure to ratify the treaty of
1884. Foster, therefore, went to Havana, where he enlisted the enthusiastic support of the Cuban planters.
This made it possible, in a special mission to Spain, to
reach an agreement with regard to Cuba and Porto
Rico. There followed in rapid succession agreements
with the Central American states, with the British West
Indies, with Austria-Hungary, and with Germany, the
last being of great importance to American export trade
because it did away with the practical embargo on
American meat products. During all these negotiations
Foster had an office in the Department of State and was
actually doing an important part of the work of the
Secretary.

There has always been a serious difference of opinion

in the Republican party as to the wisdom of these special reciprocity agreements. Made with particular and especially with neighbouring nations, their effect would inevitably be to draw these nations closely to the United States, practically to include them in the American economic system. This was certainly the effect of the reciprocity agreement with Hawaii, whether or not this was recognized at the time. Possibly Foster may have felt that similar accords would serve to bind the various Latin-American nations more closely to us, but his idea seems rather to have been that every new accord would bring some specific benefit to the United States and that the sum of all these accords would be of general advantage to this country. At that time the idea of general most-favoured-nation treaties was thoroughly unpopular, although reciprocity treaties with all nations of the world would, in a way, have brought this about. It would also have practically abolished the tariff, and this may well have been the fundamental reason for the abandonment of the system. The Democratic party in general opposed reciprocity agreements in spite of the fact that it was the party of free trade or low tariff. The reason for this may have been that the first reciprocity treaties affected the industries of the South more than those of the North. Whatever the reason, divided counsel in the Republican party and practically unanimous opposition by the Democrats soon brought about the abolition of all the agreements and little has been heard since of the matter.

CHAPTER II

THE FUR-SEAL AGREEMENTS

BEFORE this work of negotiating reciprocity agreements had been concluded Foster was appointed agent to prepare the case of the United States in the Bering Sea arbitration, which was to be held at Paris under the treaty of February 29, 1892.

The reader has already noted the origin and history of this controversy in the sketch of Secretary Blaine's second tenure of office and in the narration of Secretary Bayard's diplomacy, in earlier portions of this volume. Broadly speaking, the American contentions were two: that the United States had exclusive jurisdiction in the Bering Sea, having inherited this from Russia with the purchase of Alaska; and that the seals which inhabited the Pribilof Islands were the property of the United States. Unfortunately Secretary Blaine in his admirably phrased correspondence with Lord Salisbury had placed all the emphasis on the exclusive rights of the United States in the Bering Sea, a claim which it was later discovered could not possibly be substantiated. A better legal argument was based on American property rights in the seals, even in the face of the British counter-argument that there could be no such thing as property in wild life.

When the case of the United States was well under way Blaine retired as Secretary of State and Foster was appointed on June 29, 1892 to take his place. Counsel for the United States pointed out that the employment of a new agent would create insuperable difficulties and the President thereupon decided that there would be nothing illegal or inconsistent in permitting him to hold both positions. Foster thereafter wrote notes to the British minister signed as Secretary of State, enclosing statements on the Bering Sea case signed as agent for the United States. From certain points of view this was advantageous. Foster could speak with more authority, and he could also, as Secretary, communicate directly with the American minister in London when he wanted his assistance in enforcing points made in his memoranda as agent, or to other American diplomatic officials when he felt the American case was in need of elucidation or support.

Whether or not the American claims to exclusive jurisdiction in the Bering Sea and to property of the seal herds were justified, it was clear to all who had really studied the question that, if the seals were to be preserved from extermination, killing in the open sea must be stopped. Russia had taken the same stand in this that the United States had taken, had seized poaching vessels with the same determination to preserve the Russian herds that the United States had shown to preserve the seals of the Pribilof Islands. In this connection Foster wrote confidentially on September 16, 1892 to Andrew D. White, American minister in St. Petersburg:

"It is very important that we should, if possible, secure the concurrence of Russia, in this position assumed by us, if not as an independent proposition, at least to govern the conduct of that Government in the question which will arise or has arisen, between it and Great Britain concerning the recent seizures made by Russian cruisers in Asiatic waters adjoining the Russian seal islands. It will aid us very materially in our discussion before the Tribunal of Arbitration if the Russian Government will not recede from its attitude respecting the seizures of British and American poaching vessels, and I trust you will be able, in your confidential interviews with the Minister of Foreign Affairs and other officials of the Russian Government, to secure their adhesion to the correctness of the seizures already made. If you cannot secure their complete adhesion to this view of the question, I trust you will at least be able to have them delay any final and definite decision of the question until after the result of the Arbitration which ought not to be prolonged during the coming winter. . . . As I said to you in our interview before your departure, we feel that we are not only fighting our own battle but that we are carrying on this contest with Great Britain in behalf of Russia as well as ourselves, and that we should receive all the moral and political support possible from that Government for the success of our position before the Tribunal of Arbitration. Success for us means also success for Russia, and the preservation to that Government for years to come of a most valuable and lucrative industry."[4]

Soon after this the British Bering Sea Commission made a report which argued that to preserve fur-seal life in the Bering Sea all killing on land should be stopped. Their claim was that if the islands were guarded as perpetual breeding grounds seals could properly be captured at sea by ships of any country.

Foster wrote White in St. Petersburg on November 1, 1892 that the British commission "in support of some of the remarkable propositions upon which they base their opinion" frequently referred to statements which were made to them, so they alleged, in the Commander Islands in 1891, by a Russian official named Grebnitzki, who had been in charge of the islands for fifteen years. Foster said that this official had failed to come to Washington, although he had recently been in the United States, and instructed White to get in touch with him to talk over this British report. He was very anxious that Grebnitzki should realize the use which had been made of his alleged statements, a deduction which, if it was carried into effect, would ruin the sealing industry, in order that he might be persuaded to put on record, in the interests of both the American and the Russian Governments, what he actually believed about pelagic sealing and its disastrous effects on the industry.[5]

White had already discussed the matter with Russian officials and reported so emphatically their concurrence with the American position that Foster was able to express his gratification and that of the President "at the successful manner in which you have executed your instructions, and at the just and cordial assurances of the Russian Government."[6]

A matter of far less importance in the negotiations but exceedingly embarrassing to the American Government occurred in the Department of State. Much of

the American case depended on translations made from
the Russian archives which had been taken over at the
time of the purchase of Alaska. A certain Ivan Petroff,
a scholarly and intelligent Russian, had been engaged
in this translation, and the documents furnished by him
confirmed the American contention that Russia had
exercised exclusive jurisdiction in the Bering Sea. Petroff, apparently with the idea of assisting the American
case and thereby gaining favour for himself, had inter-
polated in the English translation whatever he thought
might be useful. Foster promptly reported the facts
orally to the British chargé d'affaires and in a letter to
the agent of Great Britain said:

"I deem it my duty to bring to your attention,
without delay, the fact that it has been discovered
by me that a number of the documents belonging to
the archives of the Territory of Alaska, now in the
possession of the Department of State, and referred
to in the Case of the United States before the Tribunal of Arbitration delivered to you on September
1st last, were incorrectly translated from the Russian
language in which the originals appear. Lithographic
reproductions of the original documents are to be
found in Volume I of the Appendix to the Case of the
United States, following page 591, and English translations of the same are given in Volume I, pages 49 to
90. It has within the last few days been ascertained
that some of these translations are incorrect, but to
what extent I have not yet been able accurately to
determine. A thorough examination is now being
made, and, at the earliest practicable date, I shall

furnish you with revised and corrected translations, and indicate the pages in the Printed Case of the United States where the erroneous translations have been quoted or referred to. I have, however, not been content to await the result of that examination, and I hasten to inform you of the above fact.'"[7]

This discovery necessitated certain last-minute changes in the American argument and greatly weakened the case, but had it not been discovered and acted on promptly by Foster, it would most certainly have been brought out by the British in a way which would utterly have destroyed public confidence in the good faith of the United States Government.

A matter of greater moment was the manner of presentation of the British case. According to the terms of the treaty both sides were to present their printed case, together with supporting evidence, on a specified date. After this evidence had been studied Great Britain and the United States were to present their counter-cases. Finally, of course, oral arguments were to be made before the arbitral court when it should meet. The British case was presented on September 5, 1892, but it was found that there was no discussion of the claim of the United States to property interest in the seals which Foster had already told the British agent was to be one of the two principal American arguments. Foster told the Honourable Michael H. Herbert, chargé d'affaires of the British Legation, orally of the painful impression this omission had made on him at first reading, but he could not formally protest until he had consulted the President, who was not in Washington. He wrote Herbert formally, however, on September 27 after discussing the matter with the President, that he was directed to say that the President had "observed with surprise and extreme regret" the omission from the British case of any evidence on the principal facts in dispute, on which the Tribunal of Arbitration must largely depend. He pointed out that there was no proof whatsoever on the vital question of the property interest of the United States in the seals of the Pribilof Islands, or on another important point, that of necessary concurrent regulations. He made his point very clear by saying:

"It must be evident to the Government of Her Britannic Majesty . . . that the treaty assumes that each party will or may have allegations to make and evidence to produce upon both questions; that the plain contemplation of the treaty is that each party shall state in his case what his propositions of law are and the evidence which will be relied upon in support of them, to the end that the other party may have a fair opportunity of showing in his Counter-Case that such evidence is untrue, or erroneous, or partial, or subject to qualification or explanation, for which purpose alone the provision for a Counter-Case was framed."[8]

He pointed out that the Government of the United States had furnished in its printed case all the evidence it planned to offer, thus giving the British Government ample opportunity to prepare its rebuttal, and added that the treaty made it manifest that each party had one opportunity only to submit evidence, that being in the original case, except, of course, that there might be

evidence in rebuttal in the counter-case. His note concluded with a paragraph which showed that he felt
deeply and that he was sure of his own ground:

"To a construction of the terms of the treaty which
leads to results so grossly unjust and so gravely prejudicial, the Government of the United States cannot
assent. It would be in its judgment, such a perversion
of the letter and such a violation of the spirit of the
treaty as would threaten to defeat its objects and be
fatal to its usefulness. It may safely be asserted that
in no judicial proceeding ever invented for the determination of disputed facts was it allowed that one
party should be at liberty to introduce his whole Case
in such a manner as to give his adversary no opportunity to present evidence in reply to it, although
afforded on his own side full means of replying to his
adversary's testimony. Such a method of trial could
not be expected to result in a just decision. Had such
a proposal been made in the present case by either of
the High Contracting Parties, when the provisions
of the treaty were being framed, it would have been
at once rejected, not only as inadmissible, but as unworthy of the Government presenting it."[9]

Foster reported on this to Robert T. Lincoln, American minister in London, instructing him to see Lord
Rosebery without delay, and to impress upon him the
astonishment of the President at the strange character
of the British case as presented, to express also the earnest hope of the authorities in Washington that Lord
Rosebery would agree with the arguments presented in

the note to Mr. Herbert. The amazement and anger of the United States Government is best expressed, however, in a personal letter which Foster wrote Lincoln on the same day. In this letter he said:

"There is a concurrence of opinion by all of us here, by counsel as well as the government officials, that the British Case as framed is a piece of 'sharp-practice' on the part of the Canadians, and that it cannot be that Lord Rosebery and the Attorney General of Great Britain were cognizant of it. The matter has created the greatest indignation on our part, and the feeling is entertained that we should not submit to it. My object in asking you to seek an interview with Lord Rosebery is that you may repeat to him what I have said to Mr. Herbert, but which we did not think best, in the first instance, to put too plainly upon paper, that a persistence in the course adopted may lead to a complete abandonment of the Arbitration."[10]

Lord Rosebery made a rather halting defense of the British position on the ground of the language of certain clauses of the treaty, an argument rather absurdly easy to refute since a particular interpretation of a single clause of a legal document can never be accepted if it contradicts the clear spirit and intent of the whole instrument, and on the ground that the right of property in fur seals depends on questions of law. Foster admitted this last point, but answered:

"I cannot conceive that the precise questions of law cannot be known, and cannot therefore be determined, until the facts out of which they arise are known; and I cannot concur with Lord Rosebery . . . that the facts concerning the nature and habits of fur-seals, and the modes by which their increase may be made subservient to the uses of man without endangering the existence of the stock, are not pertinent to the claim of the United States to a property interest. On the contrary, I regard these facts as in the highest degree important."[11]

The British Government met the American contention by submitting the evidence it had as to seal life as its complete statement on the subject. Thus a dangerous crisis in the negotiations was safely passed.

CHAPTER III

MEXICO, RUSSIA, GERMANY,

GREAT BRITAIN

PROBABLY half of Foster's time and certainly half of his interest during the months he was Secretary of State were given to preparation of the Bering Sea Arbitration. Except for the Hawaiian annexation treaty it was the most pressing work he had to do. But there were, as always, a multiplicity of matters of greater or less importance to which every Secretary of State has to give his attention.

He had not forgotten his seven years in Mexico and it must have interested him to find that the same old questions were still being discussed. Most of his notes regarding Mexico had to do with border troubles. They were principally attempts to find excuses for the United States Government for not having suppressed border raids from Texas. These had been going on for years. If Mexicans stole anything from the American side of the Rio Grande, or even were suspected of stealing anything, the Texans promptly invaded Mexican territory in pursuit of the Mexicans and to recapture their plunder. They often returned with Mexican cattle and horses. They flouted the idea of Mexican sovereignty, considering the Mexicans as an inferior race which had no national rights. With some bitterness the Mexican minister said that if the United States had a reasonable number of troops along the Rio Grande the raids could be stopped. Foster answered, quoting the Secretary of War, that it was difficult to control the situation when Mexico maintained so few troops on its own side of the border. The Mexican minister responded to this with some irony that it was at least notable that the raiders re-crossed the river as soon as possible since they were apparently safer on the left bank. Perhaps there was even more sarcasm when the Mexican minister pointed out exactly where the raiders lived and in many instances their names, facts which appeared beyond the power of the American authorities to discover. The Mexican minister knew, just as the American Government knew, that the Texans in general sympathized entirely with the raiders and not at all with the troops sent to suppress them. Foster, however, was conscious of the weakness of the American position, was probably a little ashamed of the ineffectiveness of our "superior civilization," and persuaded the War Department to send three more troops of cavalry to the border. It was the first effective step toward cleaning up a shameful situation. The federal troops were mobile, were instructed to prevent any and all invasions of Mexican territory. These first troops and their successors made the Texans understand that the Government of the United States was in earnest in prohibiting raids and as a result the number of them decreased until the raids became hardly more than a brave tradition.

With Russia, omitting the routine cases and such pressure as could be brought to bear to incline the Czar's Government to side with America in the fur-seal dispute, Foster had little to do. He succeeded, however, in consummating the extradition treaty which had been

signed in March, 1887, by Bayard on behalf of the
United States and Mr. Struve and Baron Rosen on the
part of Russia. On October 14, 1892, Foster wrote that
he was sure both Governments were impressed with the
necessity of providing some means for the reciprocal
extradition of fugitives, but that the situation was difficult because in the absence of a treaty there was no
authority in the American Executive to surrender a
fugitive to another government. This, he pointed out,
had often prevented the American Government from
surrendering a fugitive from justice to the Government
of Russia, although it would have been very glad to do
so as an act of courtesy. He said that he wanted White
to suggest to the Minister of Foreign Affairs certain
slight modifications in the Bayard-Struve Treaty, which
he felt might secure the prompt ratification of the
treaty by the Senate. He then went on to explain the
modifications which he thought would make the treaty
acceptable. The Senate of the United States, he said,
was fearful, perhaps unduly fearful, of the judicial fairness of an autocratic monarchy. This was especially the
case when it came to crimes which might be called
political, and his suggestions to White were intended to
make the treaty palatable to the Senate without, at the
same time, offending the Russian Government. As an
example he referred to one paragraph in the treaty
which excepted from the character of a political offense
attacks upon the head of the State, pointing out that
it had always been contended very strongly in this
country that whether any particular case is or is not
properly a political offense ought to be left to be determined in comity upon general principles. Foster knew

that the Russian Government placed much importance upon the provision, and, to meet its wishes as well as to obviate Senate objections, suggested that the paragraph should read: "An attempt against the life of the head of either government or against that of any member of his family when such attempt comprises the act either of murder or assassination or of poisoning, shall not be considered a political offense or an act connected with such an offense."[12] This and his other suggestions proved acceptable and on February 7, 1893 he was able to telegraph St. Petersburg that the Senate had consented to the ratification of the treaty.

With Spain there was much correspondence on minor but irritating matters. Cuba and Porto Rico levied lower duties on goods imported direct from the United States, but the Cuban and Porto Rican collectors of customs contended that if the ships made a single stop *en route* importation was not direct. Foster destroyed this contention. He had also to write interminable notes concerning the unreasonable quarantine imposed in the Spanish West Indies on all vessels from the United States after there had been in this country a few isolated cases of plague which were quickly stamped out. He was more convinced than ever that prompt dispatch of business was not in the Spanish temperament.

There were few matters up with Germany and the only correspondence of any importance which Foster carried on was in connection with the joint control of affairs in Samoa. He was, or attempted to be, the mediator but he could not correct an impossible situation which had been temporarily alleviated, not cured, by the storm which wrecked the warships of the rival powers at Apia. There was no final solution until the division of territory following the war of 1914.

Foster had the satisfaction while Secretary of preparing the President's proclamation of the convention concluded with Great Britain for the purpose of fixing the Alaskan boundary and that in Passamaquoddy Bay. He had negotiated and signed the convention concluded on July 22, 1892, providing for the delimitation of boundaries between the United States and Canada which had not been permanently marked. He had written much and made many speeches about Canadian boundary questions and welcomed enthusiastically anything which marked a step toward final settlement of these questions which he believed to be most pregnant with misunderstandings between the two countries. This convention gave authority for a joint survey of the boundary between British Columbia and Alaska and for a joint commission to determine on a method more accurately to mark the boundary between Maine and New Brunswick in the waters of Passamaquoddy Bay. The work was, perhaps of necessity, slow, and was not completed until 1905, but Foster was the man to set the machinery in motion and he retained his interest and gave his counsel until the end. On certain other questions at issue between Canada and the United States he worked vigorously, carrying negotiations toward the solution of such vexing questions as canal tolls,[13] fishing rights,[14] and the transport of Chinese immigrants across the border.[15] He considered with reason that the furthering of good relations between the Dominion and the United States was one of the most important duties of the Secretary of State.

Foster was a strict Presbyterian of the fundamentalist stripe and had all his life been interested in foreign missions. When he wrote notes, therefore, such as all Secretaries of State have to write in defense of American missionaries, it was done with zeal. In one case at least his communication might have been open to question. The British declared a protectorate over the Gilbert Islands and the British commander, a man lacking in both tact and knowledge of international practice, refused to have any dealings with the American commissioner until he should be recognized as a consul by Her Majesty's Government. Foster protested with great vigour and his protest went deeper than mere discussion of the acts of a particular officer. Citizens of the United States, he said, had during the last fifty years established themselves in several of the islands of the Gilbert group. Acquiring property and vested interests therein, they had won the confidence and esteem of the natives by their exemplary dealings and by their self-sacrificing labours as missionaries; and, supported by the benevolent contributions of the Christian churches of the United States, they had raised that remote island community to a stage of civilized order alike notable and commendable.

"As I have already said," he continued, "the germs of civilization were planted in the Gilbert Group by the zealous endeavor of American citizens more than half a century ago. The result of this work, carried on by American citizens and money, has been, in fact, to change the naked barbarism of the island natives into enlightened communities and to lay the foundations of the trade and commerce which have given those islands importance in the eyes of Europe today. Wrought by the agents of a colonizing power, this development would have naturally led to a paramount claim to protection, control, or annexation, as policy might dictate. This country, however, has slept upon its rights to reap the benefits of the development produced by the efforts of its citizens; but it cannot forego its inalienable privilege to protect its citizens in the vested rights they have built up by half a century of sacrifice and Christian endeavor. I feel certain that no country will more readily acknowledge our rights in this regard than England, which has so largely shared with the United States in the work of carrying progress and civilization to the islands of the Pacific."[16]

All this was well expressed but, having gone into the general question, there is little doubt that Foster should have realized that his action created a precedent and might seriously prejudice the rights of the American Government in the future should a similar situation arise in which the United States desired to reap the benefits of what its citizens had done. The impression given was inevitably that the United States had civilized these islands, had spent money and effort in the work, but that it did not object to having a European power become the beneficiary of all it had accomplished. It insisted, however, that such action should be done courteously. Henry White, United States chargé in London, transmitted this instruction almost verbatim to Lord Rosebery, and the British Government might well have received it with some enthusiasm.

CHAPTER IV

THE HAWAIIAN ISLANDS

DURING his short term as Secretary of State Foster had to deal with only one entirely new problem. The annexation of the Hawaiian Islands to the United States was not, of course, a new idea. Successive events had led inevitably toward it but the crisis came toward the end of 1892. The Queen was overthrown and the first act of the provisional Government was to send to Washington a commission to negotiate a treaty of annexation.

As far back as 1842 the United States had formally recognized the independence of Hawaii and had also declared that because of the volume of trade and its special interests in the islands, it would consider as an unfriendly act the attempt on the part of any European power to interfere with this independence, a position which had been often reiterated. The islands were brought into even closer relations with the United States by the commercial reciprocity treaty negotiated in 1875 and continued until 1898. This treaty made Hawaii virtually a part of the American commercial system, as Secretary Blaine put it. The United States, furthermore, had never been willing to join in an international agreement to guarantee the independence of the islands since this would forever have estopped annexation or would at least have made it very difficult.

Immediately on the overthrow of the monarchy,

John L. Stevens, American minister to Hawaii, notified
the Department of State that he had recognized the
provisional Government. Foster approved this action
in a telegram of January 28, 1893.[17] He told him that
his course in recognizing an unopposed *de facto* government appeared to have been discreet and in accordance with the facts. He said that the rule of the
Government of the United States had been uniformly
to recognize and to enter into relation with any actual
government which was in full possession of effective
power with the assent of the people. Under these conditions he was willing that the minister should recognize
the new Government and expressed his hope that the
change, besides conducing to the tranquillity and welfare of the Hawaiian Islands, might tend to draw even
closer the intimate ties of amity and common interests
so conspicuously and necessarily linking them to the
United States.

At the request of the provisional Government,
Stevens ordered marines landed in Honolulu to protect
American lives and property and also issued a proclamation granting formal protection over the Hawaiian
Islands in the name of the United States. This latter
act the Secretary of State thought might be miscon-
strued and in an instruction of February 11 he discussed
fully the meaning of protection and established the
limits to which the United States was prepared to go,
summarizing what he had said as follows:

"So far, therefore, as your action amounts to according, at the request of the *de facto* sovereign Government of the Hawaiian Islands, the cooperation

of the moral and material forces of the United States for the protection of life and property from apprehended disorders, your action is commended. But so far as it may appear to overstep that limit, by setting the authority and power of the United States above that of the Government of the Hawaiian Islands, in the capacity of Protector, or to impair in any way the independent sovereignty of the Hawaiian Government by substituting the flag and power of the United States, as the symbol and manifestation of paramount authority, it is disavowed."[18]

Foster knew that the Provisional Government would ask for annexation and, whatever the outcome of this request, he wanted the position of the United States clearly understood. He therefore sent almost identical telegrams to various American representatives abroad. His cable to Lincoln, minister in London, is an example:

"Overthrow of Hawaiian monarchy and establishment of provisional government warrants a statement of position of United States in regard to those islands. From the outset they have been objects of deep concern to this Government, and since their recognized independence we have maintained close relations of intimacy culminating in exclusive commercial reciprocity involving valuable mutual concessions. The great predominance of American interests in Hawaii is incontrovertible fact, and has repeatedly called forth declarations of the paramount interest of the United States in those islands. . . . They constitute an essential and important element in our commercial system, and their proximity and situation make them a potential factor which we could never see transferred to any other control without the gravest concern. The President directs me to recall this historical attitude to your attention, and to say that recent events have fortified our position and made our paramount concern more evident. You will carefully note and fully report by cable any governmental action adverse to or confirming our position."[19]

There was in the Department of State every disposition to meet the commissioners sent to Washington by the Provisional Government of Hawaii cordially and to proceed at once to the consideration of a treaty of annexation. The negotiations, carried on orally during successive days in the early part of February, were presided over by the Secretary. He was in favour of annexation, had believed for a long time that it was both inevitable and desirable; but this fact made him none the less solicitous of the interests of the United States. He knew not only what was right from the point of view of international law and international relations, but what points in the draft presented by the Hawaiian commissioners would be likely to cause trouble politically.

At a preliminary meeting credentials were accepted and certain general considerations brought forward by the Hawaiian commissioners. At a meeting in the Department of State on February 7, 1893, Foster said that the President had taken into consideration the letter addressed to the Secretary of State by the commissioners and had authorized him to say that the

Government of the United States was disposed to enter into negotiations for the annexation of the islands, the terms of that annexation to be arrived at through discussion.

He told the commissioners that the points contained in their proposition presented some serious embarrass-ments. In some instances, he said, it was difficult to reconcile their proposal to the Constitution and laws of the United States. He therefore put before them, largely through the method of critical comment on their own proposition, what in a general way consti-tuted the ideas of his own Government. Because the commissioners felt that the territorial form of govern-ment might not immediately meet conditions in the Hawaiian Islands, Foster said that there might be created a provisional government to exist either for a fixed or indefinite period, leaving it to the Congress of the United States at the expiration of that period to adopt such other form of government as it might deem proper. He said that under this provisional Government, although the President would appoint the Governor, Hawaiian laws would be continued in force in so far as they did not conflict with the Constitution of the United States. Within a reasonable time also he thought that American revenue, shipping, and postal laws should be extended to the islands.

The Hawaiian commissioners hoped that the Ameri-can bounty on sugar might be paid to Hawaiian pro-ducers, but this Foster saw from the beginning was an impossibility, at least without serious modifications. He said quite frankly that this was one of the danger-ous features of this scheme of annexation as presented by the commission in that it would almost certainly not be accepted by the Congress of the United States. He made the counter suggestion that a bounty of half a cent a pound be paid on Hawaiian sugar, so long as the United States should maintain a greater or equal bounty. But this suggestion was not satisfactory to the Hawaiian commissioners, who pointed out that it was a question which most vitally concerns the largest property interests in the islands. They showed that annexation would mean serious financial disadvantages to them and that their only compensation would consist in receiving a bounty equal to that paid in the United States. That the very small bounty at first suggested by Foster would be of very little assistance to the planters the chairman of the commission explained as follows:

"I think it is a perfectly proper thing to state here, and that you should know exactly what the situation is, although it would probably be disadvantageous to us if it became public. That is in connection with the sugar contracts between the planters and the sugar trust. When the contracts were made, the planters at the Islands were put into a corner. Mr. Spreckels had combined with the trust, and there was no other possible purchaser of sugar. The planters searched the world over; they made the most detailed investigation, in London, in Germany and in Australia, and there was absolutely nothing else for them to do except make a contract with the sugar trust; and one of the terms of that contract is that of any sugar bounty which they get the trust shall receive one half the benefit; so that really any bounty that is paid to the planters now goes one half to the sugar trust."[20]

It was just this contingency of annexation, the chairman added in answer to a question of the Secretary, which the sugar trust had in view when the contract was made. Foster realized that this hitherto unknown fact immensely increased the political difficulty of drawing a treaty of annexation satisfactory to both sides. He knew that the bounty, even as paid to sugar producers in America, was unpopular, that to extend its benefits to Hawaiian planters who, of necessity, employed oriental labour, would be bad political strategy; and after the admission of the Hawaiian commissioners of the interest of the sugar trust he was convinced that any mention of a bounty would not only defeat the treaty in an election year, but would involve almost certain defeat of the Republican party at the polls. This point he made so clear in private conversations with the commissioners that the matter was dropped.

The Hawaiian commissioners were very anxious that the treaty should include a promise on the part of the United States to lay a cable to Hawaii and to proceed to the development of Pearl Harbour. The Secretary said that neither of these propositions would be acceptable. He pointed out that if the United States annexed the islands the cable would be one of the first things to come as a natural result of this union and that to make any definite commitment in the matter would be a departure from American practice in the past since the Government of the United States neither built nor owned telegraphs, neither laid nor owned cables. He called to the attention of the commissioners the sensible practice of the Government to use the enterprise of individuals and private corporations for its public needs. As to immediate development of Pearl Harbour, he said that if the Government of the United States was to possess and have the sovereignty over all the waters of the Hawaiian Islands, it ought to be left to the convenience and better judgment of the Government to determine as to what steps should be taken, and what harbours should be improved. He gave earnest assurances, however, that it would be the duty of the United States, as well as to their great interest, to protect the islands, not only for the sake of the islands, as they might be a part of the nation, but for the protection of the whole Pacific coast, and because of the necessities of the navy. For these reasons he thought it unnecessary and really improper to assume the formal obligation to improve one particular harbour.

Foster was equally definite in these conversations in his opposition to the suggestion of any change of the United States immigration laws to permit the introduction to Hawaii of Chinese labourers. In general Hawaiian laws were to remain in force but the laws of the United States as to Chinese were to be extended to the Hawaiian Islands immediately upon annexation, with an additional provision that no Chinese labourers on the islands be permitted to come to the United States. It was clear that any relaxation of the rule excluding Chinese from the United States would bring instant and possibly decisive opposition to the projected treaty from Pacific coast senators.

The treaty as signed in Washington on February 15,

1893 contained only seven articles.[21] The Government of the Hawaiian Islands ceded all sovereign rights to the United States and also all public lands, buildings, and other public property. Hawaiian laws were continued in force until Congress should pass special legislation. Chinese immigration was prohibited and no Chinese in the islands were to proceed to the mainland. The public debt was assumed by the United States, which also agreed to pay an annuity to the ex-Queen and $150,000 to the Princess Kaiulani. No mention was made of the sugar bounty.

It proved impossible to secure ratification of the treaty during the last days of the session of the Senate and the incoming Cleveland Administration was opposed to annexation. The matter was only postponed, however. The case for Hawaiian annexation was too good to be destroyed by sentimental and meaningless talk of imperialism and oppression of native races. After the interval of Cleveland's Administration, another treaty of annexation was signed on June 16, 1898, following the battle of Manila Bay, and the Senate promptly gave its consent to ratification. That Foster's work five years earlier was not wasted may be seen from the fact that not only was all information collected by him available when need arose, but from the added and significant fact that all the ideas, with the exception of payments to the Hawaiian royal family, and even the exact wording of most of the paragraphs of his treaty, were embodied in the final treaty. Through his speeches and writings both before and after he was Secretary of State Foster was one of the most potent influences in America in favour of Hawaiian annexation. He was logical because thoroughly in command of the facts of the case and familiar with the history of the islands; persuasive because so completely convinced of the truth and soundness of his own position that annexation could not fail to be of advantage to both countries.

CHAPTER V

LAST YEARS

FOSTER said, and with some justice, that he was the only Secretary of State who ever left a clean desk behind him. He resigned from the Department at the end of February, 1893, eight days before the inauguration of President Cleveland, in order to prepare for the Bering Sea Arbitration, which opened in Paris on March 23 of that year. It has been noted that the American case and counter-case already had been prepared by Foster in his capacity as American agent, a position which he had continued to hold when he became Secretary of State. He was now to conduct the American case before the assembled tribunal. The promise of support for the American case which Foster had received a few months before from the Russian Government was not fulfilled and before the close of the tribunal Russia and Great Britain reached an agreement respecting the seals off the Asiatic coast which seriously prejudiced the American case.[22] The arbitral decision, handed down on August 15, 1893, was against the United States, except that seals might not be caught in the open sea between May 1 and July 31, and then only outside of a prohibited zone sixty miles off the Pribilof Islands. Foster was keenly disappointed because he knew that the decision would not protect the seal herds as was intended and even more because he knew it would make international arbitration unpopular in the United States for years to come.

After the arbitration Foster took a trip around the world, returning, as he hoped, to live permanently in Washington. But he was too well known to be left in peace and at the end of 1894 he was appointed by China to assist in her peace negotiations with Japan. He remained in the Orient for several months, acting as the close adviser of the Chinese Government and of Li Hung Chang when that great statesman proceeded himself to Japan to conduct the negotiations. He really presented the case for China, and carried on the negotiations so ably that he won the gratitude of the Chinese, so fairly that he gained the friendship of Japan. Foster's own account of these negotiations in his *Diplomatic Memoirs* makes up perhaps the most interesting chapters he ever wrote. During the next few years he was an active adviser of the Department of State on various Canadian questions including that of the Alaskan boundary, and exerted, through his speeches and writings, particularly in his books on diplomatic history and practice, strong and useful influence on public opinion. He was a delegate for China at the second Hague Conference in 1907. But on the whole his life in Washington during the last ten years became more and more secluded. He went regularly to church. He saw his personal friends and loved to discuss public affairs with them. He wrote much and occasionally appeared on the public platform. Living with his daughter and his son-in-law, Robert Lansing, he kept closely in touch with public affairs and during the first difficult period when Lansing was Counselor and then Secretary of State, or from April 1, 1914 until Foster died, his advice and assistance must have been of great value.

Chauncey Depew once made the remark that there could be written a life of John W. Foster as "handyman of the Department of State." This was meant in no derogatory sense. During a large part of his active life he lived in Washington. He was known as a profound student of international law. He understood foreign countries. His high sense of civic duty forbade him to reject any opportunity of service and the result was that he was called on repeatedly by successive Secretaries of State to assist in negotiations of one sort or another, to handle certain intricate correspondence, to advise personally on various perplexing questions. He was almost as familiar a figure in the Department during his years out of office as during the few months he was Secretary of State.

Estimates of Foster's ability vary greatly. By some he is ranked as an uninspired plodder; by others as a man of brilliant intellectual ability. Neither estimate is correct. He was far more than a plodder because he had an admirable equipment of knowledge which he knew how to apply to the problems in hand. He was an eminently safe man, but not safe because he was afraid to act, which is too often the meaning when one speaks of a safe man. He was cautious in the right sense. He wanted to be convinced of all the facts, but having them clearly in mind advanced courageously. He had no diplomatic fear of speaking out, as is evidenced by his very frank note to the British Embassy concerning what he considered the obvious unfairness of the British case as presented in the Bering Sea Arbitration. The only excuse for calling him a plodder is that he lacked both imagination and humour. And this lack makes it impossible to credit him with "brilliant" intellect. Both in the spoken and in the written word he was a little ponderous. Bryce called him "the most distinguished diplomat of our time," and this was probably true so far as experience went. He did not, however, have the vital imagination out of which springs the initiative that is the mark of a great man. He was a great citizen in his unselfish devotion to duty, in the high ideals which he lived even more than he preached. He was invaluable as a faithful servant and trusted adviser of his Government, a man of judicial temper and clarity of perception, infinitely painstaking in all that he did. "His demand on life from callow youth to ripe old age was not for a brilliant career, but for an honorable mission, a place where he might be able to do something for the world."[23] When he died, in 1917, he stood first among the older generation of Americans.

WALTER QUINTIN GRESHAM

SECRETARY OF STATE

MARCH 6, 1893, TO MAY 28, 1895

BY

MONTGOMERY SCHUYLER

FORMERLY OF THE
UNITED STATES DIPLOMATIC SERVICE

WALTER Q. GRESHAM

FROM A PHOTOGRAPH BY L. C. HANDY

WALTER QUINTIN GRESHAM

CHAPTER I

GRESHAM'S APPOINTMENT · HIS EARLIER CAREER

IT will be recalled that the focus of attention and discussion at the Democratic nominating convention in 1892 was the burning question of the tariff. Cleveland's views on that question were so much in agreement with those of Walter Quintin Gresham that the latter, a former Republican, voted for him in the election of that year and declared to his son, Otto Gresham, that he felt he ought to take the stump for Cleveland.

Before Gresham's position and views had become known publicly, there was a rumour to the effect that he intended to vote for Cleveland, and he was deluged with requests to make some statement. To a personal friend he wrote that he had made no announcement of how he should vote and that it was not his intention to do so, that he had given no interviews nor written any letters. "However, I will say to you that I expect to vote for Mr. Cleveland because I agree with him on the tariff question. . . . If I did not disagree with the Republican party on fundamental issues, I would vote its ticket, whatever I might think of its candidates."

It was this conversion of a prominent Republican

that paved the way for his appointment as Secretary of State. On January 25, 1893 President-elect Cleveland wrote to Mr. Gresham in the following terms:

"My dear Sir:—

"Will you accept the place of Secretary of State in coming administration?

"You will doubtless be surprised by this proposition but I hope you may see your way clear to accede to my request.

"You know enough of cabinet duties to make it unnecessary for me to enlarge upon their character or scope.

"I fear that your sensitiveness concerning the view that may be taken of your acceptance of the position in connection with your prior political affiliations and the part you took in the late campaign, may cause you to shrink from a fair consideration on this subject.

"I beg you, however, to believe that your sturdy regard for political duty and your supreme sincerity and disinterestedness, seen and known of all men, are proof against any and all unworthy suspicions or malicious criticism.

"In really a great emergency, the country needs your services in the place I ask you to fill. In an effort to subserve the interests of my countrymen, I need you.

"Can you not come to us? Hoping for an early reply, I am,

"Yours very sincerely,
"Grover Cleveland."[1]

Gresham did not at once accept the extraordinary offer. As little of a strict party man as he had always shown himself to be, he had voted the Republican ticket in every election since the formation of that party except in 1864, when he had been prevented by his Civil War wound from going to the polls. The offer of the highest appointive post in the power of the new Democratic President to bestow, coming as it did from a man whom it does not appear from the record that he even personally knew, was a matter for serious deliberation. Mrs. Gresham, as she relates in her biography of her husband, was strongly opposed to his acceptance. So was their son.[2] "Our reasons were perhaps not entirely unselfish. My husband's personal popularity, which Frank Hatton said was greater than that of Mr. Blaine, we did not want him to sacrifice. His motives would be misjudged and he would be maligned. We pressed home the objection that the panic then actually on, although not apparent to many, was gaining momentum and would soon break and be charged up to the men who must stem it and remove its causes, so far as they could be removed by governmental agency."

The correspondence shows that at first Gresham declined the offer on February 3, but that the continued pressure from his friends, especially Colonel Henry Watterson, and an urgent telegram from Cleveland on the 6th asking for a reconsideration of his refusal finally decided him. He wrote to the President-elect on the 7th:

"My Dear Sir:—
"I think you understand me and I believe I understand you. I have no doubt that you feel that you

need me in your cabinet, and I have finally concluded
to yield to your wish and judgment. I still entertain
misgivings, however, as to the wisdom of the step,
but I hope that neither of us will ever have cause
to regret it. I desire that you shall feel perfectly free,
even up to the last moment, to substitute someone
else in my place should circumstances seem to require
it. . . .

"Sincerely yours,
"W. Q. Gresham."[3]

Two days later, Mr. Cleveland cordially replied:

"Your letter of the 7th instant came to hand two
or three hours ago, and causes me the greatest satisfaction. I know perfectly well that only considerations
of patriotism and duty have constrained you to accede
to my wishes, and I assure you this vastly increases
my appreciation of what you have done. . . ."[4]

The independent press of the country received the
appointment with less surprise than might have been
expected and in most cases approved it. Henry Watterson gave it his powerful public approval. With the
exception of some Democratic feeling that such an office
ought not to have been given to any but an important
and "regular" party man, there was little opposition
voiced. The country seemed glad to feel that in the
troublous times which were approaching, there should
be a strong and independent man in the office of Secretary of State.

Walter Quintin Gresham was born in the family
home in Harrison County, Indiana, March 17, 1832.

He was the son of William Gresham and Sarah Davis, his wife. The Gresham family had come from Virginia to Kentucky as had the Davises, and thence migrated again to Indiana, taking up land near the present town of Lanesville. William, the father of Walter, was the son of a George Gresham, who, in 1801, in Kentucky, married Mary Pennington, the sister of Dennis Pennington, a local celebrity. Lawrence Gresham in turn was the father of this George. He was born in England and from there sent to Virginia as a boy bound out by indenture to his uncle. Lawrence, however, secured his freedom at his majority and later served in the Continental Army. Some years after the war Lawrence Gresham and his wife, accompanied by their son George, joined the stream of immigrants to Kentucky and the West.

The son of George Gresham, Colonel William, married Sarah Davis November 3, 1825. His title came from his having been elected a colonel in the state militia. He was elected sheriff of Harrison County, Indiana, and on January 26 of the next year, he was killed while arresting a desperate character. He was survived by his wife, two daughters and three sons, of whom the best known is the subject of the present sketch. The three boys grew up working the farm and going to school when possible in a log schoolhouse near by. According to a story by his wife given in her *Life of Walter Quintin Gresham*, Walter at the age of fifteen years once carried the local preacher on his back across a swollen stream which the latter was afraid to cross. On being asked if he had not been afraid to try the crossing with such a load, he answered: "Why should I when I had the man of God on my back." We shall see that a religious motive later played a part in some of Gresham's foreign policy.

Later in life the widow of William Gresham married one Noah Rumley and presently the elder children were given a half-brother, Anthony, who died in childhood, and two half-sisters, Mandy and Kate. One of the most important formative influences on young Walter Gresham was that brother of his grandmother, the locally celebrated Dennis Pennington, who was the administrator of the estate of William Gresham and his successor as sheriff of Harrison County. It is said that Dennis Pennington's frequent visits to the Gresham home and his own pronounced views had much to do with strengthening Walter Gresham and his brothers in anti-slavery ideas.

On the return of his brother Ben from the Mexican War, in which he had served in the Second Indiana Volunteers, Walter Gresham was enabled to leave the farm and take a position which Dennis Pennington had secured for him in the office of the auditor of Harrison County, at Corydon, the capital of Indiana from 1813 to 1824. He also attended an academy there and completed the course in two years, at the age of nineteen. For several terms he taught school at the log schoolhouse near the Gresham home. After a year at the Indiana State University in 1851, he began to read law with Judge William A. Porter. On April 1, 1854, on motion of Judge Porter, young Gresham was admitted to practice. Soon afterwards he formed a partnership with a Mr. Slaughter. In her biography Mrs. Gresham says: "As a lawyer, Walter Q. Gresham was a success from the start. He developed at once into a good advocate, without the florid style of oratory then so common. He possessed invective and could be impassioned, but in the main he addressed himself to the reason of his hearers, whether on the bench, on the jury, or at the hustings. He studied the reports of the English common law and chancery courts, and especially the decisions of Chief Justice Marshall and Chancellor Kent, and attempted to acquire their exactness of language and clearness of statement. Simplicity coupled with clearness is the most powerful weapon in debate. He early realized the flexibility of the equity principles of Chancellor Kent, in seeking fraud and deceit, and was able to apply them at the bar and subsequently on the bench. The moral side never escaped him."[5]

Gresham followed the usual course of the young country lawyer; he entered the local political arena with energy and was nominated for office on several occasions. He married (February 11, 1858) Matilda McGrain, daughter of Thomas McGrain, who had fled from Ireland to the United States to escape prosecution for opposition to the British Government. The young lady had been born in Louisville but had gone to school in Corydon, to which place her family had removed. When fourteen years of age and attending a party, she had met Walter Gresham and had been much impressed by the tall, handsome and well-dressed youth of nearly twenty-one. Their first home after marriage was in Corydon.

Almost coincidentally with his marriage Gresham was thrown into the beginnings of the conflict over slavery which was then overshadowing all other political questions. According to the testimony of his wife, he was not an Abolitionist as the word was then used, although he was convinced of the innate immorality of slavery. Living among those who believed in the institution as it existed (his own wife and her family being not bitter pro-slavery people, but rather anti-Abolitionists), he seems to have guarded himself from expressing opinions which might wound his hearers. Mrs. Gresham relates that as they made the twenty-mile drive from Corydon to New Albany on their wedding morning, her husband said that his confidence increased that the promptings of the human heart would settle the slavery question.[6]

Walter Q. Gresham was nominated by the Republicans of Harrison County, Indiana, in July 1860, as their candidate for the lower branch of the state legislature. Though the Republican national ticket was beaten in Harrison County, Gresham defeated his Democratic opponent by sixty votes.

Immediately after Lincoln's election the smouldering fires which had been awaiting the outcome of the popular vote burst into devastating flame and the mighty conflagration was soon under way. When the Indiana legislature assembled in January, 1861, the great task before it was to guide the destinies of that state into the channels which would keep it loyal to the Union. On the second day of the session Gresham introduced some resolutions declaring that armed resistance to the execution of the constitutional laws of Congress on the part of the citizens of any state was treason. From the committee to which they were referred the resolutions emerged with the word "treason" omitted, but, as finally adopted, they pledged "all the power of the State of Indiana to preserve the only government on earth wherein the rights of man constituted the foundation of its laws and the measure of its civil authority," and they deprecated any purpose to interfere with the right of each state to regulate its own domestic affairs. Similar resolutions were being proposed all over the country and the time taken for their discussion may have helped to postpone the actual conflict until after the inauguration of Lincoln.

Gresham had received a commission as colonel on the staff of Oliver P. Morton, the celebrated war Governor of Indiana, but his relations with him soon became strained. The young legislator drafted a bill for the military organization of the state which was passed at the special session of the legislature later in the spring and also drafted and had passed a home guard bill. Afterwards he asked for a commission as colonel or in a lower grade. His request was refused by the Governor, and he went to his home and enlisted as a private in a company which he had helped to organize. As a result of the protests of his friends, the Governor later made out for Gresham a commission as lieutenant-colonel of the thirty-eighth Indiana.

Gresham's career during the war was honourable, valorous and active in the extreme. He participated in the campaigns in Kentucky, and in the operations before Vicksburg. After the fall of that fortress he was commissioned brigadier-general. He commanded a division during Sherman's march across Georgia. On the outskirts of Atlanta he received a minie ball in the lower left leg which ended his military career and kept him on crutches for the next five years.

Gresham was nominated by the Republicans for

Congress in the autumn of 1866. He was defeated by his Democratic opponent by a small number of votes in a district normally strongly Democratic, though the state ticket and a majority of the legislature went to the Republicans or Union party, as it was called there. In the succeeding January, Gresham was made state agent to handle the finances; Morton was elected to the United States Senate and the Fourteenth Amendment was ratified. Gresham's attitude against incorporating Negro suffrage into the reconstruction acts and his efforts in this direction lost him much power and prestige in the Republican party.

He resumed the practice of law in 1865, forming a partnership in New Albany, Indiana, and retaining all his former interest in politics. In 1868 he was a delegate to the Republican convention in Chicago and favoured the nomination of General Grant. He was once more a candidate for Congress, but again was defeated by the same opponent as on the first occasion. On account of his opposition to Negro suffrage, Gresham is said to have declined to become a candidate for the United States Senate. President-elect Grant offered the collectorship at New Orleans to General Gresham in February, 1869, and asked him to be his personal adviser in that section. When Gresham declined, Grant said he admired a man who could say "no" when an office was tendered to him, more than he did one who could not accept "no" when he was asked for an office. At about this time, Gresham wrote to a friend and former partner:

"My mind is now made up; I will accept no offer, I care not what it is. I know that you will laugh when

I say that I have no political aspirations, and that I would not today go to the United States Senate if I could. I am disgusted with the whole thing, I think the Republican party is an infernally corrupt concern, and I don't care how soon it is broken up if the Democracy don't survive it."[7]

To Mrs. Gresham the world looked brighter than it did to her husband. When she first saw the city of Washington:

"It was just after General Grant's first inauguration. I saw it with young eyes. It was an enchanting place. Even the old National Hotel was a dream to me. Think of the stuffy, ill-kept rooms; the huge spittoons, not any too clean, around them and on every floor to be stumbled over; the darky servants not better kept than the rooms. And the table service was not better than we find in any country town now. Ah, but there were the terrapin, shad, and the corn bread such as we cannot get now!"[8]

President Grant, without Gresham's knowledge, on September 9, 1869 sent in his name to the Senate as United States District Judge for the District of Indiana. Notwithstanding his previous private declarations he finally accepted and took up his duties at Indianapolis, retaining the old home at New Albany. During his term of office a number of important cases were decided but nothing of sufficient general interest to be noted here except the leadership exercised by Gresham in organizing volunteer companies to preserve order and protect property at the time of the great railroad strikes of 1877.[9]

Judge Gresham declined the Republican nomination for Governor of Indiana in 1880 and also for the United States Senate. Nominally a Republican, he was never an ardent partisan and always desired to remain in a position of political independence in thought and action. He had arranged in 1882 to retire from the bench and to establish another law partnership. Before the final steps in this matter had been taken, President Arthur offered him, without his knowing that he was even being considered, the position of Postmaster General in the Cabinet. Gresham accepted. Mr. and Mrs. Gresham took the Foster home at 1405 I Street in Washington, just around the corner from the residence of General Sherman, Gresham's old commander in the war. At that time the social centre of Washington had not moved so far to the northwest as it has since and the handsome old residences still standing although shorn of their former splendor attest the fashion and wealth of H and I Streets and the district around Lafayette Park and even farther towards the present shopping and "downtown" zones.

One of the first activities of Postmaster General Gresham was an effort to suppress the lottery then actively functioning in Louisiana, which used the United States mails to disseminate its circulars throughout the country. Mail orders in payment for lottery tickets were also sent by the public through the mail in contravention of Section 4041 of the Revised Statutes. This latter activity had been stopped but the circularizing went on unabated. Even after Gresham had made a beginning, it was six years before the lottery was finally suppressed. From Louisiana it migrated to Honduras.

As Postmaster General, in his report to the President, Gresham recommended the amendment of the postal laws to suppress the Louisiana lottery; the extension of the railway mail service; cheaper postage; the reduction from three to two cents' postage on ordinary letters; and opposed the taking over of the telegraph lines as a part of the postal system.

On the death of Judge Folger, Secretary of the Treasury, Gresham was transferred to the Treasury Department. He remained there only two months. While a member of the Cabinet he took part in the presidential campaign on behalf of James G. Blaine. On November 2, 1884 Gresham accepted appointment as United States Judge for the Seventh Circuit.[10] The next day he left Washington and from that time on held court throughout his circuit, which then consisted of the states of Indiana, Illinois and Wisconsin. Many important cases were decided during the next few years, but their consideration would lead us outside the limits of the present sketch. A number of the more important were concerned with patent litigation, among them the Pullman Palace Car Company case. Considerable space is given to these cases in Mrs. Gresham's biography, where those interested may find the facts given with many details and documentary evidence.

Early in 1888 there was the usual excitement in the United States over the presidential candidates. On the Republican side, formal announcement by Blaine was made to the effect that he would not again be a candidate. This action left only one avowed candidate, John

Sherman, although there had been a certain movement in favour of Gresham. A statement made by Mr. Church Howe to the effect that President Arthur had told him in 1884 that if he, Arthur, could not get the nomination, he wanted Gresham to have it, attracted attention[11] and brought to him many of the Arthur followers. The withdrawal of Blaine brought forward a number of other candidates, including General Harrison, who had been a Blaine follower and who now felt free to declare his candidacy. The Chicago *Tribune* turned from Blaine to Gresham in February, 1888, and other newspapers followed with enthusiasm. But difficulties regarding patronage and pledges for appointments in the event of election soon began to make trouble between Gresham and the two powerful "bosses" Quay of Pennsylvania and Platt of New York. Gresham insisted on going into the convention fight unpledged to anyone and with free hands. The Republican delegates met in Chicago, June 18, 1888, and it was soon seen that from the importance of New York as a doubtful state Platt would have more real power in the convention than anyone else, and that his support was going to be used for the man who would agree to satisfy his great ambition, namely, appointment as Secretary of the Treasury. After the preliminary ballots had been taken, showing Gresham running second to Sherman in the first three, there was great activity among the Harrison forces and it was reported that the agreement was made among a number of his backers that in the event of his election Platt would be appointed Secretary of the Treasury, thus finally swinging the all-powerful New York delegation to the support of Harrison and bringing about his nomination, and subsequent election. It can be understood that Gresham was not sympathetic with the new party-management.

In the summer of 1892, there was a wide movement for Gresham to accept the presidential nomination of the People's party, or Populists, which included a number of former Republicans and Democrats, friends of his. Other friends still adhering to the old parties informed Gresham that they would vote for him and work for him. Gresham would not accept the nomination, though he made it clear that he was sympathetic with the Populists on some questions. His stand on the question of inflation had always been clear and in direct opposition to that of the new party.

CHAPTER II

GRESHAM AND HAWAII

A CERTAIN shirtsleeves brusqueness consistently characterized American diplomacy in Cleveland's second Administration, a feature which became more noticeable when the downright Olney succeeded the independent Gresham, who, compared with his successor, was of a more conciliatory disposition, but who, compared with many of his predecessors, showed qualities of decision and action. Nevertheless it was Gresham's inclination to conciliate, to make friends for his cause, and to remove obstacles by converting opponents, rather than to force his own point of view bluntly at any cost.

One of the first problems which Secretary Gresham was required to tackle was the still unsettled one of the fate of the Hawaiian Islands, which had already occupied a large share of the attention of previous Secretaries, notably of Fish, Bayard, Blaine, Frelinghuysen and Foster.

The Hawaiian diplomacy of the first Cleveland Administration, under Secretary Bayard, of developing a species of American protectorate over the islands, through what Bayard called the "peculiar reciprocities" of the treaty of 1884, as well as the earlier growth of interest on the part of the United States, has been duly noticed on previous sketches of Secretaries Bayard, Blaine and Fish. Blaine's second administration and that of his successor Foster had carried forward this policy, under President Harrison, which had ended with the negotiation of a treaty of annexation with the outlanders' revolutionary *de facto* Government that had overturned Queen Liliuokalani and her native Government. This treaty President Harrison had sent in to the Senate just before he left the White House at the end of his term.

The affairs of Hawaii were not unfamiliar to President Cleveland, who had found on entering the White House for the first time in 1885 that the convention by which Pearl Harbour was set aside for the exclusive use of the United States was still pending. At that time, after careful study of the matter, he had declared in his second annual message: "my unhesitating conviction that the intimacy of our relations with Hawaii should be emphasized. . . . The paramount influence we have there acquired, once relinquished, could only with difficulty be regained, and a valuable ground of vantage for ourselves might be converted into a stronghold for our commercial competitors." That treaty was ratified and proclaimed on November 9, 1887.

Before his second inauguration, Mr. Cleveland had a conference at Lakewood with his Secretary of State to be, at which, according to Mrs. Gresham, the Hawaiian situation was discussed. On the same authority, Gresham already had taken a position against annexation and the forward colonial policy of the United States with which the press was ringing at the time. On the seventh of March, 1893, Cleveland withdrew the convention of annexation from the Senate. Secretary Gresham advised him to send a special commissioner to

Honolulu at once. So President Cleveland sent James H. Blount, recently chairman of the House Committee on Foreign Affairs, to Hawaii to discover the "facts." The President's study of the correspondence on the case had apparently made him suspicious that the American representative in the islands had deliberately aided the revolution with a view to precipitating the annexation to the United States, his attention being especially drawn to a sentence in a dispatch from Minister Stevens under date of February 1, 1893, which said: "The Hawaiian pear is now fully ripe, and this is the golden hour for the United States to pluck it."

Blount's report of July 17, 1893 strengthened the conviction of the President. Cleveland apparently little realized the necessity under which American representatives in the more unsettled countries of the world labour, of being in close and frequent touch, not only with the government to which they may be accredited but with all other important parties and groups in what may be euphemistically described as "the opposition." In the case of the Hawaiian revolution, however, there appears to be little doubt that Stevens in his annexationist zeal had quite overstepped the limits proper to a diplomatic representative in a friendly and peaceable country. On the other hand, there seems to be little doubt but that the feeling of President Cleveland and Secretary Gresham in this matter was partly due to the fact that the treaty had been negotiated and sent to the Senate by President Harrison and that Minister Stevens had been an intimate personal friend of James G. Blaine.

It is unfortunate for the reputation of the United

States in Hawaii that during the whole time of the revolutionary disturbance and the subsequent procrastination in dealing with the situation which had developed, there was so much partisan and personal bias shown. According to the correspondence, Stevens, the American representative under Harrison, did everything in his power to overthrow the old monarchy and to establish a new government more favourable to annexation, and Blount, the special "commissioner paramount" of Cleveland, apparently made very little attempt to get at the real facts and associated only with followers of the royalist party. Another unfortunate feature was that Blount was sent not as a duly accredited diplomat, but as the personal representative of the President and his appointment was not submitted to the Senate for ratification.

Out of all the noise and partisan recrimination one thing remained evident, namely, that something would have to be done in the matter. Matters drifted on for some time, however, and Cleveland determined to get Secretary Gresham to ask the advice of the other members of the Cabinet.

Of the Cabinet papers written, that of the Attorney General, Richard Olney, later to succeed Gresham as Secretary of State, bore most weight. It is more convenient to treat of this phase of Olney's Cabinet activities here than it is under the following sketch of him as Secretary of State. On October 9 Olney addressed a letter to Secretary of State Gresham, presenting to him the results of his analysis of the Hawaiian situation and his conclusions. Some of its paragraphs are of sufficient importance to quote even in this brief study:

"The Hawaii business strikes me as not only important, but as one that may require great difficulty in the handling.

"There is no question, it seems to me, that a great wrong was done under the auspices of the United States Minister Stevens when the regularly constituted government of the Queen was supplanted and the recent, so-called, provisional government installed in its stead.

"There is no question either, I think, of the good sense, the statesmanship, and the sound morality of your proposition that this great wrong should be rectified, and that to rectify it the *status quo* at the time of its perpetration must as far as possible be restored.

"The practical conclusions I arrive at from the foregoing are these:

"1. All the resources of diplomacy should be exhausted to restore the *status quo* in Hawaii by peaceful methods and without force.

"2. If, as a last resort, force is found to be necessary—by force I mean an act or course of acts amounting to war—the matter must be submitted to Congress for its action.

"3. In addition to providing for the security of the Queen's person pending efforts to reinstate the Queen's government, and as a condition of making such efforts, the United States should require of the Queen and any other legal representatives of her government full power and authority to negotiate and bring about the restoration of her government on such reasonable terms and conditions as the United States may approve and find to be practicable. . . .

"I trust you will not regard this as an unnecessary intrusion upon your time or an uncalled-for meddling with affairs especially in your care. . . . Wishing I had something better to offer I am. . . ."[12]

As the incoming Administration had within a very few days of assuming office taken the responsibility of withdrawing from the Senate the text of the treaty which had been drawn up in the last days of the Harrison Administration and had not re-introduced it, and as the new and *de facto* Government was actually functioning in the islands, it was obvious that something had to be done. In these later days we should probably have seen the matter simply indefinitely shelved and some so-called policy of "watchful waiting" followed, but Cleveland was not the man to hesitate to right what he considered a wrong through fear of the enemies he might make. It has been charged that Gresham was instrumental in nullifying the action of the outgoing Administration and in abruptly changing its policy, on account of his long-standing personal animosity to General Harrison. Whether this be true or not, it is abundantly evident that both Cleveland himself and Olney, his Attorney General, were convinced that the United States was at least morally responsible for the overthrow of the native monarchical Government in Hawaii and the substitution of a provisional Government, and that it was the duty of the United States to take steps to bring about the renewal of the former régime, no matter how repugnant such a form of government might be to republican ideas. On October 18, 1893 Gresham made a report to the President, which gave a long summary of the case. The gist of it was that the Harrison annexation treaty was to be discarded, but it gave no hint of how or by whom this result was to be brought about.[13]

The net result of the deliberations of the Cabinet on Hawaii was that it was decided to send a new minister with a letter of credence addressed to the provisional Government. The natural result was to further befog an already complicated situation and to add one more personality to the mass of those already considering the matter.[14] On his arrival in Honolulu, Willis, the new minister, found it almost impossible to fulfil the object of his mission. He had been directed to ask for complete amnesty for all persons concerned in the uprising. "There are certain laws of my Government by which I shall abide," said Queen Liliuokalani. "My decision would be, as the law directs, that such persons should be beheaded and their property confiscated."[15]

After much futile reporting back and forth it was found by the Administration that nothing satisfactory could be accomplished, and the President came to the conclusion that he ought to lay the whole matter before Congress. He asked first Gresham and then Olney to draw up a message and finally, as Mr. James says, "using much of Olney's draft," he wrote the remarkable Hawaiian message of December 18, 1893. With the exception of rejecting Harrison's treaty, the message made no specific recommendations. It was practically a request that, in this particular matter at least, the Congress should conduct the foreign affairs of the nation, and it is illuminating in showing just how impossible it would have been for Congress to regu-

late matters which in our scheme of government belong properly to the President. After much discussion
the matter was sidetracked and it was not until January, 1895, that the Senate finally passed a resolution
approving the Administration's policy of non-intervention in Hawaii. Just nothing was the result of the
ill-considered and heedless attitude of the Administration in hastily withdrawing from the Senate a treaty
without thinking what it would have to do later on.
The provisional Government in the islands, seeing that
nothing satisfactory to any one concerned was likely
to come out of the impasse, wisely resolved to continue
itself in a more permanent form and organized a government which functioned satisfactorily until it was recognized by the United States.[16]

If Cleveland had stopped there and had contented
himself with declaring that the United States should
not profit by the uprising in the islands and the
coup d'état of January in the presence, if not under
the protection, of American marines landed at the
request of Stevens, he would probably have had the
great majority of public opinion in the United States
on his side and whether he had or not, he would have
had the satisfaction of knowing that his moral position
was impregnable. But seemingly Cleveland was under
the guidance of his Secretary of State Gresham, whose
chivalry was more worked up apparently by the fact
that it was a woman who was being deprived of her
power, than by the innate righteousness of the cause
of the Queen. His wife notes in her life of him with
obvious satisfaction: "A woman in trouble, my husband
would certainly side with her against the power, greed

and lust of man."[17] Unfortunately in this case, the power, greed and lust were on the side of the royal lady, whose private life, love of tribal revenge and bloodthirsty ways had made her reign a scandal to all the serious-minded inhabitants of the islands.

Without following what seemed to be the wish of the Administration to use force if necessary to restore the old order, the Senate on January 25, 1895 declared for a policy of non-intervention and approved the acts of the President in carrying it out, and except for the disturbance it made for some years in American domestic politics, the Hawaiian incident, in so far as it concerned the United States, came to an end. The Queen was not restored; the Republic was continued, and, as is well known, the islands were annexed to the United States in 1898.[18]

CHAPTER III

END OF THE FUR-SEAL ARBITRATION

BRAZIL: MOSQUITO INDIANS; KOREA

DEATH OF GRESHAM IN OFFICE

THE negative Hawaiian policy of Gresham was his most distinct mark—and that not an enduring one—on American foreign relations. Except for Hawaii, most of the diplomatic business which came up under his administration of the Department was matters of comparative unimportance, or questions, like that of Venezuela, which did not come to a head before his death, and which are more properly treated in the sketch of the life of his successor, Richard Olney.

One of these details concerned the winding up of the fur-seal arbitration, the previous history of which has already been set forth in this series.[19] Not long after the second Cleveland Administration came in, the arbitral tribunal at Paris, before which Mr. Foster, Gresham's predecessor in the Department, had been conducting the case of the United States, handed down its award, on August 15, 1893. It represented a complete defeat, for it stated in brief that the United States had succeeded only to rights previously held by Russia in Alaska and the adjacent waters and that these had never comprised any such claims as those which had been put forward by the United States.

Secretary Gresham promptly offered on August 21,

subject to the willingness of Congress to appropriate the funds, the lump sum of $425,000 in full settlement of the claims presented by Great Britain on behalf of captures of her subjects and their vessels for engaging in pelagic seal fishing within the waters of Bering Sea. The total of the claims as originally presented had been $542,169.26. The offer was accepted by the British ambassador, but at its next session Congress, through partisan enmity to Cleveland, refused to make the appropriation. A mixed commission was then agreed upon to adjudicate the British claims, and in December, 1897, Great Britain was allotted $473,151.26, which Congress appropriated. "Thus Congress paid $48,151.26 more than it would have had to pay if it had approved Gresham's settlement, a large price for a bit of petty factional and personal spite."[20]

A firm believer in the Monroe Doctrine, Secretary Gresham had several opportunities during the two years in which he was in charge of our foreign affairs to take action in behalf of democratic principles in Latin America. The Brazilian Republic which had been established after the overthrow of the Empire in 1889, had continued without special incident until September, 1893, when most of the Brazilian navy revolted in favour of the old régime. The harbour of Rio de Janeiro was blockaded and American shipping suffered through the efforts to re-establish the monarchy. In January of 1894, an American squadron under Rear-Admiral Benham arrived in Rio. The Admiral sent word to the President of the Brazilian Republic that he would be willing, as an individual, to intervene to bring the naval revolt to an honourable termination.

By this time American merchant ships had been fired upon and had not been allowed to unload their perishable cargoes. Admiral Benham announced that he would convoy a certain American vessel, the *Amy*, to her wharf and that he would sink any vessel that opposed her. This firm position soon ended the naval revolt and with it the movement against the Republic came to an end.[21] In connection with this action, Mrs. Gresham relates that Secretary Gresham once arrived at the British Embassy at two in the morning and demanded to see Sir Julian Pauncefote and when the latter appeared, said: "Sir Julian, I have word from Brazil that your flagship has taken Da Gama (one of the revolting admirals) aboard. You and I know it is not true, but I must be able to tell the President and Cabinet when we meet this morning that it is not true. Good morning, Sir Julian."[22]

What really disquieted Gresham, or perhaps we should say, perturbed Cleveland, was the evident signs of an attempt to weaken the Monroe Doctrine on the part of certain European powers. The outstanding example of this is, of course, the Venezuela controversy, but the Brazilian insurrection was also enlightening in this regard, to Gresham at least. We find him writing to Bayard at London:

"The critical condition of affairs in Brazil and the apparent trend of sentiment in Europe with respect to the struggle now in progress in that Republic, seem to warrant inviting your watchfulness so far at least as concerns the policy of Great Britain in this relation. . . .

"If the reported withdrawal of British protection from the operations of neutral commerce at Rio is correct, the act may be regarded as indicating a purpose at no distant day to recognize the insurgents as belligerents. . . . The Brazilian Minister at this capital . . . professes to have information that several of the most influential Governments of Europe are in sympathy with this movement and that they are affording the insurgents material aid. The consistent views of the Government of the United States touching non-intervention of the powers of Europe in the domestic questions of the American hemisphere have become well known abroad, and are firmly rooted here."[23]

It was once more as a defender of the Monroe Doctrine that Gresham took part in one of the most obstinate incidents which occurred in his time at the head of the Department of State, namely, the so-called Mosquito Coast question. This was of such long standing and so complicated that a few introductory words may not be amiss, at the risk of repeating what has been narrated in previous volumes.

Previous to 1821 the "Mosquito Coast" of Nicaragua belonged to Spain. Great Britain had acceded to this claim in the treaty of Versailles of 1783 and in that of London of 1786. The first declaration of a different point of view seems to have been in 1838, when the British vice-consul informed the Government of Nicaragua that the Mosquito Indians were an independent nation under the protectorate of Great Britain.[24] Prolonged discussions with the United States, which saw an infringement of the Monroe Doctrine, followed, and were brought to what was thought to be a satisfactory end only by the signing of the Clayton-Bulwer Treaty in 1850, Article I stipulating that both the United States and Great Britain would never "occupy, or fortify, or colonize, or assume or exercise any dominion over Nicaragua, Costa Rica, the Mosquito Coast, or any part of Central America."

This article the United States interpreted as ending all claim to British sovereignty in the Mosquito territory but the British took the position that it referred to *future* acquisitions and not to the existing status. In 1860 Great Britain, despairing of any satisfactory settlement with the United States, negotiated a treaty with Nicaragua direct—the treaty of Managua, which gave up sovereignty over the Mosquito Coast in favour of Nicaragua, and gave the Indians the right to govern themselves in all ways not incompatible with the sovereign rights of Nicaragua. In 1861 the Constitution of the Municipal Government of the Mosquito Reserve was promulgated, confirming the supremacy of the British laws already in effect there.

Discussions and recriminations continued over the precise status of the Reserve and recourse was finally had to arbitration by the Emperor of Austria to define Nicaraguan rights. His decision was given in 1881, and limited those rights to the hoisting of the Nicaraguan flag and the appointment of a commission to protect this right there. At the same time he gave to the Mosquito Indians the right to use a flag of their own, to regulate their own commerce, and to establish their own customs duties. The decision of this European arbitrator actually stated that the Mosquito territory had a separate national existence. This was not disagreeable to the general tenour of British diplomacy in that region, and certainly not disagreeable to foreign residents of all nationalities in the Reserve, including those of the United States, who were thoroughly sick of the inefficient Nicaraguan Government.

The special status for the Mosquito reservation created by the Austrian award added to the stability of that district, as distinct from the rest of Nicaragua, and led to an increase of foreign influence and investment, particularly in the establishment of banana plantations by American immigrants. The new and thriving commerce and the peaceful prosperity of the territory which followed aroused the jealousy of the less fortunate remainder of Nicaragua, and led to efforts to bring the Mosquito region more definitely under the direct government of the authorities at Managua. In May, 1892, the Government of the United States addressed to Nicaragua a communication concerning the reported increase in port charges at Bluefields, Nicaragua (the principal town in the Mosquito Reserve), on American vessels. The Nicaraguan Government answered that it was impossible for it to make a responsible reply owing to the anomalous state of things in the Reserve and intimated that it would address the British Government in order to invest its own sovereignty there with a practical meaning. Nicaragua sent a special commissioner, General Lacayo, to the Mosquito Coast in 1893 to bring about if possible by diplomatic methods the complete incorporation of the Reserve into Nicaragua. The political authority of this region was then, as it had been for some years, in the hands of leaders who claimed British nationality. When he found that he could not settle the matter peaceably, the commissioner asked for troops, which were sent, and which occupied Bluefields and proclaimed a state of siege, or martial law.

The military occupation of Bluefields by Nicaraguan forces and the proclamation of martial law were caused in part by the outbreak at this time of a war between Honduras and Nicaragua which gave rise to fears of a Honduran invasion and occupation of the Mosquito Coast. The proclamation of martial law, and the intermeddling of General Lacayo in various ways with the existing régime of the Reserve greatly antagonized the American residents, especially when the Nicaraguan commissioner placed an export tax on banana shipments. They protested, and they asked the United States Government to send down a warship to protect their rights under the Austrian award. A British warship, the *Cleopatra*, was already in the harbour, and on March 5, 1894, upon request of the British consul at the port, British marines were landed, who speedily compelled the Nicaraguans to raise the state of siege. A provisional government was then established for the Mosquito Reserve, made up of Captain Howe, the commander of the *Cleopatra;* the British consul; General Lacayo, the Nicaraguan commissioner; and the commander of the Nicaraguan troops. The provisional Government aroused the antagonism of the American residents, who saw in it a step toward the integration of the Reserve in the Nicaraguan Republic, a step which they feared would be ruinous to their industry, which had been established under the more favourable laws of the autonomous Reserve. They did not care for the general purpose of American diplomacy in dealing with the question, e.g., the incorporation of the Reserve into the Republic of Nicaragua.

The occupation of Bluefields by British marines and the setting up of a provisional government in which the local British consul and a British naval officer had prominent parts were duly reported to Secretary Gresham by the United States minister to Nicaragua. Gresham immediately directed the United States minister at London, former Secretary Bayard, to make inquiries as to the cause for Captain Howe's action. Bayard was told by Lord Kimberley, the Foreign Secretary, that the British Government had no desire nor intention to found a protectorate in Central America—that the only reason for the landing of the marines had been to protect the residents. Meanwhile an American warship, the *San Francisco*, had arrived at Bluefields to protect American interests, and the commander, Captain Watson, telegraphed to his Government that the landing of the British marines had been justifiable; that permission of the Nicaraguan commissioner had first been obtained; that the British troops had now withdrawn, leaving the Nicaraguans in full control. But Secretary Gresham, as would be natural for any United States official who was jealous of the Monroe Doctrine and for the enforcement of British obligations under the Clayton-Bulwer Treaty, wrote to Bayard objecting to the joint assumption of authority by British and Nicaraguan agents. That was not possible under the provisions of the treaty of

Managua of 1860, which had fixed the conditions under which the Reserve had been established, and the creation of the provisional Government itself seemed to raise an assumption that the Mosquito Reserve was endowed with some sort of sovereign rights. The note closed with the expression of a desire of the President that the anomalous situation in the Mosquito Reserve might be terminated, and that no foreign agency would be permitted to dictate or participate in the administration of affairs there.

An interview between Bayard and Kimberley brought out a statement by the latter that Great Britain had no desire of forming a protectorate over any part of Nicaraguan territory; it wished to act thoroughly in co-operation with the United States and to continue the Clayton-Bulwer treaty in full force and effect. In helping in the formation of the provisional Government the British consul, said Kimberley, had acted without instructions, believing the lives of the residents, as well as their property, to be in danger. It was the wish of the British Government, and its minister at Washington had been so instructed, to co-operate with the United States for the protection of the interests of both Governments against Nicaraguan violence. Gresham replied July 19, 1894, refusing to be drawn into any co-operation with Great Britain which would give body to the fiction of Mosquito self-government—neither the United States nor Great Britain, he said, could fairly sanction this abuse of Nicaraguan sovereignty. American rights in the Mosquito Reserve must be protected in the same manner as American rights in other parts of Nicaragua; that is to say, it was the Nicaraguan Government, not any Mosquito Government, which must be applied to for redress.

While this correspondence was going on, the native element at Bluefields revolted against the provisional Government, and this time American marines, from the U.S.S. *Marblehead*, were landed to quiet the disturbance and to protect foreign lives and property. The troubles on the banana coast soon ended by the Nicaraguan authorities' gaining control of the Reserve. A convention was assembled, and measures were adopted by which the Reserve was definitely integrated with the state of Nicaragua and formally recognized the constitution of that Republic.

This solution of the question was entirely satisfying to the Government of the United States, and the British Foreign Office gave expression to equal gratification. It was, then, the end of the notorious Mosquito question, which had so frequently agitated Anglo-American relations since 1848. In dealing with it Secretary Gresham had showed himself a staunch defender of the Monroe Doctrine, but the British Foreign Minister utilized the occasion by once more committing an American Secretary of State to the baleful Clayton-Bulwer Treaty, which was now rapidly becoming incompatible with the larger interests of the United States.

It is perhaps not making too extreme a statement to say that Gresham's action in the Mosquito question was the forerunner of Olney's more spectacular diplomacy in regard to the Venezuela boundary dispute.[25]

In one instruction he wrote: "The President is unable to sanction any intervention by you restrictive of the sovereign authority of Nicaragua over the territory occupied by the Mosquito Indians. Recognizing, as this Government does, the paramount rights of the Republic in that region, it ill becomes the representative of the United States to interfere to restrain the Nicaraguan Government in the exercise of those sovereign rights."[26]

Gresham held, however, that the Doctrine did not authorize Latin-American countries to escape their obligations by appeal to the United States under it. According to the testimony of the Mexican minister in Washington, in an unpublished paper, Secretary Gresham thought that: "Nicaragua had done a wrong in expelling from her territory without any trial a British subject, and Great Britain had a right to demand satisfaction on that offense, going to the extent of making war; and the United States had no right to interfere under the Monroe Doctrine as long as Great Britain did not attempt to make a permanent acquisition of territory. Gresham very properly said that Nicaragua as an independent country must accept the duties and responsibilities of such, and that if by her wrong-doing she offends other powers, she cannot ask the United States to take up her quarrels originating from acts that she had done against the opinion and advice of the United States."[27]

With this position of Secretary Gresham it is interesting to compare the declaration of President Roosevelt in his message of December 3, 1901 referring to the Monroe Doctrine: "We do not guarantee any State against punishment if it misconducts itself, provided that punishment does not take the form of the acquisition of territory by any non-American power."

During Gresham's term of office as Secretary of State, affairs with Cuba had not become so acute as they did a year or more later, but he was forced on one or two occasions to make strong representations to Spain regarding the seizure of American vessels in the vicinity of Cuba which brought expressions of regret and explanation from the Spanish Government.

The interest of the people of the United States and, therefore, of the Administration, towards Far Eastern affairs was at a very low ebb in the period of Gresham's secretaryship. Here and there were to be found a slight realization of and attention to Pacific and Oriental problems and there was a growing disposition to promote American trade and obtain a share of trade opportunities for our merchants. The American representative in Peking was very energetic but it was apparently more as an individual than as the result of any clear cut, definite policy such as that which later appeared in the days of Rockhill and Hay. As has been well observed by a keen student of our Far Eastern questions: "The pendulum had begun to swing back toward the position it occupied in the 50's but the swing had only just begun."[28] A search of the unpublished correspondence of the State Department, made for this sketch, has revealed nothing important in policy and little of general interest as to the Far East. President Cleveland's message of May 9, 1894, in response to a resolution of the Senate regarding affairs in Samoa, was accompanied by a comprehensive report by Secretary Gresham on those affairs. In this the Secretary reflected what was doubtless the general attitude of our people when he deplored our action in Samoa as a departure from the traditional policy of the United States: "Every nation and especially every strong nation must sometimes be conscious of an impulse to rush into difficulties that do not concern it, except in a highly imaginary way."

Another manifestation of Secretary Gresham's desire to help the "under dog" in the diplomatic sphere is shown by his interest in and efforts towards peace in regard to the Chinese-Japanese war. In June of 1894, a number of Chinese troops had been sent to Korea for the alleged purpose of suppressing a rebellion against the Korean Government. Japan claimed that this action was a violation of treaty rights and sent forces to occupy Seoul, the capital, and the neighbouring seaport. The rebellion having meanwhile been put down, the King of Korea asked for the withdrawal of the troops of both China and Japan. The Chinese Government appeared to be willing to withdraw its forces but Japan declined to do so until such reforms were adopted as would prevent further trouble. The King then appealed to the foreign powers to secure the withdrawal of the troops.

Secretary Gresham, in view of the provision in the treaty between the United States and Korea, which pledged the United States to use its good offices to bring about a friendly settlement of trouble with other powers, instructed the American minister at Seoul "to use every possible effort for the preservation of peaceful conditions." In view of this instruction, the minister, in concert with his local diplomatic colleagues, again requested the withdrawal of the troops, but the Japanese again declined. The King then telegraphed to his representative in Washington that the independence of the country was threatened and instructed him to appeal to the United States to intervene in favour of peace. Gresham actively took up the cause of peace between friendly nations, and in an interview with the Japanese minister expressed the hope that Japan would deal kindly and fairly with her helpless neighbour. He also cabled the United States minister at Tokyo:

"The deplorable war between Japan and China endangers no policy of the United States in Asia. Our attitude toward the belligerents is that of an impartial and friendly neutral, desiring the welfare of both. If the struggle continues without check to Japan's military operations on land and sea, it is not improbable that other powers having interests in that quarter may demand a settlement not favorable to Japan's future well being.

"Cherishing the most friendly sentiments of regard for Japan the President directs that you ascertain whether a tender of his good offices in the interests of a peace alike honorable to both nations would be acceptable to that Government."[29]

A similar tender of good offices was made to China on November 9.[30]

To Gresham's representations in favour of peace, the Japanese minister at Washington answered that his Government recognized the independence of Korea and was not seeking its territory, but that Japanese troops would not be withdrawn until needed reforms in the domestic administration had been made.

In July, the British representative had visited Secretary Gresham to ascertain whether the United States would unite with Great Britain in intervening to avert war. To this the Secretary replied that his Government could intervene only as a friendly neutral; that it had already done this; that the President did not feel authorized to go further, and that the United States could not join another power even in friendly intervention. So, as so often before and since, the United States after making a great noise did nothing.[31]

With the progress of the war and the great success of the Japanese forces on both land and sea, China and the European powers began to have apprehensions as to the far-reaching results of the war should military operations proceed too far. Again the British representative approached the Secretary to know "whether the United States would be willing to join with England, Germany, France and Russia in intervening between China and Japan," but was told that "while the President earnestly desires that China and Japan shall speedily agree upon terms of peace alike honorable to both, and not humiliating to Korea, he could not join in an intervention."

Mr. Kurino, the Japanese minister, told Mrs. Gresham that during the Sino-Japanese war he met Secretary Gresham almost daily, and received from him information as to what was going on in the diplomatic world. This information he daily cabled to his Government. "One day," said Mr. Kurino, "Secretary Gresham said to me, Japan should bring the war to a conclusion. If she continues to knock China to pieces, the powers, England, France, Germany, and Russia, under the guise of preserving order, will partition China. This information and the advice I transmitted immediately by cable to my government. And you know what we did. We ended the war almost as abruptly."[32]

Secretary Gresham's death prevented him from handling beyond its earlier stages the Venezuelan boundary question, which in its more critical phases was negotiated by Richard Olney, Gresham's successor, and it will be more properly treated in the sketch of the latter. It is pertinent to point out here, however, that if Gresham had lived the question might conceivably have been settled with less ill feeling and excitement than was actually the case. In a dispatch to Ambassador Bayard at London, dated December 1, 1894, the Secretary wrote: "England and America are fully committed to the principle of arbitration, and this government will gladly do what it can to further a determination in that sense." He believed that he could make such a statement of the case that the British Government would accept it or ask that it be submitted to arbitration. On this note Gresham was working when he became ill in April 1895. To a friend who later said that Olney had stolen her husband's thunder, Mrs. Gresham replied: "No, there was to be no ultimatum as my husband had prepared it, and Mr. Olney and President Cleveland are entitled to all the credit for such a State paper."[33]

Gresham died suddenly in office. He became ill with a cold in April, 1895, which developed into pleurisy, then into pneumonia. The end came on May 12. The President, members of the Cabinet, various members of the diplomatic corps and many friends accompanied the remains to Chicago for the funeral. In addition to his colleagues his old comrades in arms of Civil War times turned out in strength. His widow finally decided on Arlington as the most suitable place for burial and the final obsequies were held in the capital in May, 1896. Interment was made in a plot near the Lee mansion in the presence of President Cleveland and his Cabinet.

It was Gresham's misfortune as Secretary of State to be a political misfit. Cleveland, on assuming office for his second term, had chosen him as Secretary of State, partly, no doubt, on account of his known and recognized ability and probity, but also from the feeling that he wished to recognize a man who had been an eminent Republican ever since the birth of the party and who had been himself a prominent favourite for the Republican nomination for the Presidency, a man whose publicly avowed support of Cleveland had greatly contributed to his election. From the moment Gresham entered the Cabinet he was in a position almost untenable in American politics, for he was one of a body of men, chosen personally by the President, responsible only to him, and regarded not only as his advisers in matters of public policy, but as his counsellors in party politics as well. Cleveland seems to have had little if any previous acquaintance or association with Gresham. He knew of him chiefly as an anti-Harrison Republican. Although the character of Cleveland was such that he welcomed sterling honesty of purpose and singleness of mind wherever he found it and always preferred public welfare to party advantage, he had made many enemies even in his own party, on account of his sturdy support of sound money and the gold standard against the heresies of free silver, which men like Bryan had championed from a combination of ignorance and political shrewdness, as well as those he had angered during his first term as President through thwarting their schemes of private gain and advantage. As Governor Bragg, of Wisconsin, had declared years before: "They love him most for the enemies he has made." And yet at a time when he needed them most to hold the Democratic party together, the President surrounded himself in his new Cabinet with men like Gresham and Olney, who, however able they may have been as advisers, were not apt politicians and temperamentally were little able to guide him away from errors of judgment or to temper his pronouncements to meet the shifting of political breezes. Gresham, more than Olney, seems to have been ready to reach his ends through conciliation of his opponents. His untimely death, in the middle of his term of office as Secretary of State, deprived the President of a faithful friend and the United States of a Secretary of State, who, whatever may have been his defects of temperament, was an honest, courageous, loyal and devoted public servant.

The candid student must recognize, nevertheless, that Walter Q. Gresham left no mark on American foreign policy of an enduring nature. He had a strong and independent mind but before his incumbency of the Department no particular knowledge of foreign affairs, no previous contact with diplomacy. Under Cleveland's direction Gresham's handling of the one capital question, Hawaii, was negative and, in the view of subsequent history, not in accordance with the legitimate interests of the United States or with the trend of events in Hawaii itself. We may sympathize with the repudiation of any aggressive intermeddling of the United States in the affairs of Queen Lil, but we cannot recognize that Gresham or Cleveland, or Mrs. Gresham had correctly analysed the Hawaiian problem. Leaving the barbarities of that monarch out of consideration, it was a predestined fact easily then to be seen that the native race was giving way to outside peoples and outside influences—it was a matter of time only when the native Government too must give way and some foreign power would occupy the crossroads of the Pacific, a supremely strategic spot so much nearer to the coast of California than to any other land. As Captain Mahan pointed out in 1895, the very safety of the United States demanded that those islands be under the control of the United States rather than of a potential enemy of the United States.

In spite of the signs of the times which were already on the horizon and assuming large proportions, the foreign policy of the United States and the administration of the Department of State under Secretary Gresham were, it must be admitted, perhaps at the lowest ebb of activity they had reached since the Civil War. Practically, from his day on, these were to grow in importance and popular interest up to and through the World War, and it is only latterly that signs are once more becoming apparent that we are approaching a period of lassitude and reaction in interest in foreign affairs reflected in a letting down of all those standards to which we have grown accustomed, and which is without doubt a protest against the high spiritual plane to which we were urged and on which we were kept during the World War.

RICHARD OLNEY

SECRETARY OF STATE

JUNE 8, 1895, TO MARCH 4, 1897

BY

MONTGOMERY SCHUYLER

FORMERLY OF THE
UNITED STATES DIPLOMATIC SERVICE

RICHARD OLNEY

FROM A PAINTING BY HUBERT VOS

Richard Olney

RICHARD OLNEY

CHAPTER I

EARLY LIFE; ATTORNEY GENERAL IN CLEVELAND'S SECOND CABINET

WHEN Walter Quintin Gresham, Secretary of State, died on May 28, 1895, Richard Olney of Massachusetts, Attorney General in President Cleveland's second Administration, was appointed as his successor. In appointing Olney to fill the vacancy, Cleveland was in one way greatly strengthening the Cabinet. From the moment of Gresham's appointment, two years before, there had been numerous murmurs and outspoken criticism that a Republican of long standing had been given the chief place in the new Administration, simply because he had worked for and voted for Cleveland. Of Olney's staunch Democracy there could be no question. His whole life had proved the quality of his political convictions.

Thomas Olney, one of the early settlers of Salem, Massachusetts, followed Roger Williams to the settlement of Rhode Island and founded the Olney line in Providence Plantations. In that colony the family remained until Richard Olney moved from Rhode Island in 1811 and settled in Massachusetts. That Richard was the grandfather of the Richard who is the subject of the present sketch. With his migration from Rhode Island the direct line of tradition regarding the family was so broken that the later generations never knew more than that they were descended from the same family. The grandfather Richard settled in Oxford, Massachusetts, and established textile mills there. He is reported to have been a powerful man both mentally and physically, ruling his family with a rod of iron and transmitting many of his sterner qualities to his grandson. His eldest son was named Wilson Olney. He seems never to have made much mark either upon his community or upon his family. His wife was Eliza L. Butler, a descendant on her mother's side of a family of French Huguenots, whose name, originally Séjourné, had become anglicized to Sigourney. In general the family history of Richard Olney differed little from that of thousands of other New England families, brought up in the same environment and with the same traditions and outlook. Stern men followed stern men with regularity as the generations gave way to one another and left the composite product, the typical "New Englander," who has so strongly influenced our national life.

Of such a family and into such an environment Richard Olney was born at Oxford, on September 15, 1835. After early school education in the village where he was born, he graduated from Leicester Academy and then entered Brown University, where he graduated with honours. The Harvard Law School completed his education and he began the practice of law in Boston as clerk in the office of Benjamin F. Thomas, whose daughter Agnes he later married. Practice with Thomas was continued until the death of the latter. A lifelong Democrat, Olney took little active part in politics, although he several times ran for local and state offices and served one term, in 1874, in the Massachusetts legislature. As his law practice increased he seemed to drop almost entirely out of politics and to devote himself to his profession, in which he was beginning to be known as a lawyer of high standing and attainment.

His rough-hewn appearance and his uncompromising ways, which repelled rather than attracted, made him a difficult person to know well or to be intimate with and it is said that with the exception of his cousin Sigourney Butler he had no intimate friends. Grimly and as if pursued by the dictates of his Puritan conscience, he went his way straight after the object he had in mind, not allowing himself to be diverted from his goal by either pleasures or difficulties. His law offices remained the same modest set he had earlier possessed, and he did all his work himself without partners and with the help of his devoted clerk, Miss Straw, who combined in herself the attributes of stenographer, bookkeeper and secretary. She was named in Olney's will as one of his executors and trustees. His recreations seem to have been limited in early life to riding and tennis and later to walking and playing cards at home. The details of his home life show us a man wrapped up in his lonely work, not greatly loved nor caring for love and affection, and somehow becoming the family despot to whose least whim all around him were forced to accommodate themselves or suffer the penalty of his displeasure. As he grew older and the importance of his cases increased he was asked to become a director of many and important corporations and he entered the sober and unemotional life of the busy corporation lawyer.

Richard Olney's father, Wilson Olney, had first been a Whig and later on was known as a Democrat. So far as recorded Richard Olney was a lifelong Democrat, although living in Massachusetts, a state where that party was hopelessly in the minority. A list of his incursions into practical politics prior to his appointment to Cleveland's Cabinet is given by Henry James in his standard biography of Olney, entitled *Richard Olney and His Public Service*.[1] Mr. James suggests that Olney was a Democrat, "not in the least from doctrinaire sympathy with Jeffersonian principles, but because he somehow got started that way and was a born individualist to whom it was natural to incline toward the teachings of the *laissez-faire* school, and consequently also natural to incline away from protection; and perhaps, too, because he was blessed with a certain temperamental contrary-mindedness toward some of the theories that went along with the Republicanism of his day."[2]

Olney was so intellectually honest that he did his own thinking for himself and was not ready to adopt any party shibboleth which struck the popular fancy unless he personally approved it. He said once during the campaign of 1892: "No intelligent man supports a party because he thinks it is perfect, or because he approves everything it does, or everything it says. He supports it because of its general trend and tendency, of which a particular platform is only a single and partial indication."[3]

Such was the reticent, self-contained, combative and publicly unknown man to whom in February 1893, President Cleveland, in making up the list of his Cabinet for his second Administration, offered the position of Attorney General. Cleveland, it appears, had seen Olney only once before this time, but his name had been mentioned by Olney's cousin Sigourney Butler to the President in discussing appointments to the Cabinet. "Mr. Cleveland thereupon asked him to request me to come to Lakewood on the day which he named. On Sigourney's mentioning the matter to me, I at first declined to consider it or to go to Lakewood on what seemed to me a perfectly useless errand. But on reflection, it seemed discourteous not to do so and I went. Mr. Cleveland first offered me the office of Secretary of the Navy, which I positively refused. He then offered me the office of Attorney General, which I did not peremptorily decline, though I expressed my aversion to leave the practice of my profession and enter into public life. I left the matter with him in this way: I told him there was much better Cabinet material in New England than myself—men much more familiar with politics and much more ambitious in that direction—and that I could name one who, I thought, would undoubtedly accept the position. He thereupon called for the name and I mentioned John Quincy Adams of Boston. Mr. Cleveland said if I could get Mr. Adams to serve he should be delighted to have him in the Cabinet as Secretary of the Navy. He, however, insisted that, if Mr. Adams for any reason would not serve, I should consider myself booked for the position of Attorney General. I assented to the condition, not feeling in my own mind at the time the slightest doubt that Mr. Adams would readily accede to Mr. Cleveland's wishes. . . . I had counted on Mr. Adams's willingness to go into the Cabinet with so much certainty that his refusal to do so entirely upset my calculations."

Cleveland held Olney to his conditional promise to accept the Attorney Generalship in case Adams refused. "No new circumstances having intervened upon which I could fairly ground my declination of the office—considered myself fairly committed to Mr. Cleveland and arranged to be in Washington by the 4th of March," as Olney later wrote.[4]

At the time the new Administration entered office, in 1893, "the burning question," as Olney described it in the Memorandum just quoted from, "was of the immediate convocation of Congress. The campaign had been fought and won by the Democrats on the question of tariff reform. The elections had been overwhelmingly in favor of the new administration on that issue and the immediate enactment of a new tariff bill was expected by the country and would have been simply carrying out the pledges given by the Democratic Party. Nevertheless, the conclusion of the President and those whom he consulted was against a special session of Congress."

The Administration had scarcely begun when a full-fledged business depression began to make its effects felt throughout the United States and by the summer of 1893 had developed into a panic which swept banks, business houses, and even railroads into insolvency and ruin and gave birth to widespread unemployment and labour disturbances. Olney from his wide acquaintance with bankers and "big" business men was in a position to hear the comments on the Administration and doubtless kept his chief informed of what was said and thought.

President Cleveland called a special session of Congress, June 30, and then left Washington for a yacht belonging to a friend, where an operation for cancer of the jaw was performed on him. This was carefully concealed from the public and even from the Cabinet, for fear that the panic might be made worse if rumours of the President's illness should be circulated.

So weakened was Cleveland by the operation that he found it almost impossible to work on his message for the special session of Congress called for June 30. He turned to Olney for help. The latter gives the story of his part in the preparation of the message:

"After an interval of a fortnight, more or less, during which I made frequent attempts to see Mr. Cleveland, I succeeded in having an interview. He had changed a good deal in appearance, and lost a good deal of flesh, and his mouth was so stuffed with antiseptic wads that he could hardly articulate." Olney drew up a draft of a message which he took to the President's summer home at Gray Gables. He says it was approved by Cleveland practically as drawn. Professor McElroy notes, however, that a comparison of Olney's draft with the message as finally sent to Congress shows that only fifty-three out of a hundred and seventy-eight lines were adapted from the Olney draft, and Henry James points out that while Olney prepared a "forensic argument, which certainly showed a grasp of the fiscal question," it was phrased in "such needlessly challenging terms that, in reading it after reading the message, one realizes his political inexpertness." The draft had gone beyond recommending the mere repeal of the Sherman law and, in addition to asking Congress to repeal the silver purchase clauses, urged that all outstanding obligations of the Government, including both bonds and paper money, should be payable in gold coin.

It was not until October and with the aid of Republican votes that the Senate passed the bill, the House having agreed to it in August in spite of Bryan. The struggle over the bill was so violent that it greatly weakened the Democratic party and undermined the President's prestige and power both in Congress and with the public. Relying on the melodious fallacies of Bryan and the free silverites in Congress and carried off by sound without reason, Congress later on refused to sell gold bonds to the syndicate of bankers which stood ready to purchase them, needlessly costing the people of the United States millions of dollars on the price of the issue. To whatever lengths the silver craze drove the Democratic party, it showed President Cleveland and his Cabinet intelligently striving for sound money and common sense against political demagoguery and charlatanism. Never was Cleveland's sturdy independence of character and freedom from political considerations more clearly shown than in this fight for what he believed to be the right policy.

The first year of Cleveland's second Administration was so largely taken up by the claims of office-seekers that only one other decision of real importance was taken—namely, the interpretation of the Sherman anti-trust law, which was as yet new and had not been

broadly interpreted by the Supreme Court. Such decisions and opinions as had been given had taken a
narrower view than has later been done and probably
nobody at the time realized the lengths to which the
public would expect the executive to go in attempting
to restrain the trusts. In order to test the law Olney
caused the so-called sugar-trust case to be selected
and brought before the Supreme Court as rapidly as
possible. In deciding against the Government as it did,
the Supreme Court went far toward confirming the
opinion of Olney as to the availability of the law as
then interpreted to bring about any great changes in
the situation of the trusts. Readers interested in the
status of the interpretation of the anti-trust law at
that time may find additional material in his "Reports
of the Attorney-General," and in President Cleveland's
annual message of December 7, 1896. The accusations
of Republicans in the political campaign of 1904 that
Cleveland and his Attorney General had failed to enforce the law in this regard drew from Olney a notable
and vigorous "Memorandum" published in March,
1904,[5] which, however important in a fuller biography
of Olney, cannot be further noted in this sketch, which
is to concern primarily Olney as Secretary of State.

One result of the business depression and consequent
panic in the spring and summer of 1893 was the outbreak of a number of labour disturbances in various
parts of the country. One of these flashed into ominous
vigour and gave promise of serious trouble for the
Government. The firm handling of the Pullman strike,
United States troops being used to keep trains bearing
United States mail moving, gave a real notion of what

kind of man the President was. How the Administration was to deal with the situation was suggested by Olney's famous telegram to the United States district attorney in the state of California:

"See that the passage of regular trains, carrying United States mails in the usual and ordinary way, as contemplated by the act of Congress and directed by the Postmaster-General, is not obstructed. Procure warrants or any other available process from United States courts against any and all persons engaged in such obstructions, and direct the marshal to execute the same by such numbers of deputies or such posse as may be necessary."[6]

It was due to Olney's action that the injunction was resorted to, through the federal courts, to prevent obstruction of the mails. This proceeding was based upon the ground that, under the United States Constitution and laws, mails and interstate commerce were in the exclusive care of the Government of the United States and that for their protection the federal courts were competent under general principles of law to intervene by injunction; and on the further ground that under an act of Congress, passed July 2, 1890, conspiracies in restraint of trade or commerce among the several states were declared to be illegal, and the circuit courts of the United States were therein expressly given jurisdiction to prevent and restrain such conspiracies. This action inaugurated a practice which was to raise a violent issue in the domestic politics of the United States.[7]

CHAPTER II

OLNEY AND CUBA

THE two principal features of American international affairs during Richard Olney's twenty-one months of service as Secretary of State were our relations with Spain in regard to the disturbed conditions in the island of Cuba, and our sharp issue with Great Britain concerning the disputed boundary between British Guiana and the Republic of Venezuela, which latter incident gave to Olney his greatest fame. His connection with the diplomacy of President Cleveland's second Administration in regard to the Hawaiian Islands has already been noted in the previous sketch of Secretary Gresham, who leaned heavily on Olney's advice in that matter.

Its situation, size, and close community of interests with the United States have from the first days of our national existence given to Cuba an importance as great perhaps as that of any other Latin-American country. For nearly a century the island and its problems continually arose to make trouble for our statesmen and political ammunition for the enemies of successive administrations. The sympathies of the people of the United States were freely given to the revolutionists of Spanish America in their desire to throw off the autocratic yoke of Spain. When Cuba came to be the last important outpost in the possession of Spain near the American continent, the results of centuries of Spanish misrule were so evident that the efforts of the Cubans to end them brought them not only sympathy but active help from many Americans. The Spanish colonial system aimed to throw the wealth made in the trade with Spanish colonies into the hands of merchants in the home country and was followed so rigorously that it became profitable for colonial officials to connive at lawbreaking. Relatively very little of the immense sums contributed from taxation and customs went to swell the treasury of Spain and much of it remained in the hands of the local officials. Profits from smuggling and other illegal traffic on the other hand were so large that foreigners and especially Americans, on account of their geographical proximity to Cuba, were tempted to break the law whenever possible. Furthermore, the Spanish rulers of Cuba were frequently tyrants and the Spanish system gave them many opportunities of exercising their cruelty and vindictiveness. Little supervision was made from Spain as long as revenues were coming in and the Spanish representative in Havana was always a little king.

The numerous efforts at revolution and the stories spread by the Cubans throughout the United States of their persecutions made the successive administrations in Cuba most troublesome and annoying to our people and this situation was from time to time reflected in our official acts.[8] The troublesome problems and the conflicts which had arisen with the Spanish authorities in Florida, and elsewhere in our South and Southwest had also helped in making Spanish rule unpopular with our people and have been set forth in earlier volumes of this series.

The revolution by the Cubans against their Spanish

rulers that had begun in February 1895, was being closely watched by Olney, who had become Secretary of State in June of that year. In September, he reported to the President that:

"The situation of affairs in Cuba seems to me to be one calling for the careful consideration of the Executive. The Spanish side is naturally the side of which I have heard, and do hear, the most. It is, in substance, that the insurgents belong to the lowest order of the population of the Island, do not represent its property or its intelligence or its true interests, are the ignorant and vicious and desperate classes marshaled under the leadership of a few adventurers, and would be incapable of founding or maintaining a decent government if their revolution against Spain were to be successful. . . . There are, however, grounds for questioning the correctness of this view. The Cuban insurgents are not to be regarded as the scum of the earth. . . . In sympathy and feeling nine tenths of the Cuban population are with them. . . . The property class to a man is disgusted with Spanish misrule, with a system which has burdened the Island with $300,000,000 of debt, whose impositions in the way of annual taxes just stop short of prohibiting all industrial enterprise, and which yet does not fulfill the primary functions of government by insuring safety to life and security to property."

In the conclusion of his report, Olney told the President that the Cuban revolution "was just in itself, commanding the sympathy, if not the open support, of the great bulk of the population affected, and capable of issuing in an established, constitutional government" and gave his opinion that within a short time either Cuba would be smothered in its own blood, or be "in the market, for sale to the highest bidder," as Spain would never be able to suppress the rebellion. He warned the President that American "politicians of all stripes, including Congressmen," were "setting their sails, or preparing to set them, so as to catch the popular breeze," which blew in the direction of a recognition of Cuban belligerency.[9]

Congress was beginning to echo the increased annoyance of the American people at the Cuban outrages, and in its usual heedless manner in conducting its debates on foreign affairs was using such loose and vehement language that it was deeply offending Spain without producing any good results or bringing a settlement of the problem any nearer. Although numerically important, there was nothing about the revolution in organization or intelligence which could possibly make it proper for the executive to grant it a belligerent status and the efforts of our Government had to be confined to our enforcing our own municipal statutes. It took every proper and possible precaution to stop the gunrunning which was a prosperous form of trade for some of our people, and which, aided as it was by the sympathy of most of the Cubans and the laxness of the Spanish officials, was almost impossible to curb. Nearly fifty per cent of the expeditions were stopped.[10] Claims in increasing numbers were being received at the State Department of property damage and even loss of life in cases of American citizens in Cuba, and the same situation arose as has been the case with Mexico in the last fifteen years. Notes of protest from our Government cluttered up the Spanish archives and were dilatorily and evasively answered.

After long debates and much bickering, both the Senate and the House finally agreed on a concurrent resolution recognizing a state of war in Cuba, recognizing the insurgents as entitled to all belligerent rights, and tendering the good offices of the United States for a settlement of the conflict on the basis of the surrender of Spain and the granting of independence to Cuba. This was of course of no more binding value than an expression of the opinion of Congress and was naturally ignored by the Administration.

Meanwhile Richard Olney, being primarily a man of action, had determined to set the matter frankly before the Government of Spain, and on April 4, 1896, sent a note to the Spanish minister in Washington, Enrique Dupuy de Lome, with whom his official and personal relations had been close and friendly, and who had on several occasions wisely counselled his own Government on the necessities of the situation in Cuba. In this note Olney took a much wiser course than that of Congress. After pointing out with great frankness that matters were growing not better but worse, in spite of repeated explanations that the movement would be put down in a short time, Olney tendered the good offices of the United States for composing the troubles on the basis of reforms in the Government of Cuba and a more complete autonomy for that island, which should leave it, however, still a part of the Spanish dominions. After making his well meant suggestions Olney wrote:

"On all these grounds and in all these ways the interest of the United States in the existing situation in Cuba yields in extent only to that of Spain herself, and has led many good and honest persons to insist that intervention to terminate the conflict is the immediate and imperative duty of the United States. It is not proposed now to consider whether existing conditions would justify such intervention at the present time, or how much longer those conditions should be endured before such intervention would be justified. That the United States cannot contemplate with complacency another ten years of Cuban insurrection, with all its injurious and distressing incidents, may certainly be taken for granted. . . .

"In closing this communication it is hardly necessary to repeat that it is prompted by the friendliest feelings toward Spain and the Spanish people. To attribute to the United States any hostile or hidden purpose would be a grave and most lamentable error. The United States has no designs upon Cuba and no designs against the sovereignty of Spain. Neither is it actuated by any spirit of meddlesomeness nor by any desire to force its will upon another nation. Its geographical proximity and all the considerations above detailed compel it to be interested in the solution of the Cuban problem whether it will or no. Its only anxiety is that that solution should be speedy, and, by being founded on truth and justice, should also be permanent."[11]

Cuban conditions became no better but much worse and the Spanish administration was taking such steps that its policy amounted to an attempt to exterminate the Cubans. It is said that at one time there were some four hundred thousand of them confined in camps in Cuba under unspeakable conditions. In his last annual message to Congress, in December 1896, President Cleveland, after touching on the obligation of the United States to be just to both sides, said:

"I have deemed it not amiss to remind the Congress that a time may arrive when a correct policy and care for our interests, as well as a regard for the interests of other nations and their citizens, joined by consideration of humanity and a desire to see a rich and fertile country, intimately related to us, saved from complete devastation, will constrain our government to such action as will subserve the interests thus involved, and at the same time promise to Cuba and its inhabitants an opportunity to enjoy the blessings of peace."

To the above sufficiently frank statement he added, says McElroy, "this phrase, characteristically Clevelandesque: The United States is not a country to which peace is necessary."[12]

In the last days of his Administration, President Cleveland considered sending Frederic R. Coudert, the well-known international lawyer, to Cuba on a mission to the Spanish authorities, in order to see if the war which he felt to be impending might not be averted. On the refusal of Mr. Coudert to undertake the mission the matter was dropped. With the growth of Cleveland's prestige in the years since his retirement from public life, it seems strange to us now to realize that he left office as unpopular a President as ever sat in the White House and was, in the words of one newspaper, "under a greater burden of popular contempt than has ever been excited by a public man since the foundation of the government." With single-minded purpose and perfect honesty, he strove for what he thought was right, but left office feeling that he had accomplished nothing.

The Cuban problem had to be left unfinished to his successor in the Presidency and other hands took over Olney's efforts to end the thankless task.

CHAPTER III

THE VENEZUELA BOUNDARY
ULTIMATUM

IN entering on a study of the Venezuelan boundary
controversy with Great Britain, we come to the
incident of Olney's tenure of the office of Secretary of
State which attracted to him the most widespread attention and which made him one of the most talked of Secretaries in the history of the Department. In the handling
of the Hawaiian case, the Cleveland Administration
had been dealing with a primitive, island people whose
fate attracted little interest from the outside world except where other foreigners and their claims were concerned, but in the Venezuela dispute Secretary Olney
was projecting himself and the United States straight
into a contest with the strongest nation in the world.
He was entering a field which had for more than a
century been a bone of contention and the cause for
more political and electionary eloquence than any other,
for twisting the British lion's tail had long been a well-
recognized way to obtain public approval in displays
of oratory without offending any constituents. In vigorous support of the interests of the United States, or
at least of interests which the United States was supposed to have in the matter under dispute, Olney
lighted the match to the old controversy against the
historical "enemy," and quite irrespective of the merits
of the case in point, the battle was speedily on.

A brief historical resumé of the causes and development of the boundary controversy will be essential to an understanding of the incidents and the outcome of the dispute. Venezuela had formerly been a colonial possession of Spain, and shortly after declaring her independence from the mother country in 1810 had united with two of the other revolted colonies to form the Colombian federal union, which had been recognized by the United States in 1822. After the dissolution of this union in 1836, Venezuela became a separate and independent republic and as such was recognized by the United States. The recognition of the new political entity by Spain was delayed until 1845, when it ceded to Venezuela the territory which the latter had been occupying since 1810. In all treaties and agreements up to this time the boundaries had been defined only as "the same as those which marked the ancient viceroyalty and captaincy-general of New Granada and Venezuela in the year 1810."

The interest of Great Britain in boundary lines in this part of the world arose from the cession to it in 1814, by treaty, of "the Cape of Good Hope and the establishments of Demerara, Essequibo, and Berbice." No boundaries of those settlements were given in the treaty and this lack of definition soon began to make trouble. On January 28, 1841, Venezuela made a proposal to Great Britain for joint action in fixing the divisional boundaries. This proposal not having' been accepted, the Venezuelan minister in London, on October 5 of the same year, wrote to Lord Aberdeen, Secretary of State for Foreign Affairs, as follows: "The Honorable Earl of Aberdeen may now judge of the surprise of the Government of Venezuela upon learning that in the territory of the Republic a sentry-box has been erected upon which the British flag has been raised. . . . The undersigned . . . urges the necessity of entering into a treaty of boundaries as a previous step to the fixation of limits."

Lord Aberdeen replied under date of October 21 that: "Her Majesty's Government has received from the Governor of British Guiana, Mr. Schomburgk's report of his proceedings in execution of the commission with which he has been charged. . . . It appears that Mr. Schomburgk planted boundary posts at certain points of the country which he has surveyed, and that he was fully aware that the demarcation so made was merely a preliminary measure, open to further discussion between the Governments of Great Britain and Venezuela." Mr. Schomburgk, the British boundary marker, apparently went into his task with considerable care, studying the history of the case with attention and obtaining from actual exploration and from the evidence of remains such data as he could. In a later communication, the Venezuelan minister complained of the action of Schomburgk in placing several boundary posts at Point Barima and at the mouth of the Amacura. Although it was made clear that these posts had been put where they were "as the only tangible means by which the British Government could be prepared to discuss the question of boundaries," they were so offensive to the Venezuelan authorities that a succession of protests was made against them which brought about their removal, on the distinct understanding that Great Britain did not thereby abandon her claim to that position.

As the whole matter was of less vital importance to Great Britain than to Venezuela, Lord Aberdeen continued to treat it in a conciliatory way. Schomburgk, in surveying the territory, had not only located the posts mentioned but had drawn a complete dividing line running far inland and annexing to British Guiana on the west a large region also claimed by Venezuela. This line with its later extensions to the west was known as the "Schomburgk line." When it was presented to Venezuela in the report made, the latter retorted with an extravagant and vague statement of its own claims to the regions without much evidence of conquest or occupation, putting forward the Essequibo River as the proper boundary. Lord Aberdeen in reply announced certain concessions which he was prepared to make "prompted by a friendly consideration for Venezuela," amounting to a portion of the coast sufficient to insure it the free control of the mouth of this its principal river, and to prevent its being under the control of any foreign power. He also declared that he would consent to a boundary which he defined and which may be described as beginning at the mouth of the Moroco River, which is southeast of the mouth of the Orinoco and about two-thirds of the distance between that point and the Essequibo River, the boundary to run inland from that point until it included more territory than was embraced within the original Schomburgk line, although not including the region embraced within that line adjacent to the Barima and Amacura rivers and the mouth of the Orinoco River. This boundary was not, however, satisfactory to Venezuela, but as the diplomatic representative of Venezuela in Great Brit-

ain died shortly after its receipt, no answer appears
ever to have been made to it and the whole matter remained in abeyance for a long period of years, during
which Venezuela passed through a series of revolutionary disturbances. Meanwhile the discovery of gold in
the disputed territory had made the problem of settlement more difficult. With the exception of declarations made by the two Governments that they had no
intention of sanctioning any occupation by their respective nationals of the disputed regions until such time
as the boundaries might be definitely settled, no important diplomatic correspondence took place until the
year 1876.

In that year, in the words of President Cleveland,
Venezuela was confronted, upon the renewal of negotiations, by the following conditions:

"The claim by her, of a divisional line, founded upon
her conception of strict right, which her powerful opponent had insisted could not in any way be plausibly
supported, and which therefore she would in no event
accept.

"An indefiniteness in the limits claimed by Great
Britain—so great that, of two boundary lines indicated
or suggested by her, one had been plainly declared to
be 'merely a preliminary measure open to future discussion between the Governments of Great Britain and
Venezuela,' while the other was distinctly claimed to
be based not on any acknowledgment of the republic's
rights, but simply upon generous concessions and a
'desire to avoid all cause of serious controversies between the two countries.'

"A controversy growing out of this situation impossible of friendly settlement except by such arrangement and accommodation as would satisfy Great Britain, or by submission of the dispute to arbitration.

"A constant danger of such an extension of British settlements in the disputed territory as would necessarily complicate the situation and furnish a convenient pretext for the refusal of any concession respecting the lands containing such settlements.

"A continual profession on the part of Great Britain of her present readiness to make benevolent concessions and of her willingness to co-operate in a speedy adjustment, while at the same time neither reducing her pretensions, nor attempting in a conspicuous manner to hasten negotiations to a conclusion.

"A tremendous disparity in power and strength between Venezuela and her adversary, which gave her no hope of defending her territory or preventing its annexation to the possessions of Great Britain in case the extremity of force or war was reached."[13]

On November 14, 1876, the Minister for Foreign Affairs of Venezuela wrote two important communications. One was to Lord Derby, the British Foreign Secretary, referring to the interpretation of the boundary negotiations in 1846, and hoping that they might promptly be settled. The other note was to Mr. Fish, then Secretary of State of the United States. In this, after speaking of the United States as "the most powerful and the oldest of the Republics of the new continent, and called on to lend to others its powerful moral support in disputes with European nations," and outlining the controversy, the Minister concluded: "But whatever may be the result of the new steps of the Government, it has desired that the American Government might at once take cognizance of them, convinced, as it is, that it will give the subject its kind consideration and take an interest in having due justice done to Venezuela."

This note appears to be the first official communication to the American Government on the subject of the boundary dispute.

In communications at about this time to Great Britain, Venezuela suggested either the acceptance of a line such as would result from a presentation by both parties of Spanish and Dutch titles, maps, documents, and proofs, existing before the division into either Venezuela or British Guiana, or the adoption of a "conventional line fixed by mutual accord after a careful and friendly consideration of the case, keeping in view the documents presented by both sides, solely with the object of reconciling their mutual interests, and to fix a boundary as equitably as possible." The idea of Venezuela in thus abandoning its extreme pretensions was apparently to make it easier to arbitrate the line, and its appeal to us for aid was most probably with a view to the furtherance of arbitration. But as Cleveland pithily observed: "Gold beneath soil in controversy does not always hasten the adjustment of uncertain or disputed boundary-lines."[14]

In subsequent notes, the Venezuelan Government proposed arbitration of the whole boundary line, but this suggestion was first disregarded and later refused by the British Foreign Office. Up to this time the utmost the British had claimed was up to the Schomburgk line or to the boundaries mentioned by Lord Aberdeen in 1844 as a concession, and in stating that: "If Her Britannic Majesty's Government should prefer the frontier of accommodation or convenience, then it would be desirable that it should vouchsafe to make a proposition of an arrangement, on the understanding that, in order to obviate future difficulties and to give Great Britain the fullest proof of the consideration and friendship which Venezuela professes for her, my Government would not hesitate to accept a demarcation that should satisfy as far as possible the interests of the Republic," Venezuela was undoubtedly leaving the door open for an amicable arrangement which should once for all settle the controversy. The above suggestion was made in the note of the Venezuelan representative on May 19, 1879, and was answered on January 10, 1880 by Lord Salisbury, then Foreign Secretary, who stated that to argue the matter on the ground of strict right would involve many intricate questions, and that the British Government would prefer "to come to an agreement as to the acceptance of a frontier of accommodation which shall satisfy the respective interests of the two countries." Lord Salisbury then went on to outline a claim for Great Britain far beyond any limits previously discussed or even mentioned, far overlapping the Schomburgk line, "by virtue of ancient treaties with the aboriginal tribes and of subsequent cessions from Holland." The Foreign Secretary, as Cleveland says, "built up a contention in which he puts on one side a line which for the sake of pacific accommodation Venezuela no longer proposes to insist upon, and on the other a line for Great Britain so grotesquely extreme as to appear fanciful."

"This is diplomacy—of a certain sort," continues Cleveland in his later lecture on the subject, "it is a deep and mysterious science; and we probably cannot do better than to confess our inability to understand its intricacies and sinuosities; but at this point we can hardly keep out of mind the methods of the shrewd, sharp trader who demands exorbitant terms, and at the same time invites negotiation, looking for a result abundantly profitable in the large range for dicker which he has created."[15]

Numerous proposals and modifications were made by Venezuela in the next few years which failed of positive result and the controversy dragged on. Great Britain definitively refused to arbitrate the claim in a note dated February 29, 1884, for the reason that if the award should give Venezuela the full amount she claimed, "a large and important territory which has for a long period been inhabited and occupied by Her Majesty's subjects and treated as a part of the Colony of British Guiana would be severed from the Queen's dominions." Further discussion resulted in a proposed treaty agreed upon the fifteenth of May, 1885, which was to end a difference pending between the two countries regarding differential duties and other unsettled questions. An article in the treaty provided "that the undertaking to refer differences to arbitration shall include all differences which may arise between the High Contracting Parties, and not only those which arise on the interpretation of the Treaty."

But, and here is a point which strongly resembles actions taken by our own Government under different administrations, this treaty had been agreed to by Lord Granville, at the time Foreign Secretary. Less than two and a half months later Lord Salisbury had again become Foreign Secretary and his Government was "unable to concur in the assent given by his predecessors in office to the general arbitration article proposed by Venezuela, and they are unable to agree to the inclusion in it of matters other than those arising out of the interpretation or alleged violation of this particular treaty." The next year Lord Rosebery proposed that the territory between two certain lines should be equally divided between the two claimants but this was declined by Venezuela, who still insisted upon arbitration. Arbitrary and aggressive conduct on the part of local officials in the disputed territory inflamed public opinion and on January 31, 1887 Venezuela demanded the evacuation of the territory it claimed under pain of breaking off diplomatic relations, which she did on February 20.

On informal relations being resumed three years later, Great Britain said that any arrangement which did not admit the British title to the Schomburgk line would be inacceptable, but that it would be willing to arbitrate the claims to certain territory to the west of that line. A map was presented in March 1890, showing the extreme pretensions. According to Cleveland: "The trader is again in evidence. On this basis England could abundantly afford to lose entirely in the arbitration she at length conceded."[16] Further desultory correspondence followed, ending with a declaration by the Government of Venezuela on September 29, 1893 that "it is with the greatest regret that that Government sees itself forced to leave the situation produced in the disputed territory by the acts of recent years unsettled, and subject to the serious disturbances which acts of force cannot but produce; and to declare that Venezuela will never consent to proceedings of that nature being accepted as title-deeds to justify the arbitrary occupation of territory which is within its jurisdiction."[17]

There, apparently incapable of solution, the matter rested when President Cleveland assumed office for the second term. The United States throughout the more than fifty years the controversy had lasted, when it had ventured to touch the matter at all, "had done so with so uncertain a hand as to produce results negligible or worse."[18]

Throughout his knowledge of the case, Cleveland's sympathies had evidently been with Venezuela. Whether this was, as his biographer intimates, "because he was by nature disposed to suspect strong nations of designs against weaker ones,"[19] or whether his feelings towards Great Britain over the Sackville-West letter incident in his first term caused him to be unduly hostile to Great Britain, is not certain. He as well as his Secretary of State during the first years of his second term, General Gresham, and his ambassador in London, Bayard, were all strongly in favour of the principle of arbitration.

The Venezuela boundary controversy became an object of intense solicitude to the Administration apparently in the first place from a letter of the Venezuelan representative at Washington to Gresham giving a history of the case and of the alleged unauthorized acts of the British. On December 3, 1894, President Cleveland sent his annual message to Congress, in which he said: "The boundary of British Guiana still remains in dispute between Great Britain and Venezuela. Believing that its early settlement on some just basis alike honorable to both parties is in the line of our established policy to remove from this hemisphere all causes of difference with powers beyond the sea, I shall renew the efforts heretofore made to bring about a restoration of diplomatic relations between the disputants and to induce a reference to arbitration."[20]

On the following February 22, a joint resolution was passed by the Congress earnestly recommending to both parties in interest the President's suggestion that they refer their dispute as to boundaries to friendly arbitration. Through all these incidents there appeared the conviction that the United States was becoming more and more deeply concerned by the refusal of Great Britain to arbitrate except on condition that a portion of the territory in dispute should specifically be left out of the arbitration. Somewhat unduly perhaps, the Cleveland Administration was surprised that the feeble and intermittent efforts of the United States in the past had been productive of little real good and that their recent efforts at friendly mediation had practically been curtly rebuffed. The President evidently felt that Great Britain was taking advantage of the weakness of her opponent to widen and extend her claims, and taking the same attitude as he had in the case of Hawaii, was resolved that the stronger should not coerce the weaker. On the face of it this principle is excellent, but many incidents in our diplomatic history show how we have been used to exploit weakness at the expense of justice.

Before the message to Congress of December 3, 1894, Secretary Gresham had twice instructed Ambassador Bayard in London, himself a firm believer in arbitration, to urge that solution upon the British Government, but Bayard's replies showed the determination of that Government to exclude certain portions of the disputed territory from any arbitration. Secretary Gresham, however, had not given up hope of an amicable solution and was at work on a full report on the case when he was attacked by the illness which caused his death in May, 1895.

When, some ten days later, Richard Olney succeeded Gresham as Secretary of State, almost the first important problem he was called upon to study was the Venezuelan boundary situation. Into this he plunged with great energy, and early in July gave the President a draft of a note to the British Government to be transmitted by the American ambassador. After reading this draft, Cleveland wrote to him from his summer home, "Gray Gables," on Buzzards Bay: "I read your deliverance on Venezuelan affairs the day you left it with me. It's the best thing of the kind I have ever read and it leads to a conclusion that one cannot escape if he tries—that is if there is anything of the Monroe Doctrine at all. You show there is a great deal of that and place it I think on better and more defensible ground than any of your predecessors—*or mine.*

"Of course I have some suggestions to make. I always have. Some of them are not of much account and some of them propose a little more softened verbiage here and there."[21]

The "softened" version[22] was later subjected to the revision of several of the more trusted of Cleveland's advisers in the Cabinet, put in official shape and forwarded, under date of July 20, 1895. It was practically with this state paper of the first magnitude that the new Secretary of State commenced his new duties. Presentation of the note to Lord Salisbury must have been an unpleasant task indeed to Bayard, lover of peace and apostle of friendship with Britain. The mood in which it was sent may be judged from Cleveland's statement in 1901:"The seriousness of the business we had in hand was fully understood, and the difficulty or impossibility of retracing the step we contemplated was thoroughly appreciated. The absolute necessity of certainty concerning the facts which should underlie our action was, of course, perfectly apparent. Whatever our beliefs or convictions might be, as derived from the examination we had thus far given the case, and however strongly we might be persuaded that Great Britain's pretensions could not be conceded consistently with our maintenance of the Monroe Doctrine, it would, nevertheless, have been manifestly improper and heedless on our part to find conclusively against Great Britain, before soliciting her again and in new circumstances to give us an opportunity to judge of the merits of her claims through the submission of them to arbitration. . . . The Monroe Doctrine may be abandoned; we may forfeit it by taking our lot with nations that expand by following un-American ways; we may outgrow it, as we seem to be outgrowing other things we once valued; or it may forever stand as a guaranty of protection and safety in our enjoyment of free institutions; but in no event will this American principle ever be better defined, better defended, or more bravely asserted than was done by Mr. Olney in this despatch."[23]

The dispatch, which Bayard was directed to read to the Minister for Foreign Affairs, and to leave a copy of if the latter should so desire, consisted of a long history of the Venezuela boundary controversy, together with a lengthy exposition of the Monroe Doctrine and its peculiar significance, containing a unique definition of it, which has not since met generally the sanction of even American publicists. The essential purpose of the dispatch was to make it evident that the United States considered that the arbitrary rectification by Great Britain of the disputed boundary, without admission of arbitration for the entirè claims of both sides, was in effect an expansion of European territorial dominion on the American continent and thus in violation of the Monroe Doctrine.

In defense of that doctrine, and with specific reference to the Venezuela business, Olney proceeded literally to lay down the law to Great Britain. This paragraph of his celebrated note must be quoted by any commentator on Olney's diplomacy. Speaking of the possibility of European intervention in the affairs of the American republics, he said:

"The mischiefs apprehended from such a source are none the less real because not immediately imminent in any specific case, and are none the less to be guarded against because the combination of circumstances that will bring them upon us cannot be predicted. The civilized states of Christendom deal with each other on substantially the same principles that regulate the conduct of individuals. The greater its enlightenment, the more surely every state perceives that its permanent interests require it to be governed by the immutable principles of right and justice. Each, nevertheless, is only too liable to succumb to the temptations offered by seeming special opportunities for its own aggrandizement, and each would rashly imperil its own safety were it not to remember that for the regard and respect of other states it must be largely dependent upon its own strength and power. To-day the United States is practically sovereign on this continent, and its fiat is law upon the subjects to which it confines its interposition. Why? It is not because of the pure friendship or good will felt for it. It is not simply by reason of its high character as a civilized state, nor because wisdom and justice and equity are the invariable characteristics of the dealings of the United States. It is because, in addition to all other grounds, its infinite resources combined with its isolated position render it master of the situation and practically invulnerable as against any or all other powers."

Olney, contrary to a general impression, did not say specifically that the Monroe Doctrine was international law. He said that the fiat of the United States was law upon this continent upon the subjects to which it confined its interposition! And he further said, in another paragraph of the same long dispatch:

"There is, then, a doctrine of American public law, well founded in principle and abundantly supported, which entitles and requires the United States to treat as an injury to itself the forceful assumption by an European power of political control over an American state."

In directing that the views it contains should be presented to Lord Salisbury, the dispatch ends:

"They call for a definite decision upon the point whether Great Britain will consent or decline to submit the Venezuelan boundary question in its entirety to impartial arbitration. It is the earnest hope of the President that the conclusion will be on the side of arbitration, and that Great Britain will add one more to the conspicuous precedents she has already furnished in favor of that wise and just mode of settling international disputes. If he is to be disappointed in that hope, however, a result not to be anticipated, and in his judgment calculated to greatly embarrass the future relations between this country and Great Britain,—it is his wish to be made acquainted with the fact at such early date as will enable him to lay the whole subject before Congress in his next annual message."

The feelings of Lord Salisbury over the contents of the dispatch may be imagined from his remark to Bayard after the latter had presented it. The ambassador reported, August 9:

"At the conclusion of my reading and statement, his Lordship made courteous expression of his thanks, and expressed regret and surprise that it had been considered necessary to present so far-reaching and important a principle and such wide and profound policies of international action in relation to a subject so comparatively small."

The formal reply of the British Government to the Olney note as delivered by Bayard, came in the shape of two notes to the Secretary of State, dated November 26, 1895. In one of them Lord Salisbury analysed the Venezuelan boundary dispute, pointing out that Great Britain had been consistently willing to arbitrate within certain territorial limits:

"But they can not consent to entertain, or to submit to the arbitration of another power or of foreign jurists, however eminent, claims based on the extravagant pretensions of Spanish officials in the last century, and involving the transfer of British subjects, who have for many years enjoyed the settled rule of a British colony, to a nation of different race and language, whose political system is subject to frequent disturbance, and whose institutions as yet too often afford very inadequate protection to life or property. No issue of this description has ever been involved in the questions which Great Britain and the United States have consented to submit to arbitration, and Her Majesty's Government are convinced that in similar circumstances the Government of the United States would be equally firm in declining to entertain proposals of such a nature."

There was a good reason for Lord Salisbury's reluctance to arbitrate in its entirety a boundary dispute which might set a precedent for thus settling every such question that might come up on Britain's far-flung imperial frontier, no matter what the merits of the question or the scope of the territory might be. Such would have been a dangerous commitment, in the minds of many British statesmen looking ahead to the continuous boundary disputes which the Empire was frequently having in various quarters of the world where boundaries were not precisely delimited.

In the other note the British Foreign Minister animadverted at length on the nature of the Monroe Doctrine.

Her Majesty's Government, he said, "fully concur with the view which President Monroe apparently entertained, that any disturbance of the existing territorial distribution in that hemisphere by any fresh acquisitions on the part of any European State would be a highly inexpedient change. But they are not prepared to admit that the recognition of that expediency is clothed with the sanction which belongs to a doctrine of international law. They are not prepared to admit that the interests of the United States are necessarily concerned in every frontier dispute which may arise between any two of the States who possess dominion in the Western Hemisphere; and still less can they accept the doctrine that the United States are entitled to claim that the process of arbitration shall be applied to any demand for the surrender of territory which one of those States may make against another."[24]

Cleveland much later commented on these two communications as follows:

"These despatches exhibit a refusal to admit such an interest in the controversy on our part as entitled us to insist upon an arbitration for the purpose of having the line between Great Britain and Venezuela established; a denial of such force or meaning to the Monroe Doctrine as made it worthy of the regard of Great Britain in the premises; and a fixed and continued determination on the part of Her Majesty's Government to reject arbitration as to any territory included within the extended Schomburgk line. . . .

"If we had been obliged to accept Lord Salisbury's estimate of the Monroe Doctrine, and his ideas of our interest, or rather want of interest, in the settlement of the boundary between Great Britain and Venezuela, his despatches would certainly have been very depressing. It would have been unpleasant for us to know that a doctrine which we had supposed for seventy years to be of great value and importance to us and our national safety was, after all, a mere plaything with which we might amuse ourselves; and that our efforts to enforce it were to be regarded by Great Britain and other European nations as meddlesome interferences with affairs in which we could have no legitimate concern."

Despairing of obtaining in the way they had sought any satisfactory settlement by arbitration or negotiation, Cleveland submitted the exchange of notes to the Congress with a message on December 17, 1895. The President informed the Congress that in view of the failure to secure arbitration, it was now incumbent upon

the United States to determine the true boundary between Great Britain and Venezuela, and recommended
that an adequate appropriation should be made to meet
the expense of a commission to make the suggested investigation and report. The conclusion of his message
was:

"When such report is made and accepted, it will, in
my opinion, be the duty of the United States to resist
by every means in its power, as a wilful aggression
upon its rights and interests, the appropriation by
Great Britain of any lands or the exercise of governmental jurisdiction over any territory which after
investigation we have determined of right belongs to
Venezuela.

"In making these recommendations I am fully alive
to the responsibility incurred, and keenly realize all
the consequences that may follow.

"I am, nevertheless, firm in my conviction that
while it is a grievous thing to contemplate the two
great English-speaking peoples of the world as being
otherwise than friendly competitors in the onward
march of civilization, and strenuous and worthy rivals
in all the arts of peace, there is no calamity which a
great nation can invite which equals that which follows a supine submission to wrong and injustice, and
the consequent loss of national self-respect and honor,
beneath which are shielded and defended a people's
safety and greatness."

So uniformly judicious and discreet had Cleveland
been in the conduct of our foreign relations; so soli-
citously had he guarded the honour and dignity of this

Republic, not only by maintaining our own rights, but also by respecting the rights of others; so careful and conscientious in the observance of the principles of international law had been his course with regard to the insurrection in Cuba, notwithstanding the clamour of the professional "jingoes" and of hot-headed sympathizers, and notwithstanding, too, his own sympathy with the cause of the insurgents; so wisely and consistently pacific and so dignified had been his foreign policy throughout, that the people were struck with wonder and amazement when they read his famous Venezuela message, in which he asked Congress to make an appropriation for a commission to investigate the boundary line in dispute between Venezuela and Great Britain; declared that if Great Britain refused to submit the whole matter to arbitration, the United States should by every means in its power enforce the finding of our own commission; substantially made the cause of Venezuela our own, and apparently countenanced, by inference at least, that construction of the Monroe Doctrine now so much in vogue, which maintains that the relations between any part of America and any foreign power are virtually the business of this Republic.[25]

The issue had been squarely joined. Olney claimed that the Monroe Doctrine was a doctrine of *American* public law and wrote his note in such a way as to imply it to be international law itself. Lord Salisbury denied this. But this was only an academic argument after all, for professors and publicists to debate about later. How was the tangible dispute, the Venezuela boundary, to be settled? Would Great Britain accept the demand of the United States that the possession of the whole territory in dispute be arbitrated, or must there be a war between the English-speaking peoples fought over the question of the Monroe Doctrine?

Fortunately the new international problems of the Old World were to come to the assistance of the United States in its policy of maintaining inviolate the territory of the republics of the New World. The years 1895–1900 mark the rise of German commercial, military and naval power as a future menace to Great Britain's dominion of the seas and colonial empire. The growth of the German merchant marine and the agitation for a greater navy caused Britain to stir in what Lord Salisbury himself grandiloquently had called her "splendid isolation." In 1895 Great Britain had not an ally in the whole world, scarcely a dependable friend. There were several potential enemies. The day was rapidly approaching when allies might be needed. That was indicated in a spectacular way by the sudden and ominous and, as we now know, studious gesture which the German Kaiser, Wilhelm II, made to President Kruger of the South African Republic, on the occasion of his suppression of Jameson's notorious raid without the aid of friendly powers. Was it well to make of the United States at this moment another potential enemy?

Fortunately for lovers of peace between Great Britain and the United States the famous telegram of the Kaiser of January 3, 1896 took much of the attention of the British public, which was much more nearly concerned with the doings of the Germans than with ours.[26] In a confidential dispatch to Olney, No. 572, of January 15, 1896, Ambassador Bayard notes:

"There has been a welcome and unmistakable difference observable, in the manner in which the possibilities of conflict with the United States—and with Germany—were discussed and treated in this country.

"In regard to a possible collision with the United States, amazement, disappointment, genuine distress, and manifest unwillingness to accept such a possibility were chiefly discernible, but as to the German Emperor's interference in the Transvaal, a prompt joinder of issue was tendered, and readiness for contest was almost universally expressed by the general public."

James, in his *Richard Olney*, quotes a letter from John Hay to Olney, dated July 31, 1896, detailing several conversations the former had had with leading British statesmen which continues: "From what I have been able to gather in conversation I infer that most of the leading men are convinced that Lord Salisbury's tone a year ago was a mistake, and that our attitude is, on the whole, reasonable. Everybody wants the matter settled if it can be done without damage to the pride and prestige of England. Chamberlain seems afraid of making a precedent which may be injurious hereafter in Canada—and they all dread arbitration since Geneva."

Incidentally to all this, Lord Salisbury remarked to Henry White, United States chargé at London, who took occasion in June 1896, to sound out British attitude on the possible annexation of Cuba by the United States: "It's no affair of ours."[27]

The commission recommended by the President to examine into and report upon the Venezuela boundary was authorized promptly by Congress on December 21, and on January 1, 1896 five distinguished Americans were selected for membership on it, and a staff of historical scholars and experts was appointed to assist the commission. While they were at work—the British Government cordially threw open historical material on the subject for examination by them—the question of submitting the whole matter to friendly arbitration was again brought to the attention of the British Government by our ambassador in London, February 27, 1896. At the same time Olney was able to inspire a number of dispatches sent by the American correspondent of the London *Times*, which had practically the same force on Lord Salisbury—who was made cognizant of their origin by Buckle, editor of the *Times*—as did formal diplomatic notes.[28] On March 3, 1896 Lord Salisbury practically accepted the American position, as enunciated by Olney and Cleveland, by empowering the British ambassador at Washington, Sir Julian Pauncefote, to discuss the boundary question either with the representative of Venezuela or with the Government of the United States as the friend of Venezuela. Sir Julian and Olney accordingly set to work to arrange a treaty providing for arbitration, which was signed at Washington by the representative of Venezuela and the British ambassador on February 2, 1897. No part of the territory in dispute was exempted from the arbitration, which was stated to be "to determine the boundary-line between the Colony of British Guiana and the United States of Venezuela." Thus we have the singular position of having the convention negotiated between Great Britain and the United States, although signed by the former and

Venezuela. Cleveland afterwards commented: "This was a fortunate circumstance, inasmuch as the work accomplished was thus saved from the risk of customary disfigurement at the hands of the United States Senate."[29]

The arbitrators began their work in Paris in January, 1899, and made their award in October of the same year. It determined the boundary as beginning at the coast at a point considerably south and east of the mouth of the Orinoco River, thus giving to Venezuela the absolute control of that important waterway and valuable territory near it. Running inland, the line gives Venezuela a considerable amount of territory within the Schomburgk line.

Thus the lengthy controversy which had at one time threatened the good relations between two great countries was ended and as a result arose that desire for a comprehensive treaty of general arbitration between the two countries which culminated in the conclusion of such an agreement. And to such an extent have those two countries since come together in feeling and in solidarity that it would now be inconceivable to imagine them on the verge of bitterness over a boundary in South America.

One of the good results of the prolonged and bitter controversy over the Venezuela boundary was that it brought to President Cleveland and his Secretary of State a firm conviction that in the interests of the future good relations between the United States and Great Britain a general arbitration treaty between the two great English-speaking nations was an imperative necessity. Cleveland was a firm supporter of the idea of arbitration which had been discussed, especially in Pan-American affairs, for some time, but had not reached the dignity of being thought of as a practicable way of ending serious disputes.

The about-face at the British Foreign Office, due to the rise of the German menace and the new orientation of European and Asiatic international relations, was made the occasion of a praiseworthy attempt by Lord Salisbury to follow up the concession made to the United States in regard to the Venezuelan affair by proposing a general arbitration treaty calculated to settle all future issues which might arise between the two Governments. The idea was not a new one, and, as the reader of this series knows, many important questions had been settled by arbitration between the two Governments during the century preceding, from Jay's Treaty of 1795 to the great arbitrations provided for in the treaty of Washington of 1870. Charles Sumner in 1872 had introduced into the Senate a resolution proposing the establishment of an international tribunal which should be a "complete substitute for war" and declaring that refusal to accept its decision should be regarded as hostile to civilization. A general arbitration treaty between Great Britain and the United States had been proposed when over two hundred members of the British House of Commons addressed to the President of the United States and to the Congress a communication favouring such a step. This had resulted in a concurrent resolution by both houses of Congress in favour of it, in 1890, which in turn was followed by a resolution of the British House of Commons in 1893, expressing pleasure at the American declaration. President

Cleveland reported the British parliamentary resolution to Congress in the autumn of the next year.

This favourable background made it easy for Lord Salisbury to suggest in the spring of 1896 through his representative in Washington that the two countries should negotiate a formal and general arbitration treaty. At that time the Venezuela matter loomed large on the political horizon and still might easily have become a source of serious trouble. Pauncefote's idea apparently was to get rid of the Venezuela controversy by taking advantage of the public sentiment in favour of general arbitration, which had become much strengthened by that dispute.[30] Olney, in replying for the Administration, was gratified at the suggestion but did not think it advisable to merge the specific Venezuela case and a general treaty.[31] Considerable divergence of opinion arose between the two Governments, as was natural in a negotiation so novel and so weighty, but after a lengthy correspondence and many interviews, a fairly broad and comprehensive treaty was drawn up and signed in January 1897. It provided that the two countries should submit "pecuniary claims" and all other matters in difference, in respect of which either of the high contracting parties shall have rights against the other under the treaty or otherwise, to final arbitration, "provided that such matters in difference do not involve the determination of territorial claims." In territorial claims there was to be an appeal to a court of six, and an award was not to be binding if more than one member of the court dissented. Furthermore hostile measures must not be resorted to until one or both countries had invited mediation by a friendly power. And so a great step forward was made and Anglo-American relations could have been put on a basis which would have been a cause for congratulation to all concerned.

Both Cleveland and Olney took great pride in the negotiation of this treaty, which they rightly felt was a great step forward toward the cause of peace, not only of the two countries signing it, but of the entire world. On its publication, there was a great outburst of popular enthusiasm for it and Cleveland himself said: "Its ultimate ensuing benefits are not likely to be limited to the two countries immediately concerned. . . . The example set and the lesson furnished by the successful operation of this treaty are sure to be felt and taken to heart sooner or later by other nations and will thus mark the beginning of a new epoch in civilization.[32] The Committee on Foreign Relations reported it favourably, five of the six Republican members being for it, but three of the four Democratic members opposing it. And so once more blind partisan hatred of Cleveland was more powerful than patriotism. The end of the Cleveland Administration found the treaty still not acted on. President McKinley on coming into office would not make it a matter of partisan politics but recommended its ratification in his inaugural message. As has so often been the case with other important conventions, the Senate refused to approve it, May 5, although it lacked only two votes for ratification.

Naturally those who had borne the burden and heat of the negotiation were bitterly disappointed. Olney sarcastically declared: "The treaty in getting itself made by the sole act of the Executive, without leave of the Senate first had and obtained, had committed the unpardonable sin."[33]

CHAPTER IV

CONCLUSION

MANY interesting bits of gossip and recollection of how Olney administered the Department of State are given in the admirable biography by Henry James, to which reference has already been made and to which the student of Olney's life must always be indebted. It appears that he was a good executive, working hard himself and expecting hard work from his subordinates. Among the latter were Alvey A. Adee, to whom Olney was as much indebted for advice in technique and diplomatic procedure and language as were many other Secretaries and whose recent lamented death in 1925 leaves the Department without any one to take his place, and William W. Rockhill, then beginning the brilliant diplomatic career which ended with his embassies to Russia and Turkey. Olney's method of work was to take one problem at a time, devote his entire energy and attention to it, master it as a lawyer does his case, and then make prompt and positive disposition of it. His was not the kind of mind too frequently seen at the head of our foreign affairs, attempting to please everybody, and paying less attention to the necessity for studying and deciding one question after another as they come up, than to political exigencies and a desire to make no enemies. Weakness and vacillation have done more to harm our relations with foreign states in the past twenty years than all the wrong decisions ever made by the Department of State and the tendency to "pussyfoot" is becoming so strongly engrained in the traditions of that Department that it will need another Olney to bring to it fresh life and independence of character and decision. Not since the days when Elihu Root was Secretary of State have we had the firmness, intelligence and energy combined in one man which is necessary for producing a Secretary of State big enough to conduct our foreign affairs as they should be conducted.

It is apparently becoming more and more the tradition for the Secretary of State and his principal assistants to be mere rubber stamps avoiding all responsibility and all necessity for important decisions by falling back on the convenient theory that the President, being responsible for everything, should be permitted to be his own Secretary of State and that he and he alone should make every decision.

The fact is that just the contrary should be true, that the Secretary of State should be a man so big and so able to accept responsibility and make decisions that only in rare cases should matters of foreign policy be referred to the President and then only with a statement of the policy advocated by the Secretary.

One innovation made by Richard Olney was an excellent one and might well have been continued, although it never has been. In the volume of *Foreign Relations* for 1896 is printed a "Report of the Secretary of State," giving a summary of foreign relations for the year under review.[34] In spite of the fact that the heads of other departments of government have been accustomed to make annual reports of their work, this had never been done by the Department of State, and has never been continued. In other years it has been left for the President to review foreign affairs in his annual message and this is the course still followed. It is to be hoped that some future Secretary of State will have the courage to make his own report as a preface to the publication of the annual volume or volumes of *Foreign Relations*. With the present system of withholding the publication of this annual report until all confidential and controversial matters can be included in it, however, its appearance is so many years after the happenings of which it treats that it makes little difference whether it ever appears. Everything of importance or interest has appeared elsewhere except the most confidential of correspondence and its value is for the historian and for future convenience of reference alone.

Richard Olney never held public office after leaving the Department of State. It is one of the pathetic incidents of American history that Grover Cleveland and the group of men associated with him in his second Administration had so utterly lost the confidence of the radical wing of their own party, then completely in the saddle and under the pernicious leadership of William Jennings Bryan, that they remained discredited for years and their eminent abilities were not utilized as they might have been and in any other country would have been. What to do with ex-Presidents has always been a problem in the United States and will remain so until we borrow from Japan the practice of forming a board or council of "Elder Statesmen," whose advice and experience would be available to the whole people. Our ex-Secretaries of State have usually returned to the practice of their profession and, in this respect, Olney was no exception to the rule. He resumed the practice of law in the same quiet and unspectacular manner in which he had previously exercised it, and retired from public life and its responsibilities. It had been evident from the time of the Democratic convention in the summer of 1896 that Cleveland and all the saner elements in the Democratic party had lost their power and that one of the great, historical parties in the United States had deliberately turned from the constructive achievements of Cleveland—the sound money policy, the refunding of the public debt, the settlement of the Pullman strike, and the assertion of the power of the federal Government over interstate commerce as evidenced by the Debs injunctions—to give control of its future to a faction whose greater lung power gave them what reason denied. Realizing all this, Olney resisted some efforts made by his supporters to bring his name into the struggle for office, and although he always remained loyal to his party in name at least, he took no active steps to prevent it from going where it would.

After his retirement to Boston and the resumption of his law practice, Olney lent his name to several public boards in which he was interested. He was a regent of the Smithsonian Institution in Washington, a member of the Peabody Education Fund, a vice-president of the American Society of International Law, and a manager of the Franklin Union. He contributed several articles and essays to magazines and reviews, and a paper contributed to the *Atlantic Monthly* (May 1898) on "The International Isolation of the United States" made Cleveland say of him in a letter to a friend in 1900: "It seems to me strange that a man who in my judgment is largely responsible, through his *Atlantic* article, for the doctrine of expansion and consequent imperialism, should now be so impressed with the fatal tendency of imperialism, as to be willing to take Bryan as an antidote."[35] Incidentally, parts of that *Atlantic* essay are as noteworthy today as they were when written, and his remarks about the "splendid isolation" of the United States have been almost prophetic. "There is such a thing for a nation as a 'splendid isolation'—as when for a worthy cause, for its own independence or dignity, or vital interests, it unshrinkingly opposes itself to a hostile world. But isolation that is nothing but a shirking of the responsibilities of high place and great power is simply ignominious. If we shall sooner or later—and we certainly shall—shake off the spell of the Washington legend and cease to act the rôle of a sort of international recluse, it will not follow that formal alliances with other nations for permanent or even temporary purposes will soon or often be found expedient."[36]

When Olney was in his seventy-eighth year, in 1914, President Wilson offered to him the ambassadorship to Great Britain, and then the governorship of the Federal Reserve Board. He refused both of these posts. He was an old man. His wife was an invalid and needed his care. "An ambassador is nobody in these days," he is said to have remarked, "he sits at the other end of the table and does what he is told." It is well for him that he did refuse. He could not have foreseen the great trials which the outbreak of the World War was to bring on the American ambassador at London, for like Walter Hines Page, who received the post, Olney was none too well satisfied with the patient course which the Administration adopted in regard to Germany.

As war approached with Germany, Olney was rapidly dying of cancer. He retained consciousness long enough to hear of Wilson's war message to Congress. On April 8, 1917, he died.

As Secretary of State he will stand for a long while as one of the most vigorous, resolute and independent men who have ever held that office. None, in such a short term as Olney's, has achieved such important results.

APPENDICES

APPENDIX

TO SKETCH OF FRELINGHUYSEN

BIBLIOGRAPHICAL NOTE

Bibliographical data concerning the life and accomplishments of Secretary Frelinghuysen are practically non-existent beyond a eulogy pronounced by John F. Hageman before the New Jersey Historical Society at Newark, May 20, 1886, and a few notes kindly provided by some of his family. This sketch is based upon the record of his acts as Secretary of State which is to be found in the archives of the Department of State, in the printed official series *Foreign Relations*, and in the special documents printed by authorization of Congress. The references to these documents will be found in their appropriate place in the footnotes.

FOOTNOTES

[1] See *H. Rept.* 1790, 47 Cong., 1 Sess. on the subject of American intervention in the War of the Pacific. A most regrettable feature of this investigation was the unseemly altercation between Secretary Blaine and Perry Belmont, member of the House of Representatives, in the course of the public hearings of the House Committee on Foreign Relations. See also Sen. Ex. Doc. 79, 47 Cong., 1 Sess., pp. 686–701.

[2] Edward Stanwood, *James Gillespie Blaine*, 241.

[3] *Letters of Mrs. Blaine*, I, 295. Mrs. Blaine reveals bitter personal feeling against Frelinghuysen, though it is not clear to what extent this may have been shared by Blaine himself.

[4] *Foreign Relations, 1880*, 490.

[5] *Foreign Relations, 1882*, 105.

[6] Blaine to Trescot, Dec. 1, 1881, *Foreign Relations, 1881,* 143; Christiancy to Blaine, June 16, 1881, Sen. Doc. 79, 47 Cong., 1 Sess., 501.

[7] *Ibid.*

[8] These charges concerned the Cochet and Landreau claims for the discovery of guana and nitrate deposits; also the magnificose scheme of the *Société Générale de Crédit Industriel et Commercial* for the funding of Peruvian foreign obligations. See Sen. Ex. Doc. 79, *op. cit.,* 630 *et seq.* and *H. Rept.* 1790, *op. cit.*

[9] For the correspondence of Frelinghuysen relating to the Pacific question, see *Foreign Relations, 1882.*

[10] *Foreign Relations, 1883,* 727.

[11] *Foreign Relations, 1881,* 13.

[12] *Foreign Relations, 1882,* 54.

[13] *Ibid.,* 67.

[14] N. Y. *Times,* Feb. 4, 1882.

[15] *Ibid.*

[16] *Foreign Relations, 1882,* 4.

[17] *Ibid.,* 22, 65, 67, 76.

[18] Published in a special document by the Department of State.

[19] *Ibid.,* 1–8. The commission was composed of George M. Sharpe, chairman, Thomas C. Reynolds, Solon O. Thacher, and William E. Curtis, secretary.

[20] Frelinghuysen to Baker, Jan. 31, 1883, Sen. Ex. Doc. 226, 50 Cong., 1 Sess., 43.

[21] *Ibid.,* 47.

[22] The correspondence is published in Sen. Ex. Doc. 154, 48 Cong., 1 Sess.

[23] For admirable summary of facts in this dispute consult I. D. Travis, *History of the Clayton-Bulwer Treaty,* and M. W. Williams, *Anglo-American Isthmian Diplomacy.*

[24] *Foreign Relations, 1881,* 554.

[25] *Foreign Relations, 1882,* 271.

[26] *Foreign Relations, 1883*, 418.

[27] Submitted to the Senate by President Arthur on Dec. 10, 1884, Richardson, *Messages*, VIII, 256.

[28] Another expert whose advice was sought during the conference was W. P. Tisdel, who had been appointed special commissioner to the Congo by President Arthur.

[29] For correspondence relating to the Berlin Conference see Sen. Ex. Doc. 196, 49 Cong., 1 Sess., 7 *et seq.*

[30] Blaine to Comly, *Foreign Relations, 1881*, 633–639.

[31] Frelinghuysen to Carter, *Foreign Relations, 1883*, 576.

[32] C. O. Paullin, *Diplomatic Negotiations of American Naval Officers*, 282–328; Tyler Dennett, *Americans in Eastern Asia*, 450–507; and "Early American Policy in Korea," *Pol. Sci. Quar.*, III, No. 1 (March 1923); "American Choices in the Far East," *Am. Hist. Rev.*, XXX, 84–108; and "American Good Offices in Eastern Asia," *Am. Jour. Internat. Law*, XVI, 1–25.

[33] Paullin, *op. cit.*, 298.

[34] The clause proposed by Li Hung Chang read as follows: "Chosen, being a dependent state of the Chinese Empire, has nevertheless heretofore exercised her own sovereignty in all matters of internal administration and foreign relations." *Ibid.*, 315.

[35] Secretary Frelinghuysen stated in a report to the Senate Committee on Foreign Relations dated July 29, 1882 that: "The treaty . . . does not create Corean independence any more than like engagements concluded or now in process of negotiation between Corea and other western powers. . . ." Department of State, *Report Book*, 653. In a dispatch to Minister Young dated August 4, 1882 Frelinghuysen further analysed the situation in the following words: "In view of all the circumstances, I cannot but regard the administrative independence of Korea as a pre-established fact, abundantly recognized by the events of the past few years, and not created by or recognized by the conclusion of our treaty . . .

we regarded Korea as *de facto* independent, and . . . our acceptance of the friendly aid found in China was in no sense a recognition of China's suzerain power." Vol. XXX of instructions to China.

[36] It is of interest to note that Japan at one time apparently considered the idea of neutralizing Korea in a way similar to the neutralization of Belgium. See Dennett in *American Historical Review*, Vol. XXX, No. 1, October 1924, p. 96, footnote no. 21.

[37] *Foreign Relations, 1882*, 230. Frelinghuysen to Lowell.

[38] *Foreign Relations, 1884*, 215, and *Foreign Relations, 1885*, 446.

[39] *Foreign Relations, 1883*, 603. Frelinghuysen to Bingham.

APPENDIX

TO SKETCH OF BAYARD

BIBLIOGRAPHICAL NOTE

Material on the life of Thomas F. Bayard, either general or referring to his secretaryship, is scattered. There is no good comprehensive biography of the man; the only thing of the sort is a sketch prepared for use in the pre-convention campaign of 1880, Edward Spencer, *An Outline of the Public Life and Services of Thomas F. Bayard, Senator of the United States from the State of Delaware, 1869–1880, with Extracts from his Speeches and the Debates of Congress* (N. Y., 1880).

Owing to the fact that practically every question he dealt with remained unsettled at the end of his tenure, or was of no considerable importance, none of the general accounts or monographs on special subjects devotes much space to, or gives more than passing comment on, his diplomacy. By piecing together bits from one account and another something of the whole story can be made out. Among the special studies which afford some information are these: Jeanette Keim, *Forty Years of German-American Relations* (Philadelphia, 1919); John B. Henderson, *American Diplomatic Questions* (London, 1901); Lindley M. Keasby, *The Nicaraguan Canal and the Monroe Doctrine* (N. Y., 1896); Mary W. Williams, *Anglo-American Isthmian Diplomacy, 1815–1915* (Washington, 1916); John W. Foster, *American Diplomacy in the Orient* (Boston and N. Y., 1903); and Tyler Dennett, *Americans in Eastern Asia: a Critical Study of the Policy of the United States with Reference to China, Japan and Korea in the 19th Century* (N. Y., 1922).

Some information may be picked up in biographical works, especially relating to Canadians, for neither English nor

American biographies yield much on this period so far as Bayard and his diplomacy are concerned: *The Life and Letters of Sir Charles Tupper, Bart., K. C. M. G.* (E. M. Saunders, ed., London, 1916); Sir Charles Tupper, *Recollections of Sixty Years* (London, 1914); Oscar D. Skelton, *Life and Letters of Sir Wilfred Laurier* (Toronto, 1921); Sir Willoughby Maycock, *With Mr. Chamberlain in the United States and Canada* (London, 1914); *Correspondence of Sir John Macdonald: Selections from the Correspondence of the Right Honorable Sir John Alexander Macdonald, G. C. B., First Premier of the Dominion of Canada, Made by his Literary Executor, Sir Joseph Pope* (Toronto, 1921).

John Bassett Moore, *Digest of International Law* (8 vols., Washington, 1906) contains some useful material, and no study of the Samoan question can ignore Robert Louis Stevenson's *Footnote to History—Eight Years of Trouble in Samoa* (N. Y., 1897).

Much the greater part of the whole story, however, must be drawn from official documents. *Papers Relating to the Foreign Relations of the United States* (cited as *Foreign Relations, 1885, 1886*, etc.) are supplemented by numerous Senate and House *Executive Documents, Miscellaneous Documents*, and *Reports*. The American material is in turn supplemented by *British and Foreign State Papers* (London, annually), *Das Staatsarchiv: Sammlung der officiellen Actenstüke zur Geschichte der Gegenwart* (Leipzig), and *Die Grosse Politik der Europäischen Kabinette, 1871–1914* (Berlin, 1922–), although it must be said that little beyond what is found in the American sources appears except in the last named, where there are some dispatches throwing light on German policy in Samoa in relation with its other plans. A German white book, *Deutsche Interessen in Samoa* (1889) and a British blue book on Samoa (*Accounts and Papers*, 1889, lxxxvi) furnish a little not available in American sources, but nothing of considerable import.

As stated in the text, the diplomacy of this period was remarkably open and frank. The manuscript materials in the Bureau of Indexes and Archives of the Department of State do not disclose anything of real or vital significance not available in printed documents, although here and there interesting side-lights are afforded. The material in the Cleveland Papers in the Library of Congress, which the writer was allowed to use through the courtesy of Dr. Robert McElroy, may contain considerable on Bayard and his diplomacy, but until the collection has been arranged and classified—a very long task—it is impossible to assert this with conviction.

FOOTNOTES

[1] See Robert McElroy, *Grover Cleveland, the Man and Statesman* (N. Y., 1923), I, 102. Several letters among the Cleveland Papers in the Library of Congress show the advice received by the President-elect. New York *Nation*, March 12, 1885.

[2] Sen. Ex. Doc. 4, 49 Cong., 1 Sess.

[3] Department of State, *Instructions, Colombia,* XVII, *passim.*

[4] John Bassett Moore stated that it was "undoubtedly the most difficult and exciting with which he had to deal." *Bayard Memorial Addresses* (Dover, 1913).

[5] Sen. Ex. Doc. 32, 49 Cong., 1 Sess.

[6] For the extent and nature of the complaints see typical lists and correspondence in *Foreign Relations, 1887,* 459–60, 496–542; Sen. Ex. Doc. 113, 50 Cong., 1 Sess., 297 ff; H. Ex. Doc. 19, 49 Cong., 2 Sess.

[7] The protocol is in *Foreign Relations, 1887,* 427–8.

[8] Phelps to Bayard, Dec. 12, 1886, Department of State, *Instructions, Great Britain,* XXVIII, 225–6.

[9] *Sen. Report* 1683, 49 Cong., 2 Sess.

[10] Department of State, *Instructions, Great Britain,* XXVIII, 259.

[11] Sen. Ex. Doc. 113, 50 Cong., 1 Sess., 114 ff; *The Life and Letters of the Right Honourable Sir Charles Tupper, Bart., K. C. M. G.* (E. M. Saunders, ed., London, 1916) II, ch. 7; Sir Charles Tupper, *Recollections of Sixty Years* (London, 1914), ch. 9.

[12] "Bayard displayed a statesmanlike breadth and a grasp of the issues involved which had been rare at Washington." O. D. Skelton, *Life and Letters of Sir Wilfred Laurier*, I, 373.

[13] Tupper, *Recollections of Sixty Years, loc. cit.*, and Sir Willoughby Maycock, *With Mr. Chamberlain in the United States and Canada* (London, 1914), 200–2.

[14] Sen. Ex. Doc. 113, 50 Cong., 1 Sess.

[15] The testimony all hangs together on this point. Among the Cleveland Papers there is a letter from Senator Morgan, who was "convinced that a distinct purpose is to force the Administration into belligerency (commercial or, even military) with Great Britain before November." Among the same papers is a report of an Irish meeting in Chicago from a spy of the Treasury Department; he stated that a letter written by Luther Mattocks and read to the convention admitted that "to this organization alone belonged the credit of defeating the treatys."

[16] *Foreign Relations, 1888*, Part 2, 1745–1856; *Fur Seal Arbitration* (Sen. Ex. Doc., Vol. 7, Part 2, 53 Cong., 3 Sess.) II, 181–3 for Phelps's note. *H. Report* 3883, 50 Cong., 2 Sess.

[17] Sen. Ex. Doc. 143, 49 Cong., 1 Sess.; 146, 50 Cong., 2 Sess. *Alaskan Boundary Tribunal: the Counter Case of the United States* (Washington, 1903), 66.

[18] Irish troubles in England had echoes in the United States, and the Administration was criticized for not taking a more positive stand. In particular there was complaint about the case of one Dr. Gallagher arrested for complicity in one of the Irish outrages. "If by Dr. Gallagher's pardon, anger should be lessened and hostility to Her Majesty's Gov-

ernment disarmed, we should be gratified." Bayard to Phelps, Mar. 11, 1887; Department of State, *Instructions, Great Britain*, XXVIII, 398–9. Salisbury regretted that his Government was not able to comply with the wish of Secretary Bayard.

[19] H. Ex. Doc. 150, 50 Cong., 2 Sess. and *Foreign Relations, 1888*, Part 2, Supplement A.

[20] See the correspondence in Sen. Ex. Doc. 196, 49 Cong., 1 Sess.

[21] *Die Grosse Politik der Europäischen Kabinette, 1871–1914* (Berlin, 1922–) has several documents showing this. See IV, 80–1, 92, 96–7, 100–7, 143–4.

[22] A part of a telegram to Phelps read: "Our present purpose is to ascertain whether Germany proposes to assert prerogatives in Samoa which denote or flow from actual conquest. We are unprepared to admit any claim by Germany to tax or regulate trade otherwise than as stipulated in our treaty with Samoa. Our policy one of guarded reserve. Acquiescence in the destruction of the autonomy of any Pacific island is to be avoided, and each case carefully weighed as a possible precedent." Department of State, *Instructions, Great Britain*, XXVII, 646.

[23] *Ibid., Instructions, Germany*, XVII, 627.

[24] George H. Bates was the American agent. His instructions are in H. Ex. Doc. 238, 50 Cong., 1 Sess., 29–33, and his report, 137–91. Bates did not believe that a continuation of the tri-partite supervision was a practicable solution.

[25] Sen. Ex. Doc. 102, 50 Cong., 2 Sess.

[26] Department of State, *Instructions, Great Britain*, XXVIII, 399–403.

[27] The notes are in H. Ex. Doc. 238, 50 Cong., 1 Sess., 96–8, 107–21.

[28] The details may be gleaned from H. Ex. Doc. 118, 50 Cong., 2 Sess. and *Sen. Ex. Doc.* 68, 50 Cong., 2 Sess.

[29] Sen. Ex. Doc. 102, 50 Cong., 2 Sess. and *Foreign Relations, 1889*, "Germany."

[30] A half-hearted attempt by the Hawaiian King to bring Samoa under his political influence was frowned upon by Bayard. H. Ex. Doc. 238, 50 Cong., 1 Sess., 43, 45–6, 52–3.

[31] Department of State, *Instructions, Great Britain*, XXVII, 548–53.

[31a] For this question see J. B. Moore, *Digest of International Law*, V, 752 ff., where there are many excerpts from the manuscripts of the Department of State.

[32] In a letter to Senator Morgan written by R. K. Wright on January 14, 1894, the latter said that he had been in charge of one of the sections of the work from 1883 to 1885 "and then realizing the utter hopelessness of the enterprise I gave it up and became United States Consul at Aspinwall, from 1885 to 1887 under Mr. Bayard, keeping him posted as to the progress of the work there." Cleveland Papers.

[33] Department of State, *Instructions, Central America*, XIX, 2.

[34] *Foreign Relations, 1888*, Part 1, 759–67.

[35] Sen. Ex. Doc. 237, 56 Cong., 1 Sess., 520–4, 528–9.

[36] Sen. Ex. Doc. 50, 49 Cong., 1 Sess., 21–3, 46–7.

[37] Department of State, *Instructions, Central America*, XIX, 153, 166–70.

[38] *Ibid., Instructions, Great Britain*, XXVIII, 657–8.

[39] *Ibid., Instructions, Colombia*, XVII, 498–502.

[40] *Ibid., Instructions, Central America*, XIX, 33–4.

[41] *Ibid.*, XVIII, 538.

[42] Cleveland Papers.

[43] Except for the first part of the second sentence this paragraph was not included in the papers transmitted to the Senate. It is found in *Instructions, Great Britain*, XXVII, 510–13.

[44] Sen. Ex. Doc. 266, 50 Cong., 1 Sess.

[45] Department of State, *Instructions, Great Britain*, XXVIII, 497–8.

[46] *Ibid.*, Bayard to Hosmer, September 15, 1887; *Instructions, Central America*, XIX, 59–61.

APPENDIX

TO SKETCH OF BLAINE

(SECOND PART)

BIBLIOGRAPHICAL NOTE

(See pp. 265-267, Volume VII).

FOOTNOTES

[1] Gail Hamilton (Abigail Dodge), *Biography of James G. Blaine*, 620.

[2] *Ibid.*, 618.

[3] James Wilson Pierce, *Life of the Hon. James G. Blaine*, 418–421.

[4] Edward Stanwood, *James Gillespie Blaine*, 289.

[5] *Ibid.*, 305.

[6] Gail Hamilton, *op. cit.*, 652.

[7] *Congressional Globe*, 40 Cong., 3 Sess., 57–58.

[8] Blaine to Morgan, June 1, 1881. *Foreign Relations, 1881–1882*, 761.

[9] Edward Stanwood, *James Gillespie Blaine*, 359.

[10] Blaine to Comly, Dec. 1, 1881, *Foreign Relations, 1881–1882*, 637.

[11] Comly to Blaine, Aug. 29, 1881; Blaine to Comly, Nov. 19, 1881; *Foreign Relations, 1881–1882*, 627–629; 633–635.

[12] Blaine to Comly, Dec. 1, 1881, *Foreign Relations, 1881–1882*, 636.

[13] *Ibid.*, 637–638.

[14] John B. Henderson, Jr., *American Diplomatic Questions*, 214.

[15] *Ibid.*, 244.

[16] *Letters of Mrs. James G. Blaine*, II, 243, 244.

[17] *Foreign Relations, 1889*, 195–204.

[18] Report of the Secretary of State to the President, Jan. 17, 1890, *Foreign Relations, 1889*, 349–353.

[19] *Ibid.*, 353–364.

[20] John Bassett Moore, *History and Digest of the International Arbitrations to which the United States has been a Party*, I, 765.

[21] *Ibid.*, 775; John B. Henderson, Jr., *op. cit.*, 18.

[22] John Bassett Moore, *op. cit.*, I, 777.

[23] Blaine to Pauncefote, *Foreign Relations, 1890*, 366–370.

[24] John Bassett Moore, *op. cit.*, I, 792.

[25] Salisbury to Pauncefote, May 22, 1890, *Foreign Relations, 1890*, 419–423.

[26] Blaine to Pauncefote, June 30, 1890, *Foreign Relations, 1890*, 437–448.

[27] Salisbury to Pauncefote, Aug. 2, 1890, *Foreign Relations, 1890*, 456–465.

[28] Blaine to Pauncefote, Dec. 17, 1890, *Foreign Relations, 1890*, 477–501.

[29] William M. Malloy, *Treaties*, I, 745.

[30] Report of the committee of fifty citizens on the existence of secret societies in New Orleans, *Foreign Relations, 1891*, 723.

[31] *Ibid.*, 666.

[32] *Ibid.*, 667.

[33] *Ibid.*, 671.

[34] *Ibid.*, 673.

[35] Porter to Blaine, April 1, 1891, *Ibid.*, 678.

[36] *Ibid.*, 676.

[37] *Ibid.*, 685.

[38] *Ibid.*, 712.

[39] *Ibid.*, 728.

[40] Cf. Proclamation of President Balmaceda, *Ibid.*, 94.

[41] Balmaceda to Uriburu, Sept. 19, 1891, *Ibid.*, 165.

[42] Schley to Tracy, H. Ex. Doc. 91, 52 Cong. 1 Sess., 293.

[43] James D. Richardson, *Messages and Papers of the Presidents*, IX, 186.

[44] *Foreign Relations, 1891*, 273.

[45] Blaine to Egan, Jan. 21, 1891, *Foreign Relations, 1891*, 307–308.

[46] Egan to Blaine, Jan. 25, 1891, *Foreign Relations, 1891*, 309–312.

[47] *International American Conference*, I, 7.

[48] Bayard to Walker, Jan. 18, 1889, Department of State, *Instructions, Argentine Republic*, XVI, 463.

[49] Walker to Blaine, No. 1, April 5, 1889, Department of State, *Dispatches, Argentine Republic*, XXVII.

[50] *International American Conference*, I, 26.

[51] *Ibid.*, 49–54.

[52] *Ibid.*, 39–42.

[53] *Ibid.*, 61.

[54] For the debates on this subject see, *International American Conference*, I, 103–264.

[55] *International American Conference*, I, 259.

[56] *Ibid.*, 131.

[57] Roque Saenz Peña, *Escritos y Discursos*, I, 162.

[58] *International American Conference*, II, 978.

[59] *Ibid.*, 1145.

[60] *Ibid.*, 1147.

[61] José Ignacio Rodríguez, *American Constitutions*, I, 166.

[62] Edward Stanwood, *James Gillespie Blaine*, 343.

APPENDIX

TO SKETCH OF FOSTER

BIBLIOGRAPHICAL NOTE

No life of John W. Foster has been published. Materials for a biography exist largely in his own printed works. There is no collection of his letters or papers. He was Secretary of State for such a short time that he was unable to carry through any important policies, but his State Papers printed in the official publication, *Papers Relating to the Foreign Relations of the United States* (Washington, 1862 and thereafter), and on record in manuscript form in the archives of the Department give a complete picture of the period during which he was in office. As is well known to students of American diplomacy, Foster himself was an authority on the subject and the author of numerous publications. It seems proper here to enumerate the more significant, for they have been helpful in preparing this sketch. They are:

International Awards and National Honor (Washington, 1886); *Bering Sea Tribunal of Arbitration* (Washington, 1895); *Biographical Sketch of Matthew Watson Foster* (Washington and New York, 1896); *The Annexation of Hawaii* (Washington, 1897); *The Alaskan Boundary* (Washington, 1899); "A Foreign Sovereign in an American Court," *Yale Law Journal*, May, 1900, IX, 283; *A Century of American Diplomacy*, being a brief review of the foreign relations of the United States, 1776–1876 (Boston and New York, 1900); "The Treaty Making Power under the Constitution," *Yale Law Journal*, 1901, XI, 69; *Are or Is?* (Washington, 1901); *American Diplomacy in the Orient* (Boston and New York, 1903); *The Alaskan Boundary Tribunal* (Washington, 1903);

The Alaskan Boundary (Washington, 1903); *What the United States has done for International Arbitration* (Albany, 1904); *Alaskan Boundary Tribunal,* proceedings of the Alaskan Boundary Tribunal, convened in London (Washington, 1904); *Arbitration and The Hague Court* (Boston and New York, 1904); *The Proper Grade of Diplomatic Representatives* (Washington, 1904); *The Promotion of the Settlement of International Controversies by Resort to The Hague Tribunal or Reference to Special Commissions* (St. Louis, 1904); "China," *National Geographic Magazine,* Dec., 1904; *The Relation of Diplomacy to Foreign Missions* (Sewanee, Tennessee, 1906); "Questions of the Far East," *Atlantic Monthly,* April 1906, XCVII, 542–546; "Roosevelt and The Hague," *Independent,* Dec. 20, 1906, LXI, 1471.

"Annexation of Cuba," *Independent,* Oct. 25, 1906, LXI, 965; *Conditions in China* (Washington, 1906); *The Practice of Diplomacy as Illustrated in the Foreign Relations of the United States* (Boston and New York, 1906); *Armaments and the "Next War"* (Washington, 1906); "Franklin as a Diplomat," *Independent,* January 11, 1906, LX, 84–89; "Second Hague Conference and the Development of International Law as a Science," American Society of International Law, *Proceedings,* 1907; "International Responsibility to Corporate Bodies for Lives Lost by Outlawry," *American Journal of International Law,* January, 1907, I, 4–10; "Is the Forcible Collection of Contract Debt in the Interest of International Justice and Peace?" American Society of International Law, *Proceedings,* 1907; *Venezuelan Claims* Letter from Mr. Foster to Hon. S. M. Cullom, April 14, 1908 (Washington, 1908); *The Chinese Indemnity* (Washington, 1908); "Arbitration as a Judicial Remedy," American Society of International Law, *Proceedings,* 1909; "Development of International Law," *University of Chicago Magazine,* Feb. 1909, I, 136–148; *Diplomatic Memoirs* (Boston and New York, 1909); "The Japanese War Scare," *International Conciliation,* Oct.. 1910;

"Contest for the Laws of Reform in Mexico," *American Historical Review*, April, 1910; "Another Step Toward International Peace," *Independent*, June 9, 1910, LXVIII, 288–290; "America's Contribution to the Literature of International Law and Diplomacy," *Yale Law Journal*, 1900, XIII, 409; *The Foreign Wars of the United States* (Washington, 1910); *War not Inevitable* (World Peace Foundation, Boston, Pamphlet, Oct. 1911, no. 3, pt. 2); "Revision of our Neutrality Laws," *Advocate of Peace*, August, 1911; *Limitation of Armament on the Great Lakes* (Washington, 1914); "Our First Professional Diplomat," *Outlook*, Nov. 28, 1917, CXVII, 488; *War Stories for my Grandchildren* (Cambridge, 1918); "Classics as a Training for Men of Affairs," *School Review*, June, 1919; "Misconceptions and Limitations of the Monroe Doctrine," American Society of International Law, *Proceedings*, 1919.

Of the above, those which contain biographical information are the *Biographical Sketch of Matthew Watson Foster*, *American Diplomacy in the Orient*, *Diplomatic Memoirs*, and *War Stories for my Grandchildren*.

The serviceable compilations of John Bassett Moore have their usual value for the diplomacy of this period: *History and Digest of International Arbitration to which the United States has been a Party* (5 vols., Washington, 1898); and *A Digest of International Law* (8 vols., Washington, 1909).

FOOTNOTES

[1] *Diplomatic Memoirs*, II, 242.

[2] *Ibid.*, I, 12.

[3] *Ibid.*, I, 214.

[4] Instruction to United States minister at St. Petersburg, September 16, 1892, Department of State, *Instructions, Russia*, XVII, 100.

⁵ Instruction to United States minister at St. Petersburg, November 1, 1892, *Ibid.*, 111–114.

⁶ Instruction to United States minister at St. Petersburg, December 17, 1892, *Ibid.*, 129.

⁷ Note to British minister at Washington, November 2, 1892, Department of State, *Notes, Great Britain*, XXII, 130–132.

⁸ Note to British minister at Washington, September 27, 1892, *Ibid.*, 173.

⁹ Note to British minister at Washington, September 27, 1892, *Ibid.*, 180.

¹⁰ Personal letter from Mr. Foster to Mr. Lincoln, September 29, 1892, Department of State, *Instructions, Great Britain*, XXX, 66.

¹¹ Note to British minister at Washington, November 9, 1892, Department of State, *Notes, Great Britain*, XXII, 190.

¹² Instruction to the United States minister at St. Petersburg, October 14, 1892, Department of State, *Instructions, Russia*, XVII, 109.

¹³ *Foreign Relations, 1892*, 250–335, *passim*.

There was much correspondence in this matter of canal tolls. The Canadian Government by granting a substantial rebate on grain cargoes passing through the Welland Canal if their destination was Montreal or beyond and if these cargoes, before passing through the canal were transshipped at a Canadian port was clearly, if not directly, discriminating against American cargoes and ships in contravention of Article 27 of the treaty of 1871. There was also discussion as to the rights of American and Canadian nationals to carry on salvage and wrecking operations in waters contiguous to the international boundary, the Canadians claiming that this right did not extend to American citizens so far as the Welland Canal was concerned.

¹⁴ *Foreign Relations, 1892*, 317, 324, 326.

Fishing rights: Under the so-called unratified treaty of 1888 (which Great Britain, Canada and Newfoundland ratified but which failed of ratification by the United States Senate) the Canadian Government issued *modus vivendi* licenses to American fishing vessels permitting them to purchase provisions and outfits in Canadian Atlantic ports, to ship crews therein and to transship their catches therefrom to the United States.

These licenses were first issued that the vessels might have the privileges provided for in the treaty pending its ratification, but they continued after the Senate had refused ratification and, in 1892, a Canadian act of Parliament gave the Governor General in Council authority to renew the licenses from year to year. They were so renewed and issued up to December 31, 1923.

[15] *Foreign Relations, 1892*, 297–324, *passim*.

Transport of Chinese immigrants: There had been many protests in the United States, certainly not without justification, that many Chinese, who were already as a race excluded from the United States, were transported by the Canadian Pacific Railroad from Vancouver to points east where they were smuggled across the border. Foster's protests against this undoubtedly bureaucratic practice were so well put and so vigorous that the traffic was largely stopped. There was nothing to indicate any lack of co-operation with the American authorities on the part of the Canadian Government, any more than there is anything today to indicate lack of co-operation in the very much more contentious question of liquor smuggling. It is always difficult, moreover, to ask a foreign government to help enforce local laws.

[16] Instruction to United States minister at London, November 5, 1892, Department of State, *Instructions, Great Britain*, XXX, 108.

[17] Telegram of January 28, 1893, to the United States minister at Honolulu, *Ibid.*, *Instructions, Hawaii*, III, 161.

[18] Instruction to the United States minister at Honolulu, February 11, 1893, *Ibid.*, 166.

[19] Telegram to American minister at London, February 1, 1893, Department of State, *Instructions, Great Britain*, XXX, 168.

[20] Protocol of First Conference between Hawaiian Commissioners and Secretary of State, February, 1893, at Washington, Department of State, typed ms., 17.

[21] Treaty of Annexation, February 14, 1893.

[22] *Diplomatic Memoirs*, II, 25.

[23] Memorial Sermon by Reverend Charles Wood, delivered at the Church of the Covenant, Washington, December 2, 1917.

APPENDIX

TO SKETCH OF GRESHAM

BIBLIOGRAPHICAL NOTE

Little correspondence of importance has been omitted from that annual official publication, *Foreign Relations of the United States*, and in the printed congressional documents, for the period of Secretary Gresham's incumbency of the Department of State, but what has been given publicity is sometimes misleading owing to the editorial practice then prevalent of deleting portions of a text without indications. The author, in his examination of the manuscript archives of the Department, has found that in the case of Gresham, the tendency was perhaps to publish too much rather than too little. With the exception of the original sources in the published and unpublished files of the Department of State, the most useful and practically the only repository for personal papers, information on genealogical and family matters, and minor details, is the two-volume *Life of Walter Quintin Gresham* by his widow, Matilda Gresham, with an introduction by his son, Otto Gresham, published in Chicago in 1919, and this fact will explain the apparent undue amount of quotations from this work in the earlier part of this sketch. The *Life*, while naturally more of a eulogy than a biography, brings together and preserves much correspondence, particularly of an intimate and personal nature, and furnishes us with many picturesque details of the life of Gresham. It is very full and useful for this period of his life, but it is to be regretted that there is so little other material extant with which to check it.

Much relevant material and a bird's eye view of Cleveland's second Administration is given in R. M. McElroy, *Grover Cleveland, the Man and the Statesman* (2 vols., N. Y., 1923).

This work while conceived and written in a popular manner gives a very attractive picture of the man Cleveland and leaves us with the impression of a thoroughly sincere, well-meaning President who retired from office with the feeling that his Administration had been a failure and that he had no political friends.

In Willis Fletcher Johnson's *America's Foreign Relations* (2 vols., N. Y., 1921), we have a very convenient and readable compendium of the subject, which, although not original in treatment, is helpful in giving the general reader a good grasp of the theme.

Mention may also be made of Randolph G. Adams, *History of the Foreign Policy of the United States* (N. Y., 1924); P. S. Mowrer, *Our Foreign Affairs* (N. Y., 1924); "British-American Relations," by J. D. Whelpley (Boston, 1924); F. E. Chadwick, *The Relations of the United States and Spain. Diplomacy* (N. Y., 1909); A. C. Coolidge, *The United States as a World Power* (N. Y., 1910); A. B. Hart, *Foundations of American Foreign Policy* (N. Y., 1901); J. W. Foster, *A Century of American Diplomacy* (Boston and N. Y., 1900); and *American Diplomacy in the Orient* (Boston and N. Y., 1904); Henry James, *Richard Olney and his Public Service* (Boston and N. Y., 1923); J. B. Moore, *Digest of International Law* (8 vols. Washington, 1906); J. D. Richardson, *Compilation of the Messages and Papers of the Presidents, 1789–1897* (10 vols. Washington, 1896–1899); C. C. Hyde, *International Law, chiefly as interpreted and applied by the United States* (2 vols. 1923); Tyler Dennett, *Americans in Eastern Asia*, (N. Y., 1922); I. K. Travis, *History of the Clayton-Bulwer Treaty* (Ann Arbor, 1902); M. W. Williams, *Anglo-American Isthmian Diplomacy* (Wash. 1916); L. M. Keasby, *Nicaragua Canal and the Monroe Doctrine* (N. Y., 1896); Alfred L. P. Dennis, *Adventures in American Diplomacy* (N. Y., 1928). Other works of importance are cited in the bibliography appended to the sketch of Richard Olney in the present volume, below.

FOOTNOTES

[1] Matilda Gresham, *Life of Walter Quintin Gresham, 1832–1895*, II, 679. This work in two volumes with portraits Chicago, 1919) will be referred to hereafter as *Life*.

[2] *Life*, II, 679.

[3] *Life*, II, 682–683.

[4] McElroy, *Grover Cleveland*, II, 4.

[5] *Life*, I, 30.

[6] *Life*, I, 100.

[7] *Life*, I, 346.

[8] *Life*, I, 347.

[9] *Life*, I, 419.

[10] Mrs. Gresham records that it was an open secret in Washington at the time that President Arthur would have appointed Mr. Gresham to the Supreme Court had there existed a vacancy.

[11] *Life*, II, 567.

[12] *Life*, II, 836.

[13] The most convenient summary of the history of the Hawaiian problem is in "Report upon the official relations of the United States with the Hawaiian Islands" prefaced to Appendix II, of *Foreign Relations, 1894*, a bulky volume of 1437 pages. See also J. B. Moore, *Digest of International Law*, I. This was continued in the report accompanying the President's message of February 15, 1893 sending the Hawaiian Treaty to the Senate, and in Cleveland's message of December 18, 1893.

[14] The instructions given by Gresham to Willis (the new minister) are published in *Foreign Relations, 1894*, App. II.

[15] *Foreign Relations, 1894*, 1242.

[16] The President's letter to the President of Hawaii is dated August 7, 1894. See *Foreign Relations, 1894*, 358–360.

[17] *Life*, II, 741.

[18] Moore, *Digest*, I, 498–502; also *Sen. Rept.* 227, 53 Cong.,

2 Sess., 46, 65, 77; *H. Rept.* 243, 53 Cong., 2 Sess., 47, 70, 76, 79, 95, 112, 140.

[19] See ante, Vol. I.

[20] W. F. Johnson, *America's Foreign Relations*, II, 105.

[21] *Foreign Relations, 1893*, 45–148; *1894*, 57–58.

[22] *Life*, II, 781.

[23] Gresham to Bayard, No. 240, Dec. 18, 1893, Department of State, *Instructions, Great Britain*, XXX, 429.

[24] *Informes sobre la Mosquitia* (Managua, 1894), a pamphlet bound up in *Nicaraguan Memorial*, a volume in Department of State Manuscript Records on the Nicaraguan matter, pages 1–119. See also *Foreign Relations, 1894*, I, 433–480; Ex. Doc. 20, 53 Cong., 3 Sess., 1–207; Moore, *Digest*, III, 222–254.

[25] For the Bluefields incident and the incorporation of the Mosquito Reserve into Nicaragua, with diplomatic correspondence germane to the events, see M. W. Williams, *Anglo-American Isthmian Diplomacy*, 288–299, and *Foreign Relations, 1894*, Appendix I, 234–364.

[26] Gresham to the American minister to Nicaragua, No. 185, June 13, 1894, Department of State, *Instructions, Central America*, XX, 301.

[27] *Life*, II, 785. See also *Foreign Relations, 1893*, 163–173, especially the note of the Minister for Foreign Affairs of Nicaragua to the American minister, p. 165 *et seq.*, and from the Secretary of State to the American minister in London, No. 999, Nov. 23, 1894, Department of State, *Instructions, Great Britain*, XXVIII, 622.

[28] Tyler Dennett, Esquire, in personal letter to the author.

[29] Gresham to Dun, telegram, Department of State, *Instructions, Japan*, IV, 224.

[30] Gresham to Denby, telegram, Department of State, *Instructions, China*, V, 117.

[31] *Foreign Relations, 1894*, Appendix I, 5–22; 23–105; *1895*, 969.

[32] *Life*, II, 789.

[33] *Life*, II, 795.

APPENDIX

TO SKETCH OF OLNEY

BIBLIOGRAPHICAL NOTE

Most of the original sources for a knowledge of the conduct of American foreign relations under Richard Olney are naturally to be found in the collection of *Foreign Relations of the United States*, issued by the Department of State, and in the unpublished diplomatic correspondence in the archives of the same Department. These, together with Olney's personal and semi-personal papers, have been examined by Henry James, whose scholarly and interesting volume, *Richard Olney and his Public Service* (Boston and N. Y., 1923), should be consulted by all students of Olney's work.

The texts of Cleveland's messages on foreign affairs may be found in the appropriate volume of Richardson's *Messages of the Presidents*. Many of the most important and significant pronouncements of the Department of State under Olney are to be found in extracts with full references in J. B. Moore's *Digest of International Law* (8 vols. Washington, 1906), the most valuable work of its kind in existence. This should be supplemented by the later research of C. C. Hyde, *International Law, chiefly as interpreted and applied by the United States* (2 vols., N. Y., 1923).

Secondary sources which may be suggested for reading are J. F. Rhodes, *History of the United States, 1877–1896* (N. Y., 1919); Lester B. Shippee, *Recent American History* (N. Y., 1924). These works give excellent bibliographical notes and references. Of interest also are R. G. Adams, *A History of the Foreign Policy of the United States* (N. Y., 1924), and W. S. Robertson, *Hispanic-American Relations with the United States* (N. Y., 1923).

The *Bibliographical Note* appended to the life of Gresham in this series should also be consulted for other collateral reading.

FOOTNOTES

[1] (Boston and N. Y., 1923). This work will hereafter in this sketch be quoted as "James."

[2] James, 22. Perhaps it was his Puritan inheritance, a state of mind which Macaulay remarks made the Puritans stop bear-baiting, not because it gave pain to the bear but because it gave pleasure to the spectators.

[3] Speech in presiding over a rally. James, 23, 24.

[4] Both quotations above are from a Memorandum dictated by Olney, reproduced in James, 5–7.

[5] James, 208–210.

[6] Cleveland, *The Government in the Chicago Strike of 1894* (Stafford Little Lecture, Princeton University, 1904, Princeton University Press, 1913). This brief sketch in 49 pages should be consulted for details of this disturbance and its settlement.

[7] *Ibid.*, 14–15.

[8] For relations between United States and Cuba, see J. H. Latané, "Diplomacy of the United States in regard to Cuba," in *Annual Report* of the American Historical Association, for 1898.

[9] R. M. McElroy, *Grover Cleveland, the Man and the Statesman*, II, 246.

[10] E. J. Benton, *International Law and Diplomacy of the Spanish-American War* (Balto., 1908), 42.

[11] For text of note, *Foreign Relations, 1897*, 540.

[12] McElroy, *Cleveland*, II, 249.

[13] Cleveland, *the Venezuela Boundary Controversy* (Stafford Little Lecture, Princeton University Press, 1913). This little volume should be read in its entirety for details of the controversy.

[14] *Ibid.*, 25.

[15] *Ibid.*, 31.

[16] *Ibid.*, 55.

[17] *Ibid.*, 60.

[18] McElroy, *Cleveland*, II, 176.

[19] *Ibid.*, II, 177.

[20] *Foreign Relations, 1894*, x.

[21] McElroy, *Cleveland*, II, 180–181.

[22] *Foreign Relations, 1895*, I, 545–562.

[23] Cleveland, *Venezuela Boundary Controversy*, 95–96.

[24] For the note and Lord Salisbury's replies, Moore, *Digest*, VI, 535–575.

[25] Carl Schurz, "Grover Cleveland's Second Administration," *Writings*, V, 385.

[26] J. F. Rhodes, *History of the United States, 1877–1896*, 450. For the part played by the kind action of the British Government regarding American citizens in the South African Republic, see *Foreign Relations, 1896*, 562 *et seq.*

[27] James, 244.

[28] *Ibid.*, 128–129.

[29] *Venezuela Boundary Controversy*, 117.

[30] James, 144.

[31] *Foreign Relations, 1896*, 222–240, where the most important documents are given in full.

[32] McElroy, *Cleveland*, II, 243.

[33] *Ibid.*, II, 244.

[34] *Foreign Relations, 1896*, lxiii–xciii.

[35] McElroy, *Cleveland*, II, 294.

[36] James, 188.

INDEX

Prepared by DAVID M. MATTESON